Greater Syria

Greater Syria

The History of an Ambition

Daniel Pipes

OXFORD UNIVERSITY PRESS
New York   Oxford

TO PAULA

Who can find a woman of valor?
For her worth is far beyond pearls

Oxford University Press

Oxford   New York   Toronto
Delhi   Bombay   Calcutta   Madras   Karachi
Petaling Jaya   Singapore   Hong Kong   Tokyo
Nairobi   Dar es Salaam   Cape Town
Melbourne   Auckland

and associated companies in
Berlin   Ibadan

Copyright © 1990 by Daniel Pipes

First published in 1990 by Oxford University Press, Inc.,
200 Madison Avenue, New York, New York 10016

First issued as an Oxford University Press paperback, 1992

Oxford is a registered trademark of Oxford University Press

Library of Congress Cataloging-in-Publication Data
Pipes, Daniel, 1949–
Greater Syria : the history of an ambition / Daniel Pipes.
p. cm. Includes index.
1. Arab countries—Politics and government. 2. Syria—Politics
and government. 3. Syria—Foreign relations—Arab countries.
4. Arab countries—Foreign relations—Syria. I. Title.
DS63.P5   1990
956—dc20   89-34775
ISBN 0-19-506021-0
ISBN 0-19-506022-9 (pbk)

This book was written under the auspices of the Foreign Policy
Research Institute in Philadelphia. Founded in 1955, the Institute is
an independent, nonprofit organization devoted to research on
issues affecting the national interests of the United States.

1 3 5 7 9 8 6 4 2

Printed in the United States of America
on acid-free paper

Acknowledgments

I have been fortunate to work for those who encourage my research and writing. The chairman of my department at the U.S. Naval War College, Alvin H. Bernstein, arranged the maximum possible time for me to work on this book when I was a professor at the college from 1984 to 1986. As director of the Foreign Policy Research Institute since 1986, I have benefited from President Marvin Wachman's and the board of trustees' understanding that my scholarship matters as much as my administrative and editorial work. Thanks to them, I have been able to devote the time necessary to complete this undertaking.

A number of scholars have kindly read the manuscript of this book, including Fouad Ajami, John Devlin, Bernard Lewis, Ronald D. McLaurin, and Meir Zamir. I am most grateful for their comments, though they are, of course, not liable for any errors that may remain. Itamar Rabinovich read the manuscript and also very generously let me look at copies in his possession of documents from the British archives. Nancy Lane at Oxford University Press gave me the benefit of her extensive experience in publishing.

In Newport, Irene Hankinson provided excellent help with the files of clippings that provide the information in Chapter 3, while Geoffrey Schad assisted with locating books at Harvard University for Chapter 2, and Mariam A. Roustom provided all-around assistance. Robin A. Lima of the library at the Naval War College made interlibrary loan books appear rapidly and efficiently. In Philadelphia, I had excellent assistance from several students, including Jennifer Bowman, Betty Ciacci, Jennifer Holm, Youssouf Abdel-Jelil, Pauline McKean, Jennifer A. Morrissey, and Jennifer Reingold.

This book draws on articles of mine that have previously appeared in print. Permission to use this material was generously granted by the publishers of *Annals of Japan Association for Middle East Studies, Commentary, International Journal of Middle East Studies, Middle East Review, Middle Eastern Studies, The New Republic, Orbis,* and *The World & I.*

Unless otherwise noted, radio and television transcriptions derive from the Foreign Broadcast Information Service, *Daily Report*, put out daily by the National Technical Information Service of the U.S. Department of Commerce. This source also provided some newspaper and magazine references.

For the information in Chapters 2 and 4, I have relied heavily on scholarship by van Dam, Devlin, van Dusen, Ma'oz, Porath, Rabinovich, Seale, Zamir, and many of the other authors cited in the notes. As anyone familiar with this subject will quickly realize, I am deeply indebted to their work. In the interest of limiting the number of notes, however, references are provided only for direct quotes or information that derives from little-known sources.

Newport, R.I., and Philadelphia   D.P.
December 1988

Contents

Maps and Illustrations

Maps

Illustrations (*following page 100*)

Greater Syria

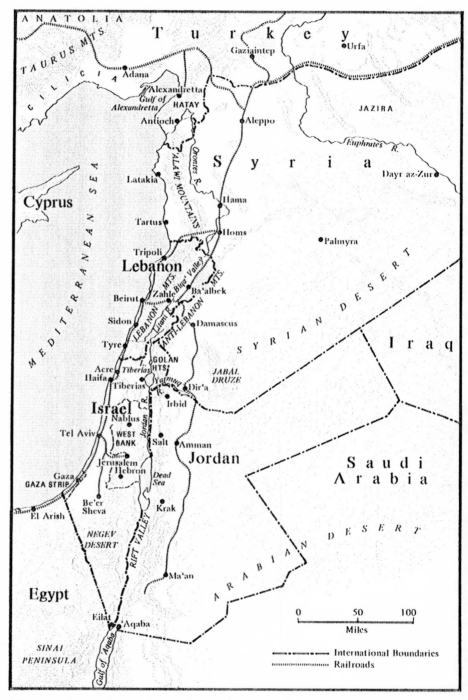

Figure 1. Greater Syria   Greater Syria refers to a region stretching from the borders of Turkey to those of Egypt, from the edge of Iraq to the Mediterranean Sea.

Introduction:
A Neglected Topic

Her Majesty's Government has stated that it considers Syria to be the
military key of Asiatic Turkey.

Lord Palmerston, 1840[1]

On first entering Syria, the observant traveler will probably be startled to go
through passport control and notice a military map of Syria on the wall, for
this map contains several anomalies. It shows the Golan Heights under Syrian
control, though they have been occupied by Israel since 1967. Syria's boundaries with Lebanon and Jordan appear not as international borders but as
something called "regional" borders. Israel does not even exist; instead, there
is a state called Palestine. And Palestine is separated from Syria by a line
designated a "temporary" border. Finally, the province of Hatay, a part of
Turkey since 1939, appears to be included in Syria; only on close inspection
can one see the "temporary" border between it and Syria.[2]

The many inaccuracies on this map reflect the Syrian rulers' profound
unwillingness to accept the actual size and shape of the country they adminis-
ter. They remember that until 1920, "Syria" referred to a region much larger
than the Syrian Arab Republic of today, a region that stretched from the
borders of Anatolia to those of Egypt, from the edge of Iraq to the Mediterranean Sea. In terms of today's states, the Syria of old comprised Syria, Lebanon,
Israel, and Jordan, plus the Gaza Strip and Alexandretta. This larger land,
known since 1920 as Greater Syria, is what they dream of reclaiming.

Pan-Syrianism—the intention to piece together a Greater Syrian nation—is
not a new phenomenon but has strongly influenced politics in the Middle East
since 1918. The division of Greater Syria after World War I proved one of the
worst of many political traumas experienced in the Middle East at that time.
Pan-Syrianism explains many of the conflicting aspirations among Syrians,
Lebanese, Palestinians, Israelis, and Jordanians; it lies behind much of the
volatility of public life in Jordan and Syria; and it partially accounts for the
Lebanese civil war and the Arab-Israeli conflict. The goal of piecing Syria's
parts together drove Jordanian foreign policy for over two decades, and it had
nearly as great a role in Iraq. The future of the West Bank is bound up with this

3

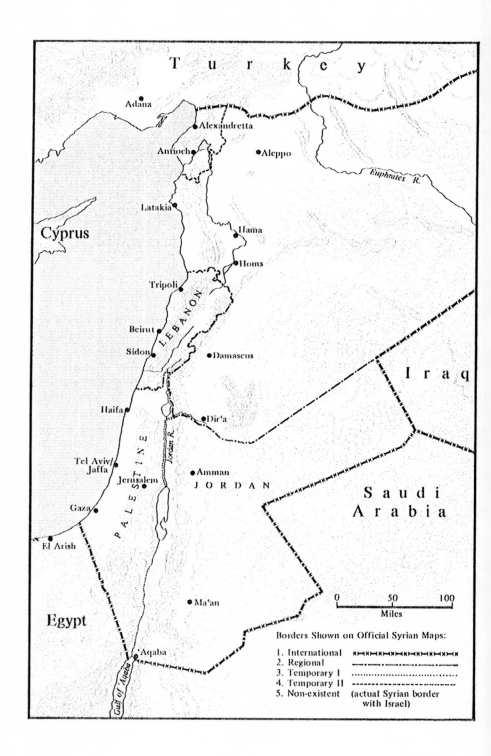

Borders Shown on Official Syrian Maps:

1. International
2. Regional
3. Temporary I
4. Temporary II
5. Non-existent (actual Syrian border with Israel)

4

dream. Pan-Syrianism helps comprehend complex interactions between Pan-Arabists, Palestinian nationalists, and state authorities.

The party that has advocated Greater Syria since 1932, the Syrian Social Nationalist Party (SSNP),[3] has had profound political importance in the twentieth-century history of the two states where it has been most active, Lebanon and Syria. As the first political party fully to embrace radical secular ideals, it incubated virtually every radical group in those two countries, with particularly great impact on the Ba'th Party. The SSNP offered the minorities, especially the Greek Orthodox Christians, a vehicle for political action and caused several of Lebanon's worst political crises. Its ideology influenced the development of Pan-Arabism (or Arab nationalism) and defined inter-Arab relations in the Levant region. Leading intellectuals such as Abu Khaldun Sati' al-Husri and Kamal Junbalat devoted considerable energy to combating Pan-Syrianism.[4]

Finally—and this may mark the apogee of its influence—the government of Hafiz al-Asad adopted Pan-Syrian ideas and made them Syrian state policy. Circumstantial evidence strongly indicates that the Syrian government has since 1974 made Greater Syria the centerpiece of its foreign policy. Thus, in addition to offering an important new perspective on the events of decades past, the study of Pan-Syrianism provides a tool for understanding the policies of the Asad regime.

Despite its critical role through the twentieth century, Pan-Syrianism receives little attention. Observers tend to view it as an aberration or a historical curiosity—and therefore as a matter of little consequence. Over a period of four decades, for example, *The Economist* has called two of Pan-Syrianism's most prominent exponents, the SSNP and King 'Abdallah of Jordan, many names. In 1947, 'Abdallah's plans were dismissed as "wishful thoughts." In 1962, the SSNP was "an activist right-wing movement of a slightly dotty kind"; it was deemed on the "lunatic fringe," "farcical," and "idiotic." By 1985, it had become "an odd little organisation."[5] Asad's efforts to build Greater Syria fare no better; *The Washington Post* has termed them a "fantasy."[6]

Editorialists are not alone in the harsh assessment of Pan-Syrianism. Most historical accounts refer to Pan-Syrianism in passing, seeing it as a quirky, inconsequential dead end. Michael C. Hudson, a scholar of Lebanese politics, called the SSNP's politics "bizarre" and its ideology "thwarted idealism twisted into a doctrine of total escape."[7] A Lebanese minister of information waved away the Fertile Crescent scheme as "stillborn."[8] Robert M. Haddad dismissed its more distant ambitions as a "hallucination."[9]

Two reasons explain why Pan-Syrianism fails to attract the serious attention it deserves. First, its adherents have a well-earned reputation for ludicrous

---

Figure 2. Syrian Military Map   The Armed Forces Administration in Damascus distributes the map on which this is based. Two points deserve special notice: the five gradations of borders and the several places where the borders diverge from reality (especially Hatay and Israel).

impracticality. 'Abdallah hawked a plan no one bought for so many years that both he and it became pathetic. From its founding in 1932 until the present time, the SSNP has fallen short in virtually everything it attempted. Quixotic conspiracies, foiled coup attempts, and a despised ideology won it a reputation for not being serious.

But while it is true that most efforts to unite Greater Syria have failed, this does not in itself render Pan-Syrianism unimportant. Failure to achieve objectives is not the main measure of an ideology's importance; were this so, many historically powerful ideologies, including Pan-Turkish nationalism, Pan-Slavic nationalism, and even Nazism, would also have to be deemed insignificant. Closer to the case at hand, Pan-Arabism has failed perhaps even more thoroughly, yet no ones disparages its role.

Indeed, fascination with radical Pan-Arabism (the ideology that calls for a single Arab state from the Atlantic Ocean to the Persian Gulf) is a second reason for the neglect of Pan-Syrianism. A sequence of dramatic events—the founding of the Arab League, the rise of Jamal 'Abd an-Nasir, the formation of the United Arab Republic—caused scholars and politicians alike to dwell on the proposed Arab nation, to the virtual exclusion of the Greater Syrian nation. There would seem to be five hundred books on the topic of Pan-Arabism for each one on Pan-Syrianism; and the ratio of political speeches must be on the order of thousands to one. It is not my intent to deny the importance of Pan-Arabism, which has indeed been a central feature of Middle East politics; but Pan-Arabism has had no monopoly and has never (with the near exception of 1958–1960) excluded a role for Pan-Syrianism.

The Pan-Arabist effort looms so large, it expropriates many of the central events in Pan-Syrian history. Several examples illustrate this. Although the anonymous placards that appeared in major cities of Syria in 1880 were the first public expressions of Pan-Syrianism, historians typically interpret them as Pan-Arabist[10] or even as Lebanese separatist.[11] The rebellion against the Turks in World War I, now invariably called the Arab Revolt, was often referred to as the Syrian revolt by its leader, Prince Faysal.[12] Further, this British ploy contained few nationalist ideas until the rebels came into contact with the Pan-Syrianists. Despite the specifically Pan-Syrian focus of the General Syrian Congress of 1919–20, it is routinely presented as a Pan-Arab gathering; one account goes so far as to change its name to the "Arab National Congress."[13] Muhammad Y. Muslih preempts the Syrian Kingdom of 1920, turning it into "the first experiment in the bewildering dream of Arab unity."[14]

Even more egregious is Christopher Sykes's statement that in the 1920s, "Arab nationalism was fixed on the dream of a Greater Syria";[15] this is as nonsensical as saying that German nationalists aspired to a strong Austria. In her otherwise excellent biography of King 'Abdallah, Mary C. Wilson almost entirely ignores the role of Pan-Syrian ideology, preferring to interpret the king's expansionary plans solely in the light of "the structure of Transjordan."[16] Perhaps most outlandish is Philip S. Khoury's referring to the standard Pan-Syrian name for Palestine, *Southern Syria,* as a term "often preferred" by radical pan-Arabists, a sleight of hand that allows him completely to ignore Pan-Syrianism.[17]

As possibly the most disregarded topic of Middle East history in the twentieth century, Pan-Syrianism cries out for investigation; my goal is to begin to recall this topic from its neglect. The pages that follow are a first step toward setting the record straight.

The topic is richly documented. Faysal's Syrian kingdom attracted great attention because of its epochal nature; 'Abdallah, a voluble man, widely promoted his Greater Syria plan for thirty years; and the Syrian Social Nationalist Party is a party of intellectuals whose organization and membership have produced voluminous materials. The Asad government has clearly shown its intentions in word and deed. There is nothing secret about Greater Syria.

At the same time, open discussion of Greater Syria ended several decades ago, and the whole subject has gone into abeyance. It is hard now to picture the vividness of the debate over Greater Syria in the interwar period and beyond; perhaps the way to conjure up the role of Pan-Syrian nationalism, then, is to compare it with Palestinian nationalism more recently. Both causes excited wide attention and profoundly influenced the politics of the Middle East, yet all the brouhaha brought neither one closer to realization.

Chapter 1 provides background information on three subjects: what Greater Syria is, what happened to it in the aftermath of World War I, and how Pan-Syrianism emerged as a political ideology. Chapter 2 records the history of Pan-Syrian efforts from 1920 to 1973, and Chapter 3 continues this account from 1974 to 1988. The earlier period was characterized by leaders making claims on each other—Palestinian on Transjordanian, Transjordanian on Syrian, Syrian on Lebanese, and so forth; in the recent period, Syrians made almost all the claims. Earlier, all efforts but one failed; in contrast, recent Syrian efforts have succeeded quite handsomely. Chapter 4 offers an explanation for Damascus's turn toward Pan-Syrianism under Hafiz al-Asad, intering this primarily as the result of domestic factors.

A few words on methods used in this study:

Widespread doubt about the importance of Pan-Syrianism prompts me to buttress my inquiry with a very extensive factual base. Accordingly, the following text—and Chapters 2 and 3 especially—includes a great number of examples and direct quotations.

Believing that religious lines—not party politics, ideology, or geography—delineate the most basic and abiding political divisions in the Greater Syria region, this account emphasizes communal affiliations. To ignore or deemphasize religion is to miss the most characteristic quality of Syrian politics. In contrast, government institutions, ideological parties, and the other trappings of modern politics sit lightly. The Ba'th Party, as Stanley F. Reed has rightly observed, has become "a clan masquerading as a political party";[18] and the same applies to much of the rest of the Western overlay in public life.

But using religious labels to identify political groups raises two possible misunderstandings. First, I am not implying that the policy advocated by a communal group derives from its theology; rather, religion is only one factor in a complex mix. That Maronites seek a separate state and the Greek Orthodox sympathize with Pan-Arabism results much less from their credos than from the fact that the former are geographically concentrated and the latter are dispersed. The 'Alawi-Sunni confrontation that shaped Syrian politics from the mid-1960s culminated centuries of conflict, economic and social as well as religious.

Second, although the members of a religious community usually hold a common position, they are never unanimous. Personal temperament, ideology, economics, and geography also influence an individual's outlook. Contrary to their communities' stands, some Christian Lebanese advocate close links between their country and Syria, while some Muslim Lebanese resist these. Although the impact of such dissidents tends to be small, the characterization of a community's stand must not be understood to apply to all its members.

Similarly, care must be taken not to equate the actions of the government with the views of its citizenry. All too often one reads about "Syria" doing this or "Egypt" doing that, whereas what is meant is "the rulers of Syria" or "the government of Egypt." Authoritarian states require special caution; but even where democracy prevails, it is wise to distinguish the authorities from the citizenry.

About the intricacy of this subject: The Japanese fondly believe that their culture is incomprehensible to outsiders, and it is indeed very subtle and diverse. But it can seem almost like child's play compared to a small country like Lebanon, for Japan is nearly one homogeneous whole, while the Levant consists of an extraordinary variety of peoples and cultures. The adjective *Levantine* applies well to the political realm, for the area at the eastern end of the Mediterranean involves intricacies on many levels.

There is Syria and Greater Syria, Mount Lebanon and Greater Lebanon, Transjordan and Jordan. Alexandretta and Hatay are the same place, as are the West Bank and Judea and Samaria. The Parti Populaire Syrien and the Syrian Social Nationalist Party are the same organization,[19] while Pan-Syrianism and Syrian nationalism are the same ideology.[20] Rivalries abound: French and British, European and Middle Eastern, Sunni and Shi'i, Arab and non-Arab, Muslim and Christian, Sunni and non-Sunni, Hashimi and Sa'udi, Faysal and 'Abdallah, monarchist and republican, Pan-Syrianist and Pan-Arabist.

These intricacies inhere in the subject. As British prime minister David Lloyd George wrote about the negotiations that followed World War I:

> In some respects the settlement of the Turkish Empire presented greater difficulties than that of any other enemy country. There was a greater variety of races and religions to be dealt with. They were more hopelessly intermingled without any trace or hope of merger. There were historical complications which had never been unraveled. There were the jealousies of Powers, each of them with real or imaginary interests—historical, religious, financial or

territorial—in some corner of this dilapidated Empire. There was a wilderness of decay and ruin.[21]

A word on the negative tone of this study. *Tension, problem, conflict,* and similar words fill the pages. With such a gloomy text, an author has to question whether his approach is overly pessimistic. Reflecting on this question brings me to the conclusion that the twentieth-century history of the Levant calls for this tone. Lloyd George's literal "wilderness of decay and ruin" disappeared in the years after World War I, only to be replaced by its political equivalent. A wide range of fundamental disagreements and deeply unsettled identities characterizes the political life of Greater Syria. It has been one of the most consistently volatile regions in the world. An author must contend with these facts.

On a personal note, my immersion in Pan-Syrian history and my efforts to bring attention to it in no sense imply an endorsement of the ideology. Quite the contrary. I am convinced that there is no such thing as a Syrian nation. (Nor, for that matter, is there an Arab nation.) The strong communal identities of the residents repudiate such an affiliation, as does the absence of a Syrian polity at any time in the region's long history. Egypt fits the definition of a nation; Greater Syria never has and never will. My views roughly correspond to those of William Yale, a member of the American commission sent to ascertain Syrian opinion in 1919, who noted that "the Moslems of Palestine and Syria have been united on a program which superficially has every sign of being Syrian nationalism, but which is basically Islamic."[22] Pan-Syrianism has force to the extent that it reflects sectarian sentiment or *raison d'état,* but there is no Greater Syrian nation.

I

GREATER SYRIA
IN HISTORY

1

Background and Changes

I haven't yet come across one spark of national feeling: it is all sects and hatreds and religions.

Freya Stark, 1928

If ever there was a country in which every conceivable influence, divine and mundane, physical and moral, inherent and extraneous, militated against national unity and the formation of a patriotic sentiment, that country was Syria before 1914.

Edward Atiyah, 1946[1]

Historic Syria to 1918

What Is Syria?

The name *Syria* derives from the Semitic term *Siryon*. In the Bible (Deuteronomy 3.9), this refers to Mount Hermon. *Syria* is originally a Greek word; its probable first literary use occurs in Aeschylus's *Persae* (84), written in 472 B.C. Herodotus, writing about 440 B.C., used *Syria* loosely in the *Histories* to refer to Cappadocia. In the Hellenistic period, the Greeks used the term *Coele Syria* to refer to the area between the Mediterranean and the Euphrates River, distinguishing it from the part of Syria in Mesopotamia. The Seleucids of the third century B.C. also used the term vaguely to mean what is now called Southwest Asia.[2] The Romans first used this term to refer to what came to be the standard area—"those regions of the Near East between Asia Minor and Egypt which belonged to the Roman Empire."[3] The Byzantines subsequently adopted the Roman usage.

Arabians conquered historic Syria in the seventh century A.D. Although they brought with them new names—*Ash-Sham* (the North),[4] *Bilad ash-Sham* (the country of Sham), *Barr ash-Sham* (the land of Sham)—they exactly retained the Romans' meaning.[5]

Disregarding the Arabic term, Europeans continued to use the name *Syria* (or *Surie*) through the centuries. (By similar token, they retained the names *Persia*, *Egypt*, and *Albania* for what local peoples called Iran, Misr, and Shqiperia.) With the expansion of European influence, the term *Suriya*—an Arabic form of the Greek name—was introduced in Arabic and Turkish, probably by Protestant missionaries. As early as 1825, a farewell letter of

Jonas King to his "brethren in Palestine and Syria," used the word *Suriya*.[6] The term gained currency in the mid-nineteenth century. Thus, the Syrian Society for the Acquisition of the Sciences and the Arts (*Jam'iya Suriya li-Iktisab al-'Ulum wa'l-Funun*) came into existence in 1847 and lasted until 1850. Founded by three American missionaries, it consisted only of Christian members. The Syrian Scholarly Society (*al-Jam'iya al-'Ilmiya as-Suriya*), founded in 1868, included Muslims as well.[7] Butrus al-Bustani, a leading figure in the development of Syrian consciousness, published a newspaper in 1860 called *Nafir Suriya* ("The Trumpet of Syria"). A book titled *Kharabat Suriya* ("The Ruins of Syria") appeared in Beirut in 1861.

The word then took hold. Muhammad Abu's-Su'ud al-Hasibi referred to Syria in a history written sometime after 1868.[8] Ilyas Dib Matar wrote a *History of the Syrian Kingdom* in 1874, and Jurji Yanni wrote a *History of Syria* seven years later.[9] Though nonpolitical in outlook, these books concentrated attention on the concept of Syria and in so doing encouraged the emerging Syrian national consciousness. Ottoman officials initially opposed the use of the term *Syria*, but eventually they, too, accepted it and even used it officially.

Historically, the name *Syria* refers to a region far larger than the one presently contained by the state called Syria. At minimum, that Syria includes an irregular rectangle bounded by the Mediterranean Sea in the west, the Taurus and Anti-Taurus Mountains in the north, and the Syrian, Arabian, and Sinai deserts in the east and south. In terms of today's political units, historic Syria comprises all of four states—Syria, Jordan, Israel, and Lebanon—as well as the West Bank, the Gaza Strip, and substantial portions of southeastern Turkey.

Europeans saw Transjordan, Palestine, and Lebanon firmly included in Syria, but they tended to define Syria minimally. Thus, the French traveler Volney wrote in 1787 that Syria comprised "the area included between two lines, one drawn from Alexandretta to the Euphrates, the other from Gaza (in the Arabian Desert) to the desert in the east."[10] In 1837, Georg Wilhelm Friedrich Hegel wrote, "in Syria we have Jerusalem." Sarah Barclay Johnson entitled her 1858 book *Hadji in Syria: or, Three Years in Jerusalem*.[11] The American University of Beirut, founded in 1866, was originally named the Syrian Protestant College.

Europeans often used the term *southern Syria* to refer to Palestine. John Lewis Burckhardt noted in 1812 that the region around Salt (in northwest Jordan) had the best pasturage "of all southern Syria."[12] The 1840 Convention of London referred to the area around Acre as "the southern part of Syria."[13] H. B. Tristam posited the Nahr al-Kalb, just north of Beirut, as the boundary of southern Syria.[14] The eleventh edition of the *Encyclopaedia Britannica*, published in 1911, explained that Palestine "may be said generally to denote the southern third of the province of Syria."[15]

Some observers, mostly those of Middle East origins, saw Syria as a yet larger entity. According to an Egyptian historian writing in the early nineteenth century, a person born in El Arish (at the north of the Sinai Peninsula) is one of the Syrians.[16] The General Syrian Congress of 1919 defined Syria to include large parts of Iraq and Saudi Arabia.[17] The French government at that time included Cilicia in Syria, as did Benoit Aboussouan, writing in 1925.[18] Antun Saʿada, founder of the Syrian Social Nationalist Party (SSNP), initially defined Syria within the minimal borders; later he added the Sinai Peninsula, all of Iraq, and even Cyprus.[19] With one exception, these larger boundaries attracted little support and had no practical importance; that exception was the joining of Iraq and Syria into a single unit, dubbed the "Fertile Crescent."

The many sizes and shapes ascribed to Syria point to a key geographical fact; like Germany, historic Syria has no firm natural boundaries hallowed by age. Instead, its contours change with each war, diplomat, or theorist. To make matters even more fluid, some divisions are more clearly delineated within the region than outside it. Small as it is, the Jordan River has historically made residents of the west and east banks "strangers, or enemies, to each other."[20] Alexander W. Kinglake noted during a trip in 1834–35 that the Jordan "is a boundary between the people living under roofs and the tented tribes that wander on the further side."[21] In short, Israel differs more from Jordan than does Jordan from Iraq. A geographer can draw a line between the Maronite and Sunni areas of Lebanon with more confidence than between Syria and Turkey. For centuries, Aleppo and Damascus served as capitals of rival regions.

This said, ecology and culture (but not politics) give historic Syria some cohesion. Like Egypt, Arabia, Yemen, and the other large traditional units of the Middle East, Syria has geographic boundaries and ecological characteristics that make it distinct from adjoining areas. With the sea on one side and the desert on the other, it is "rather like an isthmus, comparable to the Panama Isthmus between North and South America—an isthmus between Anatolia to the north and Egypt to the south, about five hundred miles long and about seventy-five miles wide, with the geographical features running north and south."[22] Syria makes up the western part of the Fertile Crescent, a dry region that supports life when—and only when—tended with great care. Geographers recognized the cohesion of the area. According to one, Emmanuel de Martonne, from the Sinai desert to Alexandretta, the country has "the same physical structure, the same climatic phenomena," while "vegetation, culture, and human societies obey the same laws."[23]

As de Martonne suggests, culture also defines Syria; its residents have important qualities in common. They share a physical typology and an extended family structure. They speak Arabic with a distinctive lilt and prepare foods in a similar fashion. As a Syrian explained in 1919 to the Paris Peace Conference, "Apart from language, the factors welding this nation into one are the soil on which it has sprung up, whence it has derived similarity of physical and moral form and been inspired by the same ideals; its traditions and customs; its common fate throughout the course of centuries; and, above all perhaps, its sufferings."[24] Less poetically, the General Syrian Congress justified its demand for a united Syria on the basis that "the people speak Arabic; they are intermarried and have many links of kinship; and commerce has for ages moved freely between them."[25]

Though universally recognized for more than two thousand years as a cohesive region, Syria is not a polity. It never acquired political form as a single state containing only Syria and nothing else. In this, it resembles New England or Scandinavia (or Germany and Italy before unification); like them, it is a region that exists outside politics. The closest a state came to covering precisely the area of Syria was for some years in the second century B.C. under the Seleucid kings. Also, the area as a whole was ruled from within for ninety years, A.D. 660–750, though it was then but a corner of the immense Umayyad Empire. Except for these two brief periods, Syria was usually the province of an empire based elsewhere, though parts were occasionally independent. A Syrian patriot wrote in 1912: "Its glories were the undoing of Syria; it hardly left the control of one master before it fell under that of another. . . . If Syria was never united, it is because it always had masters, never a proper government."[26]

From 1516 to 1918, Syria made up a small portion of the Ottoman Empire, the state based in Constantinople that extended from central Europe to southern Arabia. Ottoman rulers divided Syria into a variety of administrative districts during those four centuries. After 1864, these consisted of three vilayets (Aleppo, Damascus, and Beirut); the province of Jerusalem; and the mutasarrifiya of Mount Lebanon.[27] Except for the Maronite region of Mount Lebanon, which enjoyed a special cohesion and autonomy, these units had little more than administrative significance. They had no greater political meaning than the circuit court districts in the United States. Nor did they interfere with communications; people and goods freely traversed administrative lines.

It is important to emphasize that the territorial concepts in existence today—Palestine, Israel, Jordan, Syria, the Arab world—did not appear until very late in the Ottoman period; and Lebanon existed only in embryo.

A Splintered Society

Not only does Syria have no history as a state, but its residents historically did not consider themselves members of a Syrian nation. The area's unique features militated against any sense of common purpose. The location of Syria makes it a crossroads for conquering armies; the mountainous terrain ("less favorable to the administrator than to the outlaw and heretic")[28] makes it a refuge for vanquished and oppressed peoples; holiness makes it a destination for pilgrims and pioneers. These factors go far to explain the region's characteristic religious and ethnic diversity.

Syria hosts an extraordinarily full representation of the three major monotheisms; a remnant of almost every Middle East schism and heterodoxy lives on there. Muslim groups include Sunnis and Shi'is, the latter dividing into the Twelver and Sevener branches, known locally as Mutawalis and Isma'ilis.

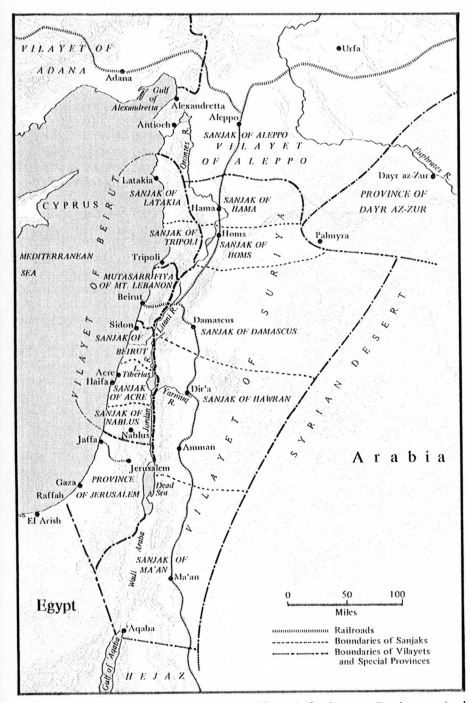

Figure 3. Ottoman Syria in 1914   Until World War I, the Ottoman Empire contained the whole of Greater Syria, though parts of it were only loosely controlled.

17

Among the Christian groups, the Eastern Orthodox are split into Greek and Syrian (Jacobite) branches. Catholics divide into five Uniate Churches—Greek (Melkite), Syrian, Armenian, Chaldaean (Nestorian), and Maronite—as well as the Latin rite. Other Christians include the Armenians (Gregorian church), Nestorians (Assyrians), and Protestants. Jews include the indigenous Sephardim and immigrant Ashkenazim.

Syria is a haven for minorities. It boasts Lebanon, the only Christian-ruled state of the Middle East, and Israel, the only country in the world where Jews form a majority of the population. Three religions are unique to Syria: the Samaritans, an early Jewish offshoot; and the 'Alawis and Druze, two secretive breakaway sects of Shi'ism. Many minor religions find a home in Syria. These include the Yazidis, a people living in the northeast of Syria, and the Ahl-i Haqq, a heresy of Islam; both of these also keep their doctrines secret. The Baha'i religion makes its headquarters in Haifa.

Several communal groups speak languages other than Arabic. Groups of Sunni Muslims speak Kurdish, Circassian, and Turkic, while Christian sects speak Armenian, Assyrian, and Syriac. In the course of the twentieth century, some Lebanese dropped Arabic for French, while Sephardic Jews abandoned Arabic and Ladino in favor of Hebrew; Ashkenazi Jews brought Yiddish and other European languages.

Some communities, especially the Greek Orthodox, are spread throughout Syria. Others have the advantage of being "compact minorities"[29] and are able to exert their will over a specific piece of land; these include the Druze, 'Alawis, and Shi'is, and most especially the Maronites.

Syria contains probably the most fractured population in the world. One Pan-Syrian nationalist goes so far as to call the region's heterogeneity its "trademark."[30] Robert de Caix, an architect of French mandatory policy, referred to confessionalism as the "virtual nationality" of Lebanon.[31] Parts of historic Syria, such as Alexandretta and Lebanon, have no majority population, only pluralities; and, as Table 1 shows, Syria as a whole has a virtual parity between Sunni Arabs and other peoples.

This plethora of ethnic and religious groups has deeply influenced public life in Syria. Historically, each religious community enjoyed strong internal bonds and lived as separately as it could from the others. Except for specific commercial or political purposes, communities did not cooperate, and there certainly was no sense of common identity as Syrians. Residents of Syria directed their first loyalties to the family; then came other genealogical relations, as well as religious, ethnic, regional, linguistic, ecological, and class ties. Other than a weak allegiance of Sunnis to the Ottoman overlord in Constantinople, ties to the state were almost nonexistent.

Communal relations in Syria were not the best. Isabel Burton, who lived some time in Damascus, exaggerated only slightly in summing up the hostilities:

> These various religions and sects live together more or less, and practise their conflicting worships in close proximity. Outwardly, you do not see much, but in their hearts they hate one another. The Sunnites excommunicate the Shiahs,

Table 1. Population of Greater Syria

	Total Population	Sunni Arab Population	Sunni Arab (%)
Alexandretta	923,000[a]	92,000	10[b]
Gaza Strip	483,000[c]	478,000	99[d]
Israel	3,960,000[e]	475,000	12[f]
Jordan	3,419,000[e]	3,145,000	92[f]
Lebanon	2,598,000[e]	623,000	24[f]
Syria	9,739,000[e]	5,300,000	54[g]
West Bank	875,000[c]	831,000	95[d]
TOTAL	21,997,000	10,944,000	50

a. Estimate for 1983 from *Başbakanlık Devlet İstatistik Entstitüsü, Genel Nüfus Sayımı: Nüfusun Sosyal ve Ekonomik Nitelikleri* (Ankara: Devlet İstatisik Entstitüsü Matbaası, 1982), Vol. 31, p. 3.

b. Elizabeth Picard, "Retour au Sandjak," *Maghreb-Machrek,* January–March 1983, p. 55.

c. Estimates for 1983 from Michael K. Roof and Keven G. Kinsella, *Palestinian Population: 1950 to 1984* (Washington, D.C.: U.S. Bureau of the Census, 1985), pp. 22, 26.

d. Israel Defense Forces, *Census of Population 1967: West Bank of the Jordan, Gaza Strip and Northern Sinai, Golan Heights* (Jerusalem: Central Bureau of Statistics, 1967), pp. XI–XII.

e. Estimates for 1983 from U.S. Bureau of Census, *World Population 1983* (Washington, D.C.: U.S. Bureau of the Census, 1983).

f. Derived from Appendix B in R. D. McLaurin, ed., *The Political Role of Minority Groups in the Middle East* (New York: Praeger, 1979).

g. See below, p. 151.

and both hate the Druzes; all detest the Ansariyyehs ['Alawis]; the Maronites do not love anybody but themselves, and are duly abhorred by all; the Greek Orthodox abominate the Greek Catholics and the Latins; all despise the Jews.[32]

Out of this came a splintered society. In the Ottoman period, Europeans and Westernized Syrians often remarked on the absence of Syrian solidarity or national sentiment. Testimony on this subject is unanimous. Lord Shaftsbury wrote in 1853 that Syria was "a country without a nation." The well-informed author of a British travel guide to Syria noted in the mid-nineteenth century that "patriotism is unknown. There is not a man in the country, whether Turk or Arab, Mohammedan or Christian, who would give a para [penny] to save the empire from ruin; that is if he be not in government pay. . . . The patriotism of the Syrian is confined to the four walls of his own house; anything beyond them does not concern him."[33] Gertrude Bell, a knowledgeable British observer, wrote in 1907 that "Syria is merely a geographical term corresponding to no national sentiment in the breasts of the inhabitants."[34] K. T. Khaïrallah noted in 1912 that

Syrian society did not exist in the past. There was nothing but distinct and often hostile groups. It was a vast cluster of disparate elements brought together through conquest and held together under one authority by terror and tyranny. Each element jealously retained its traditions, customs, and livelihood, ignoring that of its neighbor. If anything was known, it was the better to feed hatred and excite fanaticism. Society was based on a despotism of brutal force modeled on that of the ruler.[35]

Writing in 1915, T. E. Lawrence observed about the residents of Greater Syria:

> Autonomy is a comprehensible word, Syria is not, for the words Syria and Syrian are foreign terms. Unless he has learnt English or French, the inhabitant of these parts has no word to describe all his country. *Syria* in Turkish (the word exists not in Arabic) is the province of Damascus. *Sham* in Arabic is the town of Damascus. An Aleppine always calls himself an Aleppine, a Beyrouti a Beyrouti and so on down to the smallest villages.
>
> This verbal poverty indicates a political condition. There is no national feeling. Between town and town, village and village, family and family, creed and creed, exist intimate jealousies.[36]

Lawrence was mistaken about Syria not existing in Arabic; but his observation indicates how little used was this novel term as late as World War I. This situation changed only with the Arab Revolt, European occupation of Syria, and Faysal's Syrian kingdom. The chief of French information in the Middle East wrote in early 1918 that "it was absolutely impossible to create a native Syrian kingdom, even one with illusionary power." Divided into many "nations and nationalities, Syria, from a political point of view, was like dust."[37]

Scholars concur. Jacques Weulersse, the foremost student of Syrian rural life, observed in 1946 that

> for the peasant, the state is largely arbitrary, something that engages neither his life nor his heart; it is an inevitable curse that afflicts him. His absolute lack of patriotism is so striking because the reflexes of our [French] peasants are essentially patriotic. One searches vainly among Oriental [i.e., Syrian] peasants for the sacredness of the border or the holy defense of the ancestral land.
>
> His concept of the world does not extent beyond his tribe. . . . He knows no other community but that of religion. Interrogate a peasant in the Jazira, in the Anti-Lebanon, or in Ajlun, ask who he is, and he will reply that he is of this or that tribe, of this or that village, a Muslim, Christian Orthodox, or Druze; never will he tell you spontaneously that he is Iraqi, Syrian, Lebanese, or Jordanian. . . .
>
> In the course of time, the state and the countryside have, in the Orient, followed different paths. The political organism has systematically ignored the rural populaces and the latter have reciprocated. This divorce has resulted in a paradoxical situation: on the one hand, states without national territory, peoples, or patriotism; on the other, amorphous and indifferent peasant masses. States without land are matched by peasants without a nation (*patrie*).[38]

Moshe Ma'oz notes that "Syrian socio-political life was characterized by the lack of a strong central government, a multitude of regional power centers, political administrative splits, social seclusion, and communal, religious, regional, and social contrasts."[39]

The Sunnis of Syria, with their powerful sense of enfranchisement and superiority, stood out within the mix of peoples. Although making up only half the population of Syria, Sunnis constituted a majority in the Middle East at large. Beyond numbers, Sunnis had a unique sense of seeing themselves not as a community but as the dominant people. As the ruling elite of the Ottoman Empire, they were the nonethnics in a heterogeneous society—like Anglo-Saxon Protestants in the United States. Their special status was acknowledged by their often being called "Islam" and nothing more. In contrast, other religious groupings were but sects, tolerated to one degree or another, enjoying more or less political weight. This led to an assumption that Sunnis, and not Shiʻi Muslims (much less the Christians), had a right to rule. Supporting this view was the fact that between 636 and 1917, Sunnis had indeed ruled Syria, with just a few exceptions (the Fatimids and Crusaders in parts of Syria in 978–1078 and 1097–1291; also, from the early nineteenth century, Maronites and Druze controlled parts of Lebanon).

But minority peoples in Syria became increasingly unwilling to accept continued Sunni domination from the early 1800s. They sought power commensurate with their half of the population. Two developments allowed the minorities to stake a new position. Local Christians took advantage of their close connections to Europe, especially France, to force a new set of relations on the Sunni Muslims. Soon after, other groups, such as the Druze and Jews, followed the Christian example. Sunnis increasingly resented the behavior of uppity minorities; communal relations in Syria plummeted as conflict between Sunni Arabs and the minorities came to characterize the region's political life. And this applied not just to the well-known case of the Jews but also to the Maronites, Druze, Twelver Shiʻa, and ʻAlawis.

Second, the encounter with nationalism—that European ideology that holds that the state should represent a culturally cohesive people—caused an upheaval in Syrian politics. Nationalism had revolutionary implications for the Muslims, bringing in a whole new way of looking at the state. It emphasized language and territory, two essentially apolitical traits for Muslims, and it prescribed equality for all members of the nation, regardless of religion, thereby dismissing the most basic and ancient political division. It called for the transformation of a cultural region into a political union.

The presence of strongly defined religious groups in Syria raised a major question. What was the nation to which the Christians belonged? Did each denomination constitute a separate nation? Did all the Christians of Syria make a single nation? Was the population of the Christian-dominated area (i.e., Mount Lebanon) a nation? All Syrians? All residents of the Fertile Crescent? All Arabic speakers in Asia? All Arabic speakers, regardless of place?

The Christians developed ideologies to support three of these concepts: Lebanese separatism emphasized the Christian-dominated region, Pan-Syrianism stressed Syria, and Pan-Arabism dwelt on the Arabic-speaking peoples. Even if tactics differed—Lebanese separatism created new barriers, while Syrian and Arab nationalism bridged old distinctions—all three offered a way to eliminate the Sunnis' historic dominance and the minorities' historic subjugation.

The nationalist idea first arrived in Syria in the mid-nineteenth century, brought from Europe by Middle East Christians who saw it as an instrument to improve their inferior status. Sunni Muslims absorbed these ideas within a

few decades. As Western ideologies impinged, Sunnis too began to feel a need
to define the nation to which they belonged. Because they were dealing with
radically unfamiliar matters, Muslims tended to follow the lead of Middle East
Christians. And while the Muslims almost universally rejected Lebanese separatism, Islamicized versions of Syrian and Arab nationalism appealed to them.

For both Christians and Muslims before World War I, these three concep-
tions were to a fair degree compatible and overlapping. As Albert Hourani
observed:

> The supporters of Syrian nationalism were proud of their Arab culture, had
> connexions with the "Party of Decentralization," and took part in the Arab
> Congress of 1913; at the same time, they argued for the *de facto* independence
> of Lebanon. Similarly, those who spoke in terms of Arab nationalism often
> had a special feeling for the human community of Syria, and when asking for
> Arab autonomy thought primarily of Syria, with Damascus at its centre. The
> advocates of independent Lebanon, it is true, tended to think in terms of
> Muslims and Christians rather than Arabs and Turks, and wished to be inde-
> pendent of Damascus no less than Constantinople; they saw Lebanon as a
> Mediterranean country linked with western Christendom. But at the same
> time they were jealous of the autonomy of the eastern Catholic Churches,
> proud of the Arabic language and its literature, aware that they could not turn
> their backs on their Syrian and Arab hinterland of economic and cultural
> influence. There was no need, before 1914, for lines to be sharply drawn: all
> groups had a common interest in changing the policy of the [Ottoman] gov-
> ernment, and none of them seemed near to securing independence in any
> form.[40]

Before these ideas could crystallize, however, World War I permanently
upset the small, sheltered world of Syria. The outbreak of war meant having to
choose sides and preparing for possible independence.

Dividing Historic Syria, 1918–1923

The decade from 1914 to 1924 was the formative period for Greater Syria, as
well as the rest of the Middle East. The Ottoman Empire fell, European powers
moved in, boundaries were delineated, and new states came into existence, all
in ten years. Virtually every Middle Eastern political movement of the twentieth century, including Pan-Syrianism, got started during that decade.

The Syrian Kingdom

Modern Syrian political history begins with the First World War, when Syria
abruptly emerged from "the shabby obscurity of an Ottoman province"[41] to
become the focus of wide international concern. At the center of this transformation was the British government's effort to build alliances for its war effort
against Germany. Toward this end, it made vaguely worded promises of Syrian
territory to three different parties. In the Husayn-McMahon correspondence,

ten letters exchanged between July 1915 and March 1916, London promised portions of Syria to the Ottoman governor of Mecca, the Sharif al-Husayn. In the Sykes-Picot Agreement of May 1916, it divided Syria with France. In the Balfour Declaration of November 1917, it endorsed "the establishment in Palestine of a national home for the Jewish people."

British forces took control of the area from the Mediterranean Sea to Iran in a quick campaign that began with the Arab Revolt of June 1916 and ended with the conquest of Aleppo in October 1918. For the campaign in Syria, the British allied with forces from the Arabian peninsula led by Prince Faysal, the son of Sharif al-Husayn. The British agent with the Arabs was T. E. Lawrence, who later famously described his efforts in *Seven Pillars of Wisdom*. The British forces stopped short of Damascus, allowing Faysal to take the city and establish the Arab Military Government in Syria. With this act, the British indicated their favor of an Arab—not a French—administration in Damascus, while enhancing Faysal's stature.

But the Arabs controlled only part of the area that fell under British control. In an effort to meet their commitments to Arab, Frenchman, and Zionist, the British divided Syria into three military administrations, called Occupied Enemy Territory Administrations (OETAs). Britons ran a zone roughly equivalent to what later became Israel; the French received the coastal region between what are now Israel and Turkey; and Prince Faysal received Transjordan as well as everything away from the Mediterranean in today's Lebanon and Syria. Despite this sharing of duties, there was no doubt of ultimate power; the commander of the British forces, General Edmund Allenby, had command over all three zones, and the Union Jack alone flew over his residence.

To the Sunni Arabs who had joined the British, the division of Syria into three zones was both unexpected and disappointing. Called to arms to replace Turkish rule with a united Arab state, they expected Arab rule over the whole of historic Syria. This remained Faysal's goal. Although he served under Allenby, he hoped to gain control of the entire area of Syria, including the zones under British and French administration. With Allenby's assent, Faysal formally announced this intention just two days after arriving in Damascus. "I proclaim . . . in the name of our master, King al-Husayn, the formation of an absolutely independent, constitutional, and unblemished Arab government in Syria that includes the whole of Syria."[42]

Faysal's declaration marks the first operative assertion of Pan-Syrian goals. Despite his confident tone, it was but a futile hope; in this, the first call for Syrian unity foreshadowed the plethora of Pan-Syrian statements that followed in subsequent decades.

To calm the mounting displeasure of Sunni Muslims about the division of Syria, the British and French governments jointly issued a declaration in November 1918, during the last week of the war. In it, they asserted that the OETA zones had only military significance and promised "to put an end to the divisions too long exploited by Turkish policy."[43] This was, in effect, a pledge to unite Syria. Soon thereafter, French foreign minister Stéphen Pichon pri-

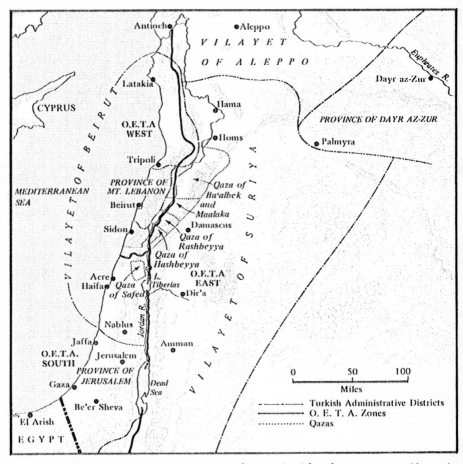

Figure 4. The Three OETA Zones in November 1918   After the conquest of Aleppo in
October 1918, the British government established three military administrations, called
Occupied Enemy Territory Administrations. The inland one was controlled by Faysal
from Damascus.

vately confirmed France's concern for Syrian unity at a closed session of the
Paris Peace Conference in March 1919. He stated that "France strongly protested against any idea of dividing Syria. Syria had geographical and historic
unity."[44] Publicly, he declared in October 1919 that the postwar peace settlement "must not lead to the partition of Syria."[45]

These fine words meant little, however, for the French government wanted
Syria for itself. It had several motives. On the deepest level, the Crusades still
rankled; many Frenchmen sought revenge for the losses of centuries earlier.
(This was symbolized by the actions of General Henri Gouraud, the conqueror
of Syria. On entering Damascus in July 1920, he allegedly went straight to the

tomb of the Muslim leader who had defeated the Crusades in 1187 and announced: "Saladin, nous voici de retour!")[46] At the same time, the French deluded themselves into thinking they had a strong position in the area: the usually perceptive Robert de Caix argued in 1915 that Syria would take "no effort at conquest, for all we have to do is reap the fruit of seven centuries of French activities."[47] More recently, the French had invested prestige in protecting the Christians of Syria and spreading French culture in the region through an ambitious network of schools.

Practical concerns also weighed on the decision to demand control over Syria. French money was committed for such major projects in Syria as the building of railroad and port facilities. The Paris government disliked the presence of a British protégé, Faysal, in Damascus;[48] it needed to protect the French position along the coast; and ties to the Maronites impelled it to heed their fears of an independent Sunni Arab kingdom in Damascus. For all these reasons, strong French currents held that Syria should become the cultural and economic preserve of France.[49]

Thus, Faysal and the French were in competition for the same piece of territory. They agreed that Syria should be under a single rule while disagreeing on who the ruler should be. In contrast, the British, Maronites, and Zionists wanted the area divided.

In the end, French opposition to Faysal's plans partially turned the British around. To have backed Faysal would have meant a collision with France, and this the British were not about to do for a protégé, no matter how helpful. Lord Milner, the colonial secretary, expressed this sentiment candidly in private correspondence: "I am totally opposed to the idea of trying to diddle the French out of Syria."[50] Prime Minister David Lloyd George put it even more directly: "For us, the friendship of France is worth ten Syrias."[51]

Wisely, Prince Faysal did not wait for the Europeans to honor their promises of Syrian unity but set up the embryo of a Sunni Arab government in Damascus. Although in theory he headed what General Edmund Allenby called a "purely provisional" military administration,[52] Faysal quickly converted his command—which covered most of Syrian territory—into a civilian authority, the Arab Syrian Government. To strengthen his regime, Faysal sought support wherever he could. For example, on 3 January 1919, he reached an agreement with the Zionists. In return for Faysal's promise "to encourage and stimulate immigration of Jews into Palestine on a large scale," he won Zionist backing for his campaign against the French. (But his agreement was contingent on Britain keeping France out of Syria; and this not being done, the accord did not take effect.) In a letter of 1 March 1919 to the Zionist Felix Frankfurter, Faysal noted that "there is room in Syria for us both."[53]

Fearing that the military administrations would become permanent, Prince Faysal went to Paris in November 1918 and stayed there until April 1919. He attended the peace conference and implored the great powers for a unified and independent Syria. A Pan-Syrian contest of sorts developed between Faysal and some Syrian agents of the Quai d'Orsay. A leader of the latter, Shukri Ghanim, delivered a long speech in February 1919 expressing the hope that there would be no "mutilation of our country, the unity of which has never been denied in spite of all the vicissitudes of its sad history."[54]

Sure of popular support for a united Syria, Faysal proposed to the peace conference that its members send a commission of inquiry to ascertain the wishes of the Syrian populace. The powers accepted this proposal in late March, to Faysal's undiplomatic glee.[55]

Negotiations with the French government almost resulted in an accord in mid-April. Both Faysal and Premier Georges Clemenceau sought to keep Lebanon and Syria together as a unit—Faysal called this area Greater Syria— but each wanted real authority over the whole of that area, and this difference in view precluded an agreement.

Faysal returned to Damascus in April 1919 to prepare for the International Commission of Inquiry (commonly known as the King-Crane Commission). Calling for "a Syria within its natural borders," he declared that "Syrians demand the independence of their natural homeland."[56] The General Syrian Congress (*Al-Mu'tamar as-Suri al-'Amm*, often translated into English as the Syrian National Congress) convened in July 1919 to prepare for the commission of inquiry. The congress, which was attended by representatives from all parts of Syria, showed overwhelming support for Faysal's demands. It pleaded in its report that "there be no separation of the southern part of Syria, known as Palestine, nor of the littoral western zone, which includes Lebanon, from the Syrian country." In response, the King-Crane Commission recommended that "the unity of Syria be preserved, in accordance with the earnest petition of the great majority of the people of Syria."[57]

But this endorsement had no influence; according to Elie Kedourie, the report of the King-Crane Commission "was as ill-informed as its influence on policy was negligible."[58] Instead, Lloyd George was concerned primarily with repairing relations with the powers. Improving relations was no easy matter; as Foreign Secretary Arthur James Balfour noted in August 1919, "France, England, and America have got themselves into a position over the Syrian problem so inextricably confused that no really neat and satisfactory issue is now possible for any of them."[59] In part, animosity aroused by the Syrian question had to do with it taking on the character of a personal feud between Lloyd George and Clemenceau.

Simultaneous with the King-Crane inquiry, the leaders of an 'Alawi revolt against the French made known their demands. The first was "agreement on the inclusion of the Syrian coast [i.e., Lebanon] within the Arab government in Syria, and the evacuation of French troops [from Lebanon]."[60]

For its part, the French government became increasingly emotional and intransigent on the issue of Syria. Faysal came to be viewed as a mere puppet of British imperialism, and his rule portrayed as contrary to the interests of either France or the Arabs. Thus, according to Maurice Barrès, a prominent commentator, "Prince Faysal has no business in Damascus, Homs, Hama, or Aleppo. France would know how to give these towns a government of Syrians. Who is Faysal for us or for the Syrians? An English man of straw, without title or merit."[61] French emotions on the issue of Syria began to affect the whole tenor of Franco-British relations.

In part to avert a degeneration in those relations and in part because he realized that British defenses had been overstretched by new responsibilities in the Middle East, Lloyd George gave in to French wishes. He decided in September 1919 that Britain would withdraw its forces from Lebanon and Syria. They would be replaced, respectively, by the troops of France and of Faysal. After reminding the French that "the Arab people . . . were bitterly opposed to the partition of Syria,"[62] the British transferred their garrisons on the first of November 1919. In return, the French implicitly gave up on their plan to put together a *Syrie intégrale.*

Faysal quickly recognized that Britain had left him to his fate. Knowing he lacked the military means to resist French forces (whose numbers in the area had increased from 2,000 in late 1918 to 180,000 in early 1920), Faysal undertook another round of diplomacy, going to Paris in October 1919 and negotiating again with Clemenceau. In January 1920, the two held their second talks within eight months, this time reaching an agreement. Faysal recognized a temporary French presence along the coast in return for Paris's acknowledgment of Syrian unity and Faysal's rule over the whole interior. The compromise came to naught, however. It met a very poor reception in Syria; and Clemenceau was replaced just two weeks later by a new premier who repudiated the agreement.

Faysal's power began to slip at this point in favor of his radical supporters. Under their pressure, he gave up on British support or French good will and instead convened a second General Syrian Congress in Damascus in March 1920. Delegates from all parts of Syria not only proclaimed Faysal king of Syria but specifically included the British and French zones within his realm. "We unanimously proclaimed the complete and unconditional independence of our country Syria, including Palestine, within its natural boundaries."[63] The congress also declared independence for Iraq and the twenty-nine Iraqis at the meeting proclaimed Prince ʿAbdallah, Faysal's elder brother, king of Iraq. In effect, Faysal had ruled out further compromise with Paris.

The congress stressed two themes—independence and unity for Syria—which then became central political passions during the French mandate. As Alaeddin Saleh Hreib wrote, "Every political demonstration, urban uprising, and rural revolt consistently made [these] two basic demands."[64] Of the two, unity had the greatest importance. According to George Antonius, "while there were many who were willing and even eager to see Independence qualified by a recourse to foreign assistance, none were for the slightest compromise on the doctrine of Unity."[65]

Faysal, now king, made further negotiations with Britain and France contingent on acknowledgment of the unity between Syria and Palestine. This had little consequence, however, as both imperial powers rejected the whole of the congress's proclamation. Paris instructed the French high commissioner in Beirut to tell Faysal that the French government considered the declaration "null and void."[66] The British foreign secretary huffed that "Great Britain does not recognize that any committee in Damascus has the right to speak about Palestine and Iraq."[67] As Paris prepared to remove Faysal, the British did nothing; indeed, they took some quiet satisfaction at the removal of the troublemakers in Damascus.[68]

In April 1920, British and French representatives met at San Remo and formalized their agreement of September 1919.[69] In accordance with the Sykes-Picot Agreement, they split Syria into two parts, southern and northern, Britain taking the former and France the latter.[70] Faysal in turn rejected these actions, but to no avail. The French army entered the Kingdom of Syria in July 1920, crushing Faysal's forces and forcing him to flee. Paris saw the conquest as permanent; later in 1920, the French prime minister replied to a question what part of Syria his government intended to rule and for how long: "The whole of it, and for ever."[71] San Remo had prevailed over Damascus.

Imposing the Mandates

The division of Syria into two mandates, British and French, was followed during the next three years by the creation of yet another six boundaries. Though exceedingly complex, the divisions of 1920 to 1923 bear close attention, for a number of them remain in place to the present. Decisions taken on the spur of the moment for fleeting imperial interests endured long after the collapse of the European empires; indeed, the careless, arbitrary nature of these divisions continues to burden politics in historic Syria. With the exception of Lebanon, the divisions corresponded neither to Ottoman provincial lines nor to any other boundaries. Indicative of their novelty was the need to refer back to ancient or medieval times to find names for some of these new entities—Iraq, Jordan, Palestine.

The British called their half of Syria the "Mandate for Palestine" and in March 1921 subdivided this territory along the Jordan River into two further parts. Land to the west of the Jordan River became Palestine and was designated for Jewish settlement. In May 1948, most of Palestine became the State of Israel. In the war following the declaration of Israel's independence, Jordan took the piece of Palestine that came to be known as the West Bank, Egypt took the Gaza Strip, and Syria took a few villages.

Land to the east of the Jordan River, Transjordan, had been ruled by King Faysal until July 1920. Subsequently, it became a power vacuum, for Paris did not claim this territory and London did not seek directly to control it (though the British authorities in Palestine tried very hard to get permission to do so). "At that moment," reported Herbert Samuel, the British high commissioner of Palestine, "Trans-Jordan was left politically derelict."[72] Local residents set up their own governments, but these were limited in power and temporary in duration.

When Faysal's older brother, Prince ʿAbdallah, moved into Transjordan (en route to expelling the French from Damascus), Winston Churchill offered the area to him, and he accepted it. At the same time, Churchill determined that the Balfour Declaration would not apply to Transjordan, excluding Jewish settlement there; this decision imbued the geographic division with religious significance. Transjordan became independent in March 1946 and was renamed Jordan in June 1949. Jordan acquired the West Bank in 1948 and lost it in 1967, when the country in effect reverted to Transjordan.

The San Remo conference bestowed the northern half of Syria to France, which termed it the "Mandate for Syria and the Lebanon." The mandate included territory up to the Taurus and Anti-Taurus Mountains in Anatolia; but French troops could not hold Cilicia against the Turkish forces of Mustafa Kemal Atatürk, and Paris formally gave up this area in the Franklin-Bouillon Agreement of October 1921. Although still seen by some as a part of Syria, this northernmost region subsequently dropped out of the consciousness of most Pan-Syrian nationalists.

Like London, Paris promptly subdivided the territory under its control into regions that carried clear religious connotations. Between September 1920 and March 1923, six new units came into existence: Lebanon, the state of Damascus, the government of Aleppo, the autonomous district of Latakia, the autonomous district of Jabal Druze, and the region of Alexandretta. In addition, Jazira province, on the far side of the Euphrates River, had few connections to Syria and was separately run by the French military. These units had the trappings of proto-states (issuing in some cases, for example, their own stamps) and in the normal course of colonial development would have become separate states at independence.

The divisions were clearly an attempt to exploit ethnic and religious differences. What French officials called *la politique minoritaire* isolated the Sunni Arabs in two regions, Aleppo and Damascus, where they formed about 85 percent of the population. Elsewhere, Sunni Arabs constituted minorities— about 30 percent of Latakia, 20 percent of Lebanon, 10 percent of Alexandretta, and 2 percent of Jabal Druze. Latakia was 60 percent 'Alawi, Lebanon 55 percent Christian, Alexandretta a bit of everything (but mostly 'Alawis and Sunni Turks), and Jabal Druze 90 percent Druze.

Paris then disconnected two of these units. Lebanon became an independent republic in May 1926, gained sovereignty in November 1943, and gained full independence when the last French troops left in December 1946. As the price for a nonaggression pact with France just before the outbreak of war with Nazi Germany, the Turkish government took control of Alexandretta in June 1939 (renaming it Hatay). Both detachments aroused great opposition, especially among Sunni Arabs. The other four units were, over the next twenty years, joined together to form the modern state of Syria. Responding to local pressure, France unified Aleppo and Damascus in January 1925, adding Latakia in June 1942 and Jabal Druze in December 1944. Full evacuation of French troops from Syria took place on 15 April 1946.

Why so many territorial cuts? They had several advantages for the British and French authorities. For one, they exacerbated communal tensions among the local population, easing European efforts to maintain control. Grateful for escaping Sunni rule, Zionists, Maronites, Druze, Shi'is, and 'Alawis had reason to want the mandatory power to stay; they therefore served the British and

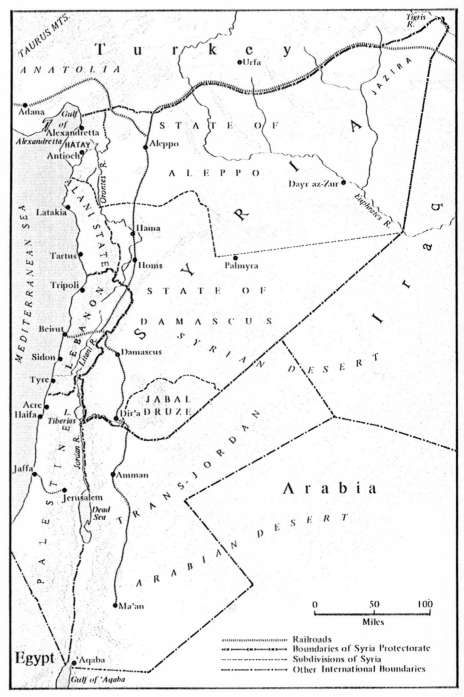

Figure 5. Divisions in Greater Syria, 1920–23 Decisions taken on the spur of the moment for fleeting imperial interests led to the complex divisions of 1920–23. These bear close attention, for many of them remain in place to the present.

French. Second, some of the new polities, such as Jordan, Lebanon and Latakia, were so weak that they depended on European patronage to remain autonomous. In some cases, they needed help just to pay the bills. The Latakia region was ruled directly by French administrators. Third, the French hoped that putting strategically important areas in the hands of minorities would allow them to retain access to these regions even after the Sunnis gained independence. Finally, French concern for the Maronites must not be underestimated; the creation of Lebanon fulfilled a Maronite dream, and the other divisions of French Syria reduced the Muslim threat to Lebanese independence.

Syria takes on new meanings after 1920, when it refers (in addition to historic Syria) to the whole region under French mandate as well as the area it specifically designated as Syria. Then, after 1946, it means the Republic of Syria, the state with its capital in Damascus. To distinguish the historic territory of Syria from these rump regions, several retronyms[73] have been devised. The pre-1918 area is variously called Geographic Syria, Greater Syria, Historic Syria, Natural Syria, or United Syria; in Arabic, *Sham* and *Bilad ash-Sham* are also used. Greater Syria (*Suriya al-Kubra*) being the most familiar term in English, it is the one adopted here.[74] The Syria of San Remo—the new state bounded by Lebanon, Turkey, Iraq, Jordan, and Israel—will be known simply as Syria; but where confusion with Greater Syria might arise, it will be called Lesser Syria.[75]

To summarize these events: Though divided into administrative provinces in 1916, Greater Syria was an integral whole within the Ottoman Empire, and it appeared likely that the region would emerge from the war as a single polity. That it did not reflected British and French imperial needs. By 1923, two European powers had divided it into eight regions. In 1949, it had become four independent countries—two run by Muslims (Syria and Transjordan), one by Christians (Lebanon), one by Jews (Israel)—while small parts were ruled by Turkey and Egypt (Alexandretta and the Gaza Strip, respectively). The same region today contains eight political units: Syria, Jordan, Lebanon, Israel, Alexandretta, the Golan Heights, the West Bank, and the Gaza Strip. Many attempts have been made to eliminate the borders that Europeans had established, but so far all have failed. Rather than ease matters, the granting of independence solidified boundaries even more firmly.

A final word about the divisions of 1918 to 1923: the British and French governments have been often—and justly—criticized for the manner in which they established themselves in the Levant. Their legacy remains heavy in the Middle East, as the divisions they created are still, after so many decades, the source of tension. Although control from Paris and London ended long ago, the heritage of their imperial needs continues to dominate public life in the Levant. A near-random geographic and ethnic hodgepodge froze into the status quo. (The deficiencies of the polity bequeathed by France and their influence on public life in Lesser Syria are discussed in the first pages of Chapter 4.) But it is easier to criticize than to offer alternatives; even the passage of seventy years does not make clear what the powers should have done. With so many antagonistic local forces and so many allegiances, some elements had to domi-

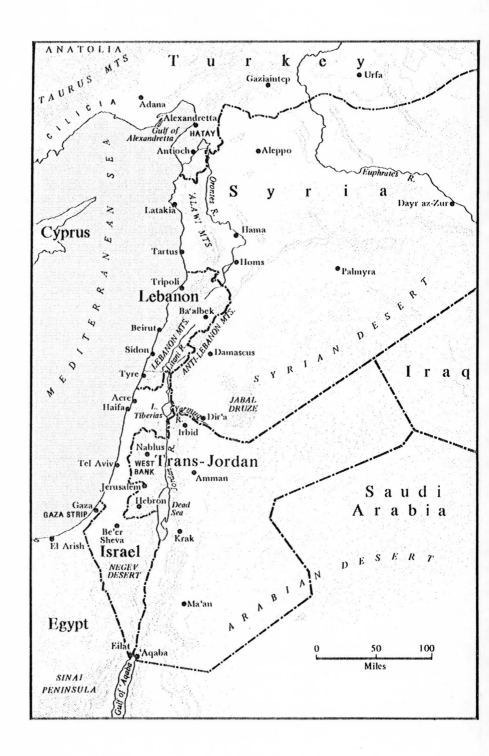

nate and some had to lose, and the results in any case would probably not be much different from what they are in fact today.

What Is the Nation?

What President Woodrow Wilson described as "the whole disgusting scramble" for Syria[76] ended with some of its inhabitants pleased and most of them resentful. Maronites and Zionists reacted most enthusiastically to the divisions; virtually their entire populations hoped to avoid Sunni Arab rule and so embraced Lebanon and Palestine. Conversely, Sunni Arabs despised the new boundaries. The rest of the population—other Christians, other Muslims, ʿAlawis, Druze—stood somewhere in between. In general, Christians favored the borders more than Muslims, while the geographically more compact minorities (Maronites, ʿAlawis, Druze, Shiʿis) accepted them more readily than did dispersed ones (such as the Greek Orthodox).

The divisions aggravated traditional differences between the religious communities and introduced new tensions. Opponents of the new order feared the borders would obstruct the two Pan-Syrian goals of unity and independence. Reflecting this sentiment, the King-Crane Commission report argued that "the separation off of the Greater Lebanon . . . would intensify the religious differences in Syria."[77] Less polite was a remark heard in the 1920s: "The British brought the Jews with their millions to Palestine, and the French brought the Armenians with their poverty and misery to Syria."[78] Dr. ʿAbd ar-Rahman Shahbandar, a prominent Sunni politician, termed the creation of an independent Lebanon part of an effort "to ignite confessional conflicts and to favor the minorities' interests."[79]

Further, territorial divisions transformed the three forms of nationalism that Christians had developed before World War I: Lebanese separatism, Pan-Syrianism, and Pan-Arabism. What had been speculative exercises within the context of the vast, hardly changing Ottoman Empire became urgent political questions in the mandatory period. Two developments had special importance: first, religious communities opted to belong to different nations; then the emergence of ideological parties in the 1930s imbued all three variants with added force. Let us look at each of the three, plus two main alternatives, the Fertile Crescent plan and state nationalism.

Lebanese Separatism

Mount Lebanon is the region of Greater Syria with the longest tradition as a political entity; Lebanese separatism harks back to the polity created by the

Figure 6. Greater Syria in 1949 The borders reached in 1949 have stayed the same, except that the Gaza Strip is no longer under Egyptian control, nor the West Bank under Jordanian control, nor the Golan Heights under Syrian rule. Further, Jerusalem has been united under Israeli rule.

Druze leader Fakhr ad-Din II at the end of the sixteenth century. Lebanese separatism flourished as a result of a conjunction of religion, ethnic affiliation, and geography. The most compact and militant of Christian groups, the Maronites, lived in Mount Lebanon, an inaccessible region which rarely came under the direct control of outside forces.

The first autonomous Lebanese government, called the Mutasarrifiya, was established in Mount Lebanon in 1860. About the same time, Bishop Niqula Murad developed an ideology of Maronite nationalism. The Mutasarrifiya so insulated Mount Lebanon from the Ottoman Empire that most of its Christian inhabitants no longer considered themselves subjects of the emperor. Instead, they looked to France for protection and culture. But Maronites wanted more than the Mutasarrifiya; after 1860, they sought to expand their territory by adding regions to the north, east, and south, as well as the city of Beirut.

The Maronites faced a conundrum: they could either add territory which would bring with it many non-Maronites, or they could keep Christians predominant and Lebanon small. Achieving ideal boundaries meant losing the large Christian majority. Keeping Christian predominance meant remaining geographically tiny. In the end, Maronite separatists opted for the former. They won their maximalist goals in September 1920, when the French authorities delineated the boundaries of the present state of Lebanon. This new area had roughly twice the size of the Mutasarrifiya and included virtually all the Maronites had sought: Tripoli in the north, the Biqa' Valley to the east, Jabal 'Amal to the south, and Beirut in the west. The pre-1920 area is known as Mount Lebanon and the post-1920 area as Greater Lebanon or simply Lebanon.

Of course, the price of expansion was that many unwilling Muslims became Lebanese, sowing the seeds of the civil war that began in 1975. Already in 1920, wise heads anticipated the consequences of including Muslims in Christian-controlled Lebanon. Robert de Caix, a high-level French official, wrote that "creating a too large Lebanon is a serious error, visible even at the time when it is committed. . . . Greater Lebanon breeds an irredentism; we have made Lebanese many Muslims who do not want to be Lebanese."[80] But Maronites long remained oblivious to this danger.

Rather, Maronites embraced the new Lebanon with enthusiasm, seeing it as the best way to avoid Sunni Arab rule. During the mandatory period, they worked for three political goals: remaining separate from Syria, retaining the new 1920 territories, and achieving independence from France. These were not easy tasks, for the Maronites needed French protection to fend off Sunni opposition to Lebanon, especially with its new provinces. To forward these ends, a number of Maronite organizations came into existence, the most important of which was the Phalanges Libanaises (*Al-Kata'ib al-Lubnaniya*), founded in 1936 by Pierre Jumayyil. The Phalanges defined their goals specifically in opposition to Syrian and Arab nationalism; the organization was founded a year after the SSNP's existence became known, part of a reaction to solidify the Lebanese state against its detractors. It was also directed against

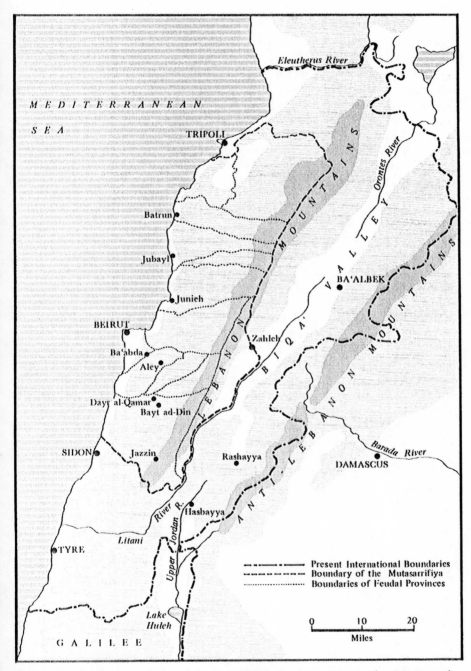

Figure 7. *The Mutasarrifiya of Mount Lebanon, 1860–1914* The Mutasarrifiya
came into existence in 1860 to give the Maronites of Lebanon some automony within
the Ottoman Empire. The region became the nucleus of the larger Lebanese unit created
by the French in 1920.

Pan-Arabism; as Jumayyil wrote, "Lebanon is a 'mission.' And this mission is incompatible with that which the Arabs aspire generally to realize."[81]

The Maronites did well for some decades; keeping the enlarged borders, Lebanon became a republic in 1926 and gained full independence in 1946. Maronites detached themselves from Greater Syria by virtue of having (like the Zionists) the necessary will, territorial base, organization, and European patronage. Separatism could not work for other minorities, however. 'Alawis and Druze tried to emulate the Maronites and win separate states for themselves, but they started too late and lacked the Maronites' resources and connections to Europe. Lebanese separatism is thus a special case, with limited though intense appeal.

Pan-Syrian Nationalism

Unlike Lebanese separatism, which arose from a spontaneous and widespread desire of Maronites to be free of Muslim rule, Pan-Syrianism first appealed to the elites and then spread more widely. It developed as a response to European ideas, not as an articulation of the needs of a portion of the Syrian population. (For proof, note the quotations on pages 19–20.) Thus, Pan-Syrianism attracted support only slowly and sporadically before World War I.

Its origins go back to the mid-nineteenth century. A Maronite intellectual, Butrus al-Bustani (1819–1883), was the first prominent thinker to stress Syria as a focus of loyalty. His writings, especially after the Druze-Maronite conflict of 1860, portrayed Syria as a distinct historical and geographical entity. The broadsheet he published, *Nafir Suriya* ("The Trumpet of Syria"), repeatedly appealed for loyalty to Syria as a way to circumvent endemic communal feuding. Bustani was quite precise about implications of the term *Syria*: it "is our fatherland . . . and the inhabitants of Syria, whatever their creed, sect, or race, are the sons of our fatherland."[82] The idea of a Syrian region had existed for millennia, but Bustani first connected it to the European concept of the nation. At the same time, he continued to see Syria within the Ottoman Empire.

Political action also followed, though slowly. In 1877, the exiled Algerian leader 'Abd al-Qadir al-Jaza'iri was contacted by Sunni leaders about the possibility of leading a movement for the independence of Greater Syria, and then becoming the region's king, but he declined.[83] An organization composed mainly of Sunni notables founded in Damascus in 1878, Independence of Syria (*Istiqlal al-Bilad ash-Shamiya*), was the first political movement to promote Pan-Syrianism, and it too looked to Jaza'iri as king of Syria.[84] In 1880–81, anonymous placards appeared in the major cities of Syria calling for Pan-Syrian nationalism; two of the three extant texts began with the salutation "O Sons of Syria!" The third began with "O Sons of the fatherland [*watan*]!"[85]

The Pan-Syrian ideology made little progress during the next twenty-five years, during the reign of Ottoman emperor 'Abd al-Hamid II. The coming to power of the Young Turks in 1908, with their efforts at centralization and Turkification, prompted new political activism on behalf of historic Syria. Already in 1908, Christians had founded the Syrian Central Committee in

Paris with the goal of promoting a united Syria under French rule. *Al-Fatat* was founded in 1911, the Decentralization Society in 1912, the Reform Committee of Beirut in 1913, the Lebanese Revival in probably the same year, and the Central Committee for Reform and Defense of Syrian Interests in 1913. That same year, the Syrian Arab Congress met in Paris. Despite these activities, the sense of a Greater Syrian nation was still weak when World War I broke out.

Greater Syria acquired a large and articulate following in the aftermath of World War I. Prince Faysal, Shukri Ghanim, the ʿAlawi rebels, and many other politicians subscribed to Pan-Syrian goals. Pro-French publicists were among the most prominent supporters. For example, George-Samné (a colleague of Ghanim's) wrote in 1920: "Ask a Syrian, be he Druze, Muslim, Maronite, Jew, Orthodox, Catholic, be he from Beirut, Aleppo, Damascus, or Jerusalem, what he wants for his country, and he will reply: the independence and unity of Syria, a federal structure on democratic and secular bases."[86] Pan-Syrianism came into its own as an ideology only with Antun Saʿada, the Greek Orthodox intellectual who founded the Syrian Social Nationalist Party (SSNP), on which much more follows in Chapters 2 and 3.

Pan-Arab Nationalism

Early in the century, *Arabs* referred only to the Arabic speakers of Southwest Asia. Egyptians, North Africans, and Sudanese were excluded. Arabians were usually seen as too far away and so were ignored. For all practical purposes, the Pan-Arabist ideology addressed just Greater Syria and Iraq. As late as March 1936, a knowledgeable observer could write that

> The leaders of the [Pan-Arab] movement are themselves extremely vague as to the meanings they attach to the terms nation, nationalism, confederation or pan-Arabism. . . . They will, on occasion, look upon Syria, Palestine and Transjordan as the Arab "nation" having a population of 5 million Arabs, or englobe the countries of Arabic-speaking peoples in Asia and think of a "nation" of 15 million Arabs. In more expansive moments they claim all Moslems as their brothers, and talk of an Arab people of 300 million.[87]

The first Pan-Arab societies were founded in 1908, in response to the Committee of Union and Progress taking power in Istanbul. Modern Pan-Arabism began with the 1933 founding of the League of Nationalist Action (ʿ*Usbat al-ʿAmal al-Qawmi*) in Syria. The Baʿth, founded in 1940 and turned into a functioning party in 1947, became the most effective organization at promoting Pan-Arabist goals. It held that "the Arabs form one nation" and called on them to unify into a single state.[88]

Although initially promoted by Christians, Pan-Arabism suits Sunni Arabs well. It rather exactly combines two contrary and powerful urges: Pan-Islam, the traditional drive to create a union of Muslims, and nationalism, the European ideal. Pan-Islam decrees that all Muslims should live together in one state under a single ruler or, failing this, that Muslim states should live at peace with one another. This vision de-emphasizes differences in language, geography, and ethnic identity in favor of the brotherhood of Islam. In contrast, national-ism exalts language, geography, and ethnic identity. Pan-Arabism's emphasis on the unity of Arabic-speaking Muslims recalls Pan-Islam; its stress on the Arabic language recalls nationalism. By substituting language for religion as the basis of political identity, it acts as a nationalized version of Pan-Islam. That Pan-Arabism serves as a bridge between two contrary ideals goes far to explain its wide appeal.

The Pan-Arabism of Christians was limited to Greater Syria and Iraq, but Sunni Arabs found this definition unnecessarily constricting, and they ex-tended its scope. On adopting the ideology, they enlarged the definition of *Arab* to include the Arabian peninsula, then Egypt and North Africa, even-tually even Somalia and Mauritania. By the 1970s, the "Arab nation" had grown to encompass Arabic speakers from Morocco to Oman. Sunnis also saw Arab unity as a smaller version of Muslim unity and imbued with an Islamic spirit and sensibilities. In the hands of Jamal ʿAbd an-Nasir of Egypt, it became the dominant ideology and he the leading politician of the Middle East. At its peak in the years 1956 to 1963, Pan-Arabism verged on becoming a civil religion.

In the process, the originators of Pan-Arabism, the Christians of Greater Syria, were alienated from Pan-Arabism. They and the other non-Muslim minorities—Druze and ʿAlawis—had two problems. First (echoing traditional Muslim expectations that non-Muslims would assimilate religiously), Sunnis saw non-Sunnis as less Arab than themselves and called on them to assimilate Sunni culture—something the non-Sunnis had no intention of doing. Second, all the minorities (though, of course, not every member of each community) feared being submerged in a sea of Sunni Arabs. As Muslims appropriated Pan-Arabism, others responded by pulling away. Some sought refuge in alternative ideologies, including Lebanese separatism, Pan-Syrianism, state nationalism, communism, and fascism. ʿAlawis and Druze turned inward to extend the power of their communities. Non-Sunni Arab members of the Baʿth Party reformulated Pan-Arabism to enhance their position by stressing the party's militantly socialist and secularist aspects.

The Fertile Crescent

Fertile Crescent plans, which hold that Greater Syria should combine with Iraq, were forwarded mainly by the Hashimi rulers of Iraq. More than Pan-Syrianists, they foresaw Syria as part of something bigger. Indeed, Nuri as-Saʿid, the longtime prime minister of Iraq, explicitly saw the Fertile Crescent as the intermediate step between Syria and the Arab nation. In a plan he put forward in December 1942, Saʿid suggested that Arab unity be reached in three steps: the formation of Greater Syria, its immediate union with Iraq, and the eventual joining of other Arab states. Revealingly, Nuri considered the order of this development unquestionable: "Obviously, the union of the various parts of historic Syria must come first."[89] While Nuri's rivals in Iraq (such as Prince

'Abd al-Illah) had other visions of the Fertile Crescent, all saw it building on Greater Syria.

State Nationalism

A new nationalism began emerging as soon as the borders had been drawn after World War I—allegiance to the polity that actually exists. Loyalty to Lebanon, Syria, Jordan, or the idea of Palestine gained in strength in a gradual but uneven fashion as schoolchildren learned the state's myths, businessmen acquired interest in its preservation, politicians controlled it, and soldiers died on its behalf. The import of this development could already be seen in 1936, when a British observer noted:

> Slowly, yet surely, the national idea is developing. In each State has been formed a Government with a permanent or semi-permanent officialdom, recruited on European lines and jealous of its power and prospects. Autarky has more than made an appearance and national defence forces have been individually organised and infused with local *esprit de corps*. Legal and political systems, grafted upon different roots, have grown quite dissimilar. Each country has . . . tended to become increasingly conscious and jealous of the boundaries fixed by the "victorious allied powers."[90]

Curiously, this process took hold much more thoroughly among Sunni Arabs in Palestine than in Lebanon. Whereas the former came to see Palestine as a valid unit, the latter continued to see Lebanon as an insult to Arab unity. Indeed, attachment to Palestine became so great that for many residents it obliterated Pan-Syrian and Pan-Arab allegiances; Arabs and Southern Syrians turned into Palestinians.

These five ways to define the nation by no means exhaused the alternatives. Other choices also existed, among which Phoenicianism and Mediterranean-ism were prominent.

French administrators were at times driven to despair by the complexity and flux of these ideologies. The distinguished high commissioner for Syria, Henri de Jouvenel, told a League of Nations commission in 1926 that France

> was faced [in Syria] with a country where nationality was in constant movement, and where it was extremely difficult to determine exactly the nationalities, which were very confused, as in that country anyone speaking of his religion called it "my nation." Everything was unstable; it was a kind of perpetual political earthquake. Further, [de Jouvenel continued,] he felt sure that members of the Commission had studied the history of Syria through the centuries, and knew therefore that this earthquake had never ceased.[91]

Today, opinions on the nation depend on whom one talks to. Palestinians (and here I must oversimplify, for each sect, class, and region has a distinct vantage point) define the nation as Palestine, Jordan's rulers define it as Jordan, and the other Sunni Arabs view it as the single Arab nation. Some

Lebanese minorities define it as Lebanon, other minorities see it as Greater Syria.

The residents of Greater Syria also disagree on the question of borders. In outline (and again this is an extremely complex matter) the Sunni Arabs of Syria feel that the boundary with Turkey should be pushed back and all the others, being artificial, should be eliminated. Syria's minorities accept the boundary with Iraq but otherwise share the Sunnis' views. In Lebanon, the Maronites, Druze, and Shi'a want the boundaries where they are, while Sunnis most want to bring them down, and Greek Orthodox are most ambivalent. Some Jewish Israelis see Israel ultimately in its 1949 borders (with minor changes), while others would extend the borders to include the West Bank and Gaza Strip. Some Palestinian Arabs see Palestine as expansionist Israelis see Israel; others go beyond this and see it including Jordan, too. Depending on era, Jordanians have seen Jordan within its present borders, with the addition of the West Bank, with the addition of all Israel, or with the addition of Syria and even Lebanon.

The boundary issue has cursed all the regions of Greater Syria since London established the three military zones in October 1918. Very few people of any community or citizenship in Greater Syria accept the borders that exist today as final. Nearly seventy years have passed since Britain and France divided Greater Syria, but disagreement over what constitutes the nation yet causes turbulence. Politics in the area between Turkey and Egypt is characterized by a geographic fluidity which does not diminish with the passage of time. The fact that most residents see the nation as a unit larger than the state they actually live in has immense implications for relations between the communities and polities making up Greater Syria. De Jouvenel's "perpetual political earthquake" remains active more than six decades later. Indeed, clashing views of the nation still underlie the much-remarked instability of the the Greater Syrian region.

Two Forms of Pan-Syrian Nationalism

Pan-Syrian nationalism has two forms, the pure and the pragmatic. Purists and pragmatists differ in their view of the great ideology of the central Middle East—Pan-Arab nationalism—the first rejecting it, the second accepting it. Purists seek a Greater Syrian state complete in itself without reference to a larger union. This position has been adopted by only one group, Antun Sa'ada and the Syrian Social Nationalist Party (SSNP). Pragmatists contend that Greater Syria forms part of the Arab nation and that its creation is a stepping stone toward a Pan-Arab polity. For them, the unification of Syria is not an end but a means toward building a much larger unit. King 'Abdallah of Jordan was the most prominent and articulate of the pragmatists. The first form is a type of *qawmiya* (nationalism), the latter a type of *wataniya* (patriotism).

Pure Pan-Syrianism

A pure Pan-Syrianist cannot accept Syria's submergence in a larger Arab entity. "Syria is for the Syrians, and the Syrians are a complete nation."[92] The SSNP argued that Greater Syria forms a nation and the Arabs do not. In contrast to the all-important Syrian nationality, it deemed the Arab, Muslim, Christian, Lebanese, and Palestinian identities meaningless. For them, Syria has no connection to an Arab state. If Syrians are a nation, then the Arabs are not; Antun Sa'ada argued that "the Arab world is many nations, not one."[93] Pure Pan-Syrianists fear a Pan-Arab order far more than they worry about existing states. Thus, when Pan-Arabism was at its height in the late 1950s, the SSNP gave its support to existing states, including the Lebanese government during the civil war of 1958.

Most Sunnis reject secularism and pure Pan-Syrian nationalism, two key aspects of the SSNP program.[94] Secularism challenges some of the basic precepts of Islam; the few Muslim thinkers who have publicly espoused the withdrawal of religion from politics have been at best ignored, at worse put on trial and executed. Almost everything about pure Pan-Syrian nationalism contradicts the spirit of Islam. It disregards religious distinctions, equates non-Muslim with Muslim, glorifies pagan antiquity, and puts undue emphasis on the history, culture, and bloodlines of a territory. Extreme attachment to a piece of territory is un-Islamic—not precisely against the religious law but very much against its spirit. Muslims found it hard enough to accept when secularists of Muslim origins, such as Kemal Atatürk or Reza Shah, exalted Turkish or Iranian nationalism in predominantly Muslim states; they found it far worse when Christians promoted Syrian nationalism in a region where Sunni Muslims constituted only half the population. (On the positive side, Pan-Syrianism did attract those few Sunni Arabs who rejected Islamic ways and wanted to reach across the religious divide.)

The intense opposition of most Sunnis toward pure Pan-Syrian nationalism doomed the SSNP's chances to achieve its ambitions. The Greek Orthodox (alone or in combination with other minorities) could not dominate a Greater Syrian state; even if they did, the experience of the Maronites—who tried to impose a minority ideology in Lebanon and failed—suggests they would not have prevailed for long.

The SSNP promoted pure Pan-Syrianism knowing full well that this position denied the validity of Pan-Arabism, a widely cherished political tenet. Sa'ada consciously adopted a controversial position, one that distinguished the SSNP not only from general intellectual trends but even from the great bulk of Pan-Syrian nationalists, who were of the pragmatic variety. The SSNP point of view also pitted it against Pan-Arabists, pious Muslims, Lebanese and Palestinian separatists, Jordanian monarchs, and Zionists. The disrepute of pure Pan-Syrianism goes far to explain why the SSNP is dismissed as eccentric; add secularism and fascism, and its frequent persecution becomes understandable.

If pure Pan-Syrianism aroused such opposition, why did the SSNP adopt it?

Because the non-Sunni minorities found it attractive. In contrast to Sunni Arabs, who tended to see Greater Syria as a more practical version of Pan-Arabism, minorities usually saw it as an end in itself. Pragmatic Pan-Syrianism was fine for Sunnis, but minorities sought something more radical—including secularism, socialism, and the glorification of antiquity. Secularism promised to bridge the historic gap between Muslims and Christians, bringing full citizenship and equality to the latter. Socialism promised new opportunities. And the glorification of pre-Islamic antiquity—the civilization that Islam vanquished—celebrated the Christians' culture.

As Orthodox Christians found pure Pan-Syrianism especially appealing, the SSNP became a primary conduit for the expression of their discontent with the status quo. Spread quite exactly in the area making up Greater Syria, the Orthodox could not hope to emulate the Maronites and retreat to their own homeland, so they tried to structure their relations with Sunnis along new lines and to bring their whole community under one roof. Pan-Syrianism promised both equality for Christians and the inclusion of most Orthodox within the confines of a single state.

The SSNP vision originated, not surprisingly, in the mind of a Lebanese Greek Orthodox, Antun Khalil Saʿada, its founder and leader from 1932 to 1949. Born in 1904, Saʿada spent critical years of his youth outside Lebanon. His father, Khalil Saʿada, lived in Egypt for several years before World War I, and Antun joined his father in São Paulo, Brazil, in 1920. Although a medical doctor, the elder Saʿada published a journal, *Al-Majalla*, which promoted independence for Syria, secularism, and anticonfessionalism. The elder Saʿada also founded the National Democratic Party in Buenos Aires and chaired the first Syrian National Congress (*Al-Muʾtamar al-Watani as-Suri*) after World War I.[95] These influences clearly affected Antun, who returned to Lebanon in 1929 and founded the SSNP in November 1932.

The family's years abroad, and especially those in Egypt, go far to account for the characteristic elements of Saʿada's thought: his deep belief in a Syrian identity, his rejection of the Arab identity, and his secularism.

Syrians constituted a small but highly influential community in Egypt from the eighteenth century on. Although they played a major role in the country's commercial, industrial, and intellectual life,[96] they never lost their separate identity or forgot their foreignness. To the contrary, the Syrians took pride in the many points of difference between them and the native population. As Egyptian nationalism grew in the late nineteenth century, the Syrians' sense of being apart became more acute. Thomas Philipp wrote that "Syrians who had arrived during the last two decades of the nineteenth century had to realize that they would remain marginal and barely tolerated in Egyptian national politics. As emigrants in a foreign surrounding, they had, indeed, been made aware of their 'Syrianness.' "[97]

The psychology of the Syrians in Egypt bore on Saʿada's ideas in several ways. First, Egyptians perceived all those from the Levant area as Syrians; if residents of Jaffa and Aleppo felt nothing in common before arriving in Egypt, they gained some sense of solidarity after living there. Second, in contrast to

Syrians living in Greater Syria, who casually equated being Syrian with being Arab, Syrians in Egypt drew a sharp distinction between the two notions. Noting that Egyptians too speak Arabic, they tended to consider themselves Syrians, not Arabs. Sa'ada's views on Syria probably originated in this perception. Third, whether Muslim or Christian or Jewish, Syrians in Egypt felt a kinship for each other (in strict contrast to those who never left Syria) and organized themselves with little regard to religion. Sa'ada's effort to ignore religion as a political force may well have derived from this outlook.

Sa'ada took ideas about the Syrian nation from others, too. The Jesuit scholar Henri Lammens argued in his influential book of 1921, *La Syrie*, that an independent Syrian nation had existed since ancient times, long before Islam and the Arab conquests. He also imbued it with a mystical quality: "A remarkably uniform race, a true national type, developed across the centuries. It was sheltered by an area whose borders—the Taurus Mountains, the Euphrates, the desert, and the Mediterranean—were marked by Providence."[98] According to Bassam Tibi, Sa'ada's idea of a Syrian nation "appears to be a synthesis of Lammens' notions with those of German and Italian popular nationalism."[99] (The extent of Lammens's influence on the Pan-Syrian movement was apparent even years later; in 1962, when Asad al-Ashkar, a former president of the SSNP, testified before a military tribunal, he was asked about the authorship of a document in his possession that argued that a Lebanese nation does not exist. In response, Ashkar claimed he could not remember whether Lammens or he had written the text.)[100]

Philip K. Hitti, a Lebanese scholar living in America, published a short book in 1926, *Syria and the Syrians in History*, in which he argued that "Syrians are Arabs only in language and culture, not in their blood."[101] Labib Zuwiyya Yamak speculated that Hitti's ideas also influenced Sa'ada.[102]

Pragmatic Pan-Syrianism

The SSNP was alone in boldly proclaiming against Pan-Arabism. All other advocates of Greater Syria, including Lebanese Muslims, Hashimi rulers, and Hafiz al-Asad, portrayed the establishment of Greater Syria as a step toward a wider Pan-Arab unity.

Pragmatists contend that Greater Syria forms part of the Arab nation and its creation is a stepping stone toward a Pan-Arab polity. For them, the unification of Syria is not an end but a means toward building a much bigger unit. Pragmatic Pan-Syrianism has two strengths over the purist version. First, it does not confront Pan-Arabism; second, it attracts Sunnis as well as minorities.

For a resident of Greater Syria, Pan-Syrian and Pan-Arab nationalism have much in common. Syria is the source and heartland of both ideologies. Both reject Syria's existing boundaries and view Lesser Syria as unworthy of deep loyalty. In both cases, Damascus is seen as the natural capital of a larger, more powerful polity. Syrian and Arab nationalism alike offer a means to turn the rump, divided state of Syria into something worthy of the citizens' loyalty; their irredentist elements offer powerful ways to mobilize the support of the

Syrian populace. Both adopt a posture of militant anti-Zionism and implicitly challenge the legitimacy of existing governments. Both reduce the pressure of domestic issues by directing popular emotions outward.

Both ideologies have radical and moderate forms, and their radical versions foresee the complete elimination of boundaries and the incorporation of all parts of the Syrian or Arab homeland into a single state. In each case, the radical vision predominated in early years and was transformed by dint of long failure into something less ambitious and more practical. Their moderate versions foresee close relations between states but not total absorption.

Whereas pure Pan-Syrian nationalism is almost exclusively the possession of non-Sunni Arab minorities, pragmatic Pan-Syrianism appeals mostly to Sunnis, who see it as a more feasible alternative to Arab nationalism. If the minorities consider Pan-Syrianism an end in itself, Sunni Arabs tend to see it as a more practical version of Pan-Arabism. They choose not to fight Pan-Arabism but to cooperate with it. That Hashimi leaders advocated this approach is hardly surprising, given the family's attachments outside Syria— its origins in the Hijaz, Husayn's dream of becoming caliph, and the uprising which aspired to control Iraq as well as Syria.

Prince Faysal, leader of the Arab Revolt and briefly king of Syria, saw a close connection between Syrian and Arab nationalism; indeed, he used the two concepts almost interchangeably. He argued in May 1919 that Syria had a right to autonomy: "Although the Arabs are one nation [*umma*]—and all of us know that the Arab provinces are one land [*bilad wahida*] in terms of history, geography, and national ties—Iraq is an independent country [*bilad musta-qilla*], unrelated to Syria, just as Syria has no relation to all the other Arab countries [*al-bilad al-'Arabiya*]."[103] Symptomatic of the confusion in Faysal's mind about these terms was a speech he gave in March 1920, in the course of which he referred to "the Syrian Arab nation," "the Arab countries," "the Arab nation," "the district of Syria," "the Syrian nation," and "the Syrian region."[104] Soon after, he talked of both a "Syrian Arab bloc" and "the Arab world."[105]

Faysal's brother 'Abdallah became the major exponent of pragmatic Pan-Syrian nationalism. Although lacking Sa'ada's intellectual ambitions, 'Abdallah did construct a coherent argument which he elaborated over many years. In addition to the speeches, declarations, and other channels available to him as ruler, he wrote two memoirs, compiled a documentary record, and even contributed to Transjordanian newspapers under a pseudonym.

'Abdallah saw no contradiction between Greater Syria and the Arab nation; to the contrary, as he tirelessly explained during three decades of residence in Transjordan, he believed the unification of Syria to be the first, most critical step toward the achievement of Arab unity. Greater Syria was the cornerstone of Arab unity, the feasible first step and the polity that he could dominate. Greater Syria—rather than the Fertile Crescent or some larger Arab entity—attracted 'Abdallah's attention because it was the smallest national unit and therefore the most realistic one he could aspire to rule. He regarded Syria as the heart of Arabism, the region whose unity had to be established before more ambitious schemes could be implemented. ʿAbdallah did not consider Greater Syria a replacement for the Arab nation but, like Egypt, one of the components that made it up. His prime minister, Tawfiq Abuʾl-Huda, explained that, once unified, Greater Syria "would participate in whatever the Arabs would agree upon as far as their union is concerned."[106] ʿAbdallah accepted Pan-Arabism, envisioning a unified Syria that would take up "its ideal place alongside a general Pan-Arab union."[107]

ʿAbdallah held Greater Syria as the key to modern Arab history. He interpreted its establishment as "the goal of the Arab Revolt"[108] and saw the decision of the General Syrian Congress of 1920 in the same light: "It obligated the Arabs to work for their genuine good and glory to strive for the union of the Syrian lands [*ad-diyar ash-Shamiya*] and the union of Syria and Iraq in the Fertile Crescent."[109] Syria was the primary objective of ʿAbdallah's 1921 military campaign and remained his chief concern thirty years later. ʿAbdallah argued in 1943 that "there will be no presence for the Arabs so long as Greater Syria remains torn apart. When it is united, the Arabs will be united."[110] Toward the end of his life, an embittered ʿAbdallah declared: "We, the Hashimis, left the Hijaz for the sake of Syria and Palestine and lost it to a barbarous Arab people."[111] The creation of a Greater Syrian state looked back to the revolt and forward to Arab unity.

This vision persuaded some Jordanians. For example, the prominent Jordanian politician Zayd ar-Rifaʿi recalls how he saw Arab unity in the late 1940s: "When I was a student at the university [in Cairo], I imagined that Arab unity had to be achieved gradually by means of four entities, not a single entity. The first entity was a union of natural Syria, for nothing distinguishes the Jordanian from the Palestinian, nor from the Syrian or the Lebanese or even the Iraqi."[112] (He saw the other three entities as being Egypt, the Arabian peninsula, and the Maghrib.)

Pan-Syrianism versus Pan-Arabism

Differing Views of the Arab

Just as Pan-Syrianists differ on Pan-Arabism, Pan-Arabists are divided in their views of Pan-Syrianism. For some Pan-Arabists, the two cannot be reconciled; for others they complement each other. The more narrowly a Pan-Arabist defines the Arab, the more sympathetic he is to Pan-Syrianism; and the wider his interpretation, the more opposed he is. The definition of an Arab, in turn, largely depends on religious identity, locale, and era. Belonging to a minority group, living in the early twentieth century, and residing in Syria make it likely that a person sees Pan-Syrianism and Pan-Arabism as compatible. Being a Sunni, living late in the century, and residing outside Syria point the opposite way.

When Christians launched Pan-Arabism, their definition of Arabs was narrow, being restricted to the Arabic speakers of the Fertile Crescent and Arabia. As we have seen, the Sunni Muslims adopted the ideology and expanded the definition of *Arab* to include all Arabic speakers without regard to geography. Fundamentalist Muslims go farther yet and see Pan-Arabism as a step toward Pan-Islam.

Much depends on the era. When Pan-Syrianism and Pan-Arabism were yet developing, from the 1880s until World War I, *Syrian* and *Arab* were nearly synonymous. An Arab then was not anyone who spoke Arabic, regardless of location, but an Arabic speaker who lived in Greater Syria or nearby (Iraq or the Arabian peninsula). There are many examples to show that *Syrian* and *Arab* were used interchangeably. The anonymous placards that appeared in Syrian cities during 1880–81, for instance, used *Syrian* and *Arab* indiscriminately. A question on one of the placards—"Where is your Arab honor, where is your Syrian fervor?"—makes it clear that the terms are synonymous. Similarly, "Arise and recover, O Arabs" is directed to the population of Syria.[113]

The first public call for the separation of the Arabic-speaking countries from the Ottoman Empire, by Negib Azoury in 1905, defined the "Arab Empire" as "stretching from the Tigris and the Euphrates to the Isthmus of Suez, from the Mediterranean Sea to the Arabian Sea." Within this large area, however, Azoury offered assurances to "respect the autonomy of the Lebanon, and the independence of the principalities of Yemen, Najd, and Iraq."[114] In effect, he was calling for a Syrian state with some form of authority over the other regions of Arabic-speaking Southwest Asia. The poet Anis al-Maqdisi hardly distinguished between the two in odes composed a short time apart. He wrote in the first, "If religion must divide us, our Arabic tongue unites our ranks." In the second, "O Syria, I wish you glory, independence, and progress."[115] Similarly, resolutions of the June 1913 Arab-Syrian Congress referred repeatedly, without elaboration, to the "Syrian and Arab" provinces.[116] The close link between these two terms led Nadim K. Makdisi to conclude that "the national awakening in Syria was characterized by a duality of nationalism, both Syrian and Arab."[117]

The meanings of *Syrian* and *Arab* diverged irrevocably when the Egyptian government adopted Pan-Arabism in the 1940s. As an Egyptian cannot be a Syrian, so an Egyptian's Pan-Arabism must differ from Pan-Syrianism.

As this implies, where one lives affects one's view of Pan-Arabism. Syrians and Egyptians define the poles: (1) A Syrian sees his country as the geographic and historic center of the Arab nation; for him, as Kamal Junbalat observed, "Arab unity begins with [Pan-Syrianism]."[118] For the Syrian, Pan-Arabism is a natural extension of Greater Syria. He tends to merge the Syrian with the Arab nation and confuse the ideologies associated with them. In contrast, Pan-Syrianism is an alien concept to the Egyptian, one that has nothing in common with Pan-Arabism. Pan-Arabism flows naturally from Pan-Syrian nationalism but has no connection to Egyptian nationalism. (2) Syrians tend to envision a radical solution—the elimination of existing boundaries and the fusion of countries into a single nation. Egyptians see Pan-Arabism as a voluntary association which allows each country to preserve its independence and identity; it serves as a bridge to develop close relations with fellow Arabic speakers in other regions. (3) Syrians must be involved in one or other of these nationalist schemes. Egyptians view Pan-Arabism more instrumentally, as the means to involve themselves in the affairs of Greater Syria, Iraq, and Arabia. When Egyptians do not seek such an involvement, Pan-Arabism falls by the side.

Most other Arabs fall somewhere on the spectrum between Syrians and Egyptians. Iraqis are perhaps closest to the Syrian vantage point, seeing Pan-Arabism as a way to extend their power by incorporating other, weaker units. Saudi Arabians approach the Egyptian view. Palestinians and Sunni Lebanese see it as the way to rally forces to their conflicts. Historically, Jordanian leaders have seen Pan-Arabism as a threat to their own leadership. Sudanese and North Africans are even farther removed than Egyptians.

Differing Views of Pan-Syrianism

The attitude of a Pan-Arabist toward Pan-Syrianism depends also on the kind of Pan-Syrianism in question. He can accept the pragmatist's goal; Greater Syria is fine so long as it helps build the Arab nation. But he has to reject the purist's vision of Syria for, as Edmond Rabbath wrote, "There is no Syrian nation. There is an Arab nation."[119] The key point is that, as an end in itself, Greater Syria is anathema to the Pan-Arabists. Just as Pan-Syrianists accept the Arab nation so long as it does not interfere with Greater Syria, Pan-Arabists accept Greater Syria so long as it is a step toward the larger polity of the Arab nation.

Pan-Arabists reject the whole premise of pure Pan-Syrianism, seeing it as a rival to their own plans. Note this condemnation of the SSNP by the pro-Iraqi Ba'thist, Kassim Sallam:

> The implicit presupposition of this Party—the disappearance of the Arab Nation—has to be severely condemned. The SSNP pretends to ignore the existence of the Arab Nation the better to exalt a deviationist and chauvinistic nationalism, that which is tied to "Greater Syria." This notion represents for the Party a geographically, historically, and politically complete society; extreme consequences follow from this view.[120]

Pan-Arabists disagree with pure Pan-Syrianists on a host of other matters as well. While the former emphasize linguistic and cultural homogeneity, the latter stress biological ties. Pan-Arabists and pure Pan-Syrianists disagree on the desirability of involving the further Arab states such as Egypt. For the former, the conflict with Israel is an internal Syrian affair in which non-Syrians have no business; Sa'ada wrote that had it not been for Pan-Arabist attacks on the SSNP, which weakened the party, "there would have been no need for Egypt or the Arabs to participate in the defense of Palestine."[121] In contrast, Pan-Arabists envision a role against Israel for every state between Morocco and Oman.

Pan-Arabists look much more favorably on pragmatic Pan-Syrianism, seeing a unified Greater Syria as a preliminary step toward the union of all Arabs and a less ambitious version of the unified Arab state. If a union of all

Arab states cannot be attained, then it makes sense to seek at least a partial one. Better a unified Greater Syria than the four small states and clutch of provinces that now exist.

Examples of such an attitude are plentiful. According to one account, some residents of Lebanon in 1918 "saw Syrian unity as a step toward Arab unity."[122] A conference of Lebanese Muslims in October 1936 called for "Lebanese sovereignty within the framework of Syrian unity as a preliminary step toward Arab unity."[123] One participant at the Conference of the Coast held in Beirut in March 1936 declared: "Gentlemen: Syrian unity is our vitality and no matter what happens, no substitute will satisfy us. And if we demand it, we do so because it is the first step toward the Arab unity that we seek."[124] Another told the same audience: "Today's educated Lebanese youth see that the interests of Lebanon lie in Syrian unity, followed by Arab unity."[125] George Antonius, an important advocate of Pan-Arabism, told David Ben-Gurion a month later that nothing bound Greater Syria to Iraq, that the really important unity was that of Greater Syria—not the Arabs. He argued that this region must be united.[126]

The Pan-Arabist Edmond Rabbath saw the unity of Syria as so vital for Arab unity that he titled his 1937 book *Syrian Unity and Arab Future*.[127] That same year, Benoit Aboussouan explained his skepticism about "exchanging the Syrian nationality for a hypothetical Arab one."[128] Likewise, the British government in the 1940s favored Greater Syria as a useful first step toward Arab unity. The League of National Action, a Pan-Arabist organization, stressed the interdependence of Syria and Lebanon. Even the Baʿth Party, that stalwart of Pan-Arabism, once advocated Greater Syrian unity. In 1945, the party publicly urged that Syria join with Jordan and Iraq at independence. Salah ad-Din al-Bitar, a founder of the Baʿth Party, criticized Syrian president Sabri al-ʿAsali for (in the words of a British diplomat) "having an isolationist policy which was placing obstacles in the way of union between Greater Syria and Iraq."[129] As a result, he ended up in jail. Baʿth demonstrations that year included slogans such as "Long live Greater Syria" and "Long live Faysal II."[130]

More recently, Greater Syria "attracts many Syrians, including those who believe in complete Arab unity but who now despair of this as an empty dream which has gone off track."[131] It even appeals to non-Syrians disappointed with Pan-Arabism. Thus, Libya's ruler, Muʿammar al-Qadhdhafi, said that "if Syria is capable of uniting Lebanon and Jordan by force we will support it in doing so."[132] He could approve a Syrian takeover because this is a step toward Arab unity.

The Failure of Pure Pan-Syrian Nationalism

Although Pan-Arabism did not succeed in unifying Arabic-speaking peoples, it did vanquish the ideological competition. Those ideologies that defy Pan-Arab nationalism have had to accommodate Pan-Arabism's moral hegemony and pay obeisance to the ideal of Arab unity. Egyptian Pharaonists disappeared;

Lebanese separatists had to acknowledge the Arab nation; and pure Pan-Syrian nationalism gave way to the pragmatic variety.

One can argue that pure Pan-Syrian nationalism was doomed from the start. It postulated a state dominated by non-Sunnis that would ignore the Sunni opposition. The history of Lebanon shows that this is not even attainable by a minority that dominates its own region; no minority coalition could achieve this agreement in the whole of Greater Syria.

The symbol of the defeat of pure Pan-Syrian nationalism was the SSNP effort to protect itself from persecution by obscuring its true views. To use the language of Islam, the party effectively engaged in *taqiya* (dissimulation to preserve the faith) of an ideological nature. It adopted a variety of covers, including pragmatic Pan-Syrianism, local patriotism, leftist rhetoric, and even Pan-Arabism.

Saʿada made pragmatic Pan-Syrian statements on occasion, touching up his plans for Greater Syria with specks of Pan-Arabism. He would portray the realization of Greater Syria as a step toward Arab liberation: "First the Social Nationalist revival of Syria, then cooperative politics for the good of the Arab world. The rise of the Syrian nation liberates Syrian power from foreign authorities and directs it toward arousing the other Arab nations, helping them progress."[133] Saʿada would go even farther at times, placing Syria in an Arab framework: the fact that "the Syrian nation [*umma*] is part of an Arab nation [*umma*] does not contravene its being a complete nation with right to absolute sovereignty."[134] Saʿada also developed a peculiar concept, "the Arabism of Syrian Social Nationalism," which attempted to square the circle by postulating Syrian leadership of the Arabs.[135] He went so far as to claim that "if there is a real, genuine Arabism in the Arab world, it is the Arabism of the SSNP,"[136] and used this to justify his argument that "the Syrian nation is the nation suited to revive the Arab world."[137]

Hints of local patriotism can be found as early as May 1944, when loyalty to Lebanon served as a useful cover and the party stated its goal to be "the independence of Lebanon."[138] Ten years later, to defend the status quo from the radical Pan-Arabist programs advocated by Jamal ʿAbd an-Nasir, the Baʿth, and others, SSNP leaders adopted a pro-Western outlook and made common cause with conservatives. This tactic culminated in the 1958 civil war in Lebanon when the SSNP joined the Lebanese government to suppress the rebels; given the party's views on the illegitimacy of Lebanon's very existence, this was a remarkable stand. It represented less a change in long-range goals, however, than an appreciation of Lebanon as refuge; SSNP leaders rightly feared that a victory by the government's opponents would close the country to them.

The party further muted its Pan-Syrian goals following 1956, when Pan-Arabism attained the peak of its popularity. But the real need for dissimulation came in 1962. As a result of the fiasco of December 1961, when it failed in an attempt to overthrow the Lebanese government, the SSNP found itself banned in Lebanon (as well as Syria). To become acceptable again in one or other of these states, it adopted three tactics. First, as in 1944, members feigned local patriotism. Those who lived in Syria pledged loyalty to the regime in Damascus; likewise, those in Lebanon portrayed themselves as devoted to the preservation of Lebanon's independence. This effort was tried out at the military tribunal set up to punish the participants in the failed coup, but it had little success, as neither the public prosecutor nor the presiding judge was fooled. The former told the judge:

> The object of the SSNP conspirators must be obvious to you and to all the world—it was none other than the implementation of the Party's basic principles [by taking power in Lebanon]. Lebanon was aware of this fact from the very beginning. But when the conspirators failed, they tried to fabricate reasons for their conspiracy, feigning concern for reform of the regime in Lebanon and for social development.[139]

The judge concurred: "Its goal being contrary to the law, the SSNP acted like a secret society and did not reveal its real doctrine to the authorities. Instead, . . . the party pretended to be working to preserve the Lebanese entity."[140] The implausibility of this tactic seems to have led to its abandonment.

Second, the party abandoned fascist doctrines and adopted the more acceptable rhetoric of the left. This transformation was completed in the late 1960s and permitted the SSNP soon after to make common cause with other groups seeking to overturn the status quo. Close relations were developed with several parties, especially the Progressive Socialist Party of Kamal Junbalat and the PLO.[141] The move from right to left appears long-lasting; by 1984, the SSNP chief was attending the anniversary celebration of the Lebanese Communist Party. Those unacquainted with the party's ideology even see it as Marxist.[142] What began as dissimulation may have, with time, become reality; the SSNP orientation today appears to be permanently aligned with the Left.

Third and most important, SSNP members took to portraying Greater Syria as the first step toward either a unified Arab front or (as was increasingly the case in later years) a single Arab nation. In other words, they adopted the protective coloring of pragmatic Pan-Syrianism, arguing that Syria constitutes one nation, whereas the Arab front consists of many nations, including, preeminently, the Syrian. Although Sa'ada scorned efforts to bring the many Arab nations together as infeasible and counterproductive, the party subsequently accepted this principle, at least outwardly. When challenged by Pan-Arabists to drop all vestiges of Greater Syria, the SSNP justified its reluctance by holding that the formation of a Greater Syrian state represents a practical and intermediate stage toward the realization of a single Arab nation.

There is a long party tradition of playing both the Pan-Syrian and the Pan-Arab themes. A 1961 SSNP leaflet describing the organization's goals included two contradictory slogans on the same page: "Syrian nationalism against Arab nationalism," and "The SSNP supports the Fertile Crescent, a historic and geographic reality, as the only valid form of union in the Middle East—without rejecting the possibility of an Arab front."[143] Along similar lines, one of the defendants at the 1962 trial stated that "the statement of faith in Greater

Syria, in the Syrian nation [*umma*], . . . is the same as belief in the Arab nation."[144]

In 1951, 'Isam al-Mahayiri, an SSNP member of the Syrian Assembly, argued that "our work for the unity of Natural Syria is the cornerstone for every sound Pan-Arab building."[145] Thirty-four years later, Mahayiri still held to the same dissimulation, telling an interviewer in August 1985 that the SSNP and Damascus "agree on clear Pan-Arab objectives."[146] In 1987, the SSNP slogan was "Commitment to the party's policy of struggle and Pan-Arabism," while the drive to unify Lebanon with Syria was presented as "consolidating the strategic ties with the center of Pan-Arab decision making in Damascus."[147] This double message makes it hard to believe that the SSNP underwent a genuine change of heart; continued references to the pure Pan-Syrian ideas of old lead to the conclusion that Sa'ada's vision had remained at the center of the SSNP ideology.

Ideological flexibility acquired new importance in the 1970s, as the party found an ally in the government of Syria. If the SSNP dissimulated by hiding its Pan-Syrianism, the government of Hafiz al-Asad (as we will see) blurred Pan-Arabism almost beyond recognition.

2

Failed Efforts
to Constitute Greater Syria,
1920–1973

Integral Syria is like the tunic of Christ.
—Henri Lammens[1]

Although the Syrian Kingdom lasted a scant hundred days, never to be recreated, its brief existence had a lasting impact on the politics and imagination of many residents in Greater Syria. Passions and dreams aroused by the kingdom retained power for decades. Most expectations of Pan-Syrian unity, even those of antimonarchists, referred back to the ephemeral but exciting success of Prince Faysal in 1920. Conversely, the division of Greater Syria decided on at San Remo met a resistance that has never disappeared. Indeed, the reluctance to accept the imposed boundaries of 1920 to 1923 has proved an abiding theme of politics in the area and a major source of political turmoil. The following two chapters record some of the tumult between 1920 and the present.

This presentation is colored by three important facts. First, every effort but one failed (and even that one—the annexation of the West Bank to Transjordan—appears to have been only a transitory success). Therefore, the story of Greater Syria lacks internal development; it is not much more than a sequence of failed efforts. Rather than deal with any of these efforts in great detail, I touch on many lightly. This chapter is an exercise in textual archeology; my task is to bring alive a forgotten issue by compiling thousands of discrete bits of information.

Second, because relations among Syria, Lebanon, the Palestinian movement,[2] Transjordan, and Iraq are so complex, with claims and counterclaims constantly traded, the following pages simplify their relations by focusing on the party on the offense. Initiatives to bring Greater Syria under the rule of Damascus are listed under Syria, initiatives by Lebanese are found under Lebanon, and so forth. (The fact that very few Pan-Syrian initiatives were mutual makes this division practical.) The Syrian Social Nationalist Party, which did not represent any state's interests, is dealt with at the end.

52

Third, the pursuit of Greater Syria divides into three phases: 1918–49, 1950–73, and 1974 to the present. A quiet second period separates the intense activity of the first and third periods. The bulk of this chapter deals with the 1918–49 phase, followed by a quick look at the 1950–73 phase and then the activities of the Syrian Social Nationalist Party. Chapter 3 then takes up the post-1974 era.

Syria

Pan-Syrianism held so strong in the aftermath of Faysal's failure that even the hand-picked agents of France expressed its ideals. In October 1920, on the occasion of the unfurling of a French-designed flag for Syria (complete with miniature tricolor), the Syrian prime minister gave a toast to "united Syria!"[3] Similarly, in April 1926, the newly chosen head of the Syrian state called for "Syrian unity with free access to the sea."[4]

The French administration responded to these sentiments by clamping down on political expression and forcing Pan-Syrian partisans into exile. Some went to Baghdad or Amman, where they urged either Faysal or 'Abdallah to reclaim Lesser Syria from the French. Others went to Egypt, which became the political center of Pan-Syrianism during the 1920s. Cairo hosted the newspaper *Al-Muqattam* (which was founded by the Syrian expatriate Faris Nimr) and the Syrian Party of Unity (*Hizb al-Ittihad as-Suri*). The party was founded in late 1918 by politicians discontented with the Hashimi leadership and seeking a republic from the Taurus and Anti-Taurus Mountains to Midian (in northwestern Arabia).[5] In 1921, members of this party founded the Syro-Palestinian Congress, which made the independence and unification of Greater Syria its goal. A Syrian National Party (*Hizb al-Watani as-Suri*), which came into existence in early 1920, sought to achieve Greater Syria through parliamentary monarchy.

Although most leaders of the Syro-Palestinian Congress, including Shakib Arsalan and Rashid Rida, saw Palestine as Southern Syria,[6] they kept this view quiet for tactical reasons, so as not to provoke both mandatory powers. In September 1921, for example, the congress described the Syrian people as "divided in two different countries, under two different masters," but held back on the customary call for Syrian unity.[7] Quite the contrary, the congress presented itself as speaking on behalf of Syrians, Palestinians, and Lebanese. The Executive Committee of the Syro-Palestinian Congress dominated exile efforts against the French until 1927, when it split into two parts and lost influence.

Inside Syria itself, the People's Party (*Hizb ash-Sha'b*), founded in 1925 with French encouragement, called for "the unification of Syria within its natural confines."[8] The Party of Syrian Union (*Hizb al-Wahda as-Suriya*), whose program was signalled by its name, also had French backing. Local leaders pursued a similar goal. For example, representatives from Dayr az-Zur and surrounding villages formed an assembly in 1925 and telegraphed the high commissioner to demand the unity and independence of Greater Syria. In 1926, they met again to repeat these demands. Notables from Syria's main cities met together to demand "the Syrian country [*al-bilad as-Suriya*] in its natural boundaries, such as existed before the World War."[9]

The Druze revolt that began in July 1925 under the leadership of Sultan al-Atrash was initially a local affair that resulted from disagreements between the Druze and their French administrators. But the Druzes' success quickly brought them the support of the Pan-Syrian nationalists, and together the two created a Provisional Syrian Government which issued a proclamation calling for "the unification of the Syrian country [*al-bilad as-Suriya*], coastal and interior, and the recognition of a single, completely independent, Arab Syrian state."[10]

The Druze revolt was suppressed in 1927, and normal political life recommenced soon afterward. A draft constitution drawn up in August 1928 declared that "the Syrian territories detached from the Ottoman Empire constitute an indivisible political unity. The divisions that have emerged between the end of the war and the present day do not diminish this unity." This claim offended the French high commissioner, who held up the constitution for two years. In the end, he replaced it with a less challenging formulation: "Syria constitutes an indivisible political unity."[11]

Syrians widely mourned the 1933 death of Prince Faysal, symbol of early Pan-Syrian hopes, and the Damascus municipality passed a resolution to raise a monument to him. A year later, the anniversary of Faysal's death was publicly commemorated. While Faysal's passing marked the end of an era of hope in unity schemes, it was also true that serious intentions to resurrect his kingdom had virtually ended with the Druze revolt. From the mid-1920s on, a monarchy had less attraction than a republic.

After another several years' suppression, French authorities allowed Syrian political life to resume in 1936. The leading political party of that era, the National Bloc (*Al-Kutla al-Wataniya*), began its activities by calling for a union of all Syria.

The discussions in 1943 to 1945 that led to the creation of the Arab League devoted considerable attention to the status of Syria. Although generally defensive, fearful of being absorbed by Iraq or Transjordan, Syrian spokesmen did occasionally utter Pan-Syrian remarks, too. The prime minister, Sa'dallah al-Jabiri, indicated in private talks in Egypt in October 1943 that his government hoped to build a Greater Syria as a means to eliminate artificial barriers. He noted, however, the many obstacles that existed—Lesser Syria had already existed for a generation and had its own identity—and insisted on two points: Lesser Syria had to have a republican government, and Damascus had to serve as the capital.[12]

Jabiri reiterated these points at the Alexandria conference in September 1944, declaring that

> the Syrian problem concerns four regions: Syria, Lebanon, Palestine, and Transjordan. . . . We insist upon unity while keeping Damascus as the capital and the republican system as a basis; but we leave its [political] form to the

choice of the country's residents. . . . We are anxious to create Greater Syria
and eliminate the divisions imposed by dominant force, international interests,
and political rivalries."[13]

A spokesman for the Syrian Legation in Washington stated in February 1946
that "Syria, Lebanon, Palestine, and Jordan are separated by artificial
borders."[14]

The appeal of Greater Syria was so universal around the time of independence that even the Ba'th Party spoke favorably of a Pan-Syrian program (as
was noted on p. 48).

Specific Syrian claims to Lebanon, Palestine, Transjordan, Iraq, and Alexandretta followed separate rhythms and need to be considered apart.

Lebanon

Syrian politicians approached the Lebanese question cautiously. Overt efforts
to bring the whole country under their control would drive the Maronites into
French arms, with the effect of indefinitely prolonging the French presence in
Lebanon. Knowing this, Syrians rarely demanded the incorporation of all
Lebanon into Syria. For example, resolutions passed by the Syro-Palestinian
Congress in 1921 and 1922 made no reference to Lebanon's boundaries.

Instead, Syrian leaders offered the Christians a compromise: Christians
could go politically their own way if they returned the (mostly Muslim) provinces added to Lebanon in 1920.[15] The Maronites faced a choice: keep the
Muslim-inhabited provinces added in 1920 but abandon French protection, or
stick with France and return those provinces. Concentrating on the return of
these provinces, especially the Biqa' Valley and Tripoli, had the virtue of splitting opinion in Lebanon and France, thereby strengthening Damascus's hand.

Syrian leaders tried to win these provinces in many ways. From 1923 to
1925, they took trips through Lebanon to encourage Sunni Muslims to agitate
for union with Syria. Guerrillas attacked parts of Lebanon during the Druze
revolt of 1925–27. Shakib Arsalan tried diplomatic pressure; in November
1925, he demanded from Henri de Jouvenel, the new French high commissioner, a plebiscite in the disputed parts of Lebanon. Similarly, the Executive
Committee of the Syro-Palestinian Congress met with de Jouvenel and
demanded a "free and direct" plebiscite in the 1920 provinces.[16] Other delegations to de Jouvenel did not bother with the nicety of a plebiscite but simply
demanded the provinces back.[17] Even the provisional chief of the Syrian government, a French-appointed official, made this demand in June 1926. A Syrian delegation sent to Paris to negotiate the 1936 treaty with France reportedly
called for "the restitution of the territories taken away from Syria and annexed
by Lebanon."[18]

Syrian politicians also took their case to the Arab leaders. During preliminary discussions leading to the establishment of the League of Arab States,
Syrian prime minister Sa'dallah al-Jabiri told the Egyptian government that,
failing the achievement of a Greater Syria union, Syria should receive back the

parts of Lebanon that had been reassigned in 1920. He claimed that the population of those parts wished this change no less than did Syrians.

Despite this campaign for the 1920 provinces, the government in Damascus eventually saw value in the presence of large numbers of Muslims in Lebanon as a guarantee of Lebanon's Arab and Muslim character. Accordingly, Damascus accepted Lebanese independence; in return, it got agreement from the Maronites to align Lebanon culturally and politically with the Arabs (and not with the French). This compromise was made public in the Alexandria Protocol of September 1944 (the founding document of the Arab League), in which all the League members, including Syria, explicitly affirmed their "respect for the independence and sovereignty of Lebanon within its present boundaries."[19] But Syrian reluctance to recognize Lebanon as a fully sovereign and separate nation remained; the symbol of this was the absence of formal diplomatic relations between the two countries.[20]

Even after Lebanon's independence, Damascus tried to gain influence in Lebanon, though it no longer challenged the state's boundaries. For example, the president of Syria, Husni az-Za'im, briefly supported an SSNP effort to overthrow the Lebanese government in June 1949, then betrayed the plot to the Lebanese police.

Palestine

From the moment he arrived in Damascus in October 1918, Prince Faysal stressed that Palestine was a part of Syria. Both the 1919 and 1920 meetings of the General Syrian Congress identified Palestine by name as an integral part of Syria. The first called for "no separation of the southern part of Syria, known as Palestine," while the second unanimously proclaimed "the complete and unconditional independence of our country Syria, including Palestine, within its natural boundaries." Faysal informed the General Palestinian Congress that met in Damascus in February 1920 that Palestine was his "right hand" and promised to work for it as for Syria and Iraq. "I assure you, according to the wishes of its people, Palestine will be a part of Syria."[21] Three months later, Faysal wrote to General Allenby that Palestine "is an inseperable [sic] part of Syria."[22] Faysal was true to his word; Damascus became a major center of anti-Zionist rhetoric and activity. It sent so many agents to Palestine that Chaim Weizmann, the Zionist leader, concluded that "the agitation against us in Palestine is conducted from Syria."[23]

Faysal was not alone in claiming Palestine as part of Syria. His rival, Shukri Ghanim, leader of the pro-French faction at the Paris Peace Conference, declared Palestine "incontestably the Southern portion of our country."[24]

Syrian hopes for Palestine did not die when the Palestinians lost interest in Greater Syria in late 1920 (on this, see pp. 66–69). Indeed, Syrian leaders responded to the growth of Palestinian nationalism by pushing harder than ever for Greater Syria. Pan-Syrianists needed Palestinian leaders to agree with them if they were plausibly to claim popular support for Greater Syria. Accordingly, the Syrian Party of Unity strenuously tried to involve in its activities a leading Palestinian organization, the Executive Committee of the Palestinian Arab Congress, though without much success. And what Palestinian leaders would support—such as calls for the "independence of Palestine, Syria and Lebanon each alone"—the Pan-Syrianists found unacceptable.[25] The two sides eventually reached a compromise, whereby the Pan-Syrianists made considerable concessions to the Palestinian separatists. Symbolic of this, the Syrian Congress became the Syro-Palestinian Congress; more importantly, it eventually dropped the demand for Syrian independence.[26]

Syrian aspirations for Palestine then abated for about a dozen years, 1924–36, with only rare indications of continued interest. For example, a Syrian delegation participated in an October 1933 demonstration in Jaffa.

The 1936–39 Arab revolt in Palestine, an event that captured the imagination of Syrians, sparked a second round of major Syrian involvement. Within the limits established by the French authorities, Syrians did whatever they could to assist the Arab Palestinians, offering sanctuary for Palestinian politicians and fighters, sending letters and petitions to the British government, engaging in demonstrations, and retaliating against Syrian Jews through a boycott and riots. The Central Committee of the Jihad collected money and arms in Syria and Lebanon which proved vital in the fight against the British and the Zionists. A group of ʿAlawi leaders characterized union with Palestine as "the highest aspiration of the Arab Muslims."[27] Speaking at the Inter-Parliamentary Congress in October 1938, Faris al-Khuri, speaker of the Syrian Parliament, asserted that Palestine and Transjordan had been wrongly divided from Syria and called for the unification of these provinces with their own country.

Damascus sponsored "The General Command of the Arab Revolt in Southern Syria (Palestine)."[28] Led by a Syrian army officer, Fawzi al-Qawuqji, this three-hundred-man unit fought alongside the Palestinians from August to November 1936. In return for Syrian backing, a leader of the revolt, ʿArif ʿAbd ar-Raziq, called himself "Commander-in-Chief of the Rebels in Southern Syria." Under Syrian pressure in 1938, the "Bureau of the Arab Revolt in Palestine" changed "Palestine" in its name to "Southern Syria."[29] Aid from Lesser Syria and Lebanon reached such proportions that the British put up a barbed-wire fence along Palestine's borders with those two countries.

With the approach of independence after World War II, Syrian politicians showed renewed interest in Palestine. Faris al-Khuri declared in January 1946 that historical, racial, and culture ties required that "Palestine, which must always remain an Arab state, unite with Syria to form a single state."[30]

This interest grew as Great Britain made plans to leave Palestine. The United Nations decision of November 1947 to partition Palestine led to riots in Damascus and Aleppo; seventy-five local Jews were killed in the latter city. Soon thereafter, Syrians began to organize volunteer forces to fight the Zionists. Fawzi al-Qawuqji, again leader of the Syrian troops, began infiltrating Palestine in January 1948, five months before the British left. He took up a position at Tubas in central Palestine and controlled areas in the north. By March, Qawuqji commanded about four thousand soldiers. The willingness of thirty parliamentary deputies to volunteer in Palestine indicates the popularity of this cause. (Only two of them actually went, however: Adib ash-Shishakli and Akram al-Hawrani.)

Regular Syrian forces joined the general Arab assault on the nascent state in May 1948, but their failure was almost total. Syrian troops did win small areas within the territory allotted to Israel under the United Nations partition plan, and these, revealingly, were quickly incorporated into Syria itself. (In contrast, Egyptian officials administered their Gaza conquest from 1948 to 1967 as part of Palestine.) Syrian attitudes came out explicitly in May 1949 during the Armistice Conference with Israel, when a Syrian delegate announced; "there is no international border between Israel and Syria. There was a political border between Syria and Palestine. We have to sign an armistice agreement not on the basis of a political border, but on the basis of an armistice line."[31]

The failure to destroy Israel was a blow to Greater Syrian aspirations, but it did not eliminate them. In a bitter comment on the military failure, one observer wrote: "And now the clear, naked truth: Mother Syria could not save Southern Syria."[32] Husni az-Za'im's offer of April 1949 to settle three hundred thousand Palestinian refugees in Syria should be seen in light of these aspirations.

Transjordan

Syrian rulers made no serious efforts to control Transjordan, but they did lay occasional claim to it in the effort to fend off King 'Abdallah's ambitions. In this spirit, Jamil Mardam, Syrian foreign minister and his country's representative at the Alexandria conference in September 1944, declared that "Greater Syria could be achieved by the annexation of Trans-jordan to Syria as it had been a southern Syrian province under the Arab regime of Faysal."[33] He also told the Transjordanians, "We are republicans. I have already noted what our intention is—to attach to Syria this part [Transjordan] that was cut from it,"[34] ending discussion of a Greater Syria ruled by 'Abdallah. Also, the Syrian prime minister made clear his lack of interest in working with 'Abdallah, telling the Transjordanian consul in Damascus that "the Syrian government favored the formation of Greater Syria but without alteration of the present republican regime [in Syria]. Transjordan was part of Syria and should be reunited with republican Syria." He suggested a plebiscite to ascertain the popular will.[35]

In ratifying the Arab League Pact, one Syrian member of parliament conditioned his affirmative vote on the pact not obstructing the unity of Syria. Shukri al-Quwwatli, the president of Syria and a longtime opponent of 'Abdallah's schemes, suggested in September 1947 that "if Transjordan really wants unity, let her people join the mother country [Syria] as a free republic."[36] But Syria's dismal showing—and Transjordan's relative success—in the war against Israel won 'Abdallah support in Syria; consequently, some of the December 1948 rioters in Syrian cities called for union with Transjordan.

The defensive nature of Syria's claim to Jordan came out especially clearly in a speech delivered by the Syrian head of state, Husni az-Za'im, in April 1949. He began by denouncing Jordanian and Iraqi claims to Syria: "The Syrian Republic wants neither Greater Syria nor [the] Fertile Crescent." Then Za'im showed his fears: "All persons entering into contact with the Government of Jordan or travelling to that country will be charged before a military court for the crime of high treason and will be sentenced to death." He concluded by staking out Syria's own claims: "As for Jordan, which is and remains a Syrian province, she will sooner or later rejoin the mother country and become the 10th province of the Syrian Republic."[37]

According to a newspaper account, the inhabitants of Ajlun in Transjordan petitioned the French high commissioner to incorporate their district into Syria.[38] Transjordanian leaders in exile sometimes supported the claim of Lesser Syria to their home territory. The most prominent of these, Dr. Subhi Abu Ghunayma, announced in April 1947 the goal of driving 'Abdallah from the throne, then setting up a republican regime "in federation with Syria."[39]

Iraq

After 1930, Iraq's imminent independence made the prospect of union with it attractive to Syrian politicans. Accordingly, Faysal met Syrian leaders in 1931–32 to discuss merging their two countries, while Syrian supporters of union paraded Faysal's picture through the streets of Damascus and circulated petitions. Prominent monarchists came out in favor of Faysal's return to Damascus and published a program which declared the unity of the Syrian territories.[40] On Faysal's death in 1933, a number of Sunni leaders "urged the people of Iraq to work for unity of Iraq and Syria under a Hashemite King, swearing allegiance to King Ghazi as successor of King Faysal of Syria." They also renewed the pledge they had made to Faysal when he became king of Syria in 1920.[41]

Much later, in the spring of 1939, Syrian students called for a union of their country with Iraq under the rule of Ghazi.

Aleppo suffered especially from the divisions of 1920–23, for the merchants there had traditionally dealt mostly with Mosul and Baghdad. Understandably, sentiment for joining Iraq to Syria was especially strong among Aleppines. Indeed, in October 1944, a parliamentarian from Aleppo asserted that "some of our [Syrian] territory has been annexed to Iraq."[42] The People's Party (*Hizb ash-Sha'b*),[43] founded in August 1948 and based primarily in Aleppo, agitated strongly for union with Iraq. Party leaders contacted Baghdad, and unity discussions were well along when Syria's first military coup took place, on 30 March 1949, aborting the People's Party initiative.

Then, just ten days after coming to power, the new ruler, Husni az-Za'im, indicated an intention of his own to sign a military pact with Iraq. Four days after that, Syrian military mission went off to Baghdad. But Za'im's means of attaining power and the abruptness of his methods offended the Hashimis in Iraq, and they gave him a cool reception. Instead, Za'im turned to alliance with Egypt, and his rejection of Iraq then became absolute. He announced: "We shall fight everything that is hatched in the Middle East under the aegis of the Fertile Crescent."[44]

This did not end Syrian efforts. Za'im was overthrown in August 1949 by Sami al-Hinnawi, who appointed People's Party members to key positions. They immediately began discussions with Baghdad with the aim of creating a union. When Prince 'Abd al-Illah of Iraq visited Damascus in September, Hinnawi called publicly for a union of the two countries. Despite keen interest on both sides, discussions again foundered. Syrians worried about the Iraqi system of monarchy and the ties with Britain; further, important politicians in both countries, including Nuri as-Sa'id in Iraq, opposed unification.

Then, as negotiations were taking place, Hinnawi fell from power in December 1949. The immediate cause was related to Iraq. Hinnawi refused to include a statement in his presidential oath about preserving Syria's republican regime (and so left open the possibility of Hashimi rule), precipitating a coup just hours before his scheduled swearing-in ceremony.

Alexandretta

Damascus wanted the return of at least Alexandretta; ideally, it sought Cilicia and the whole region south of the Taurus and Anti-Taurus Mountains. The Syro-Palestinian Congress criticized Paris for the Franklin-Bouillon Agreement of 1921, for, without consulting Syrians, it had ceded Cilicia to the Turks. Muhammad Kurd 'Ali, an influential Syrian writer, complained in 1925 that Syria's new border in the north was "not the natural geographic border of Greater Syria," which he saw running along the Taurus and Anti-Taurus Mountains.[45]

The incorporation of Alexandretta into Turkey in 1939 upset many Syrians, thereby stimulating Pan-Syrian and Pan-Arab sentiments. Syrian efforts to win the territory back coalesced in 1945 in anticipation of the San Francisco Conference. On the anniversary of the territory's loss that year, strikes took place in all major Syrian towns and petitions were delivered to the British government. Many organizations joined the government in demanding the region's return. The Syrian press called for the retrocession of Alexandretta, which had been "wrested from Syria."[46] In March 1946, Nuri as-Sa'id of Iraq mediated an agreement whereby Ankara did not insist on formal Syrian recognition of the territory's incorporation; reciprocating, Damascus did not formally demand its return. This compromise has held for nearly half a century; but while the passage of time has necessarily diminished the immediacy of the issue for Syrians, the sense of loss lives on.

Indeed, Alexandretta continued to irritate relations between the two countries after Syrian independence in 1946. Syrian prime minister Jamil Mardam announced in early 1947 that his government would submit the dispute to an international organization for a judgment. In July, the press played up a Syrian court decision in which charges against a man who entered Syria without a passport from Alexandretta were dropped—on the grounds that he had gone from one Syrian province to another. Also in 1947, the Ba'th Party called for Alexandretta's "return to the Syrian motherland [*al-watan al-umm Suriya*]."[47]

Lebanon

The wish to bring Lebanon under Damascus's rule was not one-sided; Lebanese Sunnis saw integration into Syria as the best way to avoid Maronite ambitions. For decades, Sunnis in Lebanon looked to Damascus for help in undoing their state. But they were disappointed, for the Lesser Syrian leadership showed a willingness to compromise on Lebanon, leaving the Lebanese Sunnis to act on their own behalf and spurring their radicalization.

From late 1918 to mid-1920, the Sunnis looked to Faysal in Damascus to help them avoid incorporation in a Maronite-dominated state. Even after the French conquest of Lesser Syria in July 1920, they continued to demand union with it. Sunni opposition activities took several forms. Led by residents of Beirut and Tripoli, they flooded the League of Nations and French offices in Beirut and Paris with memorials, petitions, and telegrams. Demonstrations in the city streets took place on a regular basis. Increased mosque attendance, greater celebration of Islamic holidays, and other religious acts strengthened the spirit of communal solidarity.

The Sunnis' efforts to secede became more organized in 1923, as their leaders combined efforts to petition the French and send emissaries to Europe. That year, a group of Lebanese Muslims wrote the French high commissioner:

> The attachment of Beirut province . . . to Mt. Lebanon took place without popular approval or consultation. . . . Syrian unity brings the purest good and the most universal benefit to the greatest numbers. Mt. Lebanon is a part of Syria; it is insane for it to be excluded. . . . We demand separation from Lebanon and attachment to Syria on a decentralized basis."[48]

Exiles did their share: a Lebanese group, the Central Committee of the Union of Syrian-American Associations, issued a program calling for "the unity and integrity of Syria within its natural geographic limits, from Asia Minor to the Sinai desert."[49] An exile paper in Mexico appeared under the name "United Syria" (*Suriya al-Muttahida*). Efforts to cultivate the Greek Orthodox, who joined the Sunnis in resenting Maronite domination, paid off.

The Druze revolt in Syria of 1925–27 fueled Sunni dissatisfaction. "From the end of 1925 until the summer of 1926," wrote Meir Zamir, "a wave of intensive pro-Syrian activity, unprecedented since 1920, spread throughout the coastal area. Petitions were sent to the High Commission, the French government and the League of Nations, commercial strikes were organised, numerous meetings of notables and leaders were held and articles supporting union with Syria were published in the Muslim press."[50] Sunni leaders carried petitions to the French authorities calling for union with Damascus. They also organized into committees to orchestrate unionist sentiments, coordinate with the rebels in Syria, and communicate with the Executive Committee of the Syro-Palestinian Congress.

The constitution planned for Lebanon in early 1926 would have endowed the Lebanese polity with a new permanence. Sunni Muslims who opposed this step took the occasion to express an intent to withdraw from Lebanon. They withdrew from constitutional consultations, held meetings in Damascus to protest their exclusion from Syria, and took up guerrilla warfare in the Biqaʿ Valley. In January 1926, the municipal council in the mostly Shiʿi town of Baalbek resolved not to participate in drawing up the constitution and simultaneously demanded to be joined to Syria. In February 1926, a group of prominent Muslims demanded that Lebanon be joined to "the Syrian union on a basis of decentralization."[51]

Muslim leaders of Sidon expressed their "certain wish for separation from so-called Greater Lebanon and incorporation in a Syrian union on a basis of decentralization."[52] As one Muslim explained, "Greater Lebanon was created against the Muslims. It was a matter of forming a Christian state. When the authorities created Greater Lebanon, we Muslims were sacrificed, for our country is Syria. If we one day become citizens of Greater Lebanon, it will be because this was imposed on us. We demand to be attached to Syria in a federal government."[53] Another Muslim put it more succinctly: "We want a country that can vibrate our hearts"[54]—referring, of course, to union with Syria.

Representatives from all parts of Muslim Lebanon, including members of the Lebanese parliament, met in Damascus for a June 1926 Conference of the Sons of the Coast "to express their rejection of French behavior, communalism, and their rejection of Lebanon's separation from Syria." The conference communiqué observed that "the Syrian issue is a single issue which allows no divisions. When the Syrians made up a single nation [*umma*], nationalism [*qawmiya*] bound them all together and no distinctions were made according to religion or sect."[55] Another Conference of the Sons of the Coast met two years later and called for Lebanon's inclusion in Syria. It also declared that "when the Syrian province was unified, it did not accept division; when the Syrian people was a single nation [*umma*], it was bound by national community of purpose in which there were no differences along religion or sect."[56] The participation of members of the Lebanese parliament in these meetings endowed them with special importance.

At a Beirut Conference of the Coast in November 1933, the delegates affirmed, "We very much desire to be included within a general Syrian union; outside of it there is no life for our country." Among the telegrams of support was one from the National Bloc in Syria which endorsed what it called the "Conference of the Syrian Coast."[57]

The Sunnis of Beirut were the first to accept the status quo, as economic success cushioned political disappointment. But not entirely; the residents of one Muslim quarter of Beirut refused to fly the Lebanese flag to the end of the mandate. In Tripoli, the urge to secede took longer to diminish; though active efforts there died out in 1923, the city remained a center of militancy well into the 1930s.

The prospect of a Franco-Syrian accord in 1936 inspired another round of activism among Lebanese Muslims. The Sunnis of Tripoli petitioned the League of Nations, requesting that their region, previously incorporated into Lebanon "without their agreement or consent . . . be annexed to United Syria."[58] Four persons died in Sidon in a July riot favoring union with Syria. At a Conference of the Coast in early 1936, Muslim leaders from Lebanon and Syria met with members of the newly formed SSNP to demand that the areas added to Lebanon in 1920 be returned to Syria. An SSNP member told the conference, "Fifteen thousand Lebanese youths demand Syrian unity; and if I said that fifteen thousand Lebanese youths demand unity, I am confident when I say that Lebanon, Gentlemen, is a part of Syria and the youth of Lebanon today will not be satisfied with separation from their nation [*umma*]."[59] A Communist leader announced his support for "total unity for Geographic Syria."[60]

The signing of a Franco-Syrian protocol in September 1936 provoked the Sunni Muslims of Tripoli to riot and strike to demand incorporation in Syria. When the Lebanese president visited Tripoli four days after the signing, he was met by crowds of children and youths who shouted slogans in favor of unity with Syria; they refused to obey police orders, so the incident ended in a stone-throwing fracas with the police.[61] In late 1936, the Sunni residents of Basta, a quarter in Beirut, rioted to bring about unity with Syria. The French high commissioner described their efforts: "Armed with stones, clubs, daggers, and firearms, carrying Syrian flags, the demonstrators threw themselves down Basta Street shouting 'Down with Lebanese unity! Long live Syrian unity, the unity of blood!' Reaching the Christian quarters, the demonstrators began to break shop windows, plunder their contents, and attack trolleys and cars."[62]

Ironically, this disturbance was led by Riyad as-Sulh, the Sunni politician instrumental in forging the great Lebanese compromise of 1943, the National Pact. The pact divided power between the Sunnis and Maronites: Sunnis accepted separation from Syria, and Maronites accepted Lebanon's Arab identity (which meant turning their back on France). The informal agreement of 1943 ended Sunni efforts to join with Syria, at least for several decades.

Still, a reluctance fully to accept the Lebanese polity remained widespread among Sunni Lebanese. The case of the prominent Karami family of Tripoli illustrates the continuity of this sentiment. 'Abd al-Hamid Karami, a Sunni mufti, wrote to the president of France in June 1937 demanding the incorporation of Tripoli and its region into the "motherland" of Syria;[63] it was not until 1949, after he had been Lebanon's prime minister for four years, that he accepted the National Pact of 1943—and then only with reservations. 'Abd al-Hamid's son Rashid also served as prime minister on many occasions in the 1970s and 1980s, and he, too, consistently denigrated Lebanese independence.

Not wanting to live under Maronite rule, Sunni Arabs in Lebanon initially resisted the boundaries that separated them from Syria. With time, however, they became involved in the urgent need to influence events in the Lebanese polity, and their interest in Syria subsequently waned. In the end, the willingness of Syrian leaders to compromise on Lebanon compelled the Lebanese Sunnis to come to terms with an independent Lebanon.

Sunnis living in Lebanon also reacted to events going on in Turkey. They put additional pressure on France when Atatürk forced the French to evacuate Cilicia in late 1921. The splitting of Alexandretta from Syria raised hopes among Sunnis in northern Lebanon that Tripoli would be allocated to Syria by way of compensation; a delegation of Sunnis from Tripoli went to Paris in 1937 to petition this action from the French prime minister, without success.

Palestine

Peak Interest, 1918–1920

Before World War I, the Arabs of Palestine remained loyal to the Ottoman Empire and had but a small role in the development of Pan-Syrian and Pan-Arab ideologies. Interest in these ideologies picked up only in 1918, when several Palestinians rose to high positions in Faysal's movement. Faysal's campaign evinced little support, however; few declarations were made in his favor, and quite a few of the several dozen Palestinians who joined his forces had been Ottoman soldiers taken prisoner of war.

By the end of 1918, the Arabs of Palestine agreed almost unanimously on the need for Syrian unity. Interest in Pan-Syrian unity continued to increase and peaked during the early months of 1920. Although the appeal of Greater Syria dropped off rapidly that summer, it retained a modest role in subsequent decades.

Three major Palestinian organizations forwarded Pan-Syrian ideas in the immediate aftermath of World War I: the Arab Club (*An-Nadi al-'Arabi*), the Literary Club (*Al-Muntada al-Adabi*), and the Muslim-Christian Association (*Al-Jam'iya al-Islamiya al-Masihiya*). (Note the lack of mention of Palestine in all of their names.) The first two groups went farthest, calling outright for unity with Syria under Faysal. The Arab Club was especially vehement in this regard; al-Hajj Muhammad Amin al-Husayni, who later emerged as the deadly enemy of the Hashimi family, served as its president. He recruited about two thousand military volunteers for Husayn in 1918, worked actively on Faysal's behalf in 1919, and attended the General Syrian Congress in 1920. A British diplomatic report noted that Amin al-Husayni's activities were directed "in favor of union with Sharifian [i.e., Faysal's] Syria."[64] One of the Arab Club members, Kamil al-Budayri, edited (along with 'Arif al-'Arif) a newspaper called *Suriya al-Janubiya* ("Southern Syria"), which from September 1919 advocated Palestine's incorporation in Greater Syria.

Even the Muslim-Christian Association, an organization of traditional leaders—men who would expect to rule if Palestine became independent— demanded incorporation in Greater Syria. The association held a congress (known as the First Palestinian Congress) in January-February 1919 to draw up demands for the Paris Peace Conference. Representatives of fourteen Palestinian cities and towns submitted a petition calling for Southern Syria to be "inseparable from the independent Arab Syrian government."[65] In behind-the-scenes maneuvering, the French pressured for Greater Syria resolutions and the British for an independent Palestine. Amin al-Husayni, who was pro-British at that time, called for unity between Palestine and Syria. The congress, which by one count included sixteen delegates favoring unity with Syria (two of which were pro-French) and eleven favoring Palestinian independence,[66] declared Palestine "nothing but part of Arab Syria and it has never been separated from it at any stage." They saw Palestine tied to Syria by "national [*qawmiya*], religious, linguistic, moral, economic, and geographic bonds." On the basis of this view, they called for Palestine remaining "undetached from the independent Arab Syrian Government."[67]

Musa Kazim al-Husayni, head of the Jerusalem Town Council (in effect, mayor) told a Zionist interlocutor in October 1919: "We demand no separation from Syria."[68] According to Ahmad ash-Shuqayri (the man who headed the PLO in the 1960s), the ubiquitous slogan of 1918–19 was "Unity, Unity, From the Taurus [Mountains] to Rafah [in Gaza], Unity, Unity."[69] In this spirit, the British military governor of Jerusalem received a letter from the Arab Club toward the end of 1919, declaring, "Southern Syria forms a part of the United Syria beginning from Taures [and extending to] Rafa, the separation of which we do not tolerate under any circumstances, and we are as well prepared to sacrifice ourselves towards its defense with all our power."[70] Also at that time, plans were made to unify with Syria through force of arms.

The same appeal echoed from all corners. "A woman singer named Badiʿa sang at coffee houses in the town [of Ramla] and encouraged her enraptured listeners to join Amir Faysal."[71] From San Salvador, of all places, a protest in March 1919 went out from the "Syrian Palestinians" to international leaders calling for "no separation between Syria and Palestine" and expressing hope that "Syria and Palestine remain united." The Salvadorans declared: "We trust that if Syria and Palestine remain united, we will never be enslaved by the Jewish yoke."[72]

A congress of Palestinians met in Damascus in February 1920 and strongly advocated Pan-Syrian unity. One speaker suggested that Palestine stood in relation to Syria as Alsace-Lorraine to France. According to a contemporary newspaper report,

> ʿIzzat Darwaza spoke about Palestine and [the need for] Syrian unity, then he submitted a statement for general opinion. No one disagreed with him. The discussion proceeded further on this matter; some participants wanted not to mention Palestine but to use the expression Greater Syria [*al-Bilad ash-Shamiya*] for all the regions of Syria, and they were applauded.

The congress passed four resolutions. The first noted that "it never occurred to the peoples of Northern and Coastal Syria that Southern Syria (or Palestine) is anything but a part of Syria." The second called for an economic boycott of the Zionists in "all three parts of Syria" (meaning Lesser Syria, Mount Lebanon, and the Palestine mandate, which at that time still included Transjordan). The third and fourth resolutions called for Palestine "not to be divided from Syria" and for "the independence of Syria within its natural borders."[73]

The crowning of Faysal as king of Syria in March 1920 elicited strong Pan-Syrian reactions among the Arabs of Palestine. The British military governor of Palestine received a petition (with Amin al-Husayni's signature on it) demanding the eradication of borders with Syria and the inclusion of Palestine in a Syrian union. Musa Kazim al-Husayni broke his promise not to engage in politics and spoke from the municipality building's balcony in praise of Faysal. ʿArif al-ʿArif led a mass demonstration in Jerusalem in which the participants carried pictures of Faysal and called for unity with Syria. Rumors spread about an impending general rebellion aimed at unifying with Lesser Syria.

Amin al-Husayni, just back from Damascus, introduced a new element when he reported on 1 April 1920 that the British government would be willing to recognize Faysal as ruler of Palestine as well as Lesser Syria. This report raised Pan-Syrian expectations to a fever pitch.

The sobering news from San Remo later in April—that the powers had decided to divide Palestine from Lesser Syria and keep both territories under their control—precipitated protests from all parts of Palestine. Calls went out for the independence of a united Syria stretching from Turkey to the Sinai. Horace B. Samuel recounted that the Nabi Musa riots in Jerusalem on 4 April were initiated by two young men who shouted, "Long live our King—King Feisul."[74] One historian, Taysir Jbara, believed that these two were none other than Amin al-Husayni and ʿIzzat Darwaza.[75]

As tensions between Faysal and the French rose in mid-1920, Palestinians donated money to help the Syrian cause. Although volunteers were prevented from crossing into Syria, Palestinians living in Damascus had had an important role in organizing the violence in Palestine following Faysal's coronation.

The Decline of Pan-Syrianism

These acts notwithstanding, Palestinian interest in union with Syria was always precarious. The two sides, Lesser Syrian and Palestinian, had different expectations. Prince Faysal, like many Syrians in the period 1918–20, saw the Zionists as less of a danger than the Maronites, so he worked with Jewish leaders so long as they helped him achieve Greater Syria. In contrast, Palestinian leaders saw Zionists as the preeminent problem. For them, Faysal's standing depended almost exclusively on his ability to help them against the Zionists. In late 1918, the Palestinians saw Faysal, in the words of a French diplomat, as the only Arab leader "capable of resisting the Jewish flood" into Palestine.[76] Accordingly, Faysal's willingness to deal with the Zionists diminished Palestinian backing for him.

This difference in outlook created tensions between Lesser Syrian and Palestinian leaders from the moment World War I ended in November 1918. Signs of disaffection were apparent within three months of Faysal's arrival in Damascus, and they grew with time.

In early 1919, the Muslim-Christian Association held the First Palestinian Congress which resolved that Palestine "should be part of Southern Syria, provided the latter is not under foreign control."[77] The association's Jerusalem branch went farther; calling for an independent government in Palestine to be only "politically associated" with Syria, it authorized Faysal "to represent Palestine and defend it at the Paris Conference," on the understanding that Palestine would enjoy full autonomy within a Syrian union.[78] And while 'Arif Pasha ad-Dajjani, president of the Muslim-Christian Association, insisted that "Palestine or Southern Syria—an integral part of the one and indivisible Syria—must not in any case or for any pretext be detached,"[79] he also had doubts about rule from Damascus. 'Izzat Darwaza recalled Dajjani joking that this would lead to the Syrians snatching away the Palestinians' fezzes; to which Darwaza replied, ironically, that by the same logic, Jerusalem as capital of Palestine would then snatch the fezzes of other Palestinian towns.[80] Some wanted only a cultural union with Lesser Syria.

Arguments against connections to Damascus began to appear in the press in 1919. The Arab Club was the first nationalist institution to abandon Faysal's leadership. Despite its name, the newspaper *Suriya al-Janubiya* led the campaign away from Pan-Syrianism, arguing that Lesser Syrians had become too absorbed in their conflict with France to pay enough attention to the Zionist challenge. In January 1920, when Faysal returned empty-handed from his second trip to Europe, top Palestinians began to see him as dispensable to their cause, an impression reinforced by the lack of Syrian response to the Jerusalem riots of April 1920. Despite these strains, Lesser Syrian and Palestinian leaders minimized their differences for almost two years, for both had an interest in Prince Faysal's success.

Everything changed, however, after the French took Damascus in July 1920. The attention of Lesser Syrians became entirely absorbed by French rule, leaving very little for Palestine. For Palestinians, the attraction of a Syrian connection disappeared. Why be joined to Damascus if this meant rule by Paris? Amin al-Husayni and other Palestinian figures came to recognize that the Palestinians were on their own against the British and the Zionists. From then on, they sought to establish an autonomous Arab government in Palestine which they, not politicians in Damascus, would rule.

The Third Palestinian Congress, meeting in December 1920, formalized this change in outlook when it dropped the appellation *Southern Syria* and no longer demanded that Palestine by joined with Lesser Syria. By the Sixth Palestinian Congress, in June 1923, Southern Syria had disappeared, and it remained absent in the Seventh Congress of June 1928.

When the Syrian Congress (the main exile organization dedicated to building Greater Syria) met in August 1921, Palestinians would no longer endorse the unity of Greater Syria. They even made the organization rename itself the Syro-Palestinian Congress and issue a statement calling for the "independence of Syria and of Palestine."[81] A year later, Palestinians withdrew from this congress, finding it too preoccupied with France. By May 1923, Palestinian leaders were telling Riyad as-Sulh, a Lebanese politician who urged accommodation with Zionism, that, as a Syrian, he had no business getting involved in Palestinian matters.

What accounts for this rapid collapse of Pan-Syrian sentiment in Palestine? Yehoshua Porath argues that Palestinians supported Pan-Syrianism so long as it served them and abandoned it when it no longer had utility. In contrast to Lesser Syrians, who tended to see Pan-Syrianism as an end in itself, he says, Palestinians saw it as a means, a weapon in the battle against Zionism; it was weak because it only served ulterior purposes. In the years 1918 to 1920, being treated as part of Syria had three advantages.[82] The joint Anglo-French declaration of November 1918 promised "to encourage and assist the establishment of native governments and administrations in Syria and Mesopotamia"—not Palestine.[83] This declaration made it desirable for Palestine to be seen as part of Syria. Associating with the larger Muslim population of Greater Syria offered a way to overwhelm the Jewish immigrants demographically. And alliance with Faysal gave Palestinians a relatively powerful protector.

According to Porath, Lesser Syrian absorption with its own problems caused these advantages to disappear:

> Disappointment over the moderation of the Syrians toward Zionism cooled the Palestinians' enthusiasm for the idea of Pan-Syrian unity. . . . The orientation towards Damascus was based less on the growth of nationalism around this area [of Greater Syria] than upon a given political situation. When this situation changed, the foundations of the Pan-Syrian movement collapsed.[84]

All these points are correct, but not the implication that Pan-Syrian nationalism was merely a tactic while Palestinian nationalism appealed to deep sentiments. The reverse is closer to the truth. Existing sentiments fit better within Greater Syria than Palestine. Tactical considerations motivated the rapid collapse of Pan-Syrian sentiment and its replacement by Palestinian separatism. Porath himself quotes one Palestinian leader who openly admitted this. Only days after the fall of Faysal's government, Musa Kazim al-Husayni declared, "after the recent events in Damascus, we have to effect a complete change in our plans here. Southern Syria no longer exists. We must defend Palestine."[85] Kamil ad-Dajjani explained many years after the event that "the collapse of Faysal's rule in Syria and the disappointment of the hopes which were pinned upon that rule, made Palestinians feel that the orientation toward a Greater Syria bore no fruit."[86] Palestinian nationalism originated not in spontaneous feelings but in calculated politics, and many years passed before the emotional appeal of this premeditated and novel allegiance matched that of Pan-Syrian nationalism.

Why this shift? Because Palestine served better. It allowed the Arab leaders of Palestine to speak the same political language as the Zionists and the British. Rather than refer to some outside source of authority, they claimed sovereignty for themselves, and in the process evolved from provincial notables into independent actors. Ultimately, Palestinian nationalism originated in Zionism; were it not for the existence of another people who saw British Palestine as their national home, the Sunni Arabs would have continued to view this area as a province of Greater Syria. Zionism turned Palestine into something worthy in itself. If not for the Jewish aspirations, Sunni Arab attitudes toward Palestine would no doubt have resembled those toward the territory of Transjordan, an indifference only slowly eroded by many years of governmental effort.

The evolution of the Sunnis' views in Lebanon sheds light on their coreligionists in Palestine. The two groups faced strikingly similar challenges in the period 1918–20 for, just as Zionists wanted a separate mandate for Palestine, Maronites sought a separate Lebanon. Not wanting to live under Maronite or Jewish rule, Sunnis in both areas resisted the Lebanese and Palestinian polities. But whereas Sunni Arabs of Lebanon sought reincorporation into Lesser Syria for another two decades, those of Palestine began the switch to separatism already in 1920.

Jewish nationalism stimulated an intense Palestinian identity, but Maronite nationalism never prompted a comparable feeling for Lebanon; why? Because Sunnis in Palestine had hopes of winning British favor, whereas those of Lebanon could hardly hope to win French favor. This prompted the first to adopt language and aspirations that would suit the mandatory power. Also, Sunnis in Palestine enjoyed a demographic preponderance that gave them the confidence to go it alone; those in Lebanon felt too weak to take over the state, at least before World War II. Too, Zionists did not speak Arabic, and Maronites did; this fundamentally affected the way Sunnis saw Zionists and the state they created. Finally, Sunnis saw Jews and Christians differently, for the first had always been a weak minority, while the latter represented the Muslims' principal earthly rival.

Vestiges of Pan-Syrianism

Though it initially had very little appeal, the logic of need caused Palestinian nationalism to flourish, so that it became a truly popular cause. So thoroughly has the former come to dominate that the earlier strengths of Pan-Syrian nationalism have been largely forgotten.

Nonetheless, Pan-Syrian nationalism lasted in Palestine through the interwar period and continued to find a sizable audience, as an abundance of evidence shows. *Al-Ittihad al-ʿArabi*, a newspaper published from 1925 to 1927, strongly favored Greater Syria. (Ironically, *Al-Ittihad al-ʿArabi*, meaning "Arab Unity," supported Pan-Syrianism, while *Suriya al-Janubiya*, or "Southern Syria," came to support Palestinian separatism.) A Palestinian organization founded in August 1932, the Arab Independence Party in Southern Syria (*Hizb al-Istiqlal al-ʿArabiya fi Suriya al-Janubiya*), returned to the nomenclature of Southern Syria. Its platform called Palestine "an Arab country and a natural part of Syria,"[87] and its manifestos referred to Palestine as Southern Syria.

Some leading Palestinian thinkers continued to work for a Syrian union. Ahmad al-Khalidi, a Palestinian educator, proposed two cantons in Palestine, one Jewish and the other Arab; the latter he referred to as Southern Syria.[88] In a 1934 meeting with David Ben-Gurion, Musa ʿAlami explained that an Arab federation would consist of three major states, one of which would be "Syria and western Palestine."[89] Even George Antonius, the leading Palestinian theorist of Pan-Arab nationalism, accepted this formulation. Meeting with Ben-Gurion three times in April 1936, Antonius asserted that "there was no natural barrier between Palestine and Syria, and there was no difference between their inhabitants."[90] He explained the unreality of Palestine, and that Greater Syria from the Taurus Mountains to the Sinai Desert formed a single unit. Ben-Gurion concluded from these talks that Antonius's true interest lay in the fate of Syria, not Palestine.

Pan-Syrian ideas also remained a part of Arab diplomacy. The Fourth Palestinian Congress of May 1921 called for a Palestinian delegate to be sent to the Syro-Palestinian Congress in Geneva to demand Syrian unity from the League of Nations.[91] Delegates at the Fifth Congress were told that "the inhabitants of Southern Syria see themselves and their land as an inseparable part of the rest of Syria."[92] The Palestine Delegation in Geneva demanded that Palestine not be divided from its Arab neighbors.[93] A report by the Executive Committee of the Palestinian Arab Congress in 1924 refers to "the one country of Syria" and calls Palestine "Southern Syria."[94] Remarkably, Greater Syria surfaced even in Palestinian appeals to the West. Palestinian legations meeting with Winston Churchill in March and August 1921 both called for Palestine "not [to] be separated from her Arab-neighboring sister-states."[95]

Reviving Southern Syria offered several benefits. It provided a way for Palestinians to call on assistance from Lesser Syria and Lebanon; in June 1933, the party warned the inhabitants of "Coastal" and "Interior" Syria (i.e., Lebanon and Lesser Syria) that Zionist ambitions would harm them, too.[96] It also helped mobilize efforts outside Palestine against British and Zionist activities. Exile groups continued to see Palestine as part of Syria. The Palestine National League of New York asserted in 1922 that "The Palestinians ask only to be left alone with their fellow Syrians to develop the resources of their province which has been an integral part of Syria for two thousand years."[97]

But Pan-Syrianism was not just utilitarian. Palestinians dispatched various forms of aid when political crises occurred in Lesser Syria. During the 1925–27 revolt, they sent money and food, and they demonstrated, struck, and publicized their sympathy for the Syrians. They held a general strike in March 1926 to protest the presence in Jerusalem of the French high commissioner to Lebanon and Syria. The Syrian general strike of 1936 inspired solidarity meetings and demonstrations in Palestine; in the name of Southern Syria, some of them called for immediate unity between the two regions. Palestinians also sent money to the strike committee in Syria.

The memory of Faysal and his dream of a Greater Syrian kingdom retained its impact in Palestine. In September 1933, Palestinians mourned Faysal's death and recalled the hopes they had had in him; similarly, the first anniversary of his death prompted many expressions of grief. Despite the politicians' disillusionment with Faysal, his career touched something that stirred Palestinians.

Palestinians sometimes directed their feelings of Pan-Syrian solidarity toward Transjordan. Transjordan's independence in March 1946 provided an occasion for displaying pictures of ʿAbdallah and other Hashimis in the streets of Hebron.

With time, Palestinians developed Pan-Syrian ambitions of their own. Amin al-Husayni planned, after having wrested control of Palestine from the British, to expand east and north. In 1934 he joined with Fawzi al-Qawuqji to plot ʿAbdallah's overthrow and the union of Transjordan with Palestine. Revealingly, he suggested unity between like-minded Palestinian and Pan-Syrian parties in June 1937. Husayni's terrorist agents threatened the British consul in Damascus on behalf of the "Arabs of southern Syria."[98] In his November 1941 conversation with Adolf Hitler, Husayni explained that "the Arabs were striving for the independence and unity of Palestine, Syria, and Iraq."[99] Also suggestive is an undated leaflet in Arabic distributed by the Italian government of Benito Mussolini. Addressed to "Syrians from Mt. Taurus to El Arish," it refers to "His Excellency al-Hajj Amin al-Husayni" as "the leader of Greater Palestine."[100] As Munif al-Husayni, Amin's close associate, explained many years later, it was taken for granted that "once Palestine assumes its independence, then the Palestinians will consider the idea of unity with the other Arab states."[101] Although Husayni failed to achieve even the first step of his plan—control of Palestine—this ambition helps explain the acute tensions between himself and those politicians in Amman and Damascus who envisioned Palestine as part of Syria.

Transjordan

More than any other ruler of his time, ʿAbdallah of Transjordan tried to piece Greater Syria together. During the thirty years from his arrival in Amman in March 1921 to his assassination in July 1951, Greater Syria stood at the heart of Transjordanian foreign policy. Throughout this period, ʿAbdallah claimed Damascus and sovereignty over Greater Syria on the basis of the resolution passed by the General Syrian Congress of March 1920.[102] (The congress, it will be recalled, had called for Syrian independence within its "natural boundaries" and crowned his brother Faysal as king of Syria.) These efforts affected nearly every aspect of Transjordanian relations with Great Britain, Lesser Syria, the Arab Palestinians, and the Zionists.

Early Years, 1921–1933

Shortly after French forces expelled Faysal from Damascus in July 1920, residents of several parts of Greater Syria (Hawran, Amman, Maʿan) appealed to King al-Husayn in Mecca for help. He obliged them by sending his son ʿAbdallah to lead the campaign against the French. ʿAbdallah left Mecca in September 1920 with some five hundred to one thousand soldiers and entered the far south of Greater Syria at Maʿan two months later. He then declared an intention to march on Damascus, drive out the French, and place Faysal back on his throne. Referring to himself as the "Vice-King of Syria" (Faysal being the king), 'Abdallah called on Syrians to unite their country. Some favorable responses came in, including a few from regions under French control. After waiting in Ma'an for three months, 'Abdallah moved to Amman at the beginning of March 1921.

He set off to attack French-controlled territory with an estimated eight thousand armed men, including cavalry, and more reinforcements were on the way from Lesser Syria and the Hijaz. So worried were the French about an attack on Syria that they blew up a key railroad bridge at Dir'a. The British, knowing what an attack from their territory would do to relations with France, tried to convince 'Abdallah to return home to Mecca.[103] When this failed, they attempted to placate him by offering him control over the larger but less important part of the Palestine mandate, the land to the east of the Jordan River, the area known as Transjordan. 'Abdallah accepted the British offer and in March 1921 became the prince (*amir*) of Transjordan.

Although Transjordan made up more than three-quarters of the Palestine mandate, it was a desolate corner of Greater Syria. Its territory included a single undeveloped port, a narrow band of fertile land, and a minuiscule population of less than 250,000 persons. Laurence Oliphant wrote in 1881 that Ajlun "was the largest center of population and best-built village we had seen to the east of the Jordan, though that is giving it scant praise, for the population did not probably exceed five hundred."[104] In 1936, Amman's population was a mere three thousand. Not surprisingly, high civilization was undeveloped. A historian, Suleiman Mousa, estimates a literacy rate of about 1 one percent at the end of the nineteenth century.[105]

Before 1921, Transjordan had no government or regionwide administration but served as a dusty stage for tribal warfare and banditry. The east bank was known for its destitution ("a desert country where [there] are only wandering inhabitants," according to Selah Merrill in 1881)[106] and savagery (a "no man's land, where theft, bloodshed, and murder are the commonest everyday occurrence," according to Libbey and Hoskins in 1905).[107] Insofar as there was any law and order at all, it was produced only after the pilgrims bribed the Huwaytat and Bani-Sakhr tribal confederacies that loosely lorded over the desert.

Travelers stayed away, for as J. S. Buckingham observed in 1822, "the road on the east of the Jordan was acknowledged by all to be dangerous."[108] In 1867, Jonathan F. Swift commented on his trip to the Jordan River that "fear of Bedouin marauders kept the party within a space of half a mile. . . . The banks of that stream seem to be more infested with robbers than any other part of the valley."[109] *Cook's Tourists' Handbook* of 1876 cautiously advised travelers that "tours to the East of the Jordan would require the special protection of the local sheikhs, and would involve costs for this protection."[110] For centuries, foreigners saw Transjordan primarily as an area to be traversed quickly on the way to the pilgrimage in Mecca; if not for this route, the outside world would have happily and completely ignored it.[111]

It was no wonder that 'Abdallah was initially reluctant to accept this charmless, second-rate territory as his domain, then sought to expand out of it. An ambitious man, he made no secret of his impatience to find something more worthy of his talents. Already in August 1921, after less than half a year there, he announced, "I have had enough of this wilderness of Trans-Jordania."[112] 'Abdallah wanted the whole of Greater Syria. Most of all, he sought Damascus and Lesser Syria; he also sought Palestine, especially Jerusalem; and he had unformulated hopes of bringing Lebanon under his rule. Avi Shlaim ascribed a motto to him: "All Syria to come under the leadership of a scion of the House of Hashem; Transjordan was the first step."[113]

Nor was he alone in these hopes. The Pan-Syrian nationalists who joined him in Amman kept reminding him of the need to keep striving toward Damascus. According to Albert Abramson, the chief British representative in Transjordan, they "lost no opportunity even in the presence of His Highness to talk against the French and on one occasion Civil Secretary Rashid Bey Talieh [Tali'a] reminded His Highness that the reason His Highness had come to Transjordan was to drive the French out of Syria."[114]

'Abdallah pursued this goal with two strategies. First, though but a weak and impoverished amir, he hoped to become so useful to the British and French that they would help him against his rivals and bequeath their mandates to him. Second, though lord of little more than bleak desert, he sought to gain the support of residents throughout Greater Syria. 'Abdallah even wooed the two groups most alien to him, the Zionists and the Maronites. To maintain the maximum room for maneuver, he avoided specific geographic delineations and showed a willingness to accept any part of Greater Syria to come under his control.

The British offered Transjordan to 'Abdallah in March 1921 on the clear condition that "any action hostile to Syria must be abandoned."[115] Nonetheless, the British negotiators—none other than Winston Churchill and T. E. Lawrence—held out hope to 'Abdallah that diplomatic efforts might permit him to move to Damascus. They noted that "if he succeeded in checking anti-French action for six months . . . he would also greatly improve his own chances of a personal reconciliation with the French which might even lead to his being instated by them as Amir of Syria in Damascus."[116] In his memoirs, 'Abdallah recounts this offer as far less tentative. He records Churchill saying: "If you stay here [in Transjordan], behave well, and manage your affairs properly here and in the Hijaz, we are hopeful that France will go back on its decision and will satisfy justice within a matter of months by returning to you Greater Syria [*bilad ash-Sham*]."[117]

Even in 'Abdallah's version, it is worth noting, the British promised to do nothing against French wishes. And the French rejected any thought of letting 'Abdallah rule in Damascus. Their firmness and the British desire not to spark avoidable problems with Paris meant that, so long as the imperial powers controlled Lesser Syria and Transjordan, 'Abdallah would not be moving to Damascus.

Under these circumstances, he had no choice but to mute his ambitions; all he could do was signal his intentions. He did this, for one, by filling many high positions in the Transjordanian government with Pan-Syrian politicians from other parts of Greater Syria.[118] The first Transjordanian council of ministers, formed in April 1921, contained just one member native to Transjordan. Each of 'Abdallah's five prime ministers between 1921 and 1931 came from Lesser Syria. For another, 'Abdallah had Transjordan's Organic Law, passed in April 1928, phrased to indicate his hopes about moving to Damascus: "Amman shall be considered the capital of Transjordan, but the capital may be changed by a special law to another place." (In contrast, the Syrian constitution of two years later stated firmly that "the capital of Syria is the city of Damascus.")[119] Finally, 'Abdallah repeatedly asserted his right to the throne in Syria in private conversation and correspondence.

The Drive for Damascus, 1933–1947

The death of his elder brothers in 1933 and 1935 left 'Abdallah the senior Hashimi, prompting him to assert with greater force his claims to Greater Syria and Iraq. From the early 1930s on, he made Greater Syria a regular theme, bringing it up in most of his speeches, memoranda, letters, and diplomatic discussions.

In 1936, as French rule in Syria appeared to be coming to an end, 'Abdallah recognized the urgent need to reach an agreement with Paris that would guarantee his becoming king of Syria. If he missed the chance, Syria would become a republic. To stake a position in Syria, 'Abdallah played the two sides in his characteristic manner, seeking the support of both Syrian politicians[120] and the British authorities; according to a newspaper report, he even threatened the British that failure to persuade the French to attach Syria to Transjordan would lead to "grave consequences."[121] Nothing came of these moves, for the French determined to remain in Syria.

In June 1937, 'Abdallah proposed to London that Syria, Transjordan, Palestine, and Iraq be unified in one kingdom.[122] It is noteworthy that this list of countries includes Iraq and excludes Lebanon. Iraq had a special significance for 'Abdallah, for it had been assigned to him by his father at the end of World War I.[123] When Faysal lost his own designated area, Syria, the British compensated him with the throne of Iraq. So long as Faysal was alive, 'Abdallah dared not try to bring Iraq under his control. But Faysal's death in 1933 inspired him to win what he saw as his rightful inheritance.

'Abdallah's interest in Lebanon met with complete opposition from the Lebanese authorities. The intensity of Maronite opposition to 'Abdallah's plan caused him to concede autonomy or even full independence to Lebanon. But he envisioned a Lebanon reduced to its pre-1920 borders.

'Abdallah's unity scheme attracted some support in Lesser Syria before and during World War II, as leaders there saw him as potentially helpful to the cause of Syrian independence. 'Abd ar-Rahman Shahbandar and Fawzi al-Bakri, traveled to Amman in 1939 and declared on their departure: "The artificial borders created by the various imperialist powers must be abolished

. . . long live ['Abdallah,] the living King of Syria and Transjordan."[124] Shahbandar subsequently favored 'Abdallah as king of a united Syria and provided 'Abdallah with the little reliable support he could find in Lesser Syria. Accordingly, Shahbandar's assassination in 1940 very much diminished the king's standing in Damascus. But he could still rely on the al-Atrash Druze clan; and 'Alawi chiefs in the Jazira region worked with him at times, as did the 'Alawi rebel leader, Sulayman al-Murshid.[125] Also, some monarchists continued to favor 'Abdallah as their leader (though most preferred other Hashimi or Sa'udi figures).

Lesser Syrian politicians tended to be entirely opportunistic in their dealings with 'Abdallah. Faris al-Khuri told 'Abdallah in 1941 that, at independence, Syria's republican form of government "could be reconsidered and monarchy chosen,"[126] but this was a temporary position. Similarly, the League of National Action and the National Bloc supported 'Abdallah at moments when this served their purposes. A British diplomat aptly characterized 'Abdallah's activities in Syria as "fishing in the troubled Syrian waters."[127]

To encourage his fickle supporters, 'Abdallah provided generous funds. But not being wealthy himself, this meant that pro-'Abdallah activities depended in good part on the state of the prince's purse. Although most of the money spent in Syria came from his relatives in Iraq, some of it was obtained in more exotic ways. According to Mary C. Wilson, "it was reported that he made money for disbursement in Syria by sending his cars across the border laden with merchandise which was then sold on the Syrian market where prices were much higher than in Transjordan. His winnings at the Cairo racetrack also funded a brief flutter amongst the Syrian tribes."[128] On one occasion in 1946, 'Abdallah tried to extract funds from the Jewish Agency to spend on elections in Syria.

As Pan-Arabism became a powerful ideological force, 'Abdallah shaded his Greater Syria scheme to make it more compatible with Pan-Arabism. Beginning in November 1939, he presented unified Syria less as an end in itself and more as a step toward Arab unity.

The fall of France in June 1940 encouraged 'Abdallah's Greater Syrian ambitions in two ways. First, it terminated French rule over Syria, which 'Abdallah interpreted as the cancellation of the French mandate. Second, it brought to power Winston Churchill, the colonial secretary who had looked favorably on 'Abdallah's ambitions in 1921. 'Abdallah took every occasion to remind Churchill of his earlier assurances; he also suggested that once Syria had been retaken from Vichy control, the British government should attach it to Transjordan. 'Abdallah's prospects appeared to brighten in May 1941, when the British foreign minister, Anthony Eden, offered his government's support for Arab unity and appeared to endorse Greater Syria.

But 'Abdallah's hopes were crushed a month later, when Transjordanian troops were excluded from the British and Free French forces that invaded Syria. In response, 'Abdallah encouraged petitions, demonstrations, and other forms of protest. His cabinet issued a resolution calling Transjordan "part of the bloc of the Syrian country [*bilad*] since the most ancient historical times."

The resolution made a practical argument for Greater Syria: "In view of its geographic position and natural resources, the Syrian country cannot survive economically except as a single entity."[129]

In November 1942, when Britain's position in the Middle East had recovered from Nazi attack, 'Abdallah both decreased and increased his usual demand for Greater Syria: to Zionist leaders he sketched out a state in which Lebanon and Palestine would only be federated; to the British he demanded cultural union with Iraq in addition to a full Greater Syria state.

The next major defeat for 'Abdallah occurred in March 1943, when the Egyptian government took an interest in Arab unity. As Cairo became the new fulcrum of inter-Arab activities, the balance tipped further against 'Abdallah, for Egyptian leaders opposed the Greater Syria scheme, fearing it would create a powerful rival in Damascus which could challenge Egypt's preeminent position in Arab politics. Their active rejection of Greater Syria virtually doomed the plan. From 1943 on, 'Abdallah's efforts became increasingly futile.

But he persisted in pursuit of his dream. When Arab leaders made their opposition known, he turned to the public. Figuring that the leaders had to oppose 'Abdallah's plan (for it threatened their own positions), he placed his hopes on the masses. But they responded no better. His call of March 1943 for a congress of representatives from Transjordan, Syria, and Palestine to decide "the proper form of government in Greater Syria"[130] got no response. A month later, he sent out a plea to "the people of historic Syria" to ponder the unification of Greater Syria. 'Abdallah argued for "the mending of its rifts and the realization of the idea that it was—in its natural borders—one homeland linked by national, geographic, and historical unity."[131] This call, too, was ignored. The same fate awaited his 1944 effort to put together a common front with the Iraqi government. And the Transjordanian foreign minister's 1945 claim that 50 percent of the Lebanese population welcomed incorporation into a Greater Syria comprising Palestine and Transjordan "aroused the usual protests in Christian circles."[132]

On condition that some form of Greater Syria might emerge, 'Abdallah agreed to participate in the meetings which eventually led to the establishment of the Arab League. Greater Syria was, indeed, a prominent concern during preparatory discussions to the Alexandria Conference of September 1944, but its role declined in the course of the conference; even 'Abdallah could see he faced a united Arab opposition and had no British support. The Arab states' refusal to recognize Greater Syria in the Alexandria Protocol provoked criticism by members of the Transjordanian Chamber of Deputies and led to the cabinet's resignation. With Iraqi help, 'Abdallah did extract one concession from the Arab states: Article 9 of the Arab League Pact declared that member states "which desire to establish closer cooperation and stronger bonds than are provided by this Pact may conclude agreements to that end."[133]

'Abdallah's Greater Syria campaign entered a new stage with the independence of Transjordan in March 1946 and that of Syria a month later. These developments had a mixed effect on 'Abdallah's plans. His position improved insofar as he no longer had a British overlord; it weakened in that Syria had become an independent republic. Lesser Syrian leaders now had established interests and the means to protect them from 'Abdallah.

Nonetheless, 'Abdallah persevered. In a speech from the throne in November 1946, he enshrined the "immediate unity"[134] of Greater Syria as a formal principle of his country's foreign policy. When Syrian leaders denounced 'Abdallah's ambitions, the Transjordanian prime minister called the legitimacy of the Syrian republic into question by characterizing it as an artifice of the Sykes-Picot Agreement. By now, 'Abdallah met with the automatic opposition of all Arab leaders; the Arab League passed a resolution in November 1946 declaring Greater Syria incompatible with its pact. But 'Abdallah, not one to give up, retorted: "I shall never cease my efforts to achieve the unity of Syria."[135]

In the effort to win British backing for his expansionist plans, 'Abdallah raised the specter of a Soviet threat in the Middle East. But instead of gaining London's sympathy, this ploy provoked a pained reaction, for the British authorities did not want to be seen as party to 'Abdallah's overthrow of his neighbors.

In a frenzy of frustration, 'Abdallah hardly seemed to care anymore what reaction his plans evoked. Note the transformation of his attitude toward Lebanon. Recognizing the intensity of Maronite opposition to his Greater Syria plan, he had long been willing to concede autonomy or full independence to Lebanon within its pre-1920 borders. The throne speech implicitly retracted these careful assurances of earlier years and provoked an immediate response from the Lebanese foreign minister: "We do not want Greater Syria and we do not accept it in any form. . . . We do not want Greater Syria with Lebanon or without it."[136] In March 1947, 'Abdallah threw all caution overboard and bluntly declared, "I want a state which includes Syria, Transjordan, and Lebanon. Yes, even Lebanon."[137] The Lebanese reaction can be imagined.

'Abdallah's final effort of this round was to call a conference in August 1947 for representatives of "the Syrian regions" to discuss plans for unity.[138] The response was overwhelmingly negative. Syrian and Lebanese leaders, suffering from what Nizar Kayali calls an "encirclement neurosis,"[139] declared "stupefaction" at 'Abdallah's interference in their internal affairs.[140] Responding to 'Abdallah's publication of documents in a May 1947 book, *The Transjordan White Paper*,[141] the Damascene authorities collected Syrian condemnations of his plan from many professional associations and regional councils and published them in September under the title *The Word of Syrians and Arabs on the Greater Syrian Plan*. The Union of Newspaper Editors, for example, declared the Greater Syria plan to be an "imperialist plot" and predicted its achievement would mean "the elimination of the democratic freedom which Syria enjoys." It condemned the plan as contrary to Arab unity and noted that every Arab state without exception had denounced the plan.[142] The Muslim Brethren of Syria also issued a statement strongly opposing 'Abdallah.[143] (Two years earlier, the Syrian and Lebanese Communist parties had already condemned 'Abdallah's plan in the "strongest terms.")[144]

So panicked were the Arab leaders about 'Abdallah's Greater Syria plans, as well as the alleged British support for them, that King 'Abd al-'Aziz ibn Sa'ud of Saudi Arabia requested the U.S. government to "intervene in this matter immediately" to end it. In fact, an American official did notify London about his government being "disturbed" by reports of the Greater Syria plan.[145]

Palestine Interlude, 1947–1949

Together, the unanimity of the negative response to his Greater Syria plans and events taking place in Palestine induced 'Abdallah in October 1947 to abandon Lesser Syria and turn his attention to Palestine. But he did not really give up on Greater Syria so much as redirect his efforts. Ostensibly, the impending British withdrawal from Palestine required the Arabs' undivided attention to save that area from the Zionists; in fact, 'Abdallah realized that controlling Lesser Syria was not possible, so he focused on the opportunity Palestine offered. A December 1947 assertion that "the realization of a Greater Syria which assures the protection of the Jews offers the only viable solution of the Palestine problem"[146] showed how little his thinking had really changed.

During the next three years, 'Abdallah devoted almost all his energy to Palestine. Of course, his interest in Palestine had begun much earlier; already in March 1921, before even meeting Winston Churchill, he had tried to convince the colonial secretary to place Palestine under his control. 'Abdallah then repeated this suggestion no less than four times at the Cairo Conference. But for the next decade or so, he concentrated on building Transjordan and left Palestinian matters alone. During those years, 'Abdallah cultivated allies in Palestine among the British authorities, the pro-British Arabs, and the Zionists; he also organized support in Transjordan for his claim to Palestine.

'Abdallah's active efforts to gain influence in Palestine increased in the early 1930s. A Transjordanian delegation took part in an October 1933 demonstration in Jaffa. 'Abdallah began overtly to reassert a claim in July 1934 when he arrogated the religious and political leadership of Palestine for himself. A few months later, one of his aides proposed a union of Palestine and Transjordan to the Zionists. 'Abdallah demanded that Britain unify Palestine with Transjordan in March 1936,[147] and he took on an active role mediating between the Arab Revolt and London with this same end in mind. The king was not alone in seeking Transjordanian rule over Palestine; a meeting of desert tribal leaders in June 1936 resolved to "cross the Jordan and win Palestine back from the Jews and the British."[148]

The Peel Commission of 1937 greatly encouraged 'Abdallah's ambitions. Dispatched by the British government to suggest a political solution for Palestine, the royal commission suggested dividing the mandate into three parts: one under British rule, one an independent Jewish state, one united with Transjordan. Although nearly all Arab leaders rejected this or any other form of partition, 'Abdallah and his Palestinian allies, especially Raghib Bey an-Nashashibi, favored the Peel Plan, knowing this was the most likely way for any of them to rule a portion of Palestine.

In May 1938, 'Abdallah presented a memorandum to the British government arguing that Palestine should be united with Transjordan under his rule. When his idea met wide and vociferous Arab opposition, he tried to make his intentions less evident; but ʿAbdallah was hardly one to keep a secret, and he could not resist asserting that Transjordan and Palestine were a single country. ʿAbdallah's chief minister told a British official that Transjordan should be united with Syria and Palestine so that it could "stand on its own feet."[149]

In late 1946, when the British indicated their intention to leave Palestine, all parties interested in the future of the area began maneuvering for the fight to come. The British Foreign Office favored ʿAbdallah over the other parties—Zionists, Palestinians, and the Arab states—who joined this contest. Already in September 1945, the Foreign Office had devised a plan to place nearly all Palestine under ʿAbdallah; But more significant was the permission granted ʿAbdallah to have his forces enter Palestine before the British evacuation in May 1948. Under guise of seconding troops to secure the lines of communication as the British departed, ʿAbdallah placed two thousand soldiers in Palestine by April 1948. As usual, he was forthright, announcing an intention to pursue his "rights" in Palestine.[150] He also asserted that "Palestine and Transjordan are one, for Palestine is the coastline and Transjordan the hinterland of the same country."[151] The prime minister, Samir ar-Rifaʿi, told two British journalists: "We all believe in the Greater Syria scheme, and eventually Arab Palestine, Syria and Transjordan will become one country, they must."[152]

The presence of Transjordanian soldiers ensured that a substantial portion of Palestine (the area henceforth known as the West Bank) fell under ʿAbdallah's control in the course of Israel's war of independence. Once the West Bank had been militarily secured, ʿAbdallah orchestrated its formal annexation. He claimed Palestine as part of "the security zone of the Trans-Jordan Government, which extends from the Egyptian kingdom's frontiers to the frontiers of Syria and Lebanon."[153] He did everything possible to support the United Nations mediator for Palestine, Count Folke Bernadotte, who recommended that Arab portions of Palestine be attached to Transjordan; but the UN General Assembly rejected Bernadotte's ideas in December 1948. Undaunted, ʿAbdallah turned his attention to the Palestinians who had come under his control.

He had begun the unification process in November 1948 with his coronation by the Coptic bishop of Jerusalem as king of Jerusalem. Then he convened a Palestinian Arab Congress in Jericho a month later. The congress chairman, Mayor Muhammad ʿAli al-Jaʿabari of Hebron, called for the unification of Transjordan and Palestine on the grounds that both were part of Southern Syria.[154] The congress declared ʿAbdallah "King of All Palestine" and termed the union of Palestine and Transjordan "a preliminary step toward true Arab unity."[155] On reading the resolutions, ʿAbdallah found them too weak, so he made his own changes in the text, giving it a more assertive tone. His version of the congress resolutions—and the one that was publicized—emphasized that Palestine was "part of Natural Syria."[156]

Although the Transjordanian cabinet and parliament approved these resolutions, the Arab states' intense opposition to Transjordanian expansion compelled 'Abdallah to go slowly. He waited a month, until January 1949, before having the *khutba* (the Friday prayer invocation) said in his name in Jerusalem. Only in March did he replace military rule with a civilian authority in the conquered areas. In April, Jordanian nationality was offered to all non-Jewish residents of mandatory Palestine. Just as 'Abdallah had brought Lesser Syrians into the Transjordanian government three decades earlier, he brought Palestinians from the West Bank into the Jordanian cabinet. In May, a cabinet was formed which included three Palestinians in important positions, and a fourth was soon added; a year later, six of eleven ministers came from the West Bank. In June 1949 the name of the kingdom was changed from Transjordan to Jordan. A Jordanian stamp with "Palestine" superimposed was issued in August. Customs and travel restrictions across the Jordan River disappeared in November. 'Abdallah invested in himself all the authority of the British mandatory power in Palestine in December. In March 1950, a royal decree banned the word *Palestine* from government documents; Transjordan and Palestine were henceforth replaced by the new terms, East Bank and West Bank.[157] Finally, in April 1950, the conquered territories were formally incorporated. Jordanian dinars became the only legal currency on the West Bank in September.

Final Efforts, 1950–1951

Having annexed a part of Palestine, 'Abdallah returned to his first passion, union with Lesser Syria. He tried a new tack with Great Britain, adopting the language of the Cold War and arguing for a new need for a friendly ruler in Damascus.

Now the main obstacle to Greater Syria was the Syrian government of Shukri al-Quwwatli. 'Abdallah may have had a hand in Quwwatli's overthrow in 1949 (which brought to power the first of many military rulers in Syria); as the coup was in progress, Transjordanian diplomats abroad were warned to expect a declaration from Amman in favor of Greater Syria. Whatever his role in the change of government, 'Abdallah quickly pressed the new ruler, Husni az-Za'im to form a union of their two states. To hasten the process, 'Abdallah opened his purse to encourage friends in Syria to send him "periodical petitions and telegrams declaring their unswerving devotion to the furthering of his noble intentions."[158] But Za'im responded badly to 'Abdallah's efforts, closing the border with Jordan and deploying troops along it; and the effort, as ever, came to naught.

'Abdallah openly celebrated Za'im's overthrow in August 1949, hoping his successor would look more favorably on a unity scheme. But Sami al-Hinnawi was interested in joining with Iraq, not Jordan. 'Abdallah could do little to force Damascus's hand, for the process of incorporating the West Bank absorbed most of his attention. But he did tell the visiting prime minister of Syria in November 1950, "I and the Jordanian government and the people consider ourselves a part of Syria."[159]

'Abdallah made his final plea for Syrian unity to the former prime minister of Lebanon, Riyad as-Sulh. Sulh met the king in Amman on 13 July 1951 and heard the familiar argument: "There is no doubt that the situation in [Greater] Syria is unnatural and that it is injurious to the Arabs. . . . Accordingly, [Lesser] Syria should be joined with Jordan or with the Jordan-Iraqi kingdom and the Lebanon ought to come in some form within the kingdom." Sulh answered with the usual Lebanese wariness.[160] This meeting has special interest because Sulh was assassinated by the SSNP three days later; and ʿAbdallah was killed four days after that by a Palestinian separatist. In other words, both died in connection with Pan-Syrian issues. ʿAbdallah had labored for Greater Syria right to his death.

Assessment

Given his many weaknesses and the long record of failure, it is striking that ʿAbdallah's conquest of the West Bank made him the only leader to achieve a Pan-Syrian goal between 1920 and 1970. The question arises, how did he do this? By ingratiating himself with London, the Palestinian Arabs, and the Zionists. British officials had the most importance; their support for him got him the West Bank. They viewed ʿAbdallah's plans for Palestine much more favorably than those for Syria, and for two reasons. France having no position in Palestine, there was no need to give priority to French views, so ʿAbdallah's wishes carried more weight. Also, the British saw him as the most pro-British and the most readily controlled element in the complex politics of Palestine.

ʿAbdallah also met a better reception among the Arabs of Palestine than among those of Lesser Syria. Important leaders openly sided with him and helped his cause against Palestinian separatism. ʿAbdallah reaped the benefits of this backing in late 1948, when significant Arab Palestinian leaders endorsed his efforts. Even for Zionists, ʿAbdallah's ambitions in Palestine were not entirely unwelcome, for these splintered the Arabs; also, the Zionists knew that if they had to live under any Arab leader, ʿAbdallah's rule would be by far the most bearable.

Then turn the question around. Given these strengths, why did ʿAbdallah fail to add more than the West Bank to his kingdom? Why did he have so little to show for thirty years of tireless effort? Three factors stand out. First, while ʿAbdallah saw himself as a Syrian ruler attempting to unite Syria, his many opponents saw him as a petty desert prince trying to usurp the metropolitan areas of Syria. Residents of Greater Syria—Damascenes and Jerusalemites in particular—found the notion of being ruled from Amman unattractive and slightly absurd. Transjordan suffered from the extreme meagerness of its cultural resources; had it but a single major city, the country would have carried more weight politically. The prominent Jordanian politician Zayd ar-Rifaʿi has recounted the reception he got as a student in Cairo in 1948 on saying that he came from Amman.

> My colleagues at the university used to ask me, "Where are you from?"
> "From Amman," I told them.

"And this Amman, where is it?"
"In Jordan."
"You mean in Greater Syria [*Sham*]?"[161]

No one could take Jordan very seriously as a country. The frank assessment of a Foreign Office official that "Trans-Jordan is far too small to be anything but a pure joke as an independent state"[162] was widely shared. Thus, residents of the West Bank resisted the efforts to get them to see themselves as Jordanians rather than Palestinians. What 'Abdallah termed Greater Syria his enemies considered Greater Jordan; the insistence that Transjordan must form the core of a unified Syria was ultimately unconvincing. 'Abdallah, "as he himself well realized, was trapped by the inconsequence of Transjordan."[163]

'Abdallah's long memory proved a second liability. Family prerogatives had paramount importance for him; the historical legitimacy of the Hashimi family had to be preserved and fulfilled. Through his long career as ruler of Transjordan, 'Abdallah presented himself as personally and officially "the heir to the Arab revolt"[164]—and therefore heir to the Hashimi claim to the whole of historic Syria. For 'Abdallah, the legitimacy of this claim did not diminish with time. But as the decades passed, residents of Greater Syria increasingly ignored 'Abdallah's views and rejected his pretensions. 'Abdallah's tragedy lies in his unwillingness to recognize this change. In the words of his biographer, he spent the last years of his life "like an alchemist searching for the right combination of elements that, coming together in a single fortuitous instant, would propel him on to the throne of Greater Syria."[165] His clinging to events of two or three decades past implied an obtuseness about political realities that doomed the Greater Syria scheme.

A third problem lay in 'Abdallah being too clever by half. Characteristically, he pursued two or more approaches—compatible or not—at the same time. Even before World War I he simultaneously served as vice-chairman of the Ottoman parliament and sought arms from Britain against the Turks. As the prince of Transjordan, he served British and (to a much lesser extent) French interests and at the same time tried to win popular support among residents of Greater Syria. He did this, for example, in 1936 when it appeared likely that the French would leave Syria, and again in 1948 when he sought support for annexation of the West Bank. In the end, neither side fully trusted him or supported him. As a British official, R. W. Rendel, put it, "the Amir Abdullah, though possessing many virtues, is politically short sighted, and a good deal given to petty intrigue."[166] The strategy of playing both sides accounts for much of the mistrust and ill will that 'Abdallah, an otherwise attractive man, aroused among the Arabs.

Iraq

In their more ambitious moments, some Pan-Syrian nationalists think of Iraq as part of Greater Syria. But Iraqis never consider Iraq part of the Syrian geographic and cultural unit. Some see it as completely distinct from Syria;

others—those seeking to join with Syria—see it as the eastern half of the Fertile Crescent.

Unlike *Syria*, an indigenous name of great antiquity, the term *Fertile Crescent* (*al-hilal al-khasib* in Arabic) is of recent origin. James Henry Breasted, an American historian of the ancient Middle East, popularized the term at the beginning of this century, and it spread to the Middle East with the publication of an Arabic translation of his textbook, *Ancient Times.*[167] Breasted noted that a crescent-shaped area stretching from the east shore of the Mediterranean to the north, around the Syrian Desert, south to the Persian Gulf had a central role in the development of civilization. The Fertile Crescent comprises Syria in the west and Mesopotamia (or Iraq) in the east.

Although a scholarly term of Western origin without religious or historical significance, *Fertile Crescent* entered the political vocabulary in the 1920s as part of the search for a nation. The Hashimis seem to have been the first to propose a Fertile Crescent polity. Alec Seath Kirkbride explained the background:

> King Hussein's original vision [in 1916] was that of an Arab Empire with himself at its head, but this was, clearly, not a project capable of realization immediately after the end of the First World War, so he and his sons agreed that Ali, the eldest, should succeed their father as King of the Hejaz; that Abdullah, the second, should be King of Iraq and that Faisal, the third, should become King of Syria.[168]

Two revealing points emerge from this important passage. First, the Hashimis from the beginning saw Syria and Iraq as separate polities. Second, the two areas were expected to be included in a federation that included the Hijaz as well. Loss of Syria to the French in 1920 and the Hijaz to the Saudis in 1925 left just two regions under Hashimi control, Transjordan and Iraq. A Fertile Crescent union justified the federation of these two areas. Having come into existence for dynastic interests, the Fertile Crescent remained alive only so long as it served those interests; it disappeared when the Hashimi monarchy was eliminated from Iraq in 1958.[169]

This said, Fertile Crescent aspirations were not completely limited to the Hashimis. According to Majid Khadduri, Antun Sa'ada "almost adopted the term Fertile Crescent instead of Syria as a symbol of identity, since some had objected that certain parts of 'Iraq, Sinai, and Cyprus could hardly be regarded as parts of geographical Syria."[170] Also, Rashid 'Ali al-Kaylani, the anti-Hashimi politician who came briefly to power in 1940–41, called for an Iraqi federation with Syria, Lebanon, Palestine, and Transjordan.

The Hashimis made many efforts to join Iraq with Greater Syria. 'Abdallah tried to get Winston Churchill to agree to merge it with Transjordan in March 1921. Soon after, in August 1921, his brother Faysal became king of Iraq, a position he retained until his death in September 1933. On accepting the Iraqi throne in 1921, Faysal had promised Churchill to stay out of Syrian politics, but—as former leader of the Arab forces in World War I, the short-lived king of Syria, and brother of 'Abdallah—he naturally maintained keen interest in Greater Syria. Indeed, he made repeated attempts from Baghdad to foster this

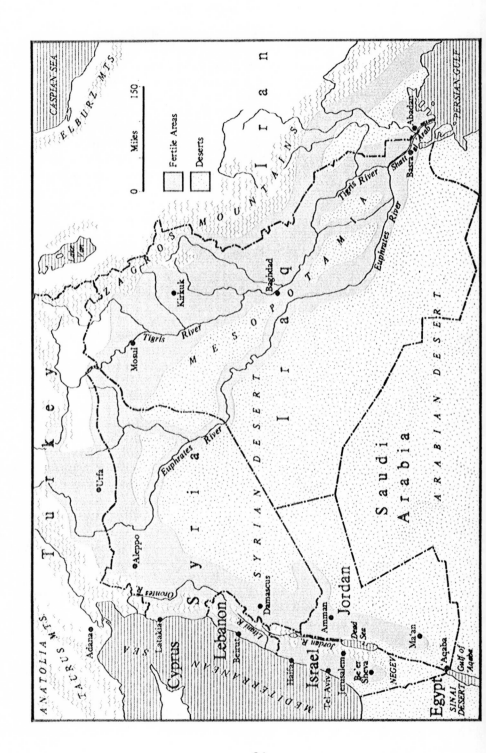

union between 1926 and 1933. He hoped to confederate Iraq with Syria, Transjordan, and Palestine, then to absorb Transjordan into Iraq.

In September 1929, Faysal talked with a high French Foreign Ministry official about uniting Syria and Iraq under his crown, then spending half a year in each capital. Two months later, Faysal proposed solving the Palestine problem by unifying Syria, Palestine, and Iraq. The full independence of Iraq in 1930 followed by membership in the League of Nations in 1932 imbued Faysal with a new status and emboldened him. A flurry of excitement occurred in 1931–32, when he discussed union with Syrian politicians. During a visit to Amman, Faysal met with delegations from Syria, Lebanon, and Palestine, all of which urged him to ascend the throne in Damascus, pending an agreement with the French authorities.[171]

The British high commissioner for Iraq concluded that Faysal "still hopes and works for the close federation under the rule of his House of all the Arab territories in Asia, and it seems that his intention is to endeavour to bring about first the union of Syria and Iraq."[172] A statue of Faysal in Baghdad was turned around to face west, at the subject's request, to indicate his plan to ride back to Damascus. Faysal stayed in contact with his lieutenant in the 'Alawi territory even after his move to Baghdad.[173] Shortly before dying, Faysal went to Europe carrying petitions signed by Syrian leaders authorizing him to speak on their behalf.

Iraqi interest in Greater Syria continued even after Faysal's death. His son Ghazi (r. 1933–39) favored Fertile Crescent schemes. Then, from the time that Ghazi's infant son Faysal II ascended the throne to the fall of the monarchy in 1958, the two leading politicians of Iraq, Prince 'Abd al-Illah and Nuri Pasha as-Sa'id, enthusiastically sought union.

'Abd al-Illah (1912–58) was the effective monarch during these years, first as regent and then as uncle of the king. To understand his position requires some familiarity with his family circumstances. 'Abd al-Illah was the son of 'Ali ibn al-Husayn, the Hashimi designated king of the Hijaz and the elder brother of princes Faysal and 'Abdallah. 'Ali did rule the Hijaz from October 1924 to December 1925, only to flee before the region's conquest by the Saudis. He lived out his days at Faysal's court in Iraq, dying in 1935. 'Abd al-Illah, feeling deprived of his rightful patrimony, used his position of power in the Iraqi court, first as regent and then as counselor, to seek his own throne in Damascus or Mecca. Toward this end, 'Abd al-Illah paid retainers to Syrian politicians and newspapers while engaging in intrigues with Syrian exiles.

The other predominant figure was Nuri Pasha as-Sa'id (1888–1958). He

---

Figure 8. The Fertile Crescent   James Henry Breasted (1865–1935), an American historian of the ancient Middle East, coined the term *Fertile Crescent* in 1916, and it spread to the Middle East with the publication of an Arabic translation of his textbook, *Ancient Times*. The term refers to a crescent-shaped area stretching from the east shore of the Mediterranean to the north, around the Syrian Desert, south to the Persian Gulf. The Fertile Crescent had a central role in the development of civilization. A number of Iraqi and Syrian plans aimed to unite this region politically.

served as Faysal's chief of staff during World War I, commanded Faysal's army when it entered Damascus in September 1918, then accompanied Faysal to Baghdad. There, Nuri served as prime minister fourteen times between 1930 and 1958, as well as six times each as minister of defense and foreign minister. Nuri's interest in Greater Syria differed fundamentally from the prince's; whereas ʿAbd al-Illah sought a new political configuration which would allow him to become king of Syria, Nuri hoped to expand Iraqi influence by bringing Lesser Syria and other regions under the control of Baghdad. ʿAbd al-Illah had a personal interest in Syria and was not tied to Iraq; Nuri wanted Iraq to lead the Arabs and did not insist on Hashimi, or even monarchical, control if not to do so helped his cause. Nuri was thus politically far more flexible than the regent.

Already in 1935, Nuri proposed that Iraq and Transjordan join together and then invite the other units of Greater Syria—Syria, Lebanon, and Palestine—to join them. British opposition to this plan caused Nuri to desist from pressing it for almost a decade. His most important Fertile Crescent plan was made public in January 1943. At that time, Nuri foresaw three stages leading to unity: First, "Syria, Lebanon, Palestine, and Trans-Jordan shall be reunited into one State." He left the form of this government, "whether monarchical or republican whether unitary or federal," to the peoples of Greater Syria themselves. Second, "there shall be created an Arab League to which Syria and Iraq will adhere at once." This league would have responsibility for foreign affairs, defense matters, and some other key issues. Finally, after this had been achieved, Nuri invited other Arab states to join the league, "at will."[174] In short, Nuri accepted ʿAbdallah's plan for Greater Syria and made two changes, adding Iraq and leaving open the form of government.

The Fertile Crescent proposal initiated intensive discussions among independent Arab states beginning in July 1943 and culminating in March 1945 with the creation of the Arab League. At first, the formation of Greater Syria was at the top of the agenda, with Hashimi leaders in Transjordan and Iraq favoring it, the kings of Egypt and Saudi Arabia suspicious of it. On the Hashimi side, ʿAbdallah expressed willingness to get started with a Syrian-Transjordanian union, while Nuri and ʿAbd al-Illah favored the inclusion of Palestine and Lebanon as well. In this instance, the Iraqis showed even more devotion to Greater Syria than ʿAbdallah.

During early 1944, Nuri traveled in Syria, Lebanon, Palestine, and Transjordan to discuss steps toward a Greater Syrian union. He claimed to have reached an oral agreement with the Syrian government for the "federatation" of Syria and Iraq, regardless of what the other Arab states chose to do, an account which may reflect his wishful thinking. In any case, sharp reactions from ʿAbdallah and the Maronites quickly followed. (To prevent Maronite displeasure, on one occasion Syrian government censors deleted Nuri's reference to Lebanon as an element of Greater Syria, but to little avail.)[175]

At an Arab meeting in Alexandria in the fall of 1944, Nuri tried to keep the possibility of Greater Syria separate from that of Arab unity, but he faced the opposition of the Egyptian and Saudi governments, both of which feared the power of a united Syria. At the insistence of Nuri, the pact founding the League of Arab States included, in Article 9, a provision permitting member states "to establish closer cooperation and stronger bonds" than those called for by the pact itself.[176]

New rounds of discussions took place once the Arab League had been established, as Nuri explored closer ties with the Syrian prime minister in 1946. Then 'Abd al-Illah took the lead, visiting Amman in February 1946 to explore ideas of unity with 'Abdallah. The two sides foresaw a common foreign policy and strong economic ties, including a single currency. Internal administrations would remain apart, at least for the time being. As usual, 'Abdallah had great hopes: "I believe that when union between Trans-Jordan and Iraq is realized other countries will follow our example. I am working for Syrian unity comprising not only Lebanon but the Syria of King Feisal."[177] More discussions followed in September 1946. Opposition within Iraq prevented these from going far, however, and the pact eventually signed in April 1947 was not a union at all but a Treaty of Brotherhood and Alliance with provisions for very modest financial and military cooperation.

The years 1950 and 1951 saw another effort toward a Hashimi union. The Iraqi government presented 'Abdallah with an innovative plan to unite the two monarchies: 'Abdallah would rule both kingdoms through his lifetime, then would be succeeded by Faysal II of Iraq (born in 1935). On this occasion, 'Abdallah proceeded cautiously; he thought that union with Iraq needed time. Then, as his interest in this scheme grew, he found that the Syrian government also sought union with Iraq, relegating what Transjordan had to offer to second-best. But the Syrian efforts also got nowhere, and so ended the first stage of Fertile Crescent efforts.

Even if Lesser Syrians, Lebanese, and Palestinians could not be induced to accept Hashimi rule, surely the two kingdoms, Iraq and Jordan, could have unified. Why did they not? The reasons illustrate the difficulty inherent in all efforts at eliminating actual boundaries. First, leaders of the two countries were working at cross purposes. Nuri wanted to extend Iraqi power; 'Abd al-Illah sought a crown for himself; and 'Abdallah dreamed of ruling at least one of the great cities of the Middle East. These differences bred mistrust, especially between 'Abdallah and Nuri, and prevented sustained cooperation.

Second, domestic groups obstructed union, especially in Iraq, where interests vested in the status quo resisted radical change. In Iraq, Kurds, Shi'is, army officers, and businessmen feared the consequences of joining with Jordan. In Syria, even politicians friendly to union preferred, in the final analysis, receipt of Iraqi money to unification with Iraq.

Third, the leaders stumbled on the same issue that constantly confronts Pan-Arabists: Who will rule? The question of ultimate authority stymied every union effort. Though they came up with some creative schemes, Transjordanian and Iraqi leaders could not agree. Faysal and 'Abd al-Illah no more forgot the ambitious dreams of the 1910s than did 'Abdallah; thirty and forty years later they were still trying—half-rivals, half-allies—to regain lost kingdoms.

Finally, the Hashimis faced a special problem: the opposition of other Arab leaders, who feared the strength of their combined forces. Syrian politicians dreaded the prospect of being surrounded. The Saudi king worried that the Hashimis united would try to regain their ancestral home in the Hijaz. Egyptian leaders saw a union as a rival in the contest to dominate Arab politics. To block Hashimi union, these rulers resorted to diplomacy, intrigue, and even public opinion. Their most important and long-lasting response was the League of Arab States. "The creation of the Arab League in 1944–5 and its policies throughout the early 1950s [wrote Reeva S. Simon] can be seen as a maneuver by the Saudis and the Egyptians to create an official forum through which to subvert Jordanian and later Iraqi attempts at union in the area north of the Arabian peninsula."[178]

Great Britain and Others

British Schemes

Outside Greater Syria itself, it was mostly Britons who supported Pan-Syrian schemes. British writers and officials adopted Greater Syria with enthusiasm, and this goal had real importance in the formulation of British policy in the Middle East. Some Frenchmen, Zionists, and a few non-Syrian Arabs were also attracted to the idea. The endorsement of Pan-Syrianism by Europeans greatly enhanced the ideology's validity and furthered its (admittedly meager) chances of success.

In an influential pamphlet issued in 1918, the Very Rev. Sir George Adam Smith argued for the unity of what he called the New Syria—by which he meant Greater Syria; Smith also held that the Syrians were not Arabs.[179] The British Naval Intelligence *Handbook of Syria*, published in 1920, defined Syria as Greater Syria.[180] Herbert Samuel, the British high commissioner for Palestine, advocated in April 1920 a loose confederation of Arab states with a seat of government in Damascus and Faysal at its head. Arnold J. Toynbee held that "the territory mandated to France is a torso without the limbs. . . . Syria is being strangled."[181]

Seeing the mandatory divisions as harmful to the Arabs' interests, a number of British civil servants agitated for their elimination and the unification of the British and French territories into Greater Syria. Some of them even resigned their positions to take up the cause of Greater Syria. Their viewpoint gained wider support in the mid-1920s when it was phrased in terms advantageous to British interests:

> From the Syrian point of view there might be much to be said for a single mandate for Syria and Palestine, which could ensure as great a measure of independence and self-government as Iraq has, while [and here British interests enter] safeguarding the country from any possible menace from the north. In such a state the bogey of the Jewish National Home, with which the unthinking Arab or Syrian allows himself to be scared today, would assume more modest proportions; for a united Syria would have nothing to fear from

a small Jewish minority and might one day grow wise enough to appreciate the value of Jewish cooperation.[182]

These twin attractions—a solution to the Palestine issue and a more secure Middle East—remained the permanent bases for British interest in Pan-Syrianism. (These two reasons also explain the later British support for Pan-Arabism. "If we treat the Arab world as a whole, Palestine can be made to appear so small that we can do anything we like with it—even give it to the Jews.")[183]

Pan-Syrian ideas gained wider currency as a result of the Arab Revolt that disrupted Palestine from 1936 until 1939. This turmoil prompted many Britons in and out of government to begin the long search for an equitable resolution to the Arab-Zionist conflict; Greater Syria attracted some of them. A number of influential voices—such as Sir Arnold Wilson and *The Times* editorial writers—proposed a Federal Syrian State to include all of Greater Syria. They reasoned that if London would deprive the Arabs of Palestine, it should give them something in return, and Greater Syria seemed like suitable compensation.

The British government then explored the idea of Greater Syria (with Iraq sometimes added). At the London Conference in early 1939 (an attempt to bring together the Arabs and Jews of Palestine, as well as the independent Arab rulers), it offered a Greater Syria scheme which met with little Arab interest. A British observer concluded that "the irritation which the proposal instantly aroused in Arabs suggests that the longing for a united Syria, often expressed by Palestine nationalists, was in fact no very deep-seated passion."[184] This diffidence was due, at least in part, to the Arabs' perception of Greater Syria as a scheme to perpetuate British power in the Middle East.

The outbreak of World War II in late 1939 made Middle East stability a high priority for the British government; toward this end, it again proposed a Greater Syria plan, hoping this would defuse the Palestine issue and so help secure the region against the Axis. A Foreign Office memorandum of September 1939 noted the artificiality of existing borders between Syria, Lebanon, Palestine, and Transjordan. The colonial secretary, Lord Lloyd, wrote in September 1940 that a federation of Palestine, Transjordan, and Syria "is not without its attraction."[185] The recipient of this message, Sir Harold Mac-Michael, the high commissioner for Palestine, agreed that Palestine and Syria formed a single unit, which he thought should be united. Winston Churchill's private secretary, Sir John Martin, held that "some form of federation (embracing Palestine, Syria, and Trans Jordan)" would reduce Arab opposition to the Zionists.[186]

The foreign minister, Anthony Eden, promised in a May 1941 speech that "His Majesty's Government for their part will give their full support to any [unity] scheme that commands general [Arab] approval."[187] As invariably happens after a senior official makes an unexpected statement, his subordinates scurried to interpret his intentions. As understood by the Foreign Office, Eden meant to endorse a Greater Syrian union followed by a general Arab union.[188] Thus, the orientalist Hamilton A. R. Gibb also saw Greater Syria as the first step toward a larger Arab union. He argued in a memorandum that if it became possible "to initiate negotiations on the future of the [Jewish] National Home as an integral part of discussions directed towards comprehensive settlement in greater Syria, the chances of reconciling Arab and Jewish claims would be immensely improved."[189] A year and a half later, Gibb proposed an even more ambitious scheme: that the British government divide the Fertile Crescent into twelve provinces unrelated to existing units, then join these together.

Humphrey Bowman, head of the Political Intelligence Department of the Foreign Office, argued in July 1941 that "it would be worthwhile to pursue a policy aiming at the formation of a federation of Syria, Lebanon, Trans-Jordan and Palestine."[190] Sir Harold MacMichael condemned the divisions of Greater Syria as "a defiance of history."[191]

Anthony Eden restated his government's support for Arab unity in a parliamentary statement during February 1943. This set off even more intense efforts within the government to ascertain what sort of unity should be encouraged. Many favored Greater Syria. Secretary of State for India Leo Amery called for the establishment of "a loose Syria-Palestine-Transjordan Federation."[192] Such senior officials as Viscount Cranborne (lord privy seal) and Sir Stafford Cripps (minister of aircraft production) echoed his view.

Sir Harold MacMichael submitted a memorandum to the Middle East War Council, meeting in Cairo in May 1943, in which he dismissed the divisions of Greater Syria and argued that "the problem of the Levant States cannot be treated piecemeal, for they are in all essentials of a single unit."[193] The War Council favored "closer political association between the Arab States or even between the States of 'Greater Syria'" but saw this as unattainable so long as the French maintained direct influence in Lebanon and Lesser Syria. It therefore suggested that "the most practical course is to encourage efforts toward economic and cultural unity, out of which some form of political confederation, at least in 'Greater Syria', may ultimately emerge."[194] But these recommendations were stillborn, for the foreign minister rejected them.

London sent emissaries to discuss unity plans with Arab leaders. Freya Stark, then on service for the British government, recorded a conversation with the Syrian foreign minister in July 1943. After the minister stated his views on Palestine, she replied: "I couldn't agree more. But don't you think that the whole question may become easier from a practical point of view if the Arab nations come together into a Commonwealth."[195] Colonel S. F. Newcombe raised the issue of union between "Syria, Palestine, Trans-Jordan, perhaps Iraq and Saudi-Arabia."[196]

The Cabinet Committee on Palestine, set up in July 1943 to plan long-term policy in Palestine, took up this issue. In September 1943, Lord Moyne, the deputy minister of state resident in the Middle East, presented the committee with an original plan for Greater Syria. He called for the creation of four polities: small Jewish and Maronite states, a separate British-protected regime for Jerusalem, and a Greater Syria comprising the remaining parts of Syria,

Lebanon, Palestine, and Transjordan. In effect, Moyne endorsed the first part of Nuri's Fertile Crescent plan; indeed, he told ʿAbd al-Illah of his agreement with Nuri that "Greater Syria would have to come first."[197] Moyne's superior, Minister of State Resident in the Middle East Richard Casey, informed the foreign minister that "partition [of Palestine] plus Greater Syria is, in my opinion, the best solution of the general Levant problem that I have yet heard."[198] Casey later went even farther, arguing "that the 'Greater Syria' plan was essential to the success of the scheme [to partition Palestine]."[199]

For their part, the authorities in Palestine concurred with Moyne and Casey. According to them, "the feeling of the Palestine Arabs would be much more favourable to the partition projects if they were to be included in a large State such as a Greater Syria and not merely lumped in with Trans-Jordan."[200]

The Cabinet Committee adopted Moyne's plan, with only slight modifications. It foresaw an emasculated Greater Syria which excluded Lebanon, the Jewish parts of Palestine, and Jerusalem. In addition to offering the standard reasons for this recommendation—to increase security and solve the Palestine problem—the committee added an economic rationale as well. It argued that the Arabs of Palestine could not survive on their own. In accord with the majority view, the report held that the creation of Greater Syria would "greatly enhance" British prestige in the area and would be "eagerly welcomed" by the Arabs.[201]

Pan-Syrianism then received an unexpected boost when Prime Minister Churchill indicated his "general agreement" with Casey's point that Greater Syria had to accompany a partition of Palestine.[202] This endorsement prompted Casey further to explain to Churchill the advantages of Pan-Syrianism:

> The best solution in sight is partition in Palestine together with the creation of Greater Syria. I do not think that partition is a workable solution by itself, there would be too much Arab resistance and too much bloodshed. But the simultaneous creation of Greater Syria would provide the necessary bait and the necessary political offset to partition from the Arab point of view. I do not believe there is any objection to Greater Syria that cannot be overcome in practice.[203]

Noteworthy is Casey's perception that Greater Syria was a "bait" so desired by Arabs that it would console them for the partition of Palestine.

The War Cabinet discussed this plan in January 1944 and approved it in principle, with the understanding that its details would be further studied— just the opening sought for many officials to express their disagreement.

In partial dissent, Sir Harold MacMichael suggested that Greater Syria be seen as a long-term, not an intermediate goal. He thought it necessary "to contemplate a transition stage, involving the creation, under the Amir [ʿAbdallah], of a new state (which might be designated 'Southern Syria') consisting of Trans-Jordan and the Arab areas of Central Palestine, as a first step towards the constitution of the Greater Syria."[204] A conference of British diplomats in the Middle East during April 1944 echoed this view; the partici-

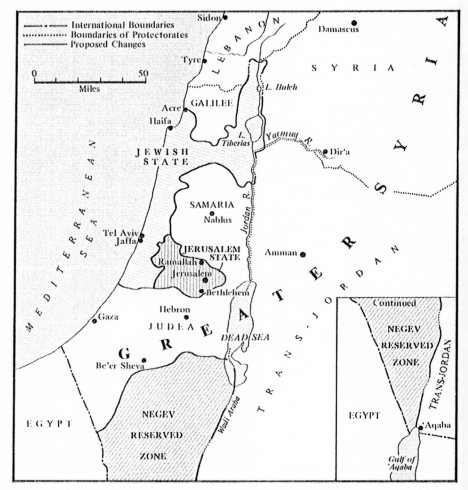

Figure 9. Plan Prepared for the British Cabinet, 1943–44   The War Cabinet gave preliminary approval in January 1944 to a Greater Syria scheme, though in the end this idea came to naught.

pants agreed that "while the project for Greater Syria should continue to have our cordial support, its establishment could not form part of our immediate policy."[205] The Colonial Office adopted this two-stage approach, but the Foreign Office rejected any delay. If Greater Syria could not be achieved, Casey wrote, "he was doubtful whether it would be worthwhile attempting partition [of Palestine] at all."[206]

In the end, MacMichael and the Colonial Office won out. The Palestine Cabinet Committee's Final Report of October 1944 recommended the partition of Palestine and the establishment of a Southern Syrian state under

'Abdallah, to include Transjordan and the Arab parts of Palestine. Despite Churchill's active support for this scheme, it was not submitted to the cabinet, and in September 1945, when it became clear that Greater Syria would fulfill neither of these goals, the Greater Syria idea was finally discarded. With this, British interest in Greater Syria came to an end.

Great Britain and 'Abdallah

It is important to note that British approval of Greater Syria did not imply support for 'Abdallah's aspirations. Many British officials had an affection for 'Abdallah and would have been happy to see his kingdom grow in size. Colonial Secretary Lord Moyne suggested in July 1941 that 'Abdallah be offered the crown of Syria. Alec S. Kirkbride, the British resident in Amman, hinted several times that he favored 'Abdallah's control over the Arab parts of Palestine. In 1947, for example, he wrote that "a greater Transjordan would not be against our interests, it might be in their favour, so even if we are not prepared to help, I see no reason why we should place obstacles in the way of Transjordan."[207]

Despite this sympathy for 'Abdallah, the British government did not endorse his plans for a Greater Syria. This had something to do with its skepticism about his political abilities. Already in 1936, the high commissioner was offering him stern advice: "I suggest it would be wiser in future if Your Highness refrains, as it is my invariable practice, from all discussion of the situation in neighboring countries."[208] Almost a decade later, a British diplomat in the field informed London: "The Amir is not equipped adequately to run his own foreign relations yet and often acts and talks unwisely."[209]

British doubts also had to do with the views of other states. By late 1941, it became apparent that French, Lebanese, Syrian, Iraqi, Saudi, and Egyptian opposition to his aggrandizement meant that support for 'Abdallah's plan would be counterproductive. Nonetheless, 'Abdallah was a good friend, and the British avoided taking a public stand against his plans for as long as they could. Time and again, the Amman government forwarded demands to London; time and again, these were tactfully left unanswered. In the end, however, London had formally to disassociate itself; as Arab rage against 'Abdallah rose to a crescendo in mid-1947, a government spokesman declared "most strongly" that reports about British support for 'Abdallah's Greater Syria plan were "quite unfounded."[210]

To pressure London, 'Abdallah argued that "the Syrian country cannot survive economically except as a single entity." But the force of his argument had the unintended—and from 'Abdallah's point of view, wholly unfavorable—result of causing some Britons to question Transjordan's viability. Officials in London considered fitting Transjordan into a larger unit, but not under 'Abdallah. P. M. Crosthwaite of the Foreign Office's Eastern Department wrote in June 1941 that "from the point of view of the inhabitants there is *nothing* to be said for the maintenance of the purely artificial frontier between Syria and Trans-Jordan, and Trans-Jordan is far too small to be anything but a pure joke as an independent state. The union of the two would in fact be a great feather in our cap."[211] Oliver Lyttleton, minister of state in the Middle East, concurred: "If Transjordan is to attain independence it can hardly stand alone, but must do so as part of a larger unit or federation, embracing Syria and the Lebanon and the inclusion of Palestine."[212]

Other officials went farther, questioning the utility of keeping 'Abdallah in power. Harold A. Caccia of the Eastern Department argued that "from historic, ethnographical and economic points of view it would be most natural to join it [Transjordan] in some way to Syria."[213] Under this arrangement, Greater Syria would come into existence, but at 'Abdallah's expense. Sir Maurice Peterson was even more direct, arguing that "Transjordan is too far from a country ever to stand alone. . . . The best answer to Abdallah is that Transjordan can only be 'independent' as part of a larger whole"[214]—that is, under the control of Damascus.

Several years later, in 1948, British officials bruited about the idea of getting 'Abdallah to renounce his claim to Damascus, or even the whole of his Greater Syria scheme. They did not follow through on this idea because 'Abdallah had gained such a reputation that nothing he said would reduce suspicions about his expansionist plans.

These views reveal just how preposterous British officials considered 'Abdallah's plans. Their silence on his ambition to rule Lesser Syria allowed 'Abdallah to maintain the illusion that he enjoyed London's support when in fact his own rule was in jeopardy. It also caused others, notably the French, to draw faulty conclusions about 'Abdallah's place in British policy.

But if the British could see through 'Abdallah's pretensions, they too showed a curious faith in the ease and utility of unity plans. Looked at from the vantage point of several decades, it is noteworthy that the voluminous British debate generated hardly a single note of skepticism—except for one voiced by T. E. Lawrence in a late 1920s letter: "When people talk of Arab confederations or empires, they talk fantastically. It will be generations, I expect—unless the vital tempo of the East is much accelerated—before any two Arabic states join voluntarily."[215] Ignoring this counsel, sober British bureaucrats in their own way showed as much dreaminess as their Arabian protégé.

France

The goal of Greater Syrian unity also had a following in France. Writings of Christian Lebanese publicists such as Shukri Ghanim and George-Samné, along with the activities of their Syrian Central Committee, introduced the concept. Other Christian thinkers also forwarded this notion, including the influential Belgian Jesuit, Henri Lammens. From them, the idea passed to colonialist groups such as the well-connected Comité de l'Asie Française. Many groups specifically sought Greater Syria. Thus, the Congrès de la Syrie (January 1919) stressed Syria's geographical unity, the Chambers of Commerce of Lyons and Marseille demanded French control of Syria "from the

Taurus [Mountains] to Egypt,"[216] and the rector of the university in Lyons publicly claimed Greater Syria for France ("*Nous réclamons la Syrie intégrale*").[217] The French Foreign Ministry, which saw in Greater Syria a boost to a French claim to the entire Levant region, backed these efforts. Premier Georges Clemenceau remarked in March 1919 that "many Syrians [are] not Arab," and "if the Syrians were put under the Arabs they would revolt."[218]

Despite the draw of Greater Syria, French authorities opposed ʿAbdallah's plans even more than did their British counterparts. Ironically, their response was shaped by the perception that the British government supported Greater Syria as a vehicle for its interests. "Time and again the French in Syria assured each other that the British, with Abdallah's connivance, were plotting an Anschluss. Time and again angry becloaked Frenchmen, muttering imprecations, shook their fists at the British soldiery as they studied the racing results on the other side of the frontier."[219] Not being privy to London's real thinking, they assumed, like ʿAbdallah, its benevolent attitude toward his aspirations.

Still, French officials warmed on several occasions to the possibility of a Hashimi prince in Lesser Syria. During the Syrian revolt of 1925, they showed some interest in Faysal returning to Damascus. This interest revived during the constitutional crisis of 1930, when they went so far as to admit that expelling him a decade earlier had been a mistake. A year later, the French minister for colonies toasted Faysal as "King of Iraq and Syria." In late 1943, as French control over Syria weakened and independence began to appear unavoidable, ʿAbdallah again appeared useful to Paris; French authorities figured that if he became sovereign in Damascus, perhaps they could retain a presence there, much as the British were arranging for Transjordan. They approached ʿAbdallah on this matter, but lack of British support for an extension of ʿAbdallah's power killed the effort. In 1945, the British consul in Beirut suspected French help for ʿAbdallah in an effort to stir up trouble for the Syrian government.

Unfortunately for ʿAbdallah, he won French officials' good will at precisely those moments when they were weakest and therefore least able to implement a policy that would benefit him.

Others

The Permanent Mandates Commission of the League of Nations, charged with overseeing the British and French mandates, implicitly recognized the existence of Greater Syria when it condemned the division of this territory. Given diplomatic restrictions, the commission put the matter as strongly as it could in 1926, when it described Syria as giving "the impression of a country which had been parceled out." Citing "oscillations" in French policy "calculated to encourage the controversies inspired by races, clans and religions," it noted with disapproval the resultant "condition of instability and unrest."[220]

Zionist leaders often supported ʿAbdallah's aspirations for Greater Syria. Insofar as it prompted him to dream of making his capital in Damascus, not Jerusalem, they saw Greater Syria as a distraction which increased their room for maneuver in Palestine. Alternatively, they saw 'Abdallah's increased strength as a way to improve the Zionists' standing in the Middle East. Rumors in Cairo held that the Zionists supported 'Abdallah's plans in return for his acceptance of a Jewish state in Palestine. Lesser Syrian leaders in May 1948 feared Israeli troops would defeat the Syrian forces, invade Syria, then evacuate and allow 'Abdallah to move into Damascus.

For the Axis powers, Greater Syria offered a virtually costless way to make trouble for the British and French in the Middle East and at the same time pick up a few friends. The Italians distributed leaflets favoring "Greater Palestine." On 30 June 1940, just after the fall of France, they announced on Radio Bari their vision of the establishment of a Greater Syrian state.[221]

Although Arab leaders normally objected to Greater Syria, seeing it as a diversion from Pan-Arabism or as a means for Hashimi aggrandizement, some of them blessed this project. For example, Prince Muhammad 'Ali, president of the Council of Regents in Egypt, proposed in 1937 that Syria, Transjordan, and Palestine be united under 'Abdallah.[222] The first secretary general of the League of Arab States, 'Abd ar-Rahman 'Azzam, supported the unification of Greater Syria in 1944 and favored its capital being in Lesser Syria.

Second Phase, 1950–1973

The drive to unify Greater Syria lost momentum between 1950 and 1973. Many developments contributed to this change. The founding of the Arab League in 1945 bestowed a legitimacy on existing political units. The four principal states of Greater Syria gained independence between 1946 and 1948. Sa'ada's execution in 1949 harmed the Syrian Social Nationalist Party. Israel's proven military strength damped the Arabs' ideas of reasserting claims to Palestine. Most importantly, Pan-Arab nationalism took center stage in the mid-1950s under the influence of Jamal 'Abd an-Nasir; his radical program of Arab unification made Egypt, a non-Syrian state, the key actor in any plans to unite the Arabs.

Circumstances specific to the individual countries also decreased interest in Pan-Syrianism. Syria suffered a long period of political instability, precluding any efforts to expand; from Za'im's *coup d'état* in March 1949 until the early 1970s, Damascus was prey, not hunter. Syrian instability diminished the desire of Lebanese Muslims to become its citizens; that those were years of economic boom in Lebanon further disenchanted Lebanese Sunnis with the idea of union. Maronites dominated in Lebanon, and they strongly rejected closer ties with Syria. Jordanians found pride in their newly independent country. Too, Jordan was isolated in Arab politics during this period, and its rulers were in no position to press claims. Palestinian nationalists had enough trouble trying to assert their rights to Palestine without taking on larger issues and, anyway, the Palestinian leadership had negligible influence.

The few Pan-Syrian efforts of the 1950–73 period can be quickly summarized.

Syria

Pro-Hashimi sentiment in Lesser Syria carried political weight until about 1955. Druze leaders had links to Jordan and promoted Hashimi interests in Syria. Some members of the Syrian Assembly relentlessly promoted the attachment of Syria to Jordan or Iraq and were every time slapped down. A January 1950 appeal for "an absolute and total"[223] union of Greater Syria and Iraq was overwhelmingly defeated when put to the vote. Later that year, one of the pro-Hashimi members of the assembly verbally assaulted the army; in retaliation, the army had him arrested on the grounds of conspiring with Jordan against the interests of the Syrian state. In the court case that followed, the prosecutor called 'Abdallah's Greater Syria project a "national crime."[224]

Syrian confrontation with Israel in 1951 gave pro-Hashimi politicians in Syria an occasion to call for a merger with Iraq, and Baghdad used the opportunity to prove itself useful to Damascus. Partially as a result of this, one of the pro-Hashimis, Hasan al-Hakim, was asked to become prime minister and form a government. But Hakim (who had been Prince Faysal's director general of posts and telegraphs in 1919) had only three months in power and faced too many domestic problems during that short period to pursue a Pan-Syrian agenda.

Adib ash-Shishakli, the ruler of Syria and a former member of the SSNP, often referred to himself as a Palestinian, declared strong interest in Jordan, and claimed Alexandretta. Right after 'Abdallah's death in July 1951, for example, he noted that "the majority of the people of Jordan are of Syrian origin. If they desire to return to their motherland, they are welcome, provided they are liberated from their treaty with Britain."[225] Shishakli delivered several speeches with Pan-Syrian overtones in early 1952.

A 1956 law gave Palestinians resident in Syria rights approximating those of Syrian nationals: "Palestinians living in the Republic of Syria upon issuance of this law are considered originally Syrian . . . with regard to rights of employment, commerce, and education—at the same time that they retain their original [Palestinian] nationality."[226] Of course, duties went along with those rights, foremost of which was the obligation to serve in the Syrian armed forces. The fact that, citizens or not, Palestinians were liable to be drafted for military service (and often were) underlines the possessive element in Syrian attitudes toward Palestine.

Syrian representatives to the United Nations occasionally vented Pan-Syrian ambitions. In May 1956, the General Assembly heard that "Palestine is nothing but southern Syria."[227] During the Six Day War of June 1967, Syria's delegate to the Security Council remarked that it was Syria "from which Palestine was severed and from the territory of which Israel was created. . . . when the world persecuted the Jews, they found a homeland in my country, Syria."[228]

In 1953, some candidates in Syrian elections explicitly called for Alexandretta to be returned to Syria. Also that year, government and press bruited about claims not just to Alexandretta but to all of Turkey south of the Taurus and Anti-Taurus Mountains. Turkish-Syrian talks in 1955 provoked emotional claims to Alexandretta. Demonstrators in Aleppo shouted, "Alexandretta is part of Syria," students protested, and deputies in the Syrian Chamber denounced.[229] When the Syrian minister in Ankara reminded his hosts of his country's feelings about Alexandretta, Turkish prime minister Adnan Menderes responded by recalling his own countrymen's feelings on losing Aleppo.

Claims to Alexandretta resurfaced after 1958, when Syria joined Egypt in the United Arab Republic (UAR). The General Congress of the UAR National Union in 1960 resolved "to take all steps official and popular to ensure the recovery of Alexandretta province," provoking an outraged Turkish reply.[230] In 1961, the second conference of the UAR General Federation of Students announced that Alexandretta was "an integral part of the UAR."[231] Four years later, the Syrian media decried the "crime" of Alexandretta having been "wrested away from Syria," calling this a "usurped portion of our homeland."[232] In addition, the Ba'th Party annually denounced the loss of Alexandretta.

Palestinians

The PLO charter, adopted in June 1964, laid a veiled claim to Jordan's territory. It stated that "Palestine with the boundaries it had during the British Mandate is an indivisible territorial unit." The charter appears to be intentionally obscure whether it referred to the mandate when it included Jordan or not, and so, in Y. Harkabi's view, the article contains a "time bomb for the Palestinians and their political future."[233] The PLO sometimes formally made a claim to Jordan. Thus, the eighth conference of the Palestine National Council, meeting in February-March 1971, resolved that "what links Jordan to Palestine is a national bond and a national unity formed, since time immemorial, by history and culture. The establishment of one political entity in Transjordan and another in Palestine is illegal."[234] The draft program of the tenth PNC conference (in April 1972) was even more forthright: "The need for struggle to overthrow the agent regime in Jordan, which is a front line of defense for the Zionist state and organically linked to Israel, has become no less urgent than the need for struggle against Zionist occupation." The fact that Palestinians make up 60 percent of the East Bank population and play a major role in all aspects of life there "implies that the two peoples be brought together into a Jordanian-Palestinian national liberation front."[235]

Individual spokesmen made more direct claims. The PLO's first chief, Ahmad ash-Shuqayri, was especially outspoken. He claimed that Jordan's 1950 annexation of the West Bank was, in fact, an annexation of the East Bank to Palestine.[236] He also made explicit that Palestine for him "stretched from the Mediterranean Sea in the west to the Syrian-Iraqi desert."[237] A PLO representative to Lebanon declared in 1966 that "Jordan is an integral part of Palestine, exactly like Israel."[238]

The Popular Democratic Front for the Liberation of Palestine drew especially close links between Jordan and Palestine; this may well result from the fact that its founder and leader, Nayif al-Hawatima, was a Christian Bedouin from the East Bank.

Jordan

Jordanian claims to the whole of Palestine remained alive even after the incorporation of the West Bank. In answer to Egyptian and Iraqi challenges, the prime minister of Jordan, Hazza' al-Majali, declared in August 1959: "We here in Jordan, led by our great king [al-Husayn] are the government of Palestine, the army of Palestine, and we are the refugees." Majali drew the obvious conclusion from this: "The Jordanian government is the sole legal representative of the Palestinians inhabiting Jordan, who possess the right to decide by legal means everything connected to their rights in Palestine."[239] Half a year later, King al-Husayn asserted that the Jordanian forces "are actually the Palestinian Army . . . which . . . awaits the final day when it shall battle to regain our usurped rights in Palestine."[240] A 1962 white paper put out by Amman called the problem of Palestine "the problem of the Jordanian homeland and the Jordanian family and the Jordanian citizen."[241] A 1964 postage stamp pictured King al-Husayn next to a map showing Jordan stretching from its actual borders to the Mediterranean[242]—cartographically eliminating Israel. The king made this same sentiment verbally explicit in 1965, stating that "the two peoples have integrated; Palestine has become Jordan, and Jordan Palestine."[243] He also declared that "those organizations which seek to differentiate between Palestinians and Jordanians are traitors who help Zionism in its aim of splitting the Arab camp. . . . We have only one army, one political organization, and one popular recruiting system in this country."[244]

Iraq

Iraq was the most active source of Pan-Syrian activity during the 1950s. The country's rulers, especially 'Abd al-Illah, continued to work for Fertile Crescent unity, looking mostly to Syria and occasionally to Jordan. Both of Syria's first two military rulers pursued unity negotiations with Iraq, only to change their minds or be overthrown before any results could be achieved. The third ruler, Shishakli, had an SSNP background and Pan-Syrian sympathies but rejected cooperation with Hashimis.

Frustrated by these developments, 'Abd al-Illah plotted Shishakli's overthrow by force. His first effort, in 1953, failed in part because Nuri opposed it and withheld the needed funds. Later that year, a second attempt proved more successful, as 'Abd al-Illah encouraged unrest in Syria and prepared military and political schemes to achieve union. While Iraqi politicians publicly proposed a federal union with Syria and Jordan in January 1954, the Iraqi army was covertly formulating plans for an invasion of Syria. But neither of these tacks succeeded; the federal union got shot down by the usual enemies of Hashimi unity—Syria, Saudi Arabia, and Egypt—and the Iraqi army resisted serious confrontation with Syria.

Shishakli's fall at the end of February 1954 offered new opportunities for Iraqi plotting. The Syrian prime minister, Sabri al-'Asali, reportedly met Iraqi leaders in Lebanon in June 1954 to plan an Iraqi invasion of Syria, but he fell from power just three days later.

As Syrian-Egyptian ties strengthened in 1956 and Syrian sentiment grew in favor of unity with Egypt, matters became urgent for the Iraqis. 'Abd al-Illah responded with the radical step of joining with the SSNP. Hashimis and the SSNP were traditional rivals; their cooperation indicated the weakness and desperation of both sides—as did 'Abd al-Illah's dependence on the use of force to achieve unity with Syria. 'Abd al-Illah contacted the SSNP in Beirut and provided it with arms and money. A variety of other Pan-Syrian, pro-Iraqi, and pro-Hashimi figures also joined this conspiracy, called the Free Syrian Movement. Muhammad Safa, a Syrian colonel cashiered by Shishakli on account of his SSNP membership, became the effective leader. Working out of Lebanon and Iraq, Safa recruited troops and made detailed plans to invade Syria, but Syrian intelligence interrupted the plot before it could be put into effect.

The last effort came in February 1958, just thirteen days after Syria and Egypt joined together in the United Arab Republic. Prodded by 'Abd al-Illah, his nephews Faysal II of Iraq and Husayn of Jordan formed the Arab Union, a federation of the two rulers (but not their states). The union found little approval, however; indeed, reaction against it contributed directly to the overthrow of the Hashimi monarchy in Iraq in July 1958. Faysal II, 'Abd al-Illah, and Nuri as-Sa'id lost their lives in the coup, and a radical republican government came to power. Already in November 1959, the ruler of that new government, 'Abd al-Karim Qasim, was pursuing a version of the Fertile Crescent plan. This amounted to no more than a propaganda ploy against Jamal 'Abd an-Nasir, however, and was quickly abandoned.

According to one observer, Syrians still worry about Iraqi designs. David Roberts writes that "however improbable it may seem to Western observers, there is a widespread Syrian fear, partly rooted in folk-lore and partly in shrewd calculation, of Iraqi ambitions for a Fertile Crescent embracing Syria." Roberts holds that "we may not have heard the last of the Fertile Crescent."[245] Nor is the notion entirely dead on the Syrian side. Moshe Ma'oz believes Hafiz al-Asad had a Fertile Crescent plan in the early 1970s and then, because of the difficulty of incorporating Iraq, reduced it to Greater Syria.[246]

These wisps notwithstanding, Iraq's involvement in Greater Syria came to an abrupt end in 1958. Since that time, Iraq has had almost no role, active or passive, in Pan-Syrian politics.

The Syrian Social Nationalist Party, 1932–1973

Background

The Syrian Social Nationalist Party (*al-Hizb as-Suri al-Qawmi al-Ijtima'i*), or SSNP, has at times been known as the Syrian Nationalist Party or the Social

Faysal ibn al-Husayn. Faysal (1885–1933) led the Arab Revolt, engaged actively in post–World War I diplomacy, served as king of the brief-lived Syrian Kingdom, then lived out his years as king of Iraq. (Temple University Libraries)

'Abdallah ibn al-Husayn. Though long in the shadow of Faysal, his younger brother, 'Abdallah (1882–1951) emerged to serve as ruler of Transjordan for three decades. During much of that time he devoted his efforts to the establishment of a Greater Syria. (UPI/Bettmann Newsphotos)

Nuri as-Sa'id, 'Abd al-Illah ibn Faysal, and King Faysal II. King Sa'ud of Saudia Arabia on a visit to Baghdad in May 1957, surrounded by the three leaders of Iraq: Nuri as-Sa'id *(to the left)*, King Faysal II *(to the right)*, and Regent 'Abd al-Illah *(between the two kings)*. Nuri and 'Abd al-Illah each had his own plan for a Fertile Crescent union that would incorporate Greater Syria. All three Iraqi rulers were murdered in the July 1958 coup. (Temple University Libraries)

Cairo Conference of March 1921. Along with the April 1920 meeting at San Remo, the Cairo Conference determined the map of the Middle East. Notable figures in this picture include: *First row* Herbert Samuel (*3rd from left*), Winston Churchill (*4th from left*), Percy Cox (*4th from right*) *Second row* Arnold T. Wilson (*far left*), Gertrude Bell (*2nd from left*), Ja'far Pasha al-'Askari (*5th from left*), T. E. Lawrence (*4th from right*). (The Bettmann Archive/BBC Hulton)

1949 Jordanian stamp showing King 'Abdallah. Transjordan was renamed Jordan in June 1949, and this stamp followed soon after. The word *Palestine* is overstamped in English and Arabic, pointing explicitly to 'Abdallah's ambitions. (Adam Garfinkle Collection)

1964 Jordanian stamp showing King al-Husayn against a map. The map pictured on this postage stamp extends Jordanian territory right to the Mediterranean Sea— completely eliminating Israel (as well as Palestine). (Adam Garfinkle Collection)

Antun Sa'ada. Sa'ada (1912–49) founded the Syrian Social Nationalist Party in 1932. In addition to its goal of creating a Greater Syrian state, the party enunciated ideological positions of great consequence for Middle East politics. (Courtesy, Majid Khadduri)

SSNP newspaper banner. A map of Antun Sa'ada's vision of Greater Syria can be seen in back of the newspaper title, *Suriya al-Jadida* (New Syria). The circle around the map contains a motto, "Syria for the Syrians."

SSNP flag being retrieved after Israeli attack on 2 August 1985. Israeli bombers destroyed the SSNP headquarters in Shtura in retaliation for a suicide attack on Israeli positions in southern Lebanon. The SSNP flag, which features a curved swastika called the red hurricane (*zawba'a*), points to the party's fascistic origins. (AP/Wide World Photos)

Hafiz al-Asad, president of Syria.   Asad became ruler of Syria at the age of forty, in 1970, and turned the most unstable country of the Middle East into a police state. By making Greater Syria a centerpiece of his policy, he achieved more to make it a reality than any other ruler of the twentieth century. (Temple University Libraries)

Nationalist Party, both abbreviated as SNP; French mistranslations of its name are also used in English—the Parti Populaire Syrien or the Parti Populaire Social, abbreviated as PPS.

Antun Saʿada, a Greek Orthodox intellectual, founded the party in Beirut as a secret organization of students in November 1932. He served as the organization's leader until 1949; the party closely reflected his personality and his ideas. Majid Khadduri observed that "never before in Syria's modern history had a leader possessed such conviction, vigilance, strength of character, and charisma"[247] (and, it can be argued, none has followed him, either). After 1949, the party was led by mediocre figures, none of whom has been able to revive it to its former position.

The SSNP stands for three main tenets: radical reform of society along secular lines, a fascist-style ideology, and Greater Syria. Although best known for its Pan-Syrian ideology, a considerable portion of the party's appeal and influence had to do with its radical reform of society and its fascist qualities. Indeed, it is hard to say which of the three features had most importance in attracting members.

The reform program is summed up in five principles: separation of church and state, prohibition of the clergy from interfering in politics, removal of barriers between sects, abolition of feudalism, and the formation of a strong army.[248] The first three principles are secularizing—they call for the withdrawal of religion (i.e., Islam) from public life—while the latter two fit under the modernizing rubric. It should be kept in mind that while these views are common, even banal in the West, they struck Lebanese and Syrians of the 1930s as novel. Together, the reform principles constitute a social transformation that account for the second *S* in the party name.

A note of caution: because Saʿada reflected the fascist thinking of the 1930s, the words *social* and *national* are sometimes joined together to form the combination *national socialist*, Hitler's coinage and the basis of the word *Nazi*.[249] This is a mistake, however, for Saʿada used the word in Arabic for *social* (*ijtimaʿi*), not *socialist* (*ishtiraki*); the proper noun form for his ideology in English is not *National Socialism* but *Social Nationalism*.

The party's fascistic qualities were expressed in Saʿada's exalted status, the party's organization, and its ideology, including the stress on bloodlines and mystical nationalism. Party rituals imitated the Fascists in many details, from the Hitler-like salute and the anthem set to "Deutschland, Deutschland über alles," to the party symbol, a curved swastika called the red hurricane (*zawbaʿa*). Before 1945, these fascist qualities offered both a powerful ideology and the means to side with the enemies of Britain and France, the two countries ruling Greater Syria. Fascists and Nazi sympathizers flocked to it as the only party in the Levant sympathetic to their viewpoint, and they appear to have formed a significant portion of the party's core membership. Some members were drawn by the fierce opposition to communism. Others sought a strong leader, something Saʿada offered in the dictatorial style of the 1930s. Adulation of Saʿada was so extreme that the SSNP slogan during his lifetime was "Long Live Syria! Long Live Saʿada!"[250] There were also strong hints of his being the prophet of a new religion. SSNP recruits were accepted into the party in a ceremony known as baptism, at which they renounced other loyalties.

Though numerically always small (estimates for 1936 range between 120 to less than 1,000 members), the SSNP exercised wide influence on radical politics in Lebanon and Syria. From its inception, when Sa'ada spent time inveighing students at the American University of Beirut, the party attracted mainly an educated elite. It was also the first party to recruit military officers, having become active in 1934 at the Homs Military Academy.[251] The SSNP never had a broad base of support but many of its members had intellectual, cultural, political, and military prominence.

A very impressive list of former members—Christians, Muslims, and others—went on to be major figures in Lebanese and Syrian life. Ghassan Tuwayni became a powerful Lebanese publisher and politician. Fayiz Sayigh left the party to become an articulate spokesman of Pan-Arabism, while Hisham Sharabi became a leading Palestinian nationalist. One of Syria's most durable military dictators, Adib ash-Shishakli (1949–54), was a former member; a second, Salah Jadid (1966–70), was possibly also a member. As head of state, Shishakli remained close to SSNP members, including his brother Salah ad-Din and 'Isam al-Mahayiri. In cultural life, too, the party had a great impact; for example, the poet Adonis ('Ali Ahmad Sa'id) identified with the party in his youth.[252]

As a well-organized and highly disciplined organization with a clear doctrine and a authoritarian leader, the SSNP had strengths others sought to copy. A number of former members took what they learned from it about political organization to begin their own parties. These included:

(1) Kamal Junbalat, the Druze leader in Lebanon, founded the Progressive Socialist Party in 1949 after negotiations to cooperate with the SSNP fell through.

(2) Adib ash-Shishakli modeled the Arab Liberation Movement (founded in August 1952) on the SSNP.

(3) Akram al-Hawrani, a leading figure in Syrian politics for many years, was one of the SSNP's first members. During his years of open association with the party, 1936–38, he helped found the National Youth Party (*Hizb ash-Shabab al-Watani*) and then in 1939 became its leader. Not only did Hawrani himself secretly remain a member of the SSNP, but he also affiliated the National Youth Party with it. Hawrani eventually broke with the SSNP[253] and cut ties between the National Youth Party and the SSNP. As in Junbalat's case, negotiations for cooperation with the SSNP failed, so Hawrani turned the National Youth Party into the Arab Socialist Party (*al-Hizb al-Ishtiraki al-'Arabi*) in January 1950. This latter organization remained independent only three years, eventually merging with the Ba'th Party in February 1953.

(4) The SSNP found a wide following among Palestinians in the early 1950s, a number of whom subsequently held high positions in the PLO. Fu'ad Shimali, a member of the party and Sa'ada's son-in-law, had a key role in Black September. Bashir 'Ubayd worked closely with the Popular Front for the Liberation of Palestine. Ahmad Jibril headed his own organization, the Popular

Front for the Liberation of Palestine–General Command. The PLO goal of "a secular democratic state" in Palestine probably reflects the SSNP background of some highly placed members. According to a generally unreliable account, Sabri al-Banna ("Abu Nidal") is said actively to have participated in the party during his student days at the American University of Beirut about 1960.[254]

(5) Georges Ibrahim 'Abdallah joined the SSNP at the age of fifteen, then quit to join George Habash. In 1980, 'Abdallah went on to found his own organization, the Lebanese Armed Revolutionary Fraction (known by its French acronym, FARL). FARL worked with Syrian intelligence and was held responsible for a rash of terrorist acts in France during the 1980s.

Even without a direct personal connection, the SSNP often provided a model for other political parties. The Phalanges Libanaises, the leading Maronite organization founded in 1936, adopted much from the SSNP; so too did An-Najjada, the Sunni organization founded a year later. Before establishing the Ba'th Party, Michel 'Aflaq and Salah ad-Din al-Bitar are said to have held long conversations with Sa'ada.[255]

The radicalism of the SSNP profoundly influenced the nature of Pan-Arab nationalism. Elsewhere in the Arab world—Arabia, Egypt, the Maghrib— Pan-Arabism first developed as a temperate doctrine advocating harmonious political relations and cooperation in finance, culture, and other spheres (what is known as moderate Pan-Arabism). But in Greater Syria, Pan-Arabism meant something far more ambitious and disruptive: the elimination of borders and the fusion of peoples (or radical Pan-Arabism). It appears that in its modern form this latter idea originated with the SSNP, whose plans to dismantle the boundaries dividing Greater Syria were subsequently transferred to the Arab nation. The Ba'th adopted SSNP-style principles in the late 1940s and then disseminated these to Egypt and throughout the Arabic-speaking countries. Radical Pan-Arabism flourished from about 1958 to 1967 and had vast political importance in the Middle East during that period. Although since overtaken by moderate Pan-Arabism, the ideology still lives on for some leaders, such as Mu'ammar al-Qadhdhafi of Libya.

The Pan-Arab theorist Abu Khaldun Sati' al-Husri, no friend of the SSNP, in the early 1950s explained the reasons for this influence:

> Until now, there has appeared no party in the Arab world that can compete with the SSNP for the quality of its propaganda, which addresses both reason and emotion, or for the strength of its organization, which is effective both overtly and covertly. By virtue of its organization, this party succeeded in creating a very powerful intellectual and political current in Syria and Lebanon.[256]

Before the SSNP came into existence, political parties in Syria and most of the Middle East represented personal interests, even if they pretended to pursue causes. The SSNP was the first true indigenous party of an ideological nature. A historian of political parties in Syria was, therefore, correct to conclude that the SSNP was founded on "a completely different basis from the parties that preceded it or followed it."[257]

Activities

The SSNP did not flinch from the radicalism of its position. To create a state that represented the Syrian identity meant eradicating the polities created by the British and French in the years after World War I—the Syrian republic, Lebanon, Israel, and Jordan. The SSNP viewed these existing states as artificial and meaningless and paid them no loyalty. With regard to Lebanon, for example, Sa'ada declared, "Above all, we are Pan-Syrian nationalists; our cause is the cause of [Greater] Syria, not that of Lebanese separatism."[258] He argued that "Lebanon should be reunited with natural Syria" and explicitly stated that his goal was "to seize power in Beirut to achieve this objective."[259]

The SSNP's devoted paramilitary forces gave it a capable militia which played a significant role in both Lebanese civil wars. In 1958, these stood with the government of Kamil Sham'un against the rebels. By the time fighting began in 1975, the SSNP had switched sides and played a small but important part in the antigovernment coalition.

The SSNP inspired many efforts to unify countries. In 1949 alone, it had connections to the three Syrian military rulers who pursued unity negotiations with Iraq, though each of them changed his mind or was overthrown before any agreements could be reached. The SSNP's willingness to use subversion and violence won it powerful allies. On at least three occasions it received external backing for planned revolutions. Syria helped a 1949 attempt to overthrow the Lebanese government; 'Abd al-Illah, uncle of the king of Iraq, supported the SSNP in an unsuccessful 1956 effort to overthrow the government of Syria; and Lebanese military officers joined the December 1961 putsch against their own government. Like almost all the SSNP did, these efforts came to naught.

Even in failure, however, they had far-reaching consequences. To take just the 1949 episode, in June of that year, the ruler of Syria, Husni az-Za'im, offered Antun Sa'ada a warm welcome and promises of arms against the Lebanese authorities. This encouraged Sa'ada to declare war on Beirut and to take steps to overthrow the government. But Za'im betrayed Sa'ada in July 1949 and delivered him to the Lebanese police, who had him executed after an eight-hour trial. Za'im's treachery had wide consequences in Syria and Lebanon. In Syria, it contributed to Za'im's overthrow a month later, for many Syrians were offended by this breach of promise. The director-general of Za'im's police, Adib ash-Shishakli, provided important assistance to the coup makers and soon after took power himself. Za'im lost his life at the hands of a soldier avenging Sa'ada. Riyad as-Sulh, one of the great figures of Lebanese politics and the premier at the time of Sa'ada's death, was assassinated by an SSNP member in July 1951. Za'im's actions engendered an ill will toward Damascus that harmed Lebanese-Syrian relations for years. In both countries, the SSNP benefited from a backlash of sympathy.

The SSNP on occasion cooperated with the Hashimis. In July 1942, it approached 'Abdallah and indicated a willingness to accept him as ruler of Greater Syria, asking in return control of certain key ministries, but 'Abdallah showed no interest. In November 1947, just as ʿAbdallah had turned his attention away from Damascus, the SSNP declared that it "does not object to the appointment of His Majesty as King of United Syria."[260] As noted earlier (p. 100), the SSNP and ʿAbd al-Illah of Iraq colluded in the Free Syrian Movement, a 1956 effort to overthrow the Syrian government. Of course, the two sides worked together only tactically. ʿAbd al-Illah provided money and arms; the SSNP supplied connections and manpower. The conspirators would almost certainly have fallen out had the plot succeeded, for each expected to rule Syria on its own; and it is unlikely that a compromise could have been achieved between ʿAbd al-Illah's quest for a throne and the SSNP's radical vision for social change.

King al-Husayn supported the SSNP in 1961–62 by giving it money and helping its efforts in Lebanon, the intent being to find allies against his principal adversary of the time, Jamal ʿAbd an-Nasir. He probably encouraged the SSNP's 1961 coup attempt in Lebanon and promised it recognition. Even later, the king retained close personal ties with several members of the SSNP resident in Amman.

Usually, the rivalry between these two main Pan-Syrian aspirants caused them openly to compete. The Hashimis rejected the SSNP's republican and secular ideas, its pure Pan-Syrian nationalism, and its claim to rule a future Greater Syrian state. In response, Antun Saʿada took ʿAbdallah on openly, declaring that "the SSNP has fought the Amman plan because of its ideology. We do not want a monarchy."[261] According to another SSNP figure, "we are against the king, for he wants to establish a state on religious bases."[262] On one occasion, the SSNP even urged military cooperation between the Lebanese and Syrian governments to resist the king's Greater Syria plan.[263]

For the SSNP, ʿAbdallah was just one of many enemies. Its irredentism, secularism, fascism, and violence assured it of almost universally hostile relations. French authorities proscribed the party during the mandate because it agitated for independence. Jamal ʿAbd an-Nasir of Egypt persecuted the SSNP because it opposed the union with Egypt (a non-Syrian state) in 1958–61. Israel fought the party because of its extreme anti-Zionism. Baʿthists rejected its pure Pan-Syrian ideology. Socialists and Communists opposed its fascism. Leaders of independent Lebanon suppressed the SSNP because it denied the state's legitimacy and the sectarian basis of its political life. Syrian rulers sought to silence a proven troublemaker.

The better to harass the SSNP, its many enemies frequently accused the party of collaborating with foreign powers and doing their dirty work. French authorities accused it of collaboration with the Axis in the 1940s; the Vichy government, ironically, continued to press this charge. Rumors of American subsidies (subsequently proven accurate) discredited SSNP candidates in the Syrian elections of 1953. Later, ʿAbd an-Nasir accused the SSNP of taking American money. A British hand was suspected in the mid-1940s and then, more plausibly, in 1961. Talk in recent years, with good reason, has centered on Romanian and Soviet aid.

With so many enemies, it is not surprising to find that the SSNP was persecuted through most of its existence. Sa'ada himself was imprisoned twice by the French, in November 1935 and August 1936, and finally executed by the Lebanese police. In Lebanon, the party has frequently alternated between legality and illegality. It was banned for the first time in March 1936 and made legal in May 1937; banned in October 1939, made legal by Kamil Sham'un in May 1944; banned in July 1949, made legal by Sham'un again in September 1958; banned in January 1962, and made legal by Kamal Junbalat in 1970. (It remained legal after 1970.) In Syria, the party was legal until 1955 (and so the party headquarters was in Damascus from 1949 to 1955) but has been banned since then. In Jordan, assassinations carried out by SSNP members caused it to be repressed during 1951–52; afraid of SSNP inroads among Palestinians, the Jordanian security services tried to eradicate the party in 1966.

Despite strong official disfavor, the SSNP on occasion won representation in the Lebanese and Syrian parliaments. In Lebanon, it took one seat in the 1957 elections. It did better in Syria, winning nine seats in 1949, one in 1953, and two in 1954. Though far too few to pass any legislation, these representatives gave the party a platform to make its views more widely known.

Conclusion:
The Historic Significance
of Greater Syria

An overview of the first half-century of activity on behalf of Greater Syria leads to several conclusions about the Pan-Syrian ideology. In particular, we shall review its importance, feasibility, mutability, weakness, and frustration.

First, evidence presented here should establish that Greater Syria was not the minor eddy of general repute but a central theme in the history of the Middle East between 1918 and 1950. It was no less important than two much better known nationalisms, the Pan-Arabist and the Palestinian. Pan-Syrian ambitions had major bearing on the course of events in Lebanon, Jordan, and Syria, and almost as much on Palestine and Iraq. It also influenced inter-Arab relations and the Arab-Israeli conflict. As a model of the ideological party, the SSNP had a major impact on a wide range of organizations.

A great number of French, British, and local politicians believed in Greater Syria as a proper unit to emerge from World War I. That it did not was a source of disappointment to such varied figures in the West as Henri Lammens, Arnold Toynbee, key officials in the British government, and business leaders in Lyons. The King-Crane Commission endorsed Pan-Syrianism, as did, implicitly, the League of Nations.

Europeans quickly reconciled themselves to the division of Syria, but the ache lasted in the Levant. Disparate revisionists in the three decades of round one—Sunnis dissatisfied in Lebanon and Palestine, 'Alawi and Druze rebels, 'Abdallah displeased with his scrap of territory, 'Abd al-Illah in search of a throne—sought solutions in the unification of Syria. In addition to those individuals most closely identified with Pan-Syrianism (Antun Sa'ada and King 'Abdallah), the ideology enjoyed support from such major actors as Faysal, Shakib Arsalan, Nuri as-Sa'id, 'Abd al-Illah, Riyad as-Sulh, 'Abd ar-Rahman Shahbandar, Amin al-Husayni, Rashid 'Ali al-Kaylani, 'Abd ar-Rahman 'Azzam, Musa 'Alami, and George Antonius.

A great number of organizations besides the Syrian Social Nationalist Party accepted and promoted Greater Syria. These included Independence of Syria, the Syrian Central Committee, the Syrian Party of Unity, the Party of Syrian Union, the two People's Parties (one founded in 1925, the other in 1948), the Syrian Congress, the Syro-Palestinian Congress, the National Bloc, the Arab Club, the Literary Club, the Muslim-Christian Association, and the Arab Independence Party in Southern Syria. Most unexpectedly, even the Ba'th Party briefly endorsed Pan-Syrianism. Important meetings blessed Greater Syria, including the two General Syrian Congresses, the First and Second Palestinian Congresses, the Conferences of the Sons of the Coast, and the Conferences of the Coast.

Greater Syria was not limited to manifestos. It caused domestic unrest and made foreign relations volatile in several countries. In Lebanon, the conviction that the country as a whole (and especially the four districts attached to it in 1920) belonged to Syria incited civil unrest through three decades. 'Abdallah worked on Greater Syria from the moment he arrived in Amman until his death three decades later. Syrian politicians frequently vented their discontent with the existing borders and made plans to control territory belonging to all five of their neighbors. Palestinian Arabs dropped Greater Syria for tactical reasons in 1920, but the idea lived on and, had they succeeded against the Zionists, probably would have been acted upon. The Fertile Crescent scheme, an enlarged version of Greater Syria, unsettled politics in Iraq until 1958; indeed, the Iraqi rulers' contradictory and futile pursuits of Damascus distracted their attention from domestic problems, with tragic consequences.

Pan-Syrianism embroiled political life in the Levant, adding another layer of complexity to an already intricate brew that included various forms of Pan-Arab and Palestinian nationalism, Pan-Islam, and local loyalties. Together these competing claims on allegiance relegated the actual state structures to an emotional void. In this way, Greater Syria denigrated the appeal of existing states and thereby contributed substantially to the well-known volatility of the Middle East.

The contest for Palestine offers a clear case of Pan-Syrian ideology entangling with other nationalisms. Pan-Syrian ambitions justified the Jordanian and Syrian governments laying title to Palestine, with great consequence. Jordan's moment came in 1948–49, when 'Abdallah's forces provided the mainstay of the Arab fighting. The dismal military record of the other Arabs suggests that had 'Abdallah not staked out a position (but had acquiesced to the radical Arab leadership in Palestine or to the Egyptian or Syrian governments), the Arab forces would have lost Palestine entirely. And had Israel won the whole of mandatory Palestine in 1948–49, including the whole of Jerusalem, the debate now taking place over the Jewish versus democratic nature of the Israeli state would have been raised earlier and in a more acute form. The issue of Jerusalem's status, never yet broached, would likely have been settled. The great post-1967 division in Israeli politics—what to do with the West Bank—might have been decided long ago.

Syria's era came several decades later, as Egypt's government retired from the conflict starting in 1974 and ending in 1982. With Egypt out, the burden fell on Syria to keep the military conflict with Israel alive. And it did; as Asad set his sights on strategic parity with Israel, the Arab-Israel war at the state level turned into a Syrian-Israel war.

But Pan-Syrianism also hindered the Arab cause against Israel. If not for the independent Jordanian and Syrian roles, the major Arab actors competing for Palestine would have been not four but two. This would have reduced inter-Arab strife, eased cooperation, and probably strengthened the Arab cause. Paradoxically, the reduction in bickering might also have increased the chances of the Arabs accepting Israel's existence.[1]

The maintenance of a distinct claim to Palestine had great domestic repercussions for Jordan, setting both ʿAbdallah and Husayn at odds with many of their own subjects and with other Arab leaders. Had ʿAbdallah not overtly planned to grab Palestine, he could have had Arab backing; had he accommodated Palestinian separatism more flexibly, he might not have been assassinated by a Palestinian tailor. Had Husayn accepted the Pan-Arabist approach during 1956–67 period, he would not have suffered so many attacks on his regime and attempts on his life; had he truly endorsed the PLO's claim to Palestine, he would have been spared more than two decades of conflict with Yasir ʿArafat; had he supported Hafiz al-Asad, he would have avoided subversion from Damascus.

The Syrian Social Nationalist Party also had a profound impact on politics in Lebanon and Syria. It introduced a panoply of new ideas to the Middle East, including the ideological party, complete political secularism, fascistic leadership, and a determination to pull down existing borders between states. The SSNP showed the way in the use of violence to destroy the established order. In a period of two decades, its radical ideas drew in a substantial portion of the intellectual leadership in Lebanon and Syria as members. Virtually every radical group in the region learned from the SSNP and imitated aspects of its program. Its repeated challenges to the Lebanese state helped undermine the prestige and status of the authorities in Beirut, while its militia had substantial roles in Lebanon's civil wars. Looking over a half-century of turmoil, David Roberts correctly noted that "the PPS has had a curiously pervasive influence through intrigue, murder and an ideology which Saʿadeh rightly foresaw would be effective in the Levant."[2]

The second conclusion concerns feasibility. Greater Syria represented a union that, for many years, was not a political fantasy but a realistic goal. Prospects were especially good about the time of the two world wars, when the established order was in flux and borders could be redrawn. Any arrangement could have succeeded in the 1918–23 period; the divisions imposed then were long seen as temporary, and with justification. A widespread, almost universal feeling existed that these would be eradicated once the imperial powers had departed; the pressing question was not whether this would happen but the exact shape, size, structure, and ideology of the larger polities that would come into being. This sentiment crested in the 1940s, only to meet with increasing disappointments after 1949.

Third, Pan-Syrianism had to change to survive. When the much-watched effort to unify Syria and Egypt in 1958–61 ended in an acrimonious collapse, the despised divisions inherited from Britain and France began to look less transient. When the best effort to overcome existing polities failed so utterly, more thought began to be put into living with them and making the best of them, and less into their elimination. Indeed, those radical enough still to aspire to wholesale changes, such as Qadhdhafi, came to be viewed as anachronistic. Pure Pan-Syrianism, especially, had to become more modest or more subtle.

Fourth, Pan-Syrianism suffered from intellectual poverty. Pan-Arabism (whether radical or moderate) attracted many thinkers who developed a powerful and nuanced argument for the Arab nation. In contrast, pure Pan-Syrianism was promoted only by Antun Sa'ada and his idiosyncratic, if talented, band of followers. The blatant self-interest of 'Abdallah, Nuri as-Sa'id, 'Abd al-Illah, and other politicians diminished their efforts. This lack of articulation went far to account for the failure of Pan-Syrianism to be established as a reputable ideology and attract a large following.

Indeed, the anti–Greater Syria position was better articulated than the pro–Greater Syria position. Note, for example, the case of Abu Khaldun Sati' al-Husri and the SSNP. Husri, perhaps the leading theoretician and exponent of Pan-Arabism, long took interest in the SSNP; he met with Sa'ada and even wrote a book about SSNP ideology. He disagreed with pure Pan-Syrianism, to be sure, but he took the SSNP seriously and argued with it respectfully. But the SSNP, reeling from its crisis in Syria, provoked Husri, and he responded in 1956 with a vicious refutation of the SSNP, dealing it a severe blow. As Bassam Tibi explained, "the massive attack of such an influential political writer as al-Husri on the SSNP, which had not yet gained a strong foothold, severely damaged its development. Husri's critique was used by all the party's opponents."[3]

Fifth, frustration far outweighed achievement. All the schemes of glory turned out badly, even the one that appeared successful. A boundary was crossed and a hitherto separate territory incorporated before 1974 only when King 'Abdallah took the West Bank in 1948. This case excepted, every move toward Greater Syria failed. Lebanese Muslims remained in Lebanon, Southern Syria became Palestine and then Israel, 'Abdaliah stayed in Amman, and the SSNP never came at all near to power. Despite widespread disapproval of the San Remo borders, they endured. Put differently, Greater Syria had no Bismarck or Cavour.

Or not before 1974. Although not likely to establish a full-fledged Greater Syria, Hafiz al-Asad has come much closer than anyone else. Quietly, Asad is achieving where others so noisily failed. Policies pursued by the Asad regime since 1974 resembled earlier Syrian claims to Palestine, Jordanian claims to Syria, and SSNP efforts to unify all four countries. There were two main differences, however. Lately, the only real effort to constitute Greater Syria emanated from Lesser Syria; Damascus became the unique predator. Also, the methods changed; Asad pursued Greater Syria with the skills of a crafty politician and the strengths of a police state. The history of failure is over; Pan-Syrianism enjoyed real success after 1974. Indeed, it had perhaps more significance in this period than at any previous time.

II

THE ERA OF
LESSER SYRIA

3

Lesser Syria's Dominance, 1974–1988

We cannot forget that Mr. Hafiz al-Asad—His Excellency the President of Syria—has declared many times that Lebanon is a part of Syria, that Palestine is a part of Syria. And if we believe that, and we have to—he has given all signs of being serious—it means that his interest in Lebanon is very genuine. He is playing the game very cautiously and intelligently.

'Abdallah Sa'idi,
a member of the SSNP[1]

While all Arabic-speaking residents of Greater Syria have been affected by the division of Greater Syria and had some role in the Pan-Syrian quest, Lesser Syrians have almost always been at the center of this effort. Alexandretta was claimed by Syria only; Sunnis in Lebanon wanted to reintegrate with Syria; the SSNP focused on Lebanese union with Syria; Palestinian Arabs looked primarily to the north; 'Abdallah hoped to sit on a throne in Damascus; Iraqi leaders dreamed of a Fertile Crescent union with Lesser Syria; and so forth.

Lesser Syria's centrality results from many factors. It has the largest territory and population of any country in Greater Syria; add to this that it carries the name of the whole region, and it naturally assumes a mantle of leadership. Because Prince Faysal made Damascus his capital, that city has a permanent claim to being the center of Greater Syria. The French *politique minoritaire* was practiced most consistently in Lesser Syria and had the most pernicious effects there. Finally, residents of Lesser Syria had prominent roles in developing many of the great ideologies of the Muslim Middle East, including Pan-Arabism, Arab socialism, and anti-Zionism. For all these reasons, Syrians see the other states as carved out from their territory and feel the most injured by the imperial divisions.

Despite Syria's centrality, its Pan-Syrian claims lay mostly dormant for fifty years, from the French conquest in 1920 to the coup by Hafiz al-Asad in 1970. During the first half of that period, French mandatory rule hindered Damascus from the serious pursuit of Greater Syria, while internal instability blocked it during the second half. Only in the mid-1970s did a Greater Syria with its capital in Damascus once again become a realistic goal.

Vestigial Claims by Others

In the third phase of Pan-Syrianism, after 1974, the PLO and Jordan continued to brandish claims to territory. But these carried less weight in the Asad era.

The PLO retained the clause in its charter which left open the possibility of making Jordan part of a future Palestinian state. From time to time, and especially in its peak years between 1974 (when the Arab League negated Jordanian rights to the West Bank) and 1982 (when Israeli forces invaded Lebanon), the PLO was more explicit. A Palestine National Council meeting in June 1974 called for a "Jordanian-Palestinian national front whose aim will be to establish a national democratic government in Jordan; this will be joined with the Palestinian entity to be established after the battle [with Israel]."[2] Yasir 'Arafat wrote later that year, "Jordan is ours, Palestine is ours, and we shall build our national entity on the whole of this land after having freed it of both the Zionist presence and the reactionary-traitor presence [of King al-Husayn]."[3] A 1975 article in the PLO magazine showed why the Jordanian regime must be overthrown. It is necessary, 'Isam Sakhnini explained,

> to cancel the Jordanian entity and to establish, in its place, a revolutionary entity. . . . Palestinian Transjordan is the basis for building the fatherland. This will be a step toward the practical realization of Greater Palestine; it will also enable those Palestinians in parts of the land to be liberated to expand from there to the west of the [Jordan] River. . . . [The land of Palestinian Transjordan] is the essential starting point for the emergence of the national entity that includes the whole Palestinian land.[4]

Faruq Qaddumi announced in March 1977 that the PLO considered Jordanians and Palestinians "one people."[5] Days later, Zuhayr Muhsin, a PLO leader long in the Syrian pay, made a similar announcement: "Once we have attained all our rights in the whole of Palestine, we must not postpone, even for a moment, the reunification of Jordan and Palestine."[6]

Yasir 'Arafat echoed these sentiments. In November 1978, he specifically answered a claim from Damascus: "Syria said the Palestinian revolution and Syria can never be separated. Al-Asad said that Palestine is the southern part of Syria. I told him that Palestine is Southern Syria and Syria is Northern Palestine."[7] 'Arafat repeated this assertion six months later: "I recall President al-Asad saying that Palestine is Southern Syria. I replied to this by saying that Syria is Northern Palestine."[8] But these PLO statements were bravado, not serious demands.[9]

Jordan's claim to the West Bank, on the other hand, still counted for something. Even during the 1974–82 heyday of the PLO, reminders of the Jordanian interest in that territory would be uttered, though sporadically and in fairly muted fashion. Prime Minister Zayd ar-Rifa'i told an interviewer in 1975:

> Jordan is Palestine. They have never been ruled as two separate states except during the British Mandate. Before 1918 the two banks of the Jordan River were a single state. When they returned to being a single state after 1948, it

was a matter of building on the earlier unity. Their families are one, as are their welfare, affiliation, and culture. Until now, despite all that happened—the Rabat summit and other decisions—tomorrow, when the Palestinian state is established on the West Bank, or any other liberated part of Palestine, I do not imagine there will be a division of the two banks. There will be special relations between them resulting from the powerful unity of the past.[10]

In answer to Ariel Sharon's repeated argument that "Jordan is Palestine," King al-Husayn asserted that "Jordan is Palestine and Palestine is Jordan."[11] In 1980, the Jordanian University in Amman sponsored a major conference on "the History of Greater Syria (Palestine)."[12] The term *Sham* was used in titles of books dealing with cultural history.[13] School textbooks held that "Palestine is the southwest part of *Bilad ash-Sham.*"[14]

Jordanian claims became bolder after the 1982 reduction of the PLO. In July 1983, Radio Amman endorsed the concept of Palestine as Southern Syria, calling this a "geographical reality," and asserted: "We agree with the Syrian officials' reiterations that Jordan is Southern Syria because geography shows that Syria is Northern Jordan."[15] The breakdown of diplomatic efforts between Jordan and the PLO in February 1986 inspired a number of efforts to reassert Amman's claims to Palestine. The king announced that he speaks "as one who feels he is a Palestinian."[16] A publication of the Jordanian government, *Occupied Land Affairs*, portrayed a map of Mandatory Palestine on its cover,[17] implying that Jordan claimed the whole of Palestine. Amman also took practical steps to reassert its presence on the West Bank. These included a larger budget, special television programming, parliamentary representation, and a host of small measures intended to reestablish a Jordanian administrative structure in the region.[18]

Whether Jordanian or Palestinian, those who supported Jordanian rule on the West Bank became distinctly bolder in 1986. 'Akif al-Fayiz, president of the Jordanian parliament, declared that "Jordan does not distinguish between its people on the East and on the West Bank. Our people is one and our family is one. We look forward to the day when the one family will resume its historic role."[19] Anwar al-Khatib, former Jordanian mayor of East Jerusalem, echoed these sentiments: "Palestine, Jordan and Syria constituted one family until the British and French occupation in 1918, which drove the wedge of boundaries among us. We do not differentiate between our people, whether they live in Jordan, Syria, or Palestine."[20]

Although Husayn had long abandoned 'Abdallah's grandiose ambitions, his statements about Jordanian rights to Palestine served to remind the world (until his dramatic renunciation of this claim in July 1988) that his grandfather's legacy had not died entirely. In fact, Husayn maintained, more discreetly than 'Abdallah ever could, that Palestine rightfully belonged within Jordan.

These Jordanian assertions aside, Pan-Syrianism has since 1974 been an almost exclusive preserve of the government in Damascus. A new era began with the coming to power of Hafiz al-Asad in 1970. Asad inherited a police state and completed its domination of Syrian public life, ending decades of

Figure 10. Jordanian Map of 1986 At a moment of Jordanian strength and PLO weakness, Jordan's Ministry of
Occupied Land Affairs published a pamphlet picturing the
whole of mandatory Palestine, suggesting (but not stating
explicitly) that this entire area should be considered
occupied Jordanian territory.

instability. He then quickly revived the Syrian claim to Lebanon. Asad pursued
the vision of Greater Syria in two complementary ways: by making verbal
claims and by building the force to implement them. The claims were important to justify Syrian expansion; the force backed up the rhetoric. The statements made and the actions taken in their support are worth noting in detail,

for they offer important insights into the regime's Pan-Syrian aspirations and the strategies it adopts.

Asad asserted rights over Lebanon, Palestine, Jordan, and Alexandretta, and most of his efforts on behalf of Greater Syria dealt separately with these component regions. Indeed, Syrian leaders used virtually identical terms with regard to the countries they aspire to control: "We and Lebanon are one country." "We and Palestine form one entity." "We and Jordan are one country."[21] Within this uniformity, however, two basic strategies coexisted. Lebanon and the PLO are both weak and fractured, and this gave Damascus the opportunity to find Lebanese and Palestinian agents. In contrast, the approach to Jordan depended on force and intimidation directed against the central government.

Lebanon

Words

Asad made a vague claim to Lebanon in August 1972: "Syria and Lebanon are a single country. We are more than brothers."[22] He made almost the same point a year later, announcing that Syria and Lebanon "are one land and one nation with two governments."[23] More ominously, the minister of information explained in January 1975, "Lebanon will not escape from the destined unity of Syria and Lebanon."[24] The entry of Syrian troops into Lebanon in June 1976 prompted a spate of Syrian claims. Asad proclaimed a month later that "through history, Syria and Lebanon have been one country and one people. . . . Our history is one, our future is one and our destiny is one."[25] Days later, a Syrian general was quoted as saying that "what is taking place presently in the region is the undoing of the Sykes-Picot agreement" (the 1916 exchange of notes that led to the division of the Levant).[26] Syria's prime minister expressed the same claim in asserting that "Southern Lebanon is like southern Syria."[27]

In May 1982, Asad referred to Lebanon as an "Arab land that belongs to us."[28] A Ministry of Information official asserted that "Lebanon and Syria are the same"[29] in August 1983. Asad declared that "Lebanon and Syria are one single people, one single nation" whose feeling of kinship "runs deeper than it does between states in the United States."[30] Interviewed by a French newspaper in May 1985, the Syrian foreign minister reminded its readership that "until the beginning of the century, we [Syria and Lebanon] formed a single country. It is true that we are now two different states, but we cannot ignore the fact that we form a single people with the same language and a common history."[31] A British diplomat recalled senior Syrian officials referring to the Biqa' Valley of Lebanon as "the usurped lands" (*al-aradi al-mughtasaba*).[32] Defense Minister Mustafa 'Abd al-Qadir Tallas told a German interviewer that "Lebanon belongs to our Great Syrian family" (*grossen syrischen Familie*).[33]

When Christian groups in Lebanon brought up the possibility of dividing the country into Christian and Muslim sections, Syrian foreign minister ʿAbd al-Halim Khaddam responded in a proprietary fashion:

> We will not permit the division of Lebanon. Any attempt at division will lead to our immediate intervention. Lebanon was part of Syria and we will recover it at the moment of an effective effort at partitioning. It should be made clear that this does not refer only to the four districts [that France took from Syria in 1920], but to Mt. Lebanon as well. Lebanon can either be united or return to Syria.[34]

Raymond Eddé, a leading Lebanese critic of the Syrian intervention, interpreted this declaration as a Syrian statement of intent to annex the Biqaʿ Valley, the town of Tripoli, and the ʿAkkar, an area to the north of Tripoli.[35] Indeed, Khaddam specified in August 1981 that "we consider Tripoli an extension of the *muhajirin* quarter of Damascus."[36]

At another point, Khaddam (who was known in Lebanon as the "Syrian High Commissioner") declared that "Syria had not consulted anyone when it entered Lebanon, nor would it consult anyone when it decides to withdraw from Lebanon."[37] Asad went even farther, remarking to a group of Lebanese parliamentarians in February 1978 that while the Lebanese army amounted to no more than gangs, Syrian troops in Lebanon constituted the legal army of Lebanon.[38] He reiterated this point in October 1983, telling a Swiss journalist that "there is only one foreign army in Lebanon, namely Israel's. The Syrians and Lebanese are one people, they are Arabs. We have the same language and the same history."[39] Once more, in July 1986, Khaddam told reporters in Paris that "the Syrian forces are present in Lebanon legitimately. . . . These forces can be present at any place they want and do not have to get permission from anybody."[40]

After his only formal visit to Lebanon as president[41] in January 1975, Asad observed: "Leaving Damascus for Shtura this morning, I had the feeling of going from one town to another within a single country, of leaving one portion of my people for another. These sentiments derive from our common way of life and our unique history. We are one and the same people, sons of the same nation."[42] The Syrian minister of economy and foreign trade, Muhammad al-ʿImadi, called for "economic unity" between Syria and Lebanon.[43]

Syrian authorities usually made sure to portray their interest in Lebanon as one based on common Arab ties. But sometimes they forgot, and made clear their real thinking. Thus, when Asad wanted to discredit Iraq's presence in Lebanon, he did it by denigrating its ties to that country. "Syria's status in Lebanon is different from that of Iraq. This is so because the human relations that exist between Syria and Lebanon do not exist between Iraq and Lebanon."[44] True enough; but this confirms that "human relations" and its synonyms are but a tactful way of pointing to the antique ties between the regions of Greater Syria.

The Syrian government construed the absence of diplomatic relations between itself and Lebanon as a sign of closeness. The information minister explained that "Lebanon and Syria are two states in harmony. It would be an offense to the rights of Lebanon and Syria to have to maintain diplomatic relations between the two."[45] Asad explained the lack of embassies by arguing that contacts of the two countries "are beyond the resources of any embassy. . . . This is a symbol of the warm fraternal relations between the two countries."[46]

But Lebanese interpret the lack of formal relations differently; for them, it indicates Syrian unwillingness to accept the sovereign existence of Lebanon. The Lebanese view was buttressed by the pressure Damascus exerted on other states to withdraw their diplomats from Lebanon. The Syrian regime used its many proxies in Lebanon to harass foreign diplomats based in Beirut; with time, these grew weary of constant intimidation and relocated their missions to Damascus. Fu'ad Butrus, the Lebanese foreign minister, once mused publicly on this issue: "I wonder if there is not a plan aiming to empty Lebanon of all diplomatic representation."[47] While some states might have withdrawn their missions from Beirut anyway, owing to the civil war, their number was probably greatly increased as a result of Syrian pressure. Among the missions either closed or left vacant were those of Afghanistan, Brazil, Canada, Chad, Costa Rica, the Dominican Republic, Egypt, Ghana, Greece, Haiti, Indonesia, Iran, Iraq, Kuwait, Libya, Malta, Nigeria, Oman, Panama, Qatar, Senegal, Sudan, Switzerland, Tunisia, the UAE, Uruguay, North and South Yemen, and Yugoslavia.[48] By 1985, only two of twenty-two Arab ambassadors remained resident in Beirut.

Deeds

The record shows that the Syrian government did more than talk big; indeed, in recent years it has extended its control over most of Lebanon. Already in the mid-1960s, the ʿAlawi village of Ghajar, at the base of Mount Hermon, was taken over by Syria in conjunction with a water diversion scheme. By early 1973, Asad had acquired virtual veto power over the major developments in Lebanon. Under heavy pressure, the Lebanese authorities acquiesced to the stationing of Syrian troops in Lebanon later that year.

The outbreak of the Lebanese civil war in April 1975 gave Asad new opportunities. The rupture of central authority and the country's fractured social condition made it easy for Damascus to find agents in Lebanon. Asad shifted support among factions in Lebanon (the Maronites, the PLO, the Druze, the Shiʿis, the SSNP, the Communists) in a masterful effort to expand Syrian influence. In addition, the Syrian government controlled two Palestinian armed units in Lebanon, those of the Palestine Liberation Army and As-Saʿiqa. When even these proved insufficient, Asad used the Syrian military forces June 1976 to intervene directly. "This move proved a watershed in the relations between the two countries: for the first time Syria realized its historic ambition and dispatched military forces into Lebanon."[49] A second intervention soon followed in September 1976.

Over a dozen years later, Syrian troops remained in Lebanon, more entrenched than ever and in control of large regions of Lebanon. Their presence was symbolized by the minute tasks in which they became involved. Looking for members of the Iraqi wing of the Ba'th Party or other leftist organizations, Syrian intelligence forces conducted house-to-house searches in Tripoli in 1979. In August 1985, Syrian soldiers enforced ceasefire agreements between warring Lebanese factions. Syrian control of the Beirut airport brought many benefits; checking passports allowed them, for example, to ban Hizbullah members from using the airport as a base for terrorism on airplanes worldwide.

Lebanese leaders dared not defy Damascus. Walid Junbalat, the Druze and leftist leader, merely had to endure several weeks of house arrest; his father, Kamal Junbalat, was (almost certainly) killed by the Syrians in March 1977. Bashir Jumayyil, the Phalangist leader and president-elect of Lebanon, was blown up just before he could assume the office of president. Bashir's brother Amin Jumayyil, the president of Lebanon, was almost dispatched in February 1988, when half a kilo of sophisticated explosives was found on his plane. After the discovery, Syrian intelligence officers at the Beirut airport immediately seized the explosive and refused to release it.

Nor were Syrian refugees in Lebanon safe. Muhammad 'Umran, one of Asad's rivals, fell to an assassin's bullet in March 1972. A critic of the regime, Zuhayr Shalaq, was kidnapped in Beirut and removed to Syria in a coffin; a similar fate befell Khalil Barayiz, who had written critically about Asad's performance in the June 1967 war.

Journalists were frequent victims of Asad's intimidation. Salim al-Lawzi, an important Lebanese publisher, had acquired embarrassing information about internal conditions in Syria, so Syrian agents tortured and killed him. A few months later, Riyad Taha, president of the Lebanese Publishers Association, was killed by four gunmen in a car. These methods were used against foreigner reporters too. After filing stories about unrest in Syria, Reuters correspondent Berndt Debusmann was shot in the back by a gunman using a silencer-equipped pistol. BBC correspondent Tim Llewellyn was threatened by Syrian agents and fled Beirut before being harmed, as did CBS correspondent Larry Pintak. One of the Syrian regime's best informed and severest critics, the Frenchman Michel Seurat (pen name Gérard Michaud), was kidnapped in Lebanon and either executed or allowed to die by a terrorist group almost certainly working for Damascus.

Asad's efforts had obvious effect. Already in 1976, he decided the presidency of Lebanon. He backed Elias Sarkis in a variety of ways, perhaps the most effective of which was to hold the presidential election under the protection of his proxy troops, the Palestine Liberation Army (PLA) and Sa'iqa. As one account described the parliamentary meeting, reluctant deputies "were herded politely at gunpoint to the makeshift parliament building by the Syrian-backed Sa'iqa guerrilla organisation in order to cast their vote for Sarkis."[50] When Beirut proved inhospitable for Sarkis's inauguration, the ceremony was moved to Shtura, where it took place under the Syrian army's firm control. A telephone conversation that took place in October 1978 between Sarkis and Asad (at the time in East Berlin) conveys the reality of Syrian power:

Elias Sarkis   No government in the world can tolerate what is taking place—being buried alive. I would like a reply to my plan for the redeployment of the Arab Deterrent Force [the Syrian forces in Lebanon] and, to begin with, an immediate cease-fire.

Hafiz al-Asad   We are in the process of studying the redeployment plan. We would like to learn the opinions of the various parties to the Lebanese crisis.

Sarkis   But, after all, I am the head of state and the only spokesman for Lebanon! I do not accept that you deal with anyone other than myself.

Asad   Dear brother, these are not the sort of issues one discusses on the telephone. In two days I will be back in Damascus and you will be welcome to come and discuss the situation in all its aspects.[51]

In 1988, the Syrian government *officially* announced its opposition to the extension of President Amin Jumayyil's term in office for another two years.

Any important meeting of Lebanese politicians took place in Damascus or involved Syrian officials. The Syrian foreign minister sat in on the Geneva conference of Lebanese leaders in late 1983. Most importantly, Asad's opposition to the May 1983 accord between Lebanon and Israel led to abrogation of that accord within a year.

Asad had achieved the long-sought Syrian role as Lebanon's kingmaker, benefactor, and discipliner. All sides acknowledged Syrian power in Lebanon. An Israeli source observed that "nothing happens in the Bekaa Valley without Syrian approval."[52] Similarly, "You don't light a cigarette here without Syrian permission" was said to be a common saying in that valley.[53] A Lebanese politician told *The Washington Post* in mid-1984: "Make no mistake about it, the real government of Lebanon sits in Damascus these days, not in Beirut."[54] Antun Lahd, commander of the Army of Southern Lebanon, a militia sponsored by Israel, held that "all big and small decisions, whether crucial or mundane, are made in Damascus and then communicated to the Lebanese authorities."[55] Yasir 'Arafat mused that no one "can move in western Beirut without the knowledge and permission of the Syrian authorities."[56] According to 'Adnan Sa'd ad-Din, a leader of the Syrian Muslim Brethren, "there are no borders between Lebanon and Syria."[57]

So great was Syrian strength that Damascus induced Lebanese leaders to make public declarations on its behalf. After meeting with Hafiz al-Asad in late 1976, President-elect Sulayman Faranjiya and other Lebanese leaders reported how their country stood to gain from the establishment of Greater Syria: "After the West Bank is returned to its sons, its inclusion in a union will cause the Palestinian concentration in Lebanon to shrink."[58] Walid Junbalat spoke of preferring "the merger of the areas under our control with Syria" over a return to "a unified Lebanon under the 1943 formula."[59]

'Asim Qansuh, leader of the pro-Syrian wing of the Ba'th Party in Lebanon,[60] was the most explicit in favoring Syrian domination. He said that no Arab country had "the right to discuss the security and stability of Lebanon with the exception of fraternal Syria."[61] Arguing that "the reattachment of Lebanon to Syria offers a panacea to all the problems suffered by Lebanon,"[62] he expressed the belief that "a mistake was made when Syrian forces entered Lebanon and did not immediately announce Lebanese-Syrian unity."[63] He declared in August 1986 that "Lebanon's troubles will only end when it is united with Syria, thus restoring the situation to its normal historical course." Qansuh described the border between the two countries as "artificial."[64]

The National Union Front, a grouping of Syrian-backed Lebanese groups put the matter more delicately in its program of August 1985: "The real expression of Lebanon's Arab identity is its distinctive relationship with and decisive and unchangeable link to Syria."[65] A cable it sent the next day to Hafiz al-Asad amplified this link, calling for "a strong Pan-Arab relationship between Lebanon and Syria to coordinate the two countries' resources in foreign policy, defense, security, economy, education, and other fields."[66] Nabih Birri, a key participant in the National Union Front, later gave more details: "There must be integration with Syria, by means of actual agreements in the economic, security, military, political, information, and educational fields."[67]

Syrian efforts to impose an end to the fighting in Lebanon culminated with a pact signed by three Lebanese militia leaders in December 1985. Familiar Syrian goals emerged from the strange language of this document:

> The most prominent meaning of Lebanon's Arabism lies in its distinguished relationship with Syria. Proceeding from this principle, relations should be based on a strategic integration concept between Lebanon and Syria because their fateful issues are one as a result of their affiliation, history, and geography, a fact that requires a high degree of coordination in various fields.[68]

In short, the militia leaders accepted Syrian dominance.

The Syrian government has even forced Pan-Syrian ideology on those stalwarts of Lebanese separatism, the Lebanese Forces. In September 1985, the Executive Committee of the Lebanese Forces under Elie Hubayqa, hitherto one of the most anti-Syrian of the Maronite leaders, succumbed to this pressure. While in Damascus, his committee "stressed the importance of bolstering the distinguished relations with Syria stemming from the unity of fate, interests, history, and geography between the two countries." After the trip, the committee issued a statement recognizing "Syria's distinctive role in Lebanon."[69] Amin Jumayyil, president of Lebanon and an opponent of this accord, also had to recognize Syrian hegemony. He told an interviewer in February 1986 that "cooperation with Syria" was the second most important aspect of solving the Lebanese problem, following only the unity of the Lebanese themselves.[70] Perhaps the most startling call for Syrian control of Lebanon came from the Maronite patriarch, Nasrallah Butrus Sfayr, who called in late 1986 for a "union merger" (*wahda indimajiya*) with Syria, particularly in economics and trade.[71]

These statements suggested a wide acknowledgment that the return of public order in Lebanon depended on the actions of the Syrian government. This made it easier for some of Asad's enemies to accept his role in Lebanese affairs. But others continued to do their best to resist Asad. The Lebanese

Forces, the coalition of Christian militias, accepted in late 1985 the need for a Syrian-imposed agreement in Lebanon but retained its long-held suspicions of Syrian motives. A spokesman demanded "that the agreement's prelude be amended to emphasize that Lebanon is a UN member and that it abides by the UN Charter and the armistice agreement in the south. In this way Lebanon . . . will not lose its identity or fall under Syrian tutelage."[72] Implicit in this concern—as in the Alexandria Protocol more than forty years earlier—was the fear that Syria would absorb Lebanon.

The Syrian Social Nationalist Party

With the Asad government's adoption of Pan-Syrianism, the Ba'th and the SSNP cooperated as never before. After decades of competition, they worked out a mutually beneficial accommodation, whereby the SSNP became a client of the Syrian state.

This development may have had something to do with personal connections as well as ideological compatibility. The Makhlufs, the family of Hafiz al-Asad's wife Anisa, had a history of involvement with the SSNP. One of Anisa's relatives, 'Imad Muhammad Khayr Bey, was a senior SSNP official until his death in 1980. Rumor in Syria portrayed Anisa as sympathetic to the party and that she influenced Asad not just to cooperate with the SSNP but also to look favorably on Greater Syria schemes.

Not all elements in the SSNP accepted Syrian patronage, leading to a series of schisms that left the party split into several factions: Maoist, rightist (led by George 'Abd al-Masih), pro-Syrian, and pro-Libyan. In'am Ra'd headed the pro-Syrian faction for some years; then, under pressure from Damascus, 'Isam al-Mahayiri succeeded him in July 1984. Ra'd took his followers with him and established the pro-Libyan wing of the party.

Mahayiri, the scion of a prominent Damascus family and a lawyer, was the party's first Syrian-born and Muslim leader. He showed exceptional willingness to do Asad's bidding. Ra'd had been docile enough to let himself be trotted out for foreign visitors (such as Jesse Jackson when he visited Syria in January 1984), but Mahayiri proved even more submissive, traveling regularly to Damascus for consultations and directions. He was thought to take orders from the head of Syrian intelligence in Lebanon, Ghazi Kan'an, and sometimes from Hafiz al-Asad himself. The Israeli defense minister, Yitzhaq Rabin, characterized the SSNP in 1985 as "entirely under the control of Syrian intelligence."[73] Mahayiri was an honorary member of the Ba'th party and a "most welcome" visitor to Damascus.[74] He much understated the case when he observed that "our relations with the Syrian regime [and] the Ba'th Party . . . are good and are developing."[75]

Syrian help brought money and arms to the SSNP militia and permitted it to become a small but significant actor in the Lebanese civil war. The party opened offices and bases in the Syrian-controlled parts of Lebanon. One estimate put SSNP strength in 1975 at three thousand troops, a sizable number for

Lebanon. The party stored away impressive arsenals and established a naval unit. Also, the party controlled a portion of territory south of Tripoli, Lebanon. The party's clear hierarchy and strict discipline increased its effectiveness, leading one on-the-spot observer to call its militia "the strongest fighting unit" of the antigovernment forces and, following Al-Fat'h, the Christians' "most important opponent."[76] Though this is an exaggeration, the SSNP forces did gain in importance following the PLO's 1982 evacuation from Lebanon.

Syrian troops in Lebanon looked out for the interests of the SSNP; thus, they on one occasion arrested five members of Hizbullah on the charge of assassinating an SSNP official. According to the Phalangists, Syrian instructors ran a military training camp in Didda, Lebanon, for the SSNP. According to Hizbullah, the two staged joint military activities. According to Israeli intelligence, Syrian forces allowed the SSNP unusually free movement in Lebanon—all signs of close ties.

In addition to military help, alliance with Damascus permitted the SSNP to use state media to promote the Greater Syria message. This is what happened when Shawqi Khayrallah was engaged as a Syrian publicist. Khayrallah had been an editor of the SSNP magazine in 1945, and he conceived of the 1961 coup in Lebanon; in a word, Khayrallah personified Pan-Syrian ideology. In 1976, he began writing editorials for the state-run Syrian radio and newspapers promoting the concept of Greater Syria. He did not mince words, on one occasion calling for the integration of Lebanon "into a Levantine [*mashraqi*] Union, currently woven by Syria, Jordan, and [Palestine]."[77] On another, identifying himself as a "unionist Lebanese," he virtually begged Damascus for a "union with Lebanon."[78]

In return for this backing, the SSNP performed a number of services. It helped the Syrian cause by providing a friendly base for Syrian troops in its home area east of Beirut. Asad relied on his SSNP allies to undertake especially difficult operations in Lebanon. For example, he deployed SSNP troops against the Iranian-backed Hizbullah in June 1986. To ensure a favorable outcome, Syrian troops took up nearby positions and intervened when the SSNP needed help.

The party was also the only Lebanese group to look beyond the Israeli presence in Lebanon and call for strikes within Israel proper. Calling Zionism a "racist movement which seeks to destroy us completely as a nation," the SSNP declared itself "in a state of continuous war against Israel regardless of any possible Israeli withdrawals from Lebanon or the land of Palestine."[79] To demonstrate its hostility, the party sent off an occasional volley of Katyushas in the direction of Israeli forces. In July 1986, it joined with the Popular Front for the Liberation of Palestine in a sea-based attack on Israel.

Most importantly, the SSNP engaged in vital acts of terrorism. Ehud Ya'ari (who called the SSNP "the oldest terrorist organization in existence") saw the party as "Syria's most reliable instrument of terror [which] is employed for particularly sensitive and dangerous operations that are beyond the capabilities of the Palestinian terror groups headquartered in Damascus."[80]

Under the aegis of Asad Khardan, the party's "commissioner for security," suicide attacks proliferated. Indeed, a spokesman claimed that about one hundred young men and women had offered their services as suicide bombers and had even recorded video cassettes with their final testaments.[81]

Thus, the man arrested for killing President-elect Bashir Jumayyil in September 1982, Habib ash-Shartuni, was a member of the SSNP. The group that claimed to have bombed the U.S. Marine barracks in October 1983 proclaimed its support for Greater Syria, making it likely that the SSNP had some role in this blast.[82] The U.S. Federal Bureau of Investigation calculated that the organization undertook seven car bombings in Lebanon in 1985 and early 1986, killing 105 persons and injuring 378.[83] The SSNP claimed responsibility for eight of the eighteen suicide bombings directed against Israel in southern Lebanon between March and November 1985. These attacks not only contributed to the Israeli decision to quit Lebanon, but they had an important role in Lebanese politics: by showing that the Syrian government could match the ferocity of Shi'i fundamentalist attacks on Israel, they added to Damascus's stature.

The importance that Asad attached to suicide attacks was clear from the attention he paid them. He personally endorsed suicide efforts in a May 1985 speech.

> I have believed in the greatness of martyrdom and the importance of self-sacrifice since my youth. My feeling and conviction was that the heavy burden on our people and nation . . . could be removed and uprooted only through self-sacrifice and martyrdom. . . . Such attacks can inflict heavy losses on the enemy. They guarantee results, in terms of scoring a direct hit, spreading terror among enemy ranks, raising people's morale, and enhancing citizens' awareness of the importance of the spirit of martyrdom. Thus, waves of popular martyrdom will follow successively and the enemy will not be able to endure them . . . I hope that my life will end only with martyrdom. . . . My conviction in martyrdom is neither incidental nor temporary. The years have entrenched this conviction."[84]

With such sponsorship at the top, a cult of the SSNP suicides was perhaps inevitable:

> Schools, streets, squares, and public institutions throughout Syria are named after the suicide bombers, and the country's most popular singer, Marcel Khalifa, has recently monopolized the top spot in the hit parade with his anthem to the suicides. Video cassettes of the bombers' "wills" are available at sidewalk kiosks, and sales are consistently brisk.[85]

Interestingly—and consistent with SSNP ideology—some of the SSNP suicides came from Syria. When asked why he joined a Lebanese movement, one of the bombers answered, "Is there a difference between Lebanon and Syria?"[86] Conversely, a sixteen-year-old Lebanese girl who attacked an Israeli convoy in April 1985 with a booby-trapped car, killing herself and two Israeli soldiers, previously had made a videotape in which she sent greetings to "all the strugglers in my nation, headed by the leader of the liberation and steadfastness march, Lt. General Hafiz al-Asad."[87] She too saw Lebanon as part of Syria. Pointing to the SSNP as "responsible for staging spectacular attacks and suicide actions,"[88] Israel retaliated by destroying the SSNP headquarters in Shtura, killing somewhere between two and fifty party members.

The party engaged in especially delicate foreign operations. May Ilyas Mansur, an SSNP member, set off a bomb on a TWA airliner in April 1986 that killed four passengers. This operation was apparently connected to the attempt by Nizar al-Hindawi, also in April 1986, to place a bomb on an El Al plane leaving London. Three SSNP members attempted to smuggle explosives from Canada into the United States in October 1987; it was only because an alert policeman in a small Vermont town noticed something amiss that they were caught.[89]

The SSNP appeared also to provide services for Asad's ally, Mu'ammar al-Qadhdhafi. A member of the party shot the top Libyan diplomat in Lebanon, 'Abd al-Qadir Ghuka, in June 1983. He later told police that the Syrian secret service hired him for the attack at the behest of Qadhdhafi, who thought Ghuka intended to defect. Libyan money increased substantially in 1986; Qadhdhafi apparently hoped to use the party as Asad did, to shield him from direct responsibility for terrorist activities. This alliance became public in October 1987, when the SSNP announced that two-hundred and fifty of its members had signed up to fight for at least six months in Qadhdhafi's war against Chad. Libyan money and training were implicit conditions of this deal.

For its part, the SSNP was naturally delighted by the Syrian regime's turn to Pan-Syrianism; after decades of tension with Damascus, it finally found an ally there in a leader committed to Pan-Syrian ideology. The SSNP leadership praised "Syria's brotherly role and heavy sacrifices"[90] and concluded that Asad genuinely aspired to a Greater Syrian union. Obstacles that prevented the SSNP from getting close to King 'Abdallah were absent with Asad, for Asad's antimonarchical and anti-Western outlook brought him much closer to the SSNP ideology. But Asad also presented a far more formidable challenge to the party than did 'Abdallah.

In one sense, the SSNP in the 1980s became stronger than ever before. No longer did it have to hide and plot clandestine coups. Instead, it enjoyed the patronage of one of the most powerful Middle East states and found freedom to maneuver in Lebanon's anarchy. Syrian help transformed the party from a moribund relic to a dynamic force. David Roberts notes that "the latest information from Lebanon and Syria suggests that the party has if anything increased its influence."[91] Ehud Ya'ari writes that "men who had been forgotten since the 1940s or 1950s have recently reappeared in the role of mentors, political mummies come back to life. Slogans that had long faded or peeled off walls have been restored with fresh paint, and the aura of action that surrounds the SSNP is once again attracting young people to the symbol of the red hurricane."[92] The party also tapped new sources of members, including Shi'is, Druzes, and Sunnis; most important, it found support among younger Christians, including even some Maronites.

At the same time, the long-term implications of alliance with Syria appeared ominous for the SSNP; Asad's support had a steep price. He sought to bring the party under Damascus's control and make it a shell for Syrian agents and an instrument of Syrian policy. The potential danger was clear; by agreeing to work so closely with Syria's rulers, the party forfeited the strength that made it an important force over the decades—its visionary politics and fierce independence. Asad's success in dictating terms restricted the SSNP's capacity for autonomous action. If money and arms from Damascus allowed the SSNP to flourish temporarily, absorption by a police state rendered its future bleak. Alliance with Damascus contained the likely seeds of the SSNP's demise.

Perhaps aware of this, the anti-Syrian wing of the SSNP deposed 'Isam al-Mahayiri as party leader in January 1987. In a coup marked by SSNP factions shooting at each other near the party headquarters in West Beirut, Jubran Juraysh replaced Mahayiri and threatened to try him before the SSNP Higher Council. The revolt seems to have been specifically provoked by a Syrian effort to use the SSNP to fight its many enemies in Lebanon—Hizbullah, the Druze, the Palestinians, and the Sunnis. But Mahayiri called on his Syrian patrons and reestablished his position in September 1987. Despite this limited reassertion of the party's independence, its influence appears to lie mostly in the past.

Palestine

Words

The claim to Palestine had two parts. It began with a rejection of the PLO's right to lead the Arabs to Palestine. Asad broached an argument in 1976 that he used often thereafter: the PLO no longer acted in the best interests of the Palestinian people.

The Syrian government ascribed PLO failure to a variety of problems: loss of purpose ("I cannot imagine what the connection is between the fighting of Palestinians in the highest mountains of Lebanon and the liberation of Palestine"),[93] treachery ("'Arafat acceded to becoming a U.S. tool against Palestine and Palestinian rights"),[94] and cowardice ("'Arafat and his supporters actually wanted to leave Beirut on the first days of the [1982] war. We told them we were against their departure and advised them to stay and resist").[95] Echoing Israelis, the Syrian government declared that "Arafat represents only himself."[96] As a result of its misbehavior, the argument went, the PLO forfeited its right to lead the Palestinian cause or to claim Palestine.

The second part of the argument asserted why Syria—rather than Jordan, Egypt, or some other state—deserved to inherit the PLO role. The Asad government offered three complementary reasons to support this claim: devotion to Palestine, correct strategy, and geographic ties.

First, as the self-proclaimed "heart, mind, shield, and sword" of Palestine and "the main state of confrontation,"[97] Syria was the natural leader of the struggle against Israel. Damascus Radio waxed poetic on this subject, calling Syria "the defender of the Palestinian issue, the shelter of the Palestinian revolution, the refuge of the Palestinian strugglers, the lungs with which the Palestinian resistance breathes, and the arena which lovingly opens its doors, heart, and capabilities to the sons of the Palestinian people."[98] It concluded that "Syria will do everything possible to protect its self-defense, because to a great extent its self-defense embodies the entire Arab defense."[99]

Past, present, and anticipated sacrifices entitled Syria to a decisive role. ʿAbd al-Halim Khaddam, the deputy prime minister and foreign minister, argued in May 1983 that "Syria is more Palestinian than some of those who try to cast doubt on Syria's position."[100] Asad asked in January 1985: "How can the Palestine question not be ours, even though we are placing all of this country's human, military, economic, and political resources at the service of this question?"

Second, alone of the front-line states, Syria had the right strategy. Damascus remained resolute, even as other states one by one betrayed Palestine by accepting Israel's existence. Indeed, Asad took credit for preventing the PLO from appeasing Israel: "Had it not been for Syria, the PLO would have agreed to the Camp David plan."[101]

Third, and most importantly, Syrian leaders claimed Palestine as a geographic part of Syria. Hafiz al-Asad liked to startle Western visitors by telling them that "Jesus Christ was a Syrian Jew."[102] In a major speech in March 1974, Asad relaunched the "Palestine is Southern Syria" campaign. He stated that "Palestine is not only a part of the Arab nation, but a principal part of Southern Syria. . . . Palestine should remain a liberated part of our Arab homeland and of our Syrian Arab region."[103] (Jordan was clearly the less principal part.) This view was reaffirmed many times. A Baʿth Party official stated in May 1978 that "the Syrian citizen considers Palestine as Southern Syria [and] the Palestinian citizen considers Syria as Northern Palestine. Both of them believe that Palestine and Syria are part of one homeland. The false borders established by the Sykes-Picot agreement . . . are no longer acceptable. Therefore the question of Palestine is strictly a Syrian issue and [only secondly] an Arab security issue."[104]

In March 1980, the Syrian prime minister declared in an interview that "to Syria, the Palestine question is not just the issue of a fraternal people but a Syrian issue."[105] Asad stated in April 1980, "Palestine is ours and Jerusalem is ours."[106] Damascus Radio announced in June 1980 that "Syria views Palestine—according to historic, cultural, and geographic factors—as its own southern province."[107] A Baʿth Party official noted on Evacuation Day (which commemorates the French departure) in April 1983 that Syria "considers its true national day, the actual evacuation day, the day when the whole of Palestine is liberated from the desecration of Zionist occupation. . . . The real day is the day when the foreign Zionist colonialists depart from Southern Syria, from Palestine."[108]

On the basis of these three claims, the Syrian government asserted its foremost role deciding Arab policy with regard to Palestine. When Henry Kissinger, the American secretary of state, visited Damascus in February 1974,

Khaddam "could not forgo the opportunity to explain that historically Palestine had been part of Syria."[109] Shawqi Khayrallah, the SSNP figure, argued for the Syrian government that the return of the Palestinians must "be based on an understanding that Palestine is Southern Syria."[110] The Syrian prime minister, 'Abd ar-Ra'uf al-Kasm, asserted in January 1981 that "the Palestinian problem cannot be solved without those to whom the issue actually belongs: the Palestinians, together with the Syrians."[111] According to Jordanian sources, in July 1980, the Syrian foreign minister insisted that his government be included, along with Jordan and the PLO, on a committee dealing with the affairs of the "occupied homeland" in Palestine.[112]

Asad told a PLO meeting in April 1981, "Syria wants Palestine as much as it wants the Golan. . . . We want Palestine first and the Golan second."[113] In August 1982, a newspaper columnist called for a "total merger" of the PLO with Syria on the grounds that this would set the Arabs on "the unique path leading to the liberation of Palestine." He then referred to Palestine being Southern Syria as an "eternal fact."[114] Syria's foreign minister vowed to a Saudi audience in May 1983: "We cannot forget the Golan because for us it is like any part of Palestine."[115] In a bellicose speech of February 1986, Asad warned the Israelis that if they tried to annex the Golan Heights, "we will work to put the Golan in the middle of Syria and not on its borders."[116]

Most revealing were Syrian leaders' private conversations with other Arabs. In a meeting with the PLO in 1976, Asad referred to Palestine as Southern Syria and announced, according to Kamal Junbalat:

> You do not represent Palestine as much as we do. Do not forget one thing: there is no Palestinian people, no Palestinian entity, there is only Syria! You are an integral part of the Syrian people and Palestine is an integral part of Syria. Therefore it is we, the Syrian authorities, who are the real representatives of the Palestinian people.[117]

King Hasan of Morocco reported how Hafiz al-Asad in 1983 told a Moroccan delegation that he well understood the Moroccan annexation of the Western Sahara (an act rejected by most Arab leaders), "because Syria [too] was cut into pieces, and the real Syria is Greater Syria." A few months later, King Hasan reported, at the Rabat Islamic Conference of January 1984, Syrian foreign minister Khaddam announced that, "With regard the issue of Palestine . . . we have less freedom than the Palestinians themselves. There is not a young person, a child, a Syrian child in primary school, or a young Syrian at the university who does not dream of the great Umayyad state [when Damascus ruled a vast empire from India to Spain]." King Hasan described taking Khaddam aside and asking him, "What is this thing you have said and what is this hotheadedness?" Khaddam answered forthrightly:

> No, this is neither hotheadedness nor anything else. You have to know, Your Majesty, that the issue of the Umayyad state for us is [like] the issue of Sahara for you. . . . The sole interlocutor [for Palestine] is Syria. If the territories are returned, they will return to the Great Umayyad state.

Hasan summarized the Syrian viewpoint: "The territories which are occupied [by Israel] are not, according to Syria, to return to [those who live in] Gaza or the Golan or the West Bank, but all the occupied territories have to return to Syria." In short, Hasan explained, the Syrians believe that " 'the sole interlocutor is me, Syria'; if the territories are returned, they will return to the great Umayyad state."[118] The testimonies of Junbalat and Hasan provide valuable insights into the mentality of the Syrian leadership.

In addition, scholars also forwarded claims to Palestine. A major study about the Arabs under Ottoman rule published in Damascus in 1974 labeled a map of the region from the north of Lebanon to the southern end of the Dead Sea "the country of Southern Syria."[119] A 1982 book titled *Syria and the Palestine Case, 1920–1949* provided many examples of this approach:

> From the Umayyad and ʿAbbasid eras [i.e., since A.D. 681], Palestine has been a part of Syria, or Sham, and it remained so for long years, through Ottoman control [i.e., until 1918]. . . .
>
> Palestine was mentioned [by the Arab geographers) only as part of Syria or *Bilad ash-Sham*. . . . It is part of the Syrian soil and was never separated from Syria through its long history. . . .
>
> Syria comprised a geographic region larger than the political and geographic region known today as Syria. It included all of Lebanon, Jordan, Palestine, parts of southern Turkey, and the province of Alexandretta. It was a compact and integral unity, a single family within clear, marked boundaries. . . .
>
> The artificial entities [after World War I] were wholly consumed in solving internal problems, to the point that they disregarded the natural and essential goal of reestablishing the unity of *Bilad ash-Sham*. . . .
>
> *Bilad ash-Sham* is a geographic, cultural, and economic unit. Its land is one, as are its hopes and agonies. Its people are related, their blood racially inter-connected. Palestine is a beloved part of this land and Palestinians are dear to Syrians. . . .
>
> There is no favoring Damascus or Jerusalem, Aleppo or Hebron; they are all part of *Bilad ash-Sham*.[120]

The book repeatedly referred to Palestine as Southern Syria and equated the Republic of Syria with Northern Syria. Existing borders between the states of Greater Syria were dubbed "imaginary and artificial."[121]

Deeds

This barrage of words was supported by major efforts by Damascus to control the weak and fractured Palestinian organizations. Although the Syrian plan of attack versus Israel changed several times—from a war of "popular liberation" in the 1960s to "strategic balance" in the 1980s—it always implied Syrian domination of the Palestinians. In particular, Damascus did everything possible to foil Palestinian acceptance of a mini-state on the West Bank. The reason was obvious; such a polity, surrounded by Jordan and Israel, would be beyond Syria's reach and almost impossible for it to dominate. The more the PLO showed interest in a West Bank solution, the greater the antagonism between it and the Syrian regime.

Initially, when the PLO was founded in 1964 by Jamal 'Abd an-Nasir, it amounted to no more than his Palestinian auxiliary. Not wanting to be left behind, Syrian leaders responded by aiding a rival organization, Yasir 'Arafat's Al-Fat'h. Syrian support increased in 1966 after radical Ba'thists came to power in Damascus. When 'Arafat succeeded in finding support from Egypt—thus reducing Syrian influence over Fat'h—Damascus countered by establishing a counter-Fat'h organization and helping the Palestine Liberation Front, led by Ahmad Jibril, a former engineering officer in the Syrian army. Jibril's organization was briefly (December 1967–October 1968) part of the Popular Front for the Liberation of Palestine, before going its own way again as the Popular Front for the Liberation of Palestine–General Command (PFLP-GC). It continued to work closely with the Syrian government.

Ostensibly the conventional military wing of the PLO, the Palestine Liberation Army (PLA) came under Syrian influence after its establishment in 1964. The PLA's three brigades have actually been directly controlled by Arab governments. The Syrian Ministry of Defense ran the Hittin Brigade from 1964 (and used it to invade Jordan in 1970). The Qadisiya Brigade began as an Iraqi tool and passed under Syrian control in 1971. (The 'Ayn Jalut Brigade has always been under Egyptian control.) The full extent of Syrian control over its two PLA brigades became apparent in 1975–76, when, exactly in step with the Syrian government, they switched sides in the Lebanese civil war.

When Syrian forces first became directly involved in Lebanon in January 1976, they wore PLA uniforms. The camouflage fooled no one. Kamil Sham'un, Lebanese minister of the interior, declared that "forces of the Syrian Army have entered Lebanese soil." When asked why he had referred to the PLA as the Syrian Army, Sham'un explained:

> It is very hard to differentiate between the Syrian Army and those military formations which are commanded by a number of Syrian officers and in whose ranks an additional number of Syrian officers fight unofficially. Let us not forget that all of the equipment and military supplies are given by Syria. . . . It is perhaps less official than the aggression by the Syrian Army, but the result is exactly the same.[122]

Even Lebanese politicians friendly to Syria, such as Rashid Karami, consistently referred to PLA troops as Syrian, not Palestinian. The deception wore so thin that by July of that year Asad gave it up and instead boasted of his cleverness: "We decided to go in under the name of the PLA. The PLA began to go into Lebanon, and nobody knew of this. Those who are speaking now in the name of Palestine [i.e., 'Arafat] . . . did not know of the army until it was inside Lebanese territory. We did not consult them."[123]

But the Vanguards of the Popular War of Liberation (*Tala'i' Harb at-Tahrir ash-Sha'biya*), better known as As-Sa'iqa, served as Damascus's main Palestinian vehicle. A classified 1979 report by the Defense Intelligence Agency (DIA) dubbed Sa'iqa "a Trojan horse maneuvering for Syria within the Palestinian movement," and noted that its aims "at any given moment are identical with those of Syria. . . . All [Sa'iqa's] exploits in the Middle East and Western Europe were authorized, and perhaps planned, by the Syrian Army G-2 [intelligence]."[124]

Sa'iqa was established in September 1966 to amalgamate the Palestinian organizations sponsored by Syria. It soon became the second largest group in the PLO, with five thousand men by late 1968. When Asad took power, he purged Sa'iqa and imposed direct control over it by appointing his ally Zuhayr Muhsin, a long-term member of the Syrian Ba'th Party, to run Sa'iqa. Muhsin, who headed it from 1970 until his assassination in 1979, was described in the DIA study as "completely subservient to the Syrian government . . . a tool of Syrian policy."[125] In addition, members of the Syrian Ba'th Party (which had already acquired Pan-Syrian overtones) staffed most of the key positions in Sa'iqa. Further, the organization was reorganized in 1976 in ways designed to increase Ba'th party control over it.

Needless to say, the Syrian government footed the whole of Sa'iqa's expenses. Further, the Syrian army provided nearly all of its equipment, while the hierarchical structure reflected close ties with the army. Many of Sa'iqa's troops were Syrian citizens who signed up after finishing a regular tour of duty in the Syrian armed forces. Indeed, Syrians made up about 50 percent of the soldiers and 75 percent of the officers. Other members were Palestinians who grew up in Syria (and who in this way discharged their Syrian military obligations). Some of Sa'iqa's training took place at the Political Officers' Training School; Syrian army instructors taught them guerrilla tactics, codes, and how to handle antiaircraft equipment. After the 1967 war, two large army bases near Damascus controlled by the Syrian General Staff were made available for training Palestinian saboteurs.

Sa'iqa served Asad as an instrument to gain control over his two primary targets, the PLO and Lebanon. With regard to the PLO, Asad sought to make Sa'iqa the decisive group within that organization. In March 1975, he proposed "to establish a single Syrian-Palestinian political leadership [and] military command";[126] 'Arafat refused, rightly seeing this as an attempt by Asad to dominate the PLO. He turned down a similar offer in 1982. Asad sent troops against the PLO in Lebanon in 1976 to this same end. On several occasions, Asad tried to replace Yasir 'Arafat as head of the PLO with Zuhayr Muhsin. On one occasion, in April 1976, 'Arafat wrote of Syrian efforts to "liquidate the PLO and to set up Zuheir Mohsin . . . as leader of the [Palestinian] resistance."[127]

Asad also used Sa'iqa to dominate Lebanon. Its forces did his dirty work in May 1969, attacking customs houses and security posts. They attacked Lebanese army positions in April 1973. In March 1976, Lebanese president Sulayman Faranjiya requested Syrian protection; rather than overtly deploy Syrian army troops around the presidential palace (which would have disturbed Lebanese sensibilities), Syrian soldiers donned Sa'iqa uniforms and pretended to be Palestinians. A month later, when several thousand troops entered

Lebanon from Syria, Kamal Junbalat condemned the Syrian army for entering "under the veil of Saʿiqa."[128]

The total obedience of the PFLP-GC, the PLA brigades, and Saʿiqa to the Syrian government became apparent in May 1976, when these organizations fought with Syria against ʿArafat's PLO. The PLA had an especially prominent role; in effect, the uniformed military of the PLO was at war with the rest of the organization.

Damascus's efforts to arrogate the claim to Palestine for itself mostly took rhetorical and military forms. But in at least one case, it also had a legal form. A Syrian decree issued in October 1984 specified that the provisions allowing Syrian nationals to pay a cash substitute for military service also "shall be applied to Palestinian Arabs who, under the laws in force, are considered as Syrians." The laws in force permitted the cash substitute only to eligible men living outside Syria, Lebanon, Jordan, and Iraq. This meant that a Palestinian living in Jordan was legally liable to serve in the Syrian armed forces unless he paid his way out.[129]

Palestinian leaders dependent on Syria had to endorse Pan-Syrianism. The communiqué of the Conference of Palestinian Engineers, meeting in Damascus in 1974, "noted with honor and pride the statement of President Asad that Palestine is the southern part of Syria."[130] Zuhayr Muhsin, leader of Saʿiqa, agreed without reservation: "There are no differences between Jordanians, Palestinians, Syrians and Lebanese. . . . We are one people. Only for political reasons do we underline our Palestinian identity. . . . Yes, the existence of a separate Palestinian identity is there only for tactical reasons."[131] It is noteworthy that the Saʿiqa organization did not mention Palestine in its name; it argued that Palestine should not be independent but part of a larger Arab unit led by Syria. The Palestinian radio station in Damascus announced in June 1983 that Syria and Palestine shared the same destiny because they were both part of Greater Syria, the one being Northern Syria, the other Southern Syria.[132]

Most explicit and remarkable, however, were the statements by Sabri Khalil al-Banna, known as Abu Nidal, the extremist Palestinian leader who depended heavily on Syrian support. Although ostensibly a Palestinian nationalist, Abu Nidal repeatedly made Pan-Syrian statements. To take just two of them: "Palestine belongs to Syria. Like Lebanon, it will be part and parcel of it," and, "In the future, after its liberation, Palestine will be an integral part of Syria."[133] Abu Nidal explained his reasoning:

> I am an ardent believer in the Greater Syrian state. . . . We [Palestinians] are Syrian citizens. For us, Syria is the mother nation, it is history, society, community, geography. Until recently, half of Lebanon was a region of Syria. As you see, we are true Syrian citizens. I myself have Syrian parents.[134] . . . Greater Syria consists of Palestine, Iraq, Jordan, and Syria. A state like Jordan did not exist in Arab history prior to the twenties. Geographically seen, Greater Syria covers the territory from the Turkish border in the north to the whole of Palestine in the south.[135]

So great was Syrian pressure that even PLO leaders not living on money from Damascus sometimes proclaimed Pan-Syrian views that they could not possibly have held. Hani al-Hasan, an aide to Yasir ʿArafat, attributed a momentary improvement in Syrian-PLO relations in mid-1977 "to historic relationships between the Syrian group of nations, of which Palestine is the southern part."[136] In July 1980, three deported West Bank figures arriving in Syria declared that "Syria and Palestine form one state with one people."[137]

It is extremely unlikely that these views expressed Muhsin's, Banna's, or the others' true feelings; it is all the more impressive, then, that the Syrian authorities succeed in making these men support their ambitions. In large part, they did so by using intimidation.

Struggle

Not surprisingly, Syrian efforts to dominate the PLO led to constant tension between the two sides. Much of the time, Syrian conflict with the PLO was conducted in code. The PLO asserted its right to "independent decision making" on the basis of its national autonomy; the Syrians denied it on the basis of Arab or Syrian national rights. In fact, they were arguing over the PLO's right to act contrary to Syrian wishes. Thus, Khalil al-Wazir, a leading PLO official, stated in August 1985 that "the Syrian regime wants to seize the independent Palestinian decision making power. This is Syria's main obsession, because we refuse to be under its control and hegemony and because we say no to it."[138] Asad replied in code as well, accusing the PLO of "concocting a plot through the slogan of independent Palestinian decision making."[139] ʿAmid Khuli, editor of *Tishrin*, drew out the implications of this debate when he threatened to "amputate the fingers of whoever exercises decision making contrary to [the Syrian] course. We will not tolerate freedom to commit treason or to sell out the cause. Palestine is Southern Syria."[140]

Occasionally, the two sides blurted out what was really on their minds. ʿArafat said that Damascus "stabbed the Palestinian revolution in the back, tried to confiscate its arms and offices, and is trying to confiscate the revolution itself."[141] Faruq Qaddumi, the PLO "foreign minister," put it even more bluntly: the Syrian aim was "to take over the PLO."[142] Already in 1975, the Democratic Front for the Liberation of Palestine held that the Syrian objective was "to expunge the identity of the Palestinian people."[143] During a 1981 undercover war between Syria and the PLO in Austria, a PLO official candidly admitted that "Syria would love to see Israel wipe out the PLO. If only the political shell of the PLO remains, they will be able to fill it with their own men."[144] ʿArafat assessed the Syrian challenge to his control of the PLO two years later in a similar way: "All this is geared toward one thing: controlling the PLO and the Palestinian revolution."[145] In 1989, a PLO radio commentary put it very bluntly: "The Syrian president believes that Palestine is a territory owned by him, that he has created it."[146]

The Syrian government replied in kind, calling ʿArafat a "traitor," an "agent of Satan," and a "prostitute."[147] Wrapping itself in the Palestinian separatist flag, it accused 'Arafat of being "a U.S. tool against Palestine and Palestinian rights"[148] and planning "to blow up the PLO from within."[149] The breach also publicly exposed the threats normally made only in private. 'Asim Qansuh, head of the Syrian-dominated Ba'th Party in Lebanon, called for the "complete liquidation of all 'Arafatists."[150] Noting these tensions, Simon Malley, a French sympathizer of the PLO, wrote in October 1982 that every Palestinian not in Syrian pay "considers the 'Alawi government of Syria his worst enemy."[151] (Conversely, according to Defense Minister Yitzhaq Rabin of Israel, "the Syrians view the PLO as their No. 1 enemy, before Israel.")[152]

The Syrian government often manhandled Palestinian leaders who defied its wishes. When a 1966 effort to subject Fat'h to Syrian control failed, Asad had 'Arafat and other Fat'h leaders arrested. Though spared the death penalty, they spent more than one month in a Syrian prison. George Habash was jailed for more than seven months in 1968. Soon after coming to power, Asad had many of Sa'iqa's leaders arrested and brought the organization under the Syrian army's control. 'Arafat was hustled to the Damascus airport and forcibly put on a plane in 1983. Salah Khalaf of the PLO announced in October 1988 that four thousand Palestinians at that time were detained in "Syria's oppressive prisons."[153]

Syrian forces attacked 'Arafat's wing of the PLO on many occasions. The desire to reduce the PLO's stature was a principal reason for the Syrian invasion of Lebanon in 1976, as well as for all the subsequent interventions. Black June targeted 'Arafat during the summer of 1981 to bring the PLO under Syria's thumb. With greater success, Asad caused a split in Fat'h in May 1983 and dominated the anti-'Arafat faction that emerged in 1985 as the Palestinian National Salvation Front (PNSF)—based in Damascus, of course. With Libyan help, Syria eliminated the last independent PLO bases in Lebanon in late 1983. Starting in 1985, Syrian-backed Shi'i forces in Beirut repeatedly battered the PLO.

Abu Nidal and the PNSF assassinated a number of 'Arafat's men in Europe, including Na'im Khadir in Brussels, Majid Abu Sharar in Rome, and 'Isam Sartawi in Lisbon. A Palestinian with close ties to 'Arafat who edited an anti-Syrian weekly in Athens was shot three times from a yard away as he left his apartment building in September 1985. Two Palestinian groups based in Damascus claimed responsibility for the March 1986 assassination of Zafir al-Masri, the newly appointed mayor of Nablus; in the West Bank itself, however, many residents directly accused Syrian operatives of the crime. The shooting of a former mayor of Hebron and current member of the PLO Executive Committee, Fahd al-Qawasma, prompted bitter comments from 'Arafat. Addressing the dead man at his burial, he said: "The Zionists in the occupied territories tried to kill you, and when they failed, they deported you. However, the Arab Zionists represented by the rulers of Damascus thought this was insufficient, so you fell as a martyr."[154] A PLO radio broadcast described Asad's policy as one designed "to kill us as Palestinians."[155] One of

'Arafat's aides echoed this sentiment when he argued that crimes committed by the Asad regime against the Palestinian people "surpassed those of the Israeli enemy."[156]

Jordan

Syrian claims to Palestine extended also to Jordan. A Damascene daily reminded its readers in August 1985 that "from the viewpoint of history, geography, and struggle, Palestine is Southern Syria and Palestine is the two banks of the River Jordan."[157] Indeed, most of the Syrian discussion of Palestine as Southern Syria can be interpreted to include Jordan as well.

Some claims specifically addressed Jordan. President Hafiz al-Asad used Greater Syria as a stick to beat King al-Husayn in March 1980. "Who divided our country? Who fragmented our nation? Who divided Arab Syria and paved the way for the occupation of Palestine and the establishment of Israel? [Arab] reactionaries did all this, in collaboration with colonialism. In the recent past, this Arab Syria extended from Sinai to the Taurus Mountains. Who divided this Syria? Where is this Syria now?"[158] In November 1980, at a time of acute tension between Syria and Jordan, Syrian radio presented the dispute as "between one Arab people in Syria and Jordan and King Husayn's regime."[159]

In March 1981, the Syrians rejected the very existence of an independent Jordan. Calling Jordan an "artificial entity," one of the state-run Syrian papers argued that the territory Jordan controls "is the land of Syria, a part of natural Syria. History has never recognized the presence of an international, or even an administrative entity separate from Syria," making the Jordanian monarchy "illegitimate."[160] Foreign Minister 'Abd al-Halim Khaddam reminded an interviewer that "not long ago—and before the Sykes-Picot Agreement—the Jordanian people were always a part of us, and they will always remain so."[161]

Over and over, Syrian officials talked about the lack of difference between Syria and Jordan. For example, Asad made the following remarks during a period of great stress with Jordan in late 1980:

> The Jordanian army is our army. It includes officers, NCOs and soldiers who are our brothers and sons, exactly like our soldiers and officers. We do not distinguish between the Syrian and the Jordanian soldier. . . . Our Jordanian soldier is exacly the same as our Syrian soldier. . . . The Jordanian army is our army; the Jordanian people are our people. When we attack the Jordanian citizens, we attack the Syrian people; when we attack the Jordanian Army, we attack the Syrian Army.[162]

'Abd al-Halim Khaddam called the Jordanian monarchy an "alien" regime "which was imported from outside this country in order to be planted and to be a tool in the hands of the British and Americans." To impugn Husayn's legitimacy, Khaddam argued that the monarchy "remained alien to this nation" because "its heart and mind remained outside the boundaries of the homeland."[163] A newspaper editorial went further: "King al-Husayn's regime has switched loyalties from British imperialism to the CIA."[164]

Starting in early 1981, the Syrian government began a campaign calling for the overthrow of the Jordanian monarchy. It began obliquely; for example, an editorial on 18 February noted that disagreements between the two countries could not be overcome "except by putting an end to the agent instruments which foment sabotage campaigns and wallow in conspiracies."[165] Three days later, a commentary described Husayn's overthrow as "a pressing Pan-Arab responsibility."[166] In April 1981, the Syrian-backed Ba'th Party of Jordan called on the masses to establish "a democratic, progressive" government in Amman that would cooperate with Damascus.[167] Then, a few days later, Asad made a remarkably candid speech explicitly calling for the elimination of Jordan. That country, he said,

> was primarily established to dismember Syria. We and Jordan are one country, one people, and one thing. The British brought the grandfather of King Husayn, carved up a part of Syria for him and told him, "You are now prince of this piece of land. . . ." But have they been able to separate us from our people in Jordan? Certainly not. Our people in Jordan are a great, noble people. Nothing links them to that king. . . . The Jordanian people now have nothing to do with the decision made by the Jordanian regime. But the day will come, perhaps very soon, when the Jordanian people will regain their right to make decisions. . . . King Husayn will discover that we are one people and that his majesty was no more than a passing, dark and rainless cloud in our historic march.[168]

The Syrian government employed other methods of verbal attack on Jordan, asserting, for example, that the regime lacked the support "of even a minority of Jordan's masses for the acts it committed."[169] Asad even had the temerity to claim that "the Jordanian rule has led to the treacherous murder of hundreds of people from all sectors of the Syrian population. . . . Such acts had been unknown to Syria in its entire history."[170]

These statements in time of hostility provided the context for effusions when relations between Syria and Jordan were warm. On a visit to Jordan in June 1975, for example, Asad repeatedly asserted that "Syria and Jordan are one people and one country. We have been so in the past and we will, God willing, be so again in the future."[171] To anyone ignorant of Syrian intentions, this sounds like the standard (and therefore innocuous) rhetoric of Pan-Arabism; but to those familiar with Asad's Pan-Syrian irredentism, it signaled his real purposes. Jordanian officials were, of course, aware of this goal; accordingly, they shied away from all Syrian proposals that would have made integration between the two countries irreversible. When relations were at their warmest in 1976, however, rumors spread of a joint Syrian-Jordanian confederation that would dominate Lebanon and the West Bank.

Syria had many ways of pressuring Jordan. Backing the PLO, which threatened the Jordanian monarchy in the late 1960s, gave it one source of leverage. Direct military pressure offered another; in September 1970, Syrian armored units participated in the PLO revolt against the Jordanian government. In November 1980, Asad mobilized thirty-five thousand soldiers near the border with Jordan. The next month, Syrian jets attacked suspected Muslim Brethren bases in central Jordan. Asad exerted great power over Jordan by helping antigovernment elements within the country and threatening to use his much larger military forces.

Amman was subject to systematic use of terror by Damascus. Consider the following sequence. On 11 February 1985, King al-Husayn and Yasir 'Arafat announced an agreement that the Syrian and Soviet governments strongly opposed. Eleven days later, four months of terrorist attacks began, including a bomb at the American Research Center in Amman; an explosion in an airliner of the Jordanian carrier, Alia; a hand-grenade attack on Alia offices in Athens; a rocket attack on the Jordanian embassy in Rome; a rocket attack on an Alia plane in Athens; an Alia plane hijacked in Beirut and blown up; a bomb attack on Alia offices in Madrid; and the assassination in Turkey of a Jordanian diplomat who also happened to be the brother-in-law of the Jordanian commander-in-chief. Syrian agents also attacked Jordanian diplomats in India and Lebanon.

In response, a Jordanian radio commentary remarked that "the Damascus regime has set up special apparatuses for terrorism, assassination, and crime against those who oppose it in the Arab arena."[172] Jordanian radio had on an earlier occasion gone even farther: "The fascist sectarian regime in Syria is not satisfied with the slaughter of Syrian citizens domestically . . . but is creating armed terrorist groups whose aims are . . . to carry out its terrorist acts outside Syria and throughout the Arab arena."[173]

Asad's ability to get his way with King al-Husayn was dramatically demonstrated in November 1985, when the king wrote an open letter apologizing for Jordan's having harbored Syrian members of the Muslim Brethren. He also promised to throw them out of Jordan, which he did. Asad then rewarded Husayn with an invitation to Damascus, and this was quickly accepted.

Alexandretta and General Claims

Alexandretta continued to be shown on official Syrian maps as part of Syria. A Syrian general was quoted as pointing to this fact and then adding meaningfully: "Draw your own conclusions."[174] The region was mentioned occasionally as one of the Syrian territories to be regained; it was also portrayed as Syrian in a wide variety of contexts, such as news and weather reports. In an annual ritual, the Syrian government renewed its claim to Alexandretta on the anniversary of its loss of the province. 'Alawis made up about 12 percent of Alexandretta's population; the combination of their discontent under Turkish rule and the coming to power of 'Alawis in Damascus brought unrest to the province, much of it sponsored by Damascus. The troubles peaked in the late 1970s, leading to virtual civil war between the government and the local Ba'th Party, whose goal was to unite the province with Syria. A recent visitor noted a graffito in a poor quarter of Alexandretta, "Save us, O Hafiz [al-Asad]."[175] In preparation for the Mediterranean games of 1987, the Syrian government did succumb to Turkish pressure and printed a map showing Hatay within Turkey, but this was a one-time exception probably designed to insure Turkish participation in the games. Commenting on the event, State Minister Hasan Celal Güzel of Turkey noted: "We, on every occasion, remind Syria that Hatay is an inseparable part of Turkey and claims on this province damage Turkish-Syrian relations."[176]

Alexandretta is less than one-fifth the size of mandatory Palestine; so the fact that the Syrian foreign minister stated in 1980 that "Turkey usurped five times the area of Palestine from Syria" implies that Syria considers its "usurped" territory to include not just Alexandretta but an area twenty-five times its size, or the equivalent of England.[177] This is about the area of Turkey south of the Taurus and Anti-Taurus Mountains, the region that historically formed a portion of Greater Syria. Although this territory became part of the Turkish republic already in 1921, the Asad government apparently still considered it part of Greater Syria and therefore a lost province.

The statement by Muhammad Mashariqa, assistant regional secretary of the Ba'th Party, that Cyprus is the "heart" of the Middle East possibly harked back to Sa'ada's later view of Cyprus as part of Greater Syria.[178]

In addition to the region-by-region claims documented here, Damascus on occasion also asserted title to the whole of Greater Syria. On the eve of a visit by the Lebanese president to Damascus in August 1976, a newspaper noted that the two presidents would examine "new ties between Lebanon and its twin Syria, both those states' ties with their twin Jordan, as well as the ties of all these with their twin Palestine," and suggested the creation of a federal state for all four, with one army and one cabinet.[179] A few months later, a Syrian official included Alexandretta as well: "this steadfast region [Syria] lost its southern part—Palestine; Alexandretta has been detached, Lebanon and Jordan were taken away."[180] A Syrian official told a U.S. reporter in May 1981: "Surely everyone understands that all of Syria, Lebanon and Jordan are historically part of natural Syria."[181]

Syrian leaders sometimes discussed the history of Greater Syria and its divisions—pointedly, often when addressing a French audience. Just before President François Mitterrand arrived in Syria in November 1984 (the first visit ever by a French head of state to Syria), Hafiz al-Asad bitterly recalled that "when France entered our countries they were united; when it left, they were disunited."[182] Along similar lines, a Damascus newspaper declared it intolerable that "the Sykes-Picot logic of 1916 regain the upper hand and re-divide the [Greater Syrian] region."[183] A school textbook published in Syria in the early 1980s used the term *bilad ash-Sham* and referred disparagingly to Lesser Syria, Lebanon, Palestine, and Jordan as "mini-states" (*duwaylat*).[184]

Although Greater Syria existed for the most part in only a de facto manner, it did have some legal basis in Lesser Syria. For example, in September 1984, Hafiz al-Asad decreed cash an acceptable substitution for military service for those Syrian conscripts living outside Syria, unless the conscript lived in

Lebanon, Jordan, or Iraq. The exception of these countries implies that they in some manner form part of Syrian territory.[185]

Views on Syrian Intentions

Most knowledgeable observers agreed on the profound importance of Greater Syria for the government of Hafiz al-Asad. A prominent Syrian dissident, the former ambassador to Paris, wrote that "Asad's objective, even when he was but minister of defense [1966–70], was to inherit 'Abd an-Nasir's place in the Arab world, to create the Greater Syria which 'Alawis keep on dreaming about, and to group Jordan, Palestine and Lebanon under his banner."[186]

Lebanese across the political spectrum were convinced of Syrian ambitions toward their country. Major Sa'd Haddad, commander of a southern Lebanese militia, saw the Syrian goal as declaring Lebanon "an inseparable part of Greater Syria."[187] Accordingly, he believed that "Syria does not want to withdraw from Lebanon. Why? Because Syria came to Lebanon not to help this or that party. It entered Lebanon to annex it to Syria on the premise that Lebanon is part of Syria."[188] Haddad's successor, General Antun Lahd, assessed Syrian intentions similarly: "Syria is my foremost enemy. The Syrians have always wanted to annex or dominate my country."[189] Bashir Jumayyil charged that Damascus kept troops in Lebanon to make Lebanon part of Greater Syria. His brother Amin, the president of Lebanon during 1982–88, accused Asad of wanting to annex Lebanon.[190] Samir Ja'ja', the Phalangist military leader, feared that Syria "aims to reclaim Greater Syria and doesn't believe Syrian statements that Lebanon is a sovereign state."[191] Karim Paqraduni, deputy to Ja'ja', noted that "Syria has not been content with occupation. It has begun annexing occupied Lebanese territory."[192]

Kamal Junbalat, leader of the Lebanese Druze, was perhaps the political figure most willing to discuss the question of Pan-Syrianism (not surprisingly, as he wrote a book on the SSNP in the early 1950s). Junbalat believed that the Syrian authorities "do not want to forget the days before the divisions of 1919, when the people of Natural Syria—Lebanese, Palestinians, Jordanians, and Syrians—formed a single people." Although Junbalat satirically called Asad "the lion of Greater Syria," he professed to being unsure whether Asad would persevere in his Pan-Syrian project.[193] With regard to Palestine, "Syrians sometimes consider themselves the only legitimate representatives of Palestine, which is for them no more than the south of Natural Syria." Despite the ostensible Pan-Arabist outlook of the Ba'th politicians in Syria, "they believed and continue to believe that all Palestinians are part of the Syrian people, and Palestine is Southern Syria."[194] As for his own country, Junbalat observed that "in Damascus, they are always dreaming of Lebanon."[195]

The SSNP was also convinced that Syrian authorities were sincere on the issue of incorporating Lebanon. As one of them told an interviewer: "We cannot forget that Mr. Hafiz al-Asad—His Excellency the President of Syria— has declared many times that Lebanon is a part of Syria, that Palestine is a part of Syria. And if we believe that, and we have to—he has given all signs of being serious—it means that his interest in Lebanon is very genuine. He is playing the game very cautiously and intelligently."[196]

Crown Prince Hasan of Jordan, echoing these views, acknowledged Syrian hopes for a Greater Syria and observed that "the Syrians say there are no Palestinians, Jordanians, Lebanese—that they are all southern Syrians."[197]

The Palestinians also explicitly discussed Pan-Syrianism. An Arabic newspaper published in Jerusalem observed accurately: "Some say that the Syrian leaders want to revive the Greater Syria plan, provided it is 'made in Damascus'—having always rejected it in the past when it was 'made in Amman' or 'made in Baghdad.'"[198] At a time when the PLO operated out of Lebanon, Yasir 'Arafat argued that "the Syrian army wants to stay in Lebanon not to combat the Phalanges or defend the National Movement, but to dominate the PLO, and more especially Al-Fat'h."[199] 'Arafat's assistant Salah Khalaf maintained that Damascus aimed "to establish Greater Syria on the ruins of Lebanon."[200]

Egyptian leaders viewed Asad's ambitions in the same light. Anwar as-Sadat accused Asad (whom he often called "the lion of Greater Syria")[201] of starting the Lebanese crisis to create a Greater Syria. Husni Mubarak explicitly stated his opposition to Asad's Greater Syria plans. "For a Greater Syria to be established," he told a French newspaper, "Lebanon has to accept its [own] disappearance and Jordan has to accept its [own] disintegration. Lebanon and Jordan definitely cannot accept such a thing. Moreover, Egypt will absolutely not accept Lebanon and Jordan becoming part of Syria. Egypt is not alone in rejecting this; the whole Arab world will reject it."[202] Shortly after the Syrian invasion of Lebanon, the newspaper *Al-Ahram* published a political cartoon on this subject; it showed a fat figure with "Imperialism" written on it charming a cobra snake labeled "Suriya al-Kubra" arising out of a basket dubbed "Fascism." The humor lies in a pun: *Suriya al-Kubra* means both "Syria the Cobra" and "Greater Syria."[203] A dozen years later, an editorial in the same paper pointed to Syrian plans "to liquidate the Palestinian entity by dispersing it and annexing it to the plan of Greater Syria."[204]

Israelis of all persuasions agreed on Syrian intentions. Among Likud politicians, Yitzhaq Shamir stated in July 1983 that "Syria wants to control all of Lebanon and will not settle for the control it now has over a large part of this territory."[205] Moshe Arens repeatedly brought up this matter. He understood the Syrian objective in Lebanon to be "to control Lebanon and turn it into a satellite or perhaps a part of Greater Syria."[206] Benjamin Netanyahu wrote that the Syrian government had "methodically pursued" Greater Syria for decades.[207] A foreign ministry spokesman termed Syria's tactics for building Greater Syria "slicing the salami."[208] On the Labour side, Shimon Peres believed that Asad was "striving to attain leadership in the Arab world and to realize the age-old Syrian dream of a Greater Syria."[209] The president of Israel (and a former chief of intelligence), Chaim Herzog, termed these Pan-Syrian ambitions "most troublesome to Syria's Arab neighbors."[210]

Maurice Couve de Murville, a former prime minister of France, wrote that

"Greater Syria is an old matter which is not forgotten and doubtlessly will never be forgotten."[211] More forcefully, Claude Cheysson, the foreign minister, called the division of Lebanon between Greater Syria and Greater Israel "our nightmare."[212]

David Roberts, the British ambassador to Syria and then Lebanon, stressed the appeal of the Pan-Syrian dream:

> The theory of "Greater Syria" decisively influenced Syrian thinking in the crucial 1930s and has done so ever since. . . . The only consistent strand discernible throughout [the Asad] period has been the "Greater Syria" policy. . . . The residual concern, when everything else is stripped away, is Syrian determination to dominate the Levant, i.e. "Greater Syria." . . . It would be dishonest not to admit that the doctrine somehow expresses the feelings of almost everyone who has lived for any length of time in Syria. . . . The doctrine of "Greater Syria" is a powerful and active political myth." . . . [It] is endemic in Syrian politics and pervades Ba'thists of all complexions.[213]

According to *The Economist*, "a good many Syrians still cling to the doctrine of Greater Syria."[214]

Many senior American officials recognized the role of Pan-Syrianism in Asad's policy. Henry Kissinger concluded from his experience mediating between Syria and Israel that the "Syrians considered Palestine part of 'Greater Syria.'"[215] President Ronald Reagan noted Syrian ambitions on several occasions. He observed that "Syria for many years has talked about a thing called Greater Syria, in which they believe much of Jordan and much of Lebanon truly should belong to them."[216] At the same time, Secretary of State George P. Shultz contended that Syria "seems determined to make Lebanon once again a satellite or province of 'Greater Syria.'"[217] Other politicians also emphasized this ambition; for example, Congressman James H. Scheuer of New York called Greater Syria "a tenacious dream" of the Syrians.[218]

Specialists on Syria of varying viewpoints recognized the role of Pan-Syrianism. Fouad Ajami held that Asad's "vision of greater Syria" caused him to dismiss Palestinian nationalism no less than did the Likud Party of Israel.[219] Najib E. Saliba argued that "even after some 60 years of separation, it is still doubtful whether Syria has finally reconciled herself to the loss of [the four districts], or to the loss of all Lebanon for that matter."[220] Adeed Dawisha wrote:

> A fundamental motivation of Syrian policies toward Lebanon has been a conviction of the indivisibility of Syria and Lebanon. The concept of a "Greater Syria" continues to permeate the psyche not only of the Syrian political elite, but also, more broadly, of Syria's mass population. . . . And, generally, Syrians do tend to hold to the belief that their country's boundary with Lebanon was artificially drawn up by France to suit the latter's colonial ambitions and interests.[221]

Israel's two leading specialists on Syria concurred. According to Itamar Rabinovich:

Underlying the Syrian state's attitude to Lebanon was the view that the whole of Lebanon and, even more so, the territories added to it by the French in 1920 were part of Syria. The explicit Syrian demands to reintegrate Lebanon or parts of it faded during the years, but an implicit claim was maintained through the refusal to establish diplomatic relations with Lebanon.[222]

Similarly, Moshe Ma'oz wrote in his political biography of Hafiz al-Asad: "Although rejected by the Ba'th Party, which advocated pan-Arab unity, the notion of a Greater Syria has been revived in a different guise by Asad."[223]

In 1977, Patrick Seale, a British journalist close to the Asad government, wrote that Asad

sees Syria's immediate neighbors, Lebanon and Jordan, as a natural extension of its territory, vital to its defence. This three-nation grouping is already a *fait accompli*—although in the low-profile Assad manner, without fanfare. Assad now rules by proxy in Lebanon, while the progressive integration with Jordan is well advanced. If the Palestinians ever recover a West Bank homeland, they too will inevitably join this complex.[224]

Six years later he confirmed this assessment:

Every Syrian believes that the current boundaries of Syria are artificial and that it is the right of Syria to extend its terrain to include the whole land of Greater Syria [*Sham*]—that is, the whole eastern coast of the Mediterranean and the Jordanian desert. The notion of Greater or "Natural" Syria remains a powerful influence . . . [which] attracts many Syrians. . . .

There is no doubt that Hafiz al-Asad believes that active political decision making for the whole of the Arab East must be taken in Damascus alone. He refuses to recognize the right of Palestinians to independent decision making; this is the essence of his rivalry with Yasir 'Arafat. Nor does he concede this right to the Lebanese; this explains his rivalry with Beirut. And so too would he like to prevent King Husayn from exercising this right.

In the struggle with competing power centers of the region, the self-interest of Damascus demands the subjugation of the PLO, Beirut, and even Amman to the will of Syria. It should go without saying to note that the other sides refuse this point of view clearly and vehemently.

Lebanese believe that Syrian egoism sacrificed every opportunity to preserve their national unity. Many Palestinians, and especially on the West Bank, accuse Hafiz al-Asad of causing them to miss the last chance to save their land from Zionist imperialism.[225]

Annie Laurent and Antoine Basbous concluded a book analyzing Syrian and Israeli policies toward Lebanon with the observation that "Greater Syria, that is, the pure and simple annexation of Lebanon," was long the dream of Syrian rulers.[226] On her own, Laurent argued that "heir to this past and to this myth, Syria does not recognize the independence of Lebanon."[227]

Charles Saint-Prot declared that "for the Syrian rulers, the map of Palestine is too important to leave to the Palestinians alone; Palestine being the south of Greater Syria, they consider the Palestinian problem a Syrian problem. . . . [Asad] has shown himself more an adherent of Antun Sa'ada's theory of

Greater Syria . . . than the Ba'th's theory of Arab unity."[228] Dominique
Chevallier noted that "the Syrian Arab Republic does not forget 'Greater
Syria,' *Bilad ash-Sham,* an area in which it evaluates the consequences of every
event and for which it accepts no settlement without first assessing its own role
and giving its agreement."[229]

Similarly, Gudrun Krämer held: "Among other matters, the claim to control Lebanon and the national Palestinian movement is on the Syrian side
grounded in the fact that in Ottoman times most of Lebanon as well as Palestine and today's Jordan were economically and administratively part of 'natural Syria,' which in turn belonged to Greater Syria."[230]

Two of Damascus's guiding principles, according to John F. Devlin, are the
unimportance of Pan-Arabism and the claim that Greater Syria "is Syria's
special sphere of interest in which other states intrude only at the risk of Syrian
hostility."[231] The Marxist scholars who edit *MERIP Reports* interpreted the
Syrians' invasion of Lebanon in 1976 as a step toward the creation of "a
Syrian-dominated confederation including Jordan and Lebanon. The role of
the Palestinians . . . is to be no more than an adjunct to their diplomatic
maneuvers."[232] Naomi Joy Weinberger noted the constancy of Syrian efforts:

> Whether Syria's regional goals were cast in terms of a proposed federation, a
> "nucleus of confrontation," or a zone of influence, the intended components
> were always the same. Indeed, they were always identical geographically to
> the contours of the earlier Greater Syria scheme, except for ambiguity as to
> how much of Palestine could feasibly be incorporated.[233]

William Harris set out Asad's two "clear, unchanging" objectives in Lebanon
at the beginning of a detailed and knowledgeable survey on this subject:
"direct control over regions perceived as immediately critical for the security
and stability of Syria" and "stable decisive influence over a reformed central
government Beirut."[234]

While most observers condemned Syria's effort to establish rule over
Greater Syria, a few did approve. Mu'ammar al-Qadhdhafi was one:

> We support Syria if it annexes Lebanon tomorrow by any method. We will
> give it our total support without any argument. . . . When I say the unity of
> Syria and Lebanon, I do not mean the colonization of Lebanon by Syria or
> Syria's crushing of the Lebanese. . . . These are two states which can be placed
> within one state, as originally they were one. If Syria takes action, we must
> support it by all our means.[235]

'Abd as-Salam Jallud, Qadhdhafi's deputy, supported Syria's intervention in
Lebanon because this "will lead to the realization of Greater Syria."[236] A
Saudi weekly seemingly endorsed this view when it referred to "the south-
western part of Syria, known as Palestine."[237] Surprisingly, Kamal Junbalat,
the Druze leader assassinated by the Asad government, looked on Pan-
Syrianism with sympathy. "Can this tendency to seek the former provinces of
Historic Syria be called imperialism?" he asks. "Not entirely," came his
answer.[238] The capture of French citizens in Lebanon as hostages made Paris
tolerant toward Syrian goals in Lebanon. For example, President François

Mitterrand reportedly told Asad that "France respects and supports Syria's great and main role in Lebanon."[239]

Despite the voluminous record of Damascus's ambition, some observers have deprecated Asad's Pan-Syrian designs. A primitive version of this was heard fairly often from American diplomats. A senior State Department figure told Congress in October 1983, "I do not believe Syria has any intention of redrawing the political boundaries between it and Lebanon or any basic desire to absorb Lebanon. . . . Syria's interest in Lebanon is that it not be a threat to Syria."[240] Expressing the same thought more graphically, another U.S. official observed: "The Syrians in Lebanon are like a dog who has been chasing a car every day it comes down the street. Finally one day the dog catches the car and then he doesn't know what to do with it."[241] An official U.S. government study of Syria asserted that the Pan-Syrian ideology "has faded."[242]

The more sophisticated argument against Pan-Syrianism acknowledged its importance for Damascus but doubted whether efforts would really be made to implement this ambitious ideology. Moshe Ma'oz and Avner Yaniv presented this viewpoint at the end of a volume titled *Syria under Assad*.

> The standard articulation of Syria's long-term aspirations, be it by President Assad, one of his more prominent colleagues or through the official organs of the Ba'ath Party, suggests limitless or at least exceedingly far reaching goals. . . . Such statements of the country's goals imply a relentless drive towards the creation of a Greater Syria, to include Lebanon, the Alexandretta area, Jordan and Israel. . . . [But] none of the areas of Syrian activities discussed in this volume offers any evidence that such a grandiose dream is an accurate representation of Syria's *operational* goals.[243]

This is an odd conclusion in light of the fact that Damascus today occupies more than half of Lebanon, exercises great leverage over Jordan, dominates a major part of the PLO, and has virtually incorporated the SSNP. The inability to see these facts cannot be the result of equivocation by the Asad regime, which has boasted of its ambitions and pursued them with strategic vision. Why, then, such disbelief by well-informed and experienced observers?

The reasoning behind this may be found in another remark of Ma'oz, that Asad "does not aspire literally to recreate Greater Syria."[244] By this he meant that Asad does not intend to eradicate boundaries and incorporate neighboring states. Similarly, Lebanese foreign minister Elie Salim argued that Syria does not seek a Greater Syria, only influence over its neighbors.[245] True enough, but this is too absolute a definition of Greater Syria. A Syria in which Damascus enjoys predominant influence over Lebanon, Palestine, and Jordan is also a Greater Syria. Whether satrapy, protectorate, or satellite, the adjacent states would still be subject to Asad's wishes.

Some observers think only in terms of the formal eradication of state boundaries; in fact, almost the same degree of control can be attained without having to undo borders. Krämer put it well: "The Syrian leadership appears not to seek territorial expansion—the resurrection of the old Greater Syria— but regional hegemony."[246] Anything more than this would create too many troubles, as Harris noted:

> Syria's interests in Lebanon may not amount to anything as crude as the wish to annex Lebanon; this would be impossible within the Arab context and would ultimately be dangerous to Syria. Syria's interest, however, implies a very special understanding of such terms as "sovereignty" and "territorial integrity." To Damascus it is simply inconceivable that Lebanon, as a "twin state," should have a foreign and security policy which differs to any great extent from that of Ba'athist Syria. . . . Syrian leaders make no secret of their view that policy should be made in Damascus and followed in Beirut. As long as Lebanese politicians understand this fundamental of Syrian-Lebanese relations, Damascus is content to leave them their titles, their fiefdoms and their façade of national autonomy.[247]

An unnamed American diplomat in Damascus went a bit far when he argued that "One problem Washington has is that a lot of people [there] see Greater Syria as a notion involving territory. It is not a territorial concept."[248] Still, the emphasis on influence is a useful corrective, for Asad sought control, not a change in borders.

Paucity of imagination also accounts for the persistent disbelief about Syrian intentions. So seldom does one state explicitly state its intention to dominate its neighbors, as does Syria, that many analysts simply cannot put credence in this ambition. True, the grandiloquent declarations of military dictators should be assessed skeptically, but three considerations argue for taking Syrian claims seriously: the long record antedating Asad of desire for union, the Asad regime's statements and actions over more than a decade, and the consensus of informed observers from all parts of the political spectrum. Asad is closer today to putting Greater Syria together than any leader since Faysal in 1920. Noting how much Syrian attention is directed to expansion, and then factoring in the recurrent, repetitious, and consistent claim to control these areas, it is reasonable to deduce that Greater Syria has occupied a central place in Asad's foreign policy since 1974.

This conclusion raises several questions. Does Pan-Syrianism result from ideological conviction, Realpolitik, or some combination of the two? How much does Greater Syria inhere to Syrian political culture and how much is it tied to the specific policies of Hafiz al-Asad? Do motives behind Pan-Syrianism lie primarily in the realm of domestic or foreign politics? The final chapter takes up these issues.

4

Changes in Lesser Syria

Seen from Damascus, the doctrine of "Greater Syria" was never more relevant than it is today.

Ambassador David Roberts[1]

What accounts for the unexpected revival of Pan-Syrianism in recent years? Why did Hafiz al-Asad resurrect a seemingly moribund ideology?

In part, he did so because of changes on the ground. On the one hand, Asad came to power in 1970 and imposed, for the first time since independence in 1946, a strong, durable, and stable government on Syria. This then reopened the way to pursue the long-dormant goal of a united Syria. On the other hand, neighboring states turned inward. Lebanon experienced a complete breakdown of order; Egypt signed a peace treaty with Israel and dropped out of the inter-Arab arena; Iraq became wholly consumed by war with Iran; and the oil-exporting countries lost power as their revenues declined. Internal conflicts plagued the PLO. As Asad's rivals became preoccupied with other matters, the field opened to Syrian aggrandizement.

Political developments made Pan-Syrianism an operational ideology. But this was not enough, for the creation of an opportunity does not explain why it was exploited. Expansionist ambitions require political motivation. Here, several factors came into play:

The discrediting of Pan-Arabism. A series of events in the 1960s—the collapse of Syria's union with Egypt, Egypt's war in Yemen, and the Arabs' disastrous defeat by Israel in June 1967—dimmed the prospects of uniting the Arabs. This inaugurated a search for alternative allegiances which gained new support for many ideologies, including fundamentalist Islam, Palestinian nationalism, Egyptian nationalism, and Pan-Syrian nationalism.

Disappointment in other Arab leaders. Sadat's readiness to negotiate with Israel immediately after hostilities ended in 1973 undercut Damascus's harder-line position, leaving Asad in the lurch. Learning from this experience, Asad resolved to find new allies. Thus impelled, he sought to develop a regional axis around Syria that he could dominate and control. In this context, Greater Syria served as "a useful paradigm"[2] for the regional grouping Asad sought to build.

Asad's own outlook. Personally, Asad was drawn to the Greater Syria goal. Although little is known about Asad, several facts point to this conclusion. First, there is the cumulative record of his many Pan-Syrian statements, as noted in Chapter 3. Then there are his many connections to the SSNP: Asad grew up in a time and place when its ideology enjoyed great strength, his wife's family (the Makhlufs) had long-standing ties to the party, and Asad himself effected the conciliation between the SSNP and the government in Damascus that had eluded his predecessors.

The needs of domestic politics. The tensions—religious, ethnic, political, economic—that drove Syrian politics led the country's rulers to find a foreign policy that would do two things: facilitate their own grip on power and make their rule as acceptable as possible to the populace.

While all four of these factors undoubtedly encouraged Asad's turn to Greater Syria, I shall stress the last of them. The first three, important as they are, result from either external or personal considerations, and so are unlikely to drive the fundamental reorientation of a state's ideology. Rather, domestic factors usually determine the main directions in interstate relations. Other reasons can account for specific actions, but the central lines of a state's foreign policy invariably derive from the nature of its domestic life. This universal truth of politics—what the Germans call the *Primat der Innenpolitik*—has special validity for authoritarian states, which are typically preoccupied with retaining power; for them, international relations serve as a key vehicle for preserving control of the state.

Applying this rule to Syria under Asad suggests that the decisive explanation for the drive toward Greater Syria lies in the rulers' need to stay in power. Indeed, that is the thesis to be presented here.

To establish this point requires the reader's immersion in domestic Syrian politics, and especially in those exceedingly complex developments that took place between 1955 and 1974; it also requires an understanding of Sunni-'Alawi dynamics. I shall argue that the adoption of Pan-Syrianism took place in four stages:

1955–1958	Pan-Arabism preeminent
1958–1961	Disillusion with Pan-Arabism
1963–1966	Stress on Syria
1970–1974	Turn to Pan-Syrianism

Several writers have dealt very capably with first two stages,[3] so these shall be touched on only lightly here; in contrast, the third and fourth stages, which are more obscure, will be studied in some detail.

The exact process by which Asad adopted Pan-Syrianism is, unfortunately, something about which almost no direct information is available publicly. In contrast to earlier years, when a profusion of inside rumors, documents, and memoirs reached print, Syrian decision making in the Asad era is almost entirely closed to the outside world. Procedures in Damascus are as unknown as those of the Kremlin. The virtual absence of solid information makes it necessary to explain the turn toward Greater Syria from the outside, by looking at circumstantial evidence and other fragments of information.

Before beginning the story of the the rise of Pan-Syrianism, however, a few of Lesser Syria's population figures ought to be noted, for they provide the backdrop to much of the discussion that follows. In the 1980s, Sunni Muslims constituted about 68.9 percent of the population, Christians 14.1 percent, ʿAlawis 11.5 percent, Druze 3 percent, and Ismaʿilis 1.5 percent. The largest of the Christian groups, the Greek Orthodox, made up 4.7 percent of the total population. Linguistically, Syria was more homogeneous, with 82 percent speaking Arabic, 8 percent Kurdish, 4 percent Armenian, 3 percent Turkoman, and 3 percent Circassian. The Kurds, Turkomans, and Circassians, who together constituted 14.5 percent of the population, were virtually all Sunni Muslims. Their strong ethnic ties separated them, however, from the Arab Sunnis. Combining these figures, the Arabic-speaking Sunni Muslims made up about 54.4 percent of the population.

There was also a geographic aspect to Syria's divisions. Roughly 10 percent of the Sunni Arabs were Bedouin and had a different outlook and political needs; they should not be counted along with the sedentary Sunni Arabs. This left a core population of somewhat less than half Syria's populace.

The uneven distribution of some ethnic and religious groups enhanced their importance. Of Syria's thirteen provinces, Sunnis made up a majority in all but two, Latakia and Jabal Druze (now called Suwayda). In the first, ʿAlawis made up 62.1 percent of the population, and Greek Orthodox there numbered 12.8 percent. Druze dominated Jabal Druze with 87.6 percent, and Christians numbered 11 percent, leaving Sunnis with only 2 percent. While the many fracture lines among the populace affect public life in Syria, the one separating the ʿAlawis from the core population of sedentary Sunni Arabs has had during the past generation, as we shall see, the greatest importance.

The Need for an Ideology of Irredentism

Lesser Syria is a remnant, something that emerged after the powers delineated the boundaries of the neighboring regions. This fragmented piece of territory came into existence not for geographic or cultural reasons, nor because of actions taken by its residents, but as a result of European maneuvering. No one planned the Syria of San Remo,[4] and, at the moment of independence, less than half the population saw itself as Syrian Arab. This basic fact explained many of the country's key characteristics: its weak national identity, weak government legitimacy, frequent changes of government, military rule, hostility toward foreigners, communal tensions, the success of radical ideologies, and irredentism.

Weak loyalties. Attachment toward the Syrian state is weak. Especially in the first years after independence, virtually all its citizens actively disdained their state and sought something else. Sunnis had designs on the territories of the country's five neighbors. Members of the SSNP wanted Lesser Syria submerged in Greater Syria. Baʿthists wanted it joined to a single Arab nation. ʿAlawis hoped to retain their independence or associate with Lebanon. Druze sought autonomy or a deal with Transjordan. Unpoliticized elements disliked the random boundaries because they restricted trade, family communications, and the like. As a Bedouin told a researcher in the early 1950s, "Though I have a Syrian passport—still I don't feel I am so."[5] Even the head of state deprecated the republic of Syria, and he expressed his feelings publicly. Adib ash-Shishakli referred to Syria in October 1953 as "the current official name for that country which lies within the artificial frontiers drawn up by imperialism"[6]—a remarkable statement for a president to make. A placard on the Syrian side of the border with Lebanon expressed this sentiment most concisely: "We make war on frontiers" (*muharib al-hudud*).[7]

The disaster of unity with Egypt between 1958 and 1961 and the passage of time reduced this sense of artificiality, to be sure, but it was never entirely overcome. Even today, residents of Syria continue to see their polity as a temporary rump unit and do not wish to devote their energies, much less their lives, to it.

Weak government legitimacy. The unwillingness of citizens to offer their allegiance to the government undermines the central government's claim to legitimacy. This has had two clear consequences: political instability and military rule. Weak legitimacy reduces the political leaders and to a great extent explains why Syria became the banana republic of the Middle East. Twenty-one changes of government occurred in the twenty-four years between 1946 and 1970 (including three in one year and a regime which lasted only several days). It also explains why soldiers came to power in 1949 and then dominated almost every subsequent Syrian government. Military rule remained even after 1970, when instability had been mastered.

Xenophobia. The Levant's division embittered Sunni relations with the outside world. Sunnis felt betrayed by Britain for cutting Greater Syria in half, setting up a Jewish homeland in Palestine, splitting Jordan off, and letting the French vanquish Faysal in Damascus. They hated the French for destroying the Syrian Kingdom, giving so much territory to Lebanon, dividing the Syrian remnant into ethnic states, and then transferring Alexandretta to Turkey. They resented Turkey for taking Alexandretta. They responded angrily to Prince 'Abdallah's attempts to move his throne to Damascus and feared Iraqi efforts at union. They saw the Zionists as usurpers in a key part of Syria. By 1946, Syrian Sunnis felt betrayed by the minorities, all their neighbors, and both great powers. Nothing in subsequent years diminished this feeling.

This long list of evildoers helps explain the negative cast of Syria's foreign policy. Resentments run deep, xenophobia outweighs patriotism, conspiracies are suspected, and the outside world is mistrusted. After many talks with Syrian leaders, Henry Kissinger concluded that "the injustice of foreigners is burned deep into the Syrian soul. Asad said to me that Syria had been betrayed before World War I by Turkey, after it by Britain and France, and more recently by the United States, which had created the State of Israel. When a people is convinced that all its troubles come from abroad, morbid suspicion becomes a national style."⁸ This factor goes far to explain the bellicose edge of Syrian foreign relations.

Sunni-minority tensions. The French colonial experience in North Africa predisposed French administrators in the Levant to expect unmitigated hostility from Sunni Muslims. To balance this antipathy, they sought to build a counterweight to the Sunnis by establishing close relations with the minority communities. The minorities were encouraged to think that their interests ran contrary to those of the Sunni Arabs. French ties with them were cemented through a policy of favoritism. Minorities paid lower rates of taxes while having more spent on their welfare. Maronites, ʿAlawis, and Druze received autonomous areas of their own; because these made it possible to escape Sunni domination, they quickly acquired real political popularity and importance. Official languages in the minority states revealed French intentions: in Damascus and Aleppo, Arabic was the only official language; in Lebanon, Arabic was the first official language and French the second; in Latakia and Jabal Druze, French was equal with Arabic.⁹

In return for these benefits, the minorities served France faithfully. ʿAlawis, Armenians, Assyrians, Circassians, Druzes, Ismaʿilis, and Kurds joined the French in the Troupes Spéciales du Levant, numbering about fifteen thousand by the mid-1930s. Armenian soldiers served the mandate against Druze rebels with such ferocity, the latter complained to the French in February 1926.¹⁰ Some Maronites celebrated every year the anniversary of the French victory in July 1920 over Prince Faysal. Druze and ʿAlawis did all they could to hold on to their own districts when incorporation of their areas into the Sunni territory appeared likely in 1936. The former toyed with joining Prince ʿAbdallah; the latter rebelled against Sunni rule.

The minorities' embrace of French rule provoked a powerful reaction from Sunni Arabs. Not only did Sunnis have to suffer the ignominy of rule by foreign Christians and endure the indignity of having their domain, the whole of historic Syria, subdivided, but, to make matters worse, the minorities escaped their grasp and gleefully profited from French rule. Minorities also began to act with a new and, for Sunnis, most distasteful self-assurance. In short, minority complicity with the imperial rulers added new political differences to the already existing religious ones. *La politique minoritaire* worked.

French success in exacerbating communal tensions spawned twofold problems for Syria when the country became independent. First, Sunnis remembered and resented the minorities' behavior—their good relations with the French, their willingness to do the colonialists' dirty work, and their readiness to exploit the boundaries put in place by Paris. Second, ʿAlawis and Druze felt only weak allegiance to the Syrian state (though Sunni suspicions about the minorities maintaining ties to France after independence were unfounded). Many events, especially the post-1946 minorities' rebellions, expressed this alienation.

Radical ideologies. Surmounting the citizens' weak loyalty to the state has been the Syrian leaders' most persistent and urgent political challenge. This problem has been exacerbated by the other factors noted above—the state's instability, the persistence of military rule, and tensions between Sunnis and non-Sunnis. It explains two other characteristic elements of Syrian political life, radical ideologies and irredentism.

Syrian citizens aspire to replace Lesser Syria's arbitrary, truncated form with something grander and more inspiring; at the same time, their strongest commitments go to their ethnic or religious group. The state, unloved, sits in between. To establish a viable state, the government in Damascus needs goals capable of attracting long-hostile communities. Mere maintenance of order and protection of the citizenry does not suffice; rulers must find ambitious projects to legitimize themselves by dislodging old affiliations and winning loyalty.

A comparison with Egypt highlights the Syrian rulers' predicament. With its five thousand years of history, Egypt is a polity that has a meaning for its residents and does not depend on the actions of politicians. Egyptians know what country they belong to, regardless of who the rulers are or what policies they pursue. Freed from the obsessive worry of defining national identity and borders, Egyptian leaders can devote themselves to governing. In contrast, a hole in the map came to be the republic of Syria, and its raison d'être must constantly be addressed. To make matters worse, whereas Egypt has a homogenous population, Syria's is extremely varied. Far more than Egyptian leaders, therefore, Syrian leaders must fit their actions within an ideological context.

Irredentism. The rulers therefore adopt irredentist goals. The sense of injustice that pervades Lesser Syrian political culture makes bellicosity against neighbors an easy way for them to gain popularity. And pervasive communal tensions within Syria make external adventure the one dependable glue. Together, these make ideological irredentism the almost inevitable recourse of an unpopular Syrian state.

In brief, ideology and irredentism compensate for arbitrariness. Ideology attracts the citizenry by endowing the government with moral purpose; pushing back the borders promises meaningful territory. Over the years, Syrian leaders have come to depend heavily on these essential activities; thus they tend to rely on radical programs domestically and aggressive behavior abroad. Indeed, efforts to remake society and expand territorially began right after World War I and have remained long-term features of Lesser Syrian politics.

Best of all, of course, is a project that combines these two—a radical ideology calling for an expansion of Syrian power. Pan-Syrianism and Pan-Arabism both fulfill these criteria. Not surprisingly, each of the two has played a very large role in the public life of modern Syria.

Initially the two were rather similar and the delineation between them was vague. Both held Syria to be the heart of any unification efforts, and they aspired to comparable boundaries. But the emergence of a Ba'thist version of Pan-Arabism—advocating a larger version of Pan-Arabism—shattered this harmony. Indeed, the Ba'th Party took on an anti–Pan-Syrian cast in the course of its long rivalry with the SSNP. In the 1950s, politically minded Syrians had to choose between the two ideologies, and most opted for the Baʿth vision. Its heyday was from 1955 until 1958.

From Baʿth to Neo-Baʿth

Led by the Baʿth Party,[11] the Syrian government began seeking a union with Egypt as early as 1955. But Jamal ʿAbd an-Nasir, Egypt's charismatic ruler, accepted its offer only three years later, and even then he required the Syrians to submit to many conditions. One of these was that all Syrian political parties dissolve themselves, and so eager was the Baʿth Party for union that it agreed to this act of political suicide. Less than three weeks of discussions were needed to create a joint political structure, and the United Arab Republic (UAR) came into existence in February 1958. The UAR was the vehicle of some very high hopes; many observers saw it as the first step toward an all-Arab union.

But the experiment came quickly to grief, in large part because ʿAbd an-Nasir monopolized power and excluded the Syrians. In the words of a later report, the "officers and civil servants of the Egyptian intelligence service turned up in every directorate"[12] in Syria. As a result, Syrians came to see the UAR less as a union of two countries than as a disguised form of Egyptian imperialism. Discontented elements in Syria included businessmen, who suffered from nationalization; politicians, who lost power; and military officers, who seethed under Egyptian dominance.

After a long three and a half years, a group of conservative Syrian officers regained independence for their country in September 1961 by seceding from the UAR. The United Arab Republic had both consummated and destroyed Baʿth hopes. When the party reconstituted itself in 1961, its new leadership differed from that before 1958 in several ways: it was minority by confession, military by profession, and anti–Pan-Arab unity by ideology. Each of these changes is worth noting in detail.

Minorities

The UAR experience sobered many Pan-Arabist enthusiasts, dashing their expectations that quick moves could achieve Arab unity. But whereas some Sunnis continued to seek union with other Arab states, nearly all the minorities lost interest in this goal.

The UAR fulfilled the minorities' worst fears about Pan-Arabism. Egypt's tens of millions of Sunni Arabs far outnumbered the heterogeneous Syrian population, and ʿAbd an-Nasir ran roughshod over minority sensibilities. The union led to an increase of Sunni power within Syria proper, to the virtual exclusion of the minorities. In contrast to their usual 20 percent of the cabinets (both before and after the union with Egypt), minorities nearly disappeared from the four Syrian cabinets of the UAR years. For minorities, Pan-Arabism meant being swamped. To make matters worse, while UAR regulations prohibited free travel by Syrians to Lebanon for work, Egyptian peasants gained the right to emigrate to Syria.

Even those minority elements who were Ba'thists had a change of heart and turned against 'Abd an-Nasir with anger. Their reaction had great importance because minorities began to take hold of the Ba'th in 1961. They rose to power in two parallel but separate ways—one civilian, the other military.

The UAR debacle transformed the Ba'th Party. The membership was alienated by the leaders' hasty and unilateral disbanding of the party in 1958 (to comply with 'Abd an-Nasir's conditions for union),[13] a decision that looked even more foolish as the union soured. Held responsible for the failed union, the party lost ground among the Syrian population at large. In the 1959 elections, for example, it won only about 100 out of 9,445 seats. The leadership further disgraced itself by dithering and contradicting itself on the issue of Syrian secession from the UAR, some welcoming it, others rejecting it. Disillusioned with democratic methods, Ba'th leaders turned their organization into a dictatorial party of the vanguard type.

When the union ended in 1961, these developments deeply affected efforts to reconstitute the party. While many Sunni Ba'thists had drifted away, minority members, especially those in the more remote provinces, remained faithful and kept the party structure intact when the formal apparatus had disappeared. Thus, as Ba'thism lost appeal to the general population, its branches in rural and minority areas filled with members who had lost interest in Pan-Arabism. This was especially the case in Latakia, the predominantly 'Alawi area.

The Military Committee

Minorities also gained strength through the Ba'th Party's military wing. Again, the UAR stimulated these changes. 'Abd an-Nasir transferred five hundred Syrian officers to Egypt, hoping this would keep them out of harm's way. Instead, a group of the officers formed the small, clandestine Military Committee (*al-Lajna al-'Askariya*) of the Ba'th Party in 1959. This committee, which developed in complete isolation from the party hierarchy in Syria, reflected the peculiar composition of officers belonging to the party. All five of its original members were of minority origins. The three top figures (Muhammad 'Umran, Salah Jadid, and Hafiz al-Asad) were 'Alawis, while the other two ('Abd al-Karim al-Jundi and Ahmad al-Mir) were Isma'ilis. When the committee was expanded, the Fatimiya minorities ('Alawis, Isma'ilis, and Druze) filled nine of the fourteen positions, and five of those were 'Alawis.

Although the Military Committee came into existence to reassert Syrian independence, it had no role in the secession from the UAR. The committee gained strength only after the Ba'th Party came to power in the coup of March 1963.

By discrediting the civilian leaders of the party, the UAR disaster had the effect of boosting military officers, and these eventually took their place. The thinkers, politicians, and party activists who dominated before 1958 had almost disappeared by 1966. Syria's Regional Command, for example, included no soldiers before 1960; after that, they increasingly dominated it. Indeed, every Ba'thist officer who played a major role between then and 1970 had been a member of the Military Committee, and its three founders dominated Syrian politics in the quarter-century after 1963.

Regionalism

Syrian leaders need irredentism and ideology; so when the UAR soured Pan-Arabism for Syrians, another vision had to take its place. Ba'thists split between those (such as the party founders Michel 'Aflaq and Salah ad-Din al-Bitar) who remained faithful to Pan-Arabism and those (including the Military Committee leaders) who stressed the importance of Syria. The former came to be known as Nationalists (*Qawmiyun*), the latter as Regionalists (*Qutriyun*). Regionalists made Syria (not the Arab nation) their primary field of action. Indeed, they concentrated so intensely on Syria that 'Aflaq, the Ba'th ideologue, accused them of working for a provincial separatism (*iqlimiya*) resembling that of the SSNP.[14] Sati' al-Husri, the theoretician of Pan-Arabism and keeper of its flame, wrote disapprovingly about "the strange matter of Ba'thists taking up Syrianism" after 1961.[15]

The regionalist heresy tended to attract minorities; Sunnis tended to stick with Pan-Arabism. Not surprisingly, the Military Committee, with its mostly minority makeup, opted for regionalism. This began a self-perpetuating cycle: as the Ba'th Party's change attracted more minority members, Sunnis found the party less appealing. Nonetheless, the turn toward Syria appears to have been in tune with the general mood in Syria, for the travails of union with Egypt strengthened the sense of a Syrian identity. Many Syrians who had abandoned their dream of immersion in the Arab nation found an attractive substitute in the Syrian nation. Those who had previously dismissed the existing polity as meaningless newly appreciated it.

Disillusion with Pan-Arabism was expressed as early as August 1960, when the Ba'th Party's Fourth National Congress stated, in the party's characteristically stilted language that "in the minds of a part of the people [a circumlocution for the minorities], the concept of Pan-Arabism is associated with Islamic sectarianism and subordination to the United Arab Republic [i.e., Egypt]."[16] Ba'th leaders also codified the party's shift from Pan-Arabism. Ambitious Ba'th rhetoric about the "eternal mission" of the unified Arab nation gave way at that meeting to modest talk of confederation between existing Arab states. The congress declared it sufficient to "work for Arab unity as an ultimate goal, and not as a political plan intended for immediate execution."[17] The decision to downplay Pan-Arabism was confidential at the time, and, although published in a volume of documents in Beirut in 1965, it appears to remain to this day little known to the Syrian public.

For a substitute political ideology, the Regionalists chose radical social transformation. This became clear at the party's Sixth National Congress in October 1963, when the central Ba'th goal was officially changed from Pan-

Arabism to a form of Leninist socialism. A key document, *Some Theoretical Propositions*, made this new priority explicit: "Socialism is the true goal of Arab unity. . . . Arab unity is the obligatory basis for constructing a socialist society."[18] In other words, Pan-Arabism was to be the means; economic and social transformation was the end.

From 1963 on, Pan-Arabism no longer drove the Ba'th Party in Syria. Avraham Ben-Tzur dubbed the party that came out of all these alterations the Neo-Ba'th, a useful term, for the party had changed in every respect. John F. Devlin explained:

> The Ba'th Party, which started with unity as its overwhelming top priority, which was prepared to work within a variety of Middle Eastern political systems, which wanted social justice in the society, had pretty much disappeared by the early 1960s. In its place arose Ba'th organizations which focused primarily on their own region, which advocated, and created where possible, authoritarian centralized governments, which rested heavily on military power and which were very close to other socialist movements and were less distinctively Ba'thist.[19]

Munif-ar-Razzaz, a disillusioned Ba'thist, noted that it was widely believed that the Ba'th Party ruled Syria; but, after 1961, there were actually two parties— "the military Ba'th Party and the Ba'th Party, and real power lay with the former."[20] Razzaz further argued (as paraphrased by Martin Seymour) that the military Ba'th

> was and remains Ba'thist only in name: that it was and remains little more than a military clique with civilian hangers-on: and that from the initial founding of the Military Committee by disgruntled Syrian officers exiled in Cairo in 1959, the chain of events and the total corruption of Ba'thism proceeded with inexorable logic.[21]

Further changes in government only confirmed the evolution away from Pan-Arabism. Salah ad-Din al-Bitar observed, with reason, that the 1966 coup "marked the end of Ba'thist politics in Syria."[22] Michel 'Aflaq put the same sentiment more pungently: "I no longer recognize my party!"[23] Most of the decisions reached in 1963 remained in place a quarter of a century later, though Asad abandoned the goal of a radical social and political transformation.

The shift away from Pan-Arabism began in 1958 and was effectively completed eight years later. Other changes during this turbulent period included the ending of democratic elections, the radicalization of politics, and the political rise of two new elements—the armed forces and the 'Alawi community. It remains to be seen how Pan-Syrianism became the ideology of the Syrian state between 1970 and 1974.

The 'Alawi Heresy to 1920

By 1966, Syrians had become disillusioned with Pan-Arabism and turned to Lesser Syria. But what caused them to turn to Pan-Syrianism? The fourth and last stage in the evolution from the Arab nation to the Syrian nation remains to be accounted for. A theoretical explanation is not hard to find, for (as noted earlier) the political culture of Syria requires a combination of radical ideology and irredentist claim. Therefore, when Pan-Arabism had been discredited, Pan-Syrianism was the only alternative doctrine that could fully replace it.

How specifically did this shift come about? What was the mechanism of change? Disaffection of the Syrian populace from their ʿAlawi-dominated government appears to have been the major factor. Therefore, to understand the political dynamics of the period after 1966, it is vital to appreciate the place of the ʿAlawi religion in Syria, the historic relations between Sunnis and ʿAlawis, and the twentieth-century ascent of the ʿAlawis. Profound changes in ʿAlawi-Sunni relations established the context for Syrian public life in the 1970s; and so, before proceeding with the rise of Pan-Syrianism in the Asad era,[24] we first turn back several hundred years and consider the ʿAlawis' place in politics, then follow their changes through the twentieth century.

People and Faith

ʿAlawi is the term that ʿAlawis (also called ʿAlawites) usually apply to themselves; but until 1920, they were known to the outside world as Nusayris or Ansaris. The change in name—imposed by the French upon their seizure of control in Syria—has significance. Whereas Nusayri emphasizes the group's differences from Islam, ʿAlawi suggests an adherent of ʿAli (the son-in-law of the Prophet Muhammad) and accentuates the religion's similarities to Shiʿi Islam.[25] Consequently, opponents of the Asad regime habitually use the former term; supporters of the regime use the latter.

ʿAlawis today number approximately 1.3 million, of whom about a million live in Syria. They constitute nearly 12 percent of the Syrian population. Three-quarters of the Syrian ʿAlawis live in Latakia, a province in the northwest of Syria, where they make up almost two-thirds of the population.

ʿAlawi doctrines date from the ninth century A.D. and derive from the Twelver or Imami branch of Shiʿi Islam (the sect that predominates in Iran). In about A.D. 859, one Ibn Nusayr declared himself the *bab* ("gateway to truth"), a key figure in Shiʿi theology. On the basis of this authority, Ibn Nusayr proclaimed a host of new doctrines[26] which, to make a long story short, make ʿAlawism into a separate religion. According to Ibn Kathir (d. 1372), where Muslims proclaim their faith with the phrase "There is no deity but God and Muhammad is His prophet," ʿAlawis assert "There is no deity but ʿAli, no veil but Muhammad, and no *bab* but Salman."[27] ʿAlawis reject Islam's main tenets; by almost any standard they must be considered non-Muslims.

Some ʿAlawi doctrines appear to derive from Phoenician paganism, Mazdakism and Manicheanism. But by far the greatest affinity is with Christianity. ʿAlawi religious ceremonies involve bread and wine; indeed, wine drinking has a sacred role in ʿAlawism, for it represents God.[28] The religion holds ʿAli, the fourth caliph, to be the (Jesus-like) incarnation of divinity.[29] It has a holy trinity, consisting of Muhammad, ʿAli, and Salman al-Farisi, a freed slave of Muhammad's. 'Alawis celebrate many Christian festivals, including Christmas, New Year's on 1 January, Epiphany, Easter, Pentacost, and Palm Sunday. They honor many Christian saints: St. Catherine, St. Barbara, St. George, St. John the Baptist, St. John Chrysostom, and St. Mary Magdalene. The Arabic equivalents of Christian personal names such as Gabriel, John, Matthew, Catherine, and Helen are in common use. And 'Alawis tend to show more friendliness to Christians than to Muslims.

For these reasons, many observers, especially missionaries, have suspected the 'Alawis of a secret Christian proclivity. Even T. E. Lawrence described them as "those disciples of a cult of fertility, sheer pagan, antiforeign, distrustful of Islam, drawn at moments to Christianity by common persecution."[30] The Jesuit scholar Henri Lammens unequivocably concluded from his research that "the Nusayris were Christians" and that their practices combined Christian with Shi'i elements.[31]

The specifics of the 'Alawi faith are hidden not just from outsiders but even from the majority of the 'Alawis themselves. In contrast to Islam, which is premised on direct relations between God and the individual believer, 'Alawism permits only males born of two 'Alawi parents to learn the religious doctrines. When deemed trustworthy, these are initiated into some of the rites at sixteen to twenty years of age; other mysteries are revealed later and only gradually. Religious secrecy is strictly maintained, on pain of death and being reincarnated as a vile animal. Whether the latter threat is made good, mortals cannot judge, but the first certainly is. Thus, the most renowned apostate from 'Alawism, Sulayman Efendi al-Adhani, was assassinated for divulging the sect's mysteries. Even more impressive, at a time of sectarian tension in the mid-1960s, the suggestion that the 'Alawi officers running the country publish the secret books of their religion caused Salah Jadid to respond with horror, saying that, were this done, the religious leaders "would crush us."[32]

Women do most of the hard labor; they are prized "precisely because of the work they do that men will not do except grudgingly, finding it incompatible with their dignity."[33] Women are never inducted into the mysteries ("Would you have us teach them whom we use, our holy faith?")[34]; indeed, their uncleanliness requires their exclusion from all religious rituals. Females are thought to retain the pagan cult of worshipping trees, meadows, and hills, and to have no souls.[35] In all, women are treated abominably; but one consequence of this disrespect is that they need not be veiled and enjoy greater freedom of movement than do Muslim women.

Unveiled women and several other 'Alawi practices—in particular, that wine drinking is permitted and that some ceremonies take place at night—long excited Muslim suspicions about 'Alawi behavior. Then, too, the obsessive secrecy inherent in the religion suggested to many Sunnis that the 'Alawis had something to hide. But what? Over the centuries, the Sunnis' imaginations supplied a highly evocative answer: sexual abandon and perversion.

Thus, the theologian al-Ash'ari (874–936) held that 'Alawism encouraged male sodomy and incestuous marriages, and the founder of the Druze religious doctrine, Hamza ibn 'Ali (d. 1021), wrote that 'Alawis consider "the male member entering the female nature to be the emblem of their spiritual doctrine."[36] Accordingly, 'Alawi men freely share their wives with coreligionists. These and other accusations survived undiminished through the centuries and even circulated among Europeans.[37] A British traveler of the early 1840s, who was probably repeating local rumors, wrote that "the institution of marriage is unknown. When a young man grows up he buys his wife."[38] Even 'Alawis believed in the "conjugal communism" of their religious leaders.[39] Such calumnies remain a mainstay of the anti-'Alawi propaganda circulating in Syria today.

Although the charges are false, 'Alawis do reject Islam's sacred law, the Shari'a, and therefore indulge in all manner of activities that Islamic doctrine strictly forbids. 'Alawis ignore Islamic sanitary practices, dietary restrictions, sexual mores, and religious rituals. Likewise, they pay little attention to the fasting, almsgiving, and pilgrimage ceremonies of Islam; indeed, they consider the pilgrimage to Mecca a form of idol worship. "Spiritual marriages" between young (male) initiates and their religious mentors probably lie at the root of the charges of homosexuality.

Most striking of all, 'Alawis have no prayers or places of worship; indeed they have no religious structures other than tomb shrines. Prayers take place in private houses, usually those of religious leaders. The fourteenth-century traveler Ibn Battuta described how they responded to a government decree ordering the construction of mosques: "Every village built a mosque far from the houses, which the villagers neither enter nor maintain. They often shelter cattle and asses in it. Often a stranger arrives and goes to the mosque to recite the [Islamic] call to prayer; then they yell to him, 'Stop braying, your fodder is coming.'"[40] Five centuries later another attempt was made to build mosques for the 'Alawis, this time by the Ottoman authorities; despite official pressure, these were deserted, abandoned even by the religious functionaries, and once again used as barns.

Beyond specific divergences, nonconformity to the Shari'a means that 'Alawi life follows its own rhythms, fundamentally unlike those of Muslims. 'Alawis do not act like Sunni Muslims, with only slight differences; rather, they resemble Christians and Jews in their pursuing a wholly distinct way of life. Matti Moosa noted that, "like the other extremist Shiites . . . the Nusayris had total disregard for Muslim religious duties."[41] Ignaz Goldziher put it succinctly: "This religion is Islam only in appearance."[42] It is important to make this point very clear: 'Alawis have never been Muslims and are not now.

Yet, as Ibn Battuta's account suggests, there is a permanent inconsistency in the 'Alawi wish to be seen as Muslim. In his case, it was mosques built and then neglected; at other times, it is some other half-hearted adoption of Islamic ways. 'Alawis have a long history of claiming Islam when this suits their needs and ignoring it at other times. In short, like other sects of Shi'i origin, 'Alawis practice *taqiya* (religious dissimulation). This might mean, for example, praying side by side with Sunni Muslims but silently cursing the Sunni caliphs. The apostate 'Alawi, Sulayman Efendi al-Adhani, recounted having been sworn to dissimulate about his religion's mysteries.[43] An 'Alawi saying explains the sentiment behind *taqiya*: "We are the body and other sects are but clothing. However a man dresses does not change him. So we remain always Nusayris, even though we externally adopt the practices of our neighbors. Whoever does not dissimulate is a fool, for no intelligent person goes naked in the market."[44] Another 'Alawi phrase expresses this sentiment succinctly: "Dissimulation is our righteous war!" (*al-kitman jihadna*).[45]

A British traveler observed in 1697 that the 'Alawis are

> of a strange and singular character. For 'tis their principle to adhere to no certain religion; but camelion-like [*sic*], they put on the colour of religion, whatever it be, which is reflected upon them from the persons with whom they happen to converse. . . . No body was ever able to discover what shape or standard their consciences are really of. All that is certain concerning them is, that they make much and good wine, and are great drinkers.[46]

A hundred and fifty years later, Benjamin Disraeli described the 'Alawis in a conversation in the novel *Tancred*:

> "Are they Moslemin?"
> "It is very easy to say what they are not, and that is about the extent of any knowledge we have of them; they are not Moslemin, they are not Christian, they are not Druzes, and they are not Jews, and certainly they are not Guebres [Zoroastrians]."[47]

Sulayman Efendi al-Adhani explained this flexibility from within:

> They take on the outward practices of all sects. If they meet [Sunni] Muslims, they swear to them and say, "We are like you, we fast and we pray." But they fast improperly. If they enter a mosque with Muslims, they do not recite any of the prayers; instead, they lower and raise their bodies like the Muslims, while cursing Abu Bakr, 'Umar, 'Uthman, and other [major figures of the Sunni tradition].[48]

Taqiya permitted 'Alawis to blow with the wind. When France ruled, they portrayed themselves as lost Christians. When Pan-Arabism was in favor, they became fervent Arabs.[49] More than ten thousand 'Alawis living in Damascus pretended to be Sunnis in the years before Asad came to power, only revealing their true identities when this became politically useful.[50] During Asad's presidency, concerted efforts were made to portray the 'Alawis as Twelver Shi'is.

Relations with Sunnis

Mainstream Muslims, Sunni and Shi'i alike, traditionally disregarded 'Alawi efforts at dissimulation; they viewed 'Alawis as beyond the pale of Islam—as non-Muslims. Hamza ibn 'Ali, who saw the religion's appeal lying in its perversity, articulated this view: "The first thing that promotes the wicked Nusayri is the fact that all things normally prohibited to humans—murder, stealing, lying, calumny, fornication, pederasty—are permitted to he or she who accepts ['Alawi doctrines]."[51] Abu Hamid al-Ghazali (1058–1111), the Thomas

Aquinas of Islam, wrote that the 'Alawis "apostacize in matters of blood, money, marriage, and butchering, so it is a duty to kill them."[52]

Ahmad ibn Taymiya (1268–1328), the still highly influential Sunni writer of Syrian origin, wrote in a *fatwa* (religious decision) that "the Nusayris are more infidel than Jews or Christians, even more infidel than many polytheists. They have done greater harm to the community of Muhammad than have the warring infidels such as the Franks, the Turks, and others. To ignorant Muslims they pretend to be Shi'is, though in reality they do not believe in God or His prophet or His book." Ibn Taymiya warned of the mischief their enmity could do: "Whenever possible, they spill the blood of Muslims. . . . They are always the worst enemies of the Muslims." In conclusion, he argued that "war and punishment in accordance with Islamic law against them are among the greatest of pious deeds and the most important obligations" for a Muslim.[53]

From the fourteenth century on, Sunnis used the term *Nusayri* to mean pariah. 'Alawis had had no recognized position in the *millet* (sectarian) system of the Ottoman Empire. An Ottoman decree from 1571 notes that "ancient custom" required 'Alawis to pay extra taxes to the authorities and justified this on the grounds that 'Alawis "neither practice the fast [of Ramadan] nor the ritual prayers, nor do they observe any precepts of the Islamic religion."[54] Sunnis often saw food produced by 'Alawis as unclean and did not eat it. According to Jacques Weulersse, "no 'Alawi would dare enter a Muslim mosque. Formerly, not one of their religious leaders was able to go to town on the day of public prayer [Friday] without risk of being stoned. Any public demonstration of the community's separate identity was taken as a challenge [by the Sunnis]."[55]

Sunnis were not alone in reading 'Alawis out of Islam—mainstream Shi'is did likewise. And 'Alawis in turn saw both groups as deficient.

> Sunni heresiographers excoriated Alawi beliefs and viewed the Alawis as disbelievers (*kuffar*) and idolators (*mushrikun*). Twelver Shi'i heresiographers were only slightly less vituperative and regarded the Alawis as *ghulat*, "those who exceed" all bounds in their deification of Ali. The Alawis, in turn, held Twelver Shi'is to be *muqassira*, "those who fall short" of fathoming Ali's divinity.[56]

There was one exception to this consensus that 'Alawis were not Muslims. Toward the end of the nineteenth century, as Christian missionaries began taking an interest in the 'Alawis, Ottoman authorities tried to bring them into Islam. The French already had special ties to their fellow Catholics, the Maronites, and the authorities in Istanbul feared a similar bond being created with the 'Alawis. So they built mosques in the 'Alawi areas, built schools to teach Islam, pressured 'Alawi religious leaders to adopt Sunni practices, and generally tried to make the 'Alawis act like proper Muslims. This isolated case of Sunnis reaching out to 'Alawism came to an end after a few decades and had very little impact on 'Alawi behavior.

The Islamic religion reserves a special hostility for 'Alawis. Like other post-

Islamic sects (such as the Baha'is and Ahmadis), they are seen to contradict the key Islamic tenet that God's last revelation went to Muhammad, and this Muslims find utterly unacceptable. Islamic law acknowledges the legitimacy of Judaism and Christianity because those religions preceded Islam; accordingly, Jews and Christians may maintain their faiths. But 'Alawis are denied this privilege. Indeed, the precepts of Islam call for apostates such as the 'Alawis to be sold into slavery or executed. In the nineteenth century, a Sunni shaykh, Ibrahim al-Maghribi, issued a *fatwa* to the effect that Muslims may freely take 'Alawi property and lives; and a British traveler records being told, "these Ansayrii, it is better to kill one than to pray a whole day."[57]

Frequently persecuted—some twenty thousand were massacred in 1317 and half that number in 1516[58]—the 'Alawis insulated themselves geographically from the outside world by staying within their own rural regions. Jacques Weulersse explained their predicament:

> Defeated and persecuted, the heterodox sects disappeared or, to survive, renounced proselytism. . . . The 'Alawis silently entrenched themselves in their mountains. . . . Isolated in rough country, surrounded by a hostile population, henceforth without communications with the outside world, the 'Alawis began to live out their solitary existence in secrecy and repression. Their doctrine, entirely formed, evolved no further.[59]

E. Janot described the problem: "Bullied by the Turks, victim of a determined ostracism, fleeced by his Muslim landlord, the 'Alawi hardly dared leave his mountain region, where isolation and poverty itself protected him."[60] In the late 1920s, less than half of one percent lived in towns, just 771 'Alawis out of a population of 176,285.[61] In 1945, just 56 'Alawis were recorded living in Damascus[62] (though many others may have been hiding their identity). For good reason, "the name Nusayri became synonymous with peasant."[63] The few 'Alawis who did live away from their mountains routinely practiced *taqiya*. Even today, 'Alawis dominate the rural areas of Latakia but make up only 11 percent of the residents in that region's capital city.

Centuries of hostility took their toll on the 'Alawi psyche. In addition to praying for the damnation of their Sunni enemies, 'Alawis attacked outsiders. They acquired a reputation as fierce and unruly mountain people who resisted paying the taxes they owed the authorities and frequently plundered Sunni villagers on the plains. John Lewis Burckhardt observed in 1812 that those villagers "hold the Anzeyrys [Ansaris] in contempt for their religion, and fear them, because they often descend from the mountains in the night, cross the Aaszy ['Asi, or Orontes River], and steal, or carry off by force, the cattle of the valley."[64]

Matters seemed to be even worse in 1860, when Samuel Lyde added that "nothing is thought of thus killing a Mussulman as a natural enemy, or a Christian as an unclean thing."[65] About the same time, a British travel-guide writer warned of the cool reception to be expected from the 'Alawis: "They are a wild and somewhat savage race, given to plunder, and even bloodshed, when their passions are excited or suspicion roused." With wonderful understatement, the author concluded, "their country must therefore be traversed with caution."[66]

'Alawis retreated to the mountains because of persecution; they then remained there, shielded from the world at large, lacking political power beyond their region's confines, isolated from the larger polities around them, almost outside the bounds of historical change. The survival well into the twentieth century of archaic practices made the 'Alawi region (in Jacques Weulersse's turn of phrase) a "fossil country." Little changed in that country because "it is not the Mountain that is humanized; man, rather, is made savage." 'Alawis suffered as a result: "the refuge they had conquered became a prison; though masters of the Mountain they could not leave."[67]

Governments had difficulty subduing the 'Alawi territory; indeed, it only came under Ottoman control in the late 1850s. Pacification of the region then led to Sunni economic inroads and the formation of an 'Alawi underclass. As badly educated peasants lacking in political organization or military strength, 'Alawis typically worked farms belonging to Sunni Arab landlords, receiving but a fifth of the produce. Ottoman agents would often exact double or triple the taxes due in the Latakia region.

'Alawis were so badly off after World War I that many of the youth left their homeland to work elsewhere. Sons left to find menial labor or to join the armed forces. Many thousands of daughters went off at the age of seven or eight years to work as domestics for urban Sunni Arabs. Because many of them also ended up as mistresses (one estimate holds that a quarter of all 'Alawi children in the 1930s and 1940s had Sunni fathers),[68] both Muslims and 'Alawis saw this practice as deeply shameful. In some cases, daughters were even sold. It is no exaggeration to say, as does one indigenous historian, that 'Alawis "were among the poorest of the East."[69] The Reverend Samuel Lyde went even further, writing in 1860 that "the state of ['Alawi] society is a perfect hell upon earth."[70]

The political effects of poverty were exacerbated by the nature of these divisions, which followed geographic and communal lines. Sunnis who lived in the towns enjoyed a much greater wealth and dominated the 'Alawi peasants. Jacques Weulersse described in 1934 how each community "lives apart with its own customs and its own laws. Not only are they different but they are hostile . . . the idea of mixed marriages appears to be inconceivable."[71] In 1946, he added that "the antagonism between urban and rural people goes so deep that one can almost speak of two different populations co-existing within one political framework."[72] A generation later, Nikolaos van Dam observed, "Urban-rural contrasts were sometimes so great that the cities seemed like settlements of aliens who sponged on the poverty-stricken rural population. . . . In the course of time, the Alawi community developed a strong distrust of the Sunnis who had so often been their oppressors."[73] This 'Alawi resentment of Sunnis has proven enormously consequential in recent years.

The Rise of the 'Alawis, 1920–1970

The 'Alawis' ascent took place over the course of half a century. In 1920, they were still the lowly minority just described; by 1970, they firmly ruled Syria. This stunning transformation took place in three stages: the French mandate (1920–46), the period of Sunni dominance (1946–63), and the era of 'Alawi consolidation (1963–70).

The French Mandate, 1920–1946

According to Yusuf al-Hakim, a prominent Syrian politician, the 'Alawis adopted a pro-French attitude even before the French conquest of Damascus in July 1920. "The 'Alawis saw themselves in a state of grace after hell; accordingly, they were dedicated to the French mandate and did not send a delegation to the [General] Syrian Congress."[74] So intensely did they oppose Prince Faysal, the Sunni Arab ruler of Syria in 1918–20 whom they suspected of wanting to dominate them, that they launched a rebellion against his rule in 1919, using French arms. According to one well-informed observer, the 'Alawis cursed Islam and prayed "for the destruction of the Ottoman Empire."[75] General Gouraud received a telegram in late 1919 from seventy-three 'Alawi chiefs representing different tribes, who asked for "the establishment of an independent Nusayri union under our absolute protection."[76]

Two years later, the 'Alawis rebelled against French rule under the leadership of Salih al-'Ali, an event that the Asad government has proudly pointed to as an anti-imperialist credential. But a close look[77] suggests that the revolt had more to do with the fact that the Isma'ilis had sided with France; given the state of Isma'ili-'Alawi relations, this led to hostilities between the 'Alawis and the French. As soon as the French authorities granted autonomy to the 'Alawis, they won 'Alawi support.

Indeed, the establishment of French rule after World War I benefited the 'Alawis more than any other community. French efforts to cooperate with the minorities meant the 'Alawis gained political autonomy and escaped Sunni control; the state of Latakia was set up on 1 July 1922. They also gained legal autonomy; a 1922 decision to end Sunni control of court cases involving 'Alawis transferred these cases to 'Alawi jurists.[78] The 'Alawi state enjoyed low taxation and a sizable French subsidy. It also acquired its own flag and postage stamps. Not surprisingly, 'Alawis accepted all these changes with enthusiasm. As an anti-'Alawi historian later put it, "At the time when resistance movements were mounted against the French mandate, when Damascus, Aleppo, and the Hawran witnessed continuous rebellions on behalf of Syrian unity and independence, the Nusayris were blessing the division of the country into tiny statelets."[79]

In return, 'Alawis helped maintain French rule. They turned out in large numbers when most Syrians boycotted the French-sponsored elections of January 1926.[80] They provided a disproportionate number of soldiers to the government, forming about half of the eight infantry battalions making up the

Troupes Spéciales du Levant,[81] serving as police, and supplying intelligence. As late as May 1945, the vast majority of Troupes Spéciales remained loyal to their French commanders. ʿAlawis broke up Sunni demonstrations, shut down strikes, and quelled rebellions. ʿAlawis publicly favored the continuation of French rule, fearing that France's departure would lead to a reassertion of Sunni control. Henri de Jouvenel, the French high commissioner for Syria (1925–27), quoted a leading ʿAlawi politician telling him: "We have succeeded in making more progress in three or four years than we had in three or four centuries. Leave us therefore in our present situation."[82]

Pro-French sentiment was expressed especially clearly in 1936, when the temporary incorporation of the ʿAlawi state into Syria provoked wide protests. A March 1936 petition referred to union with the Sunnis as "slavery."[83] On 11 June 1936, an ʿAlawi leader wrote a letter to Prime Minister Léon Blum of France, reminding him of "the profoundness of the abyss that separates us from the [Sunni] Syrians," and asking him to "imagine the disastrous catastrophe that would follow" incorporation.[84]

Days later, six ʿAlawi notables (including Sulayman Asad, Hafiz al-Asad's grandfather) sent another letter to Blum in which they made several points: ʿAlawis differ from Sunnis religously and historically; ʿAlawis refuse to be joined to Syria, for it is a Sunni state and Sunnis consider them unbelievers (*kafirs*); ending the mandate would expose the ʿAlawis to mortal danger; "the spirit of religious feudalism" makes the country unfit for self-rule; therefore, France should secure the ʿAlawis' freedom and independence by staying in Syria.[85]

An ʿAlawi note to the French government in July 1936 asked: "Are the French today ignorant that the Crusades would have succeeded if their fortresses had been in northeast Syria, in the Land of the Nusayris? . . . We are the people most faithful to France."[86] Even more strongly worded was a petition of September 1936, signed by four hundred fifty thousand ʿAlawis, Christians, and Druzes, which read:

> The ʿAlawis believe that they are humans, not beasts ready for slaughter. No power in the world can force them to accept the yoke of their traditional and hereditary enemies to be slaves forever. . . . The ʿAlawis would profoundly regret the loss of their friendship and loyal attachment to noble France, which has until now been so loved, admired, and adored by them.[87]

Although Latakia lost its autonomous status in December 1936, the province continued to benefit from a "special administrative and financial regime."[88]

ʿAlawi resistance to Sunni rule took a new turn in 1939 with the launching of an armed rebellion led by Sulayman al-Murshid, the "half-sinister, half-ludicrous figure of the obese, illiterate, miracle-working 'god.'"[89] Murshid, a bandit who proclaimed himself divine, challenged Sunni rule with French weapons and some five thousand ʿAlawi followers. In the words of a 1944 British consular report, "The local Alaouite leaders, whose conception of the new order in Syria is a Nationalist Government who will treat them after the fashion of the French, upholding their authority and condoning their excesses, are doing their best to combine, and the movement appears to be supported by the French."[90] Murshid succeeded in keeping Damascus's authority out of the 'Alawi territories.

Right up to independence, 'Alawi leaders continued to submit petitions to the French in favor of continued French patronage. For example, a manifesto signed by twelve leaders in March 1945 called for all 'Alawi soldiers to remain under French command and for French arbitration of disputes between the 'Alawi government and Damascus.[91]

Sunni Dominance, 1946–1963

It was the Sunnis, and especially the urban Sunni elite, who inherited the government when the French mandate ended in 1946. Even after independence, 'Alawis continued to resist submission to the central government. Sulayman al-Murshid led a second revolt in 1946, ending in his execution. A third unsuccessful uprising, led by Murshid's son, took place in 1952. The failure of these efforts led 'Alawis to look into the possibility of attaching Latakia to Lebanon or Transjordan—anything to avoid absorption into Syria. These acts of resistance further tarnished the 'Alawis' already poor reputation among Sunnis.

When they came to power, the Sunni rulers in Damascus spared no effort to integrate Latakia into Syria (in part because this region offered the only access to the sea). Overcoming armed resistance, they abolished the 'Alawi state, 'Alawi military units, 'Alawi seats in parliament, and courts applying 'Alawi laws of personal status. These measures had some success; 'Alawis became reconciled to Syrian citizenship after the crushing of a Druze revolt in 1954 and henceforth gave up the dream of a separate state. This change of outlook, which seemed to be a matter of relatively minor importance at the time, in fact ushered in a new era of Syrian political life: the political ascent of the 'Alawis.

Once they recognized that their future lay within Lesser Syria, the 'Alawis began a rapid rise to power. Two key institutions, the armed forces and the Ba'th Party, had special importance in their transformation.

Even though the special circumstances which had brought them into the military lapsed with the French departure, 'Alawis and other minorities continued after independence to be overrepresented in the army. Old soldiers remained in service, and new ones kept coming in. Given the Sunni attitude toward 'Alawis, the persistence of large numbers of 'Alawis in the armed forces is surprising. This anomaly resulted from several factors. First, the military retained its reputation as a place for the minorities. Patrick Seale observed that Sunni landed families, "being predominantly of nationalist sentiment, despised the army as a profession: to join it between the wars was to serve the French. Homs [Military Academy] to them was a place for the lazy, the rebellious, the academically backward, or the socially undistinguished."[92] For the non-Sunnis, however, Homs was a place of opportunity for the ambitious and talented.

Second, the Sunni rulers virtually ignored the army as a tool of state;

fearing its power in domestic politics, they begrudged it funds, kept it small, and rendered military careers unattractive. Third, the dire economic predicament of the ʿAlawis and other rural peoples meant that they could not pay the fee to exempt their children from military service. More positively, those children saw military service as a means to make a decent living.

Accordingly, although the proportion of ʿAlawis entering the Homs Military Academy declined after 1946, ʿAlawis remained overrepresented in the officer corps. A report from 1949 stated that "persons originating from the minorities" commanded "all units of any importance" in the Syrian military.[93] (This did not mean just ʿAlawis; for example, the bodyguard of President Husni az-Zaʿim in 1949 was entirely Circassian.) ʿAlawis formed a plurality among the soldiers and some two-thirds of the noncommissioned officers. According to one count, they constituted 65 percent of the noncommissioned officers in 1955.

Sunni leaders apparently believed that reserving the top positions for themselves would suffice to control the military forces. Accordingly, minorities filled the lower ranks and for some years found it difficult to rise above the company level. Ironically, this discrimination actually served them well; as senior officers engaged in innumerable military *coups d'état* between 1949 and 1963, each change of government was accompanied by ruinous power struggles among the Sunnis, leading to resignations and the depletion of Sunni ranks. Wags claimed, with some justice, that there were more officers outside the Syrian army than inside it. Standing apart from these conflicts, the non-Sunnis, and ʿAlawis especially, benefited from the repeated purges.[94] As Sunni officers eliminated each other, ʿAlawis inherited their positions. With time, ʿAlawis became increasingly senior; and, as one ʿAlawi rose through the ranks, he brought his kinsmen along.

Purges and counterpurges during the 1946–63 period bred a deep mistrust between the officers. Never knowing who might be plotting against whom, superior officers frequently bypassed the normal hierarchy of command in favor of kinship bonds. As fear of betrayal came to dominate relations between military men, having reliable ethnic ties gave minority officers great advantage. In circumstances of almost universal suspicion, those officers within reliable networks could act far more effectively than those without. Sunnis entered the military as individuals, while ʿAlawis entered as members of a sect; the latter, therefore, prospered. ʿAlawi ethnic solidarity offered a far more enduring basis of cooperation than the shifting alliances formed by Sunni officers.

In addition to the military, ʿAlawis also acquired power through the Baʿth Party. From its earliest years, the Baʿth held special attraction for Syrians of rural and minority backgrounds, including the ʿAlawis, who joined in disproportionately large numbers (especially at the Baʿth Party's Latakia branch). Rural migrants who went to Damascus for educational purposes constituted a majority of the membership in the Baʿth Party. They tended to be students of lower-middle-class origins, the sons of ex-peasants newly arrived in the towns. In Aleppo, for example, the Baʿth claimed as members as many as three-quarters of the high school students in some schools. One of the founders of the party was an 'Alawi, Zaki al-Arsuzi, and he brought along many of his (rural) coreligionists to the Ba'th.

In particular, two doctrines appealed to the 'Alawis: socialism and secularism. Socialism offered economic opportunities to the country's poorest community. (The Ba'th's socialism was unclear, however, until the 1960s; only when the minorities took over did this feature become prominent). Secularism—the withdrawal of religion from public life—offered the promise of less prejudice to a despised minority. What could be more attractive to members of a downtrodden religious community than a combination of these two ideologies? Indeed, these aspects drew 'Alawis (and other poor rural minorities) to the Ba'th more than its Pan-Arab nationalism.

The only rival to the Ba'th was the SSNP, which offered roughly the same attractions. The two competed rather evenly for a decade, until the Ba'th eliminated the SSNP through the Maliki affair in 1955. From then on, especially in Syria, 'Alawis were associated predominantly with the Ba'th.[95]

'Alawi Consolidation, 1963–1970

Three changes in regime marked the 'Alawi consolidation of power: the Ba'th *coup d'état* of March 1963, the 'Alawi coup of February 1966, and the Asad coup of November 1970.

'Alawis had a major role in the coup of 8 March 1963 and took many of the key government positions in the Ba'th regime that followed. Between 1963 and 1966, sectarian battles pitting minorities against Sunnis took place within the military and the Ba'th Party.

First the military. To resist President Amin al-Hafiz, a Sunni, and to consolidate their new position, 'Alawi leaders flooded the military with cosectarians. In this way, minority officers came to dominate the Syrian military establishment. When seven hundred vacancies opened in the army soon after the March 1963 coup, 'Alawis filled half the positions. So restricted were Sunnis, some graduating cadets were denied their commissions to the officer corps. While 'Alawis, Druze, and Isma'ilis held politically sensitive positions in the Damascus region, Sunnis were sent to regions distant from the capital. Although communal affiliation did not drive every alliance,[96] it provided the basis for most enduring relationships. 'Alawi leaders such as Muhammad 'Umran built key units of members from their own religious community. Sunni officers often became figureheads, holding high positions but disposing of little power. In retaliation, Hafiz came to see nearly every 'Alawi as an enemy and pursued blatant sectarian policies, for example, excluding 'Alawis from some positions solely on the basis of communal affiliation.

Even 'Alawi officers who resisted confessionalism eventually succumbed to it. Political events solidified ties between 'Alawis, reducing the tribal, social, and sectarian differences that historically had split them. Itamar Rabinovich, a foremost student of this period, explains how confessionalism acquired a dynamic of its own:

J'did [Salah Jadid, ruler of Syria 1966–70] was among those who (for political reasons) denounced 'Umran for promoting "sectarianism" (*ta'ifiyya*) but ironically he inherited the support of many 'Alawi officers who had been advanced by 'Umran. . . . The 'Alawi officers promoted by 'Umran realized that their overrepresentation in the upper echelons of the army was resented by the majority, and they seem to have rallied around J'did, by then the most prominent 'Alawi officer in the Syrian army and the person deemed most likely to preserve their high but precarious position. It was also quite natural for [Amin al-]Hafiz . . . to try to gather Sunni officers around himself by accusing J'did of engaging in "sectarian" politics. . . . The solidarity of [Jadid's] 'Alawi supporters seems to have been further cemented by the feeling that the issue had assumed a confessional character and that their collective and personal positions were at stake.[97]

The same factors caused Druze officers—also overrepresented in high military offices—to throw in their lot with the 'Alawis in 1965.

A similar dynamic occurred in the Ba'th Party. Just as 'Alawis filled more than half of seven hundred military vacancies, so they moved in numbers into the party. To make their recruitment possible, ideological requirements for admission were relaxed for two years after March 1963. Many party officials brought in members of their family, tribe, village, or sect. As an internal Ba'th Party document of 1966 explained the problem, "friendship, family relationship and sometimes mere personal acquaintance were the basis" of admission to the party, leading to "the infiltration of elements alien to the party's logic and points of departure."[98] While 'Alawis brought in other 'Alawis, many Sunnis were purged. Membership quintupled in the year after its accession to power, transforming the party from an ideological to a sectarian affiliation. The Ba'th became an entirely different institution during its first two and half years in power (March 1963 to late 1965).

These changes culminated in Hafiz's decision in February 1966 to purge thirty officers of minority background from the army. Hearing of his plan, a group of mainly 'Alawi Ba'thist officers preempted Hafiz and took power on 23 February in Syria's bloodiest-ever change of government (about fifty persons died). Once in office, they purged rival officers belonging to other religious groups—first the Sunnis and Druze, then the Isma'ilis—further exacerbating communal tensions. 'Alawi officers received the most important postings and acquired unprecedented power. The Regional Command of the Ba'th Party, a key decision-making center, included no representatives at all during the 1966–70 period from the Sunni urban areas of Damascus, Aleppo, and Hama. Two-thirds of its members, however, were recruited from the rural and minority populations in Latakia, the Hawran, and Dayr az-Zur. The skewing was even more apparent among military officers on the Regional Command; during 1966–70, 63 percent came from Latakia alone.

The 'Alawi hold on power provoked bitter complaints from other communities. A Druze military leader, Salim Hatum, told the press after he fled Syria that 'Alawis in the army outnumbered the other religious communities by a ratio of five to one. He noted that "the situation in Syria was being threatened by a civil war as a result of the growth of the sectarian and tribal spirit." He also observed that "whenever a Syrian military man is questioned about his free officers, his answer will be that they have been dismissed and driven away, and that only 'Alawi officers have remained." Playing on the Ba'th slogan, "One Arab nation with an eternal mission," Hatum mocked the rulers in Damascus, saying that they believe in "One 'Alawi state with an eternal mission."[99]

'Alawi domination did not ensure stability. Two 'Alawi leaders, Salah Jadid and Hafiz al-Asad, fought each other for supremacy in Syria through the late 1960s, a rivalry that ended only when Asad prevailed in November 1970. In addition to differences in outlook—Jadid was more the ideologue and Asad more the pragmatist—they represented diverse 'Alawi sects. The September 1970 war between the PLO and the Jordanian government was the decisive event in Asad's rise to power. Jadid sent Syrian ground forces to help the Palestinians, but Asad refused to send air cover. The defeat of Syrian armor precipitated Asad's bloodless *coup d'état* two months later. This, Syria's tenth military *coup d'état* in seventeen years, was to be the last for a long time to come. It also virtually ended intra-'Alawi fighting.

The man who won the long contest for control of Syria, Hafiz ibn 'Ali ibn Sulayman al-Asad,[100] was born on 6 October 1930 in Qardaha, a village not far from the Turkish border and the seat of the 'Alawi religious leader. Hafiz was the ninth of his father's eleven children. The family belonged to the Numaylatiya branch of the Matawira tribe. (This means Asad's ancestors came from Iraq in the 1120s.)

Hafiz's grandfather and father had completed the transition from peasant to minor notable, so that the family was relatively well-off by the time he was born. Thus, while Qardaha consisted mostly of dried mud houses, he grew up in a stone building. In later years, however, Asad cultivated a story of poverty, recounting to visitors, for example, about having to drop out of school until his father found the sixteen Syrian pounds to pay for his tuition.[101] True or not, Hafiz was a smart child and the first of his family to attend school. His parents sent him in 1939–40 to live in the nearby town of Latakia for studies. The next academic year, he returned to the Qardaha school. From 1944 to 1951, he was back in Latakia, attending the Collège de Lattaquié, a top high school.

Early in 1948, when only seventeen years old, Asad went to Damascus and volunteered in the Syrian army to help destroy the nascent state of Israel, only to be rejected as underage. Upon graduation in 1951, he enrolled in the Homs Military Academy and then transferred to the just-formed Aleppo Air School. Asad distinguished himself as a combat pilot and graduated as an officer in 1955. Assigned that year to the Mezze Air Base (outside Damascus), he was soon sent to Egypt for a six-month training course in jet aircraft. Back in Syria during the Suez war, he shot one time at a British aircraft, without hitting it. In mid-1958, just after marrying Anisa Makhluf, Asad went to the Soviet Union for eleven months, where he learned how to fly the MiG-15s and -17s which had just arrived in Syria. There, he picked up a bit of the Russian language.

During the UAR years, he commanded a night-fighter squadron of MiG-19s near Cairo.

Asad had been active in politics as early as 1945. While at the Collège de Lattaquié, he served as president of the Students' Committee, then went on to be elected president of the National Union of Students. While still a student, he was jailed by the French authorities for political activities. Asad joined the Ba'th Party soon after its creation in 1947 (making him one of the party's earliest members). Even as he rose through the military ranks, he remained active in the Ba'th Party. In 1959, during his exile in Egypt, Asad helped found the Military Committee and organized its activities. By that time, he had also begun the decade-long process of consolidating his position within the Syrian armed forces.

The dissolution of the UAR in September 1961 precipitated a difficult two years for Asad. In short order, he found himself in jail in Egypt, Syria, and Lebanon. He spent a month and a half in an Egyptian jail by virtue of being a Syrian soldier stranded near Cairo. Asad was a powerful figure by that time, so on his return to Syria, the conservative leaders who had taken power in Damascus forced him to resign his commission as captain and put him in a minor position in the Department of Maritime Transportation. Asad hardly showed up for work, spending his time instead participating in Military Committee activities.

He ended up in Lebanese and Syrian jails for his part in the failed putsch in March 1962. He fled to Tripoli, Lebanon, where he was apprehended by the authorities and jailed for nine days, then extradited back to Syria, where he spent another few days in prison. This misadventure notwithstanding, Asad continued to engage in conspiratorial politics and played an important role in the March 1963 Ba'th coup. He was rewarded for his efforts with a recall to the military and a meteoric rise through the ranks, going from captain in early 1963 to major-general in December 1964 and field marshall in 1968. (He resigned from the military in 1970 or 1971.) Asad took command of the key air force base at Dumayr after the 1963 coup and quickly established his control over the entire air force—his power base during the subsequent years of turmoil.

The 1963 coup gave Asad his first taste of adminstration and authority, and right from the start he proved very competent at both. His timely support for the rebellion in February 1966 proved decisive in the events that brought 'Alawis to power; his reward was to be appointed defense minister just twenty minutes after the new regime had been proclaimed. This new position gave Asad an opportunity to extend his authority beyond the air force, especially to the combat forces of the army. He was already the most powerful figure in the country in 1968, but he bided his time before taking complete control. The moment came in November 1970, when he simultaneously ousted his last rival, Salah Jadid, and culminated the 'Alawi rise to power in Syria.

How did the 'Alawis take over? Three theories have emerged to explain this unexpected development. One, favored by those unsympathetic to the Asad regime, sees a long-term conspiracy. Annie Laurent suggested that, "determined to get their revenge" after the failure of Sulayman al-Murshid, "the 'Alawis put into effect a strategy of setting up cells in the army and the Ba'th Party, and this won them power in Damascus."[102] Adherents of this view date the 'Alawi ascent to 1959, the year of the Military Committee's formation. Why, they ask, did leaders of this group keep its existence secret from the party authorities? This furtiveness suggests that the Military Committee from the beginning had a sectarian agenda. Matti Moosa argued that "it is almost certain that the officers were acting not as Baathists, but as Nusayris, with the intent of using the Baath and the armed forces to rise to power in Syria. The formation of the Military Committee was the beginning of their plan for a future takeover of the government."[103]

This speculation is confirmed by the 1960 clandestine meeting of 'Alawi religious leaders and officers (including Hafiz al-Asad) that reportedly took place in Qardaha, Asad's hometown. "The main goal of this meeting was to plan how to forward the Nusayri officers into the ranks of the Ba'th Party. They would then exploit it as a means to arrive at the rule in Syria."[104] Three years later, another 'Alawi meeting in Homs is said to have followed up the earlier initiatives. Among other steps, it called for the placement of more 'Alawis in the Ba'th Party and army. Further secret meetings of 'Alawi leaders appear to have taken place later in the 1960s.[105]

Analysts better disposed toward Asad tend to discount not just these meetings and a premeditated drive for power, but the sectarian factor more generally. John F. Devlin, for example, denied that the disproportion of 'Alawis in the army implied 'Alawi dominance of Syria. He would resist seeing "every domestic disagreement in terms of a Sunni-'Alawi clash." For him, the fact that 'Alawis reached power was basically accidental: "The Ba'th is a secular party, and it is heavy with minorities."[106] Alasdair Drysdale called it "reductionist" to focus on ethnicity, arguing that this was one of many factors—geography, class, age, education, occupation—that defined the ruling elite.[107] According to Yahya M. Sadowski, "sectarian loyalties play an insignificant role in the Ba'th, and even confessional bonds are only one among many avenues by which patronage is extended."[108]

The truth lies between conspiracy and accident. The 'Alawis did not "plan for a future takeover" years in advance, nor was it mere chance that the Ba'th Party was "heavy with minorities." 'Alawi power resulted from an unplanned but sectarian transformation of public life in Syria in which the Ba'th-military-'Alawi triad rose as an integral whole. Michael van Dusen explained: "From 1946 to 1963, Syria witnessed the gradual erosion of the national and eventually subnational political power of the traditional elite, not so much through the emergence of new and especially dynamic elites but rather by internal conflict."[109] Translated from the jargon of political science, van Dusen is saying that internal divisions caused non-Ba'th civilian Sunnis to lose power. This provided an opening that Ba'thist officers of 'Alawi origins exploited.

But which of these three aspects had the most importance? Were these

Ba'thists who happened to be 'Alawi soldiers, or were they soldiers who happened to be Ba'thists and 'Alawis? A third formulation is most accurate: these were 'Alawis who happened to be Ba'thists and soldiers. A chapel excluded the church. Without deprecating the critical roles of party and army, the 'Alawi affiliation ultimately defined the rulers of Syria. Sunni responses to their new rulers bear out this view.

'Alawi Dominion since 1970

The impact of the 'Alawis' taking power can hardly be exaggerated. Sunni Muslims saw Syria as their patrimony and interpreted the rise of the 'Alawis as an act of usurpation. Conservative and wealthy Sunnis of Damascus and Aleppo formed the landlord class and owned the great commercial enterprises. They knew how to keep power through changes in government and shifting ideologies, having held nine-tenths of the administrative posts in the years before 1914 and virtually maintained this monopoly through the mandate period, despite French efforts to disenfranchise them. It was the Sunnis who then inherited the government at independence.

This domination by the urban Sunni elite came to an end with the 'Alawi takeover. In the process, some deeply held assumptions and long-standing relationships were reversed. Martin Kramer notes the rich irony inherent in the reversal of roles:

> The Alawis, having been denied their own state by the Sunni nationalists, had taken all of Syria instead. Arabism, once a convenient device to reconcile minorities to Sunni rule, now was used to reconcile Sunnis to the rule of minorities. The cause of Sunni primacy, once served by having Alawis recognized as Muslims, now demanded that the Alawis be vilified as unbelievers.[110]

An 'Alawi ruling Syria is like an untouchable becoming maharajah in India or a Jew becoming tsar in Russia—an unprecedented development shocking to the majority population which had monopolized power for so many centuries. The rise of this despised minority signaled "the complete social, economic and political ruin of the traditional Syrian political elite." Michael van Dusen correctly described this as "the most significant political fact of twentieth century Syrian history and politics."[111]

Monopolizing Power

Between 1966 and 1970, 'Alawis increasingly controlled key military and political positions in Syria, while Sunni representation in the officer corps was about half that in the general population. After 1970, 'Alawis predominated in almost every one of the regime's elite military organizations, such as the air force officer corps and the army's Third Armored Division. They controlled every army division and strike unit. The rule of thumb was simple: if they wore distinctive uniforms, they were 'Alawis. According to Moshe Ma'oz,

'Alawis made up 60 percent of the officer corps; by contrast, Sunnis constituted just 27 percent and were overrepresented in noncombat units and functional commands.[112]

With time, Asad narrowed the range of his key allies, surrounding himself with coreligionists, fellow tribesmen, and his own family. An exact pecking order emerged: 'Alawis belonging to other tribes held key positions in the military command; members of Asad's tribe filled higher posts (such as the head of military intelligence); and close relatives (sons, brothers, cousins, nephews, brothers-in-law) filled the very most sensitive and powerful offices of state.

The forty thousand-strong Defense Brigades were commanded first by (brother) Rif'at al-Asad, then by (son) Basil al-Asad. In 1986, Basil took over security at the Presidential Palace. Cousins Haydar, 'Adnan, and Muhammad al-Asad headed the special units in charge of the Damascus area. Brother Jamil al-Asad commanded the Murtada militia in Latakia, and his son Fawwaz ran security for the region. Kamil al-Asad commanded the Urgent Action Group, a force used against the Turkish government which trained in Qardaha, the Asad hometown. 'Adnan Makhluf, the brother of Asad's wife, commanded the president's personal force, the Republican Guard. Family members also controlled the Self-Defense Militia, the Youth of 'Ali, and security in Hama and Aleppo, the two leading sources of antiregime activities. Even in Lebanon, the head of Syrian military intelligence, Ghazi Kan'an, was a cousin.

'Alawi dominance extended to politics too. Thirty of the Central Committee's seventy-five members were 'Alawis. But more than any other act, Asad's taking over the presidency for himself in February 1971 symbolized the new paramountcy. His 'Alawi predecessor had maintained a Sunni as the nominal head of state, but, even knowing how deeply distasteful this step was to Sunnis, Asad felt confident enough of his power base to take it.

Regime actions pointed to an effort to make 'Alawi dominance permanent. 'Alawis received opportunities far out of proportion to their numbers. In 1978, for example, 97 out of the 100 students sent to the U.S.S.R. from Tartus province were 'Alawi, 2 were Sunni, and 1 Christian. According to opposition sources, 270 or 286 out of the 300 students training in the artillery school in Aleppo in June 1979 were of 'Alawi origins.[113] This bias made it possible for 'Alawis to staff all levels, not just of the armed forces but also of the bureaucracy. A PLO journal summed up the situation after 1970:

> With al-Asad's presidency, the era of sectarian rule began in Syria. The most important characteristic of such rule is the expulsion of the majority from the government and the army. The Air Force is the exclusive monopoly of the ['Alawi] sect. All of the intelligence services are sectarian. All of the division commanders belong to that sect. Ninety percent of the cadets in military schools are members of the sect. The diplomatic corps is sectarian. Interstate foreign trade is sectarian, and consequently economic power is in the hands of that sect.[114]

'Alawis benefited from the Asad regime in other ways too. The bulk of government spending was concentrated in Latakia, the poorest region of Syria and the one where most ʿAlawis lived. Roads, railroads, ports, an airport, industrial plants, and irrigation works were among the major capital projects. Syria's third university, Tishrin, was established in the city of Latakia.[115] The government put up money for the Meridien chain to build a luxury hotel in Latakia; that city also hosted a broadcasting station and a new "republican palace." Even U.S. aid to Syria was funneled to Latakia. Government contracts spawned a new class—rich ʿAlawis. Sunni merchants viewed the commercial success of the ʿAlawis with profound displeasure.

State patronage permitted ʿAlawis to make their presence felt in parts of Syria where they had never lived. ʿAlawi peasants received from the Asad government large tracts of land outside Latakia, especially in Homs and Hama provinces. Working for the state took them to all the regions of Syria. ʿAlawis also moved into the cities in large numbers after 1970, searching for the better education and employment that government patronage made available. According to Kamal Junbalat, ʿAlawis even came to comprise a majority of the population in Homs,[116] though this seems unlikely. They took advantage of disasters that befell the Sunnis; thus, the February 1982 massacre of Sunnis brought thousands of ʿAlawis to Hama.

ʿAlawis were seen to be using their new power to take revenge for centuries of abuse. Mutaʿ Safadi, a Baʿthist, recounted his experience:

> There were hundreds of prisoners in the Mazza [jail] after 18 July [1963, the date of an abortive pro-ʿAbd an-Nasir coup in Syria], and I was one of them. No one remembered anyone like the prison warden, who gave free rein to torture and probing. During hundreds of nights, his escort did not hold back on the whip or electricity or punches or slaps, or insults against beliefs with the most malicious phrases. Despite this, the attentive among the prisoners understood the conspiratorial plan. They therefore prohibited themselves from hating every ʿAlawi—even though the warden was an ʿAlawi, as was the leader of the torture team. Most of their assistants were ʿAlawis who showed their ʿAlawi-hood by abusing the beliefs of those being tortured.[117]

Twenty years later, non-ʿAlawis found it harder to hold back. Riyad at-Turk, a leader of the Communist Party of Syria, explained in 1983: "Psychologically there are already two states, one Sunni and the other ʿAlawi. A veteran of fifteen years in the Party left us to rejoin his ʿAlawi clan. . . . Even I, a Communist, a Marxist-Leninist, experience a certain mistrust when I see an ʿAlawi."[118] Resentment against ʿAlawis grew very strong indeed. As a PLO editorial showed, not everyone displayed the forbearance of these two men:

> The [ʿAlawi] sectarian minority has toppled Syria's nationalist stand and replaced it with a narrow sectarian stand with one central purpose: to maintain the sect's power in the face of threats to it from the oppressed [Sunni] Muslim majority. . . . The defeat of ʿAlawi Islam and its sectarian plan in Syria and Lebanon is an urgent, major task. . . . ʿAlawi Islam is a cancer that destroys the entire Arab body.[119]

A vicious circle set in: Sunni Arabs became increasingly alienated, so the rulers closed ranks and came to depend even more on ʿAlawi support; and as the regime took on a more 'Alawi cast, Sunni discontent deepened. At the same time, the drive to please 'Alawis reduced the government's ideological character. As catering to the 'Alawis became the top priority, the Ba'th element (calling for Pan-Arab nationalism) virtually disappeared. It was a case, as the Muslim Brethren put it, of "the Nusayri sect inheriting the Ba'th Party."[120] By the mid-1970s, Asad's rule degenerated into arbitrariness and favoritism.

New Policies

In addition to 'Alawi power, Sunnis deeply resented three policies of the Asad government: secularism, socialism, and foreign relations.

Many Sunnis found it intolerable that the government called for the exclusion of religion from public life, termed Islam outdated, and denigrated Muslim practices. Especially contentious were efforts to drop Islamic instruction in the schools. This was bad enough in itself; worse was for 'Alawis to mandate and carry out the policy. Partly for these reasons, some Sunnis deemed the 'Alawis even more hated rulers than the French.

A socialist order benefited 'Alawis and other poor rural peoples and hampered the Sunni merchants. Nationalization programs that began in 1965 destroyed the leading Sunni families of Syria's cities. Expansion of the public sector harmed capitalists and alienated the traditional urban elite. An 'Alawi officer reportedly explained that socialism "enables us to impoverish the townspeople and to equalize their standard of life to that of the villagers. . . . What property do we have which we could lose by nationalization? None!"[121] By the 1980s, this process was well along, with the state controlling most of the country's agriculture, manufacturing, and service industries.

External involvements, especially with Lebanon, Israel, and the PLO, also contributed to communal tensions within Syria. The civil war in Lebanon weighed heavily on Syrian politics. Fighting in Tripoli, Lebanon, pitting 'Alawis against Sunnis, provided a specific model for the strife in Syria. Already in 1964, Muta' Safadi, the prominent Ba'thist, saw the Lebanese civil war of 1958 as a catalyst for the chain of events leading to Syria's severe "sectarian complex."[122] When Damascus allied with the Maronites against the Sunnis of Lebanon, Syrian Sunnis responded with anger and fear. Dark conspiracy theories followed about 'Alawis joining forces with the "Maronite Crusaders" against the Muslims of Lebanon.[123] Sunnis envisioned a grand 'Alawi-Maronite-Zionist alliance; or they claimed that Asad sent Syrian forces to Lebanon to get non-'Alawi officers and soldiers out of the way. Fundamentalist Sunnis initiated these allegations—a preacher in Damascus attacked the rulers as "impious" for their actions in Lebanon and was thrown in jail[124]—but they quickly spread to Sunnis of all outlooks. Indeed, the Muslim Brethren can fairly be said to represent a much larger, if less active, body of opinion among Syrian Sunnis.

Accusations against 'Alawis acquired such force that Asad eventually had to recognize them and respond. He denied as "groundless" all charges that "Syria is siding with Muslims against Christians or that it is siding with Christians against Muslims."[125] Even Asad's subsequent switch in Lebanon and his attack on the Maronite forces did him little good; Sunnis portrayed this change as a symptom of his lack of principle.

Asad's stance vis-à-vis Israel also caused him domestic problems. Before coming to power in 1966, ʿAlawis, like other minorities in the Arab world, had never taken much interest in the conflict against Israel. Along with the Maronites, Greek Orthodox, Druze, Shiʿis, Kurds, and Copts, they typically had more pressing problems than Israel's existence, expansion, or disappearance. For example, a June 1936 letter to the French prime minister signed by six ʿAlawi notables, including Asad's grandfather, expressed solidarity with the Zionists in Palestine:

> Those good Jews brought civilization and peace to the Arab Muslims, and they dispersed gold and prosperity over Palestine without damage to anyone or taking anything by force. Despite this, the Muslims declared holy war against them and did not hesitate to massacre their children and women, despite the British presence in Palestine and the French in Syria. Thus, a black fate awaits the Jews and other minorities in case the Mandates are cancelled and Muslim Syria is united with Muslim Palestine.[126]

Annie Laurent and Antoine Basbous consider the ʿAlawis even more receptive to the West than other minorities: "There is no one [in Syria] more pro-Western, more pro-Lebanon, pro-Christian, and even pro-Jewish . . . and anti-Syrian than the ʿAlawis, as their recent history proves."[127]

Accordingly, Sunni Arabs suspected the ʿAlawi regime of indifference, even treachery, to the struggle with Israel. They spun elaborate conspiracy theories around the fact that Hafiz al-Asad commanded the air force in 1967 when the Golan Heights fell to Israel almost without a fight.[128] Still in the same post, they noted, he refused to supply air cover for a Syrian expedition to help the PLO against the Jordanian government in 1970. In recent years, Asad prohibited the PLO from using Syria as a base for operations and finished Israel's work by expelling it from Lebanon in late 1983.

Sunnis drew harsh conclusions. Asad's enemies accused him of

> abandoning the Golan in 1967, betraying the Palestinians in 1970, sabotaging an Iraqi offensive against Israel in 1973, permitting the massacre of Palestinians at Tel Zaʿtar in 1976, cutting up the Lebanese National Front and attempting to divide the Palestinian resistance, playing partition games with the Israelis in Lebanon, stabbing Arab Iraq in the back when it was attacked by Khomeini's Iran, [and] attempting to liquidate the PLO and Yasir ʿArafat at Tripoli in 1983.[129]

The *Charter* of the Islamic Front in Syria condemned Asad: "Although most of the regimes in the region took part in serious practices against the Palestinian case and the resistance, the sectarian regime in Syria outstripped them all in its indulgence in this crime."[130] The National Alliance for the Liberation of Syria summed up the Sunni indictment: Asad is motivated in all his actions "by a burning hostility to Arabs and Islam in that all his crimes are in the interest of the Zionist enemy."[131] The Muslim Brethren discerned "an international

Jewish-'Alawi conspiracy" against Sunni Muslims in general and Palestinians in particular.[132] Indeed, it claimed that "collusion between the Asad regime and the Zionist enemy" underpinned the whole of Syrian foreign policy.[133]

To make up for the known indifference of his community on the question of Israel and the doubts about his own record, Asad adopted an extreme and uncompromising position against Israel. He tried to eliminate suspicions by acting more implacably anti-Zionist than the Sunnis. Anwar as-Sadat led his country's opinion on Israel, but Hafiz al-Asad could only follow. While Asad probably cared little about the fate of the Palestinians or control of Jerusalem, he adopted this cause to protect his reputation within Syria.[134]

Sunnis believed that Asad was laying the groundwork for the day when 'Alawis lose power in Damascus. They suspected him of breaking off a part of Syria to establish a separate, 'Alawi-dominated state; of preparing the isolated Jazira region (in northeast Syria) as a refuge; of turning the region from Latakia to Tartus as an 'Alawi bastion; of settling forty thousand 'Alawis in the north Lebanese town of Tripoli as a first step toward an enlarged 'Alawi state along the Mediterranean, possibly under the rule of Hafiz al-Asad's brother, Rif'at (nicknamed *Amir as-Sahil*, "Prince of the Coast"). Kamal Junbalat foresaw Homs as the capital of an 'Alawi state, and Yasir 'Arafat held that 'Alawis who moved into northern Lebanon came from Alexandretta, Turkey.[135] The settlement of 'Alawis in Hama after February 1982 was also seen as part of a plot.

Annie Laurent wrote in 1983: "The day when danger compels the 'Alawi community to withdraw to the mountains from which they come (in the northwest of Syria, along the Mediterranean coast), the 'Alawi state will no longer be an academic hypothesis and Tripoli might become its southern end." Four years later, she interpreted the 'Alawi efforts as even more systematic: "Since 1970, Hafiz al-Asad has put into effect a complete program intended to transform the 'Alawis' region into a viable state with Latakia its capital. A soaring birth rate and a program of colonization (in Hama, Homs, and Tripoli) provide the security for [their home region]."[136]

The Sunnis had many grievances against 'Alawi rule. They disliked 'Alawi domination of power and the suppression of the Muslim Brethren. They resented the socialism which reduced their wealth, the indignities against Islam, and what they perceived as cooperation with Maronites and Zionists. They suspected the 'Alawis of plotting to set up their own state. Many of the stories that circulated among Sunnis about their 'Alawi rulers appear implausible to an outside observer. But it is precisely this that makes matters so explosive: anything can be believed, nothing strikes the Sunnis as too outlandish.

Sunni Alienation and Pan-Syrianism

Sunni Opposition

Asad's years in power reversed traditional roles, so that Sunni resentment of the 'Alawis came to resemble the old 'Alawi hostility toward Sunnis. Combining old and new grievances, these two groups surely loathed each other more than any other two groups in Syria. Their hostility had many political implications; one of these was the turn to Pan-Syrianism.

Sunni agitation led by the Muslim Brethren began soon after 'Alawis moved into positions of power and occasioned six violent revolts in the cities of Syria. The Muslim Brethren of Syria, like its eponym in Egypt, was a fundamentalist Islamic organization; that is, it sought to establish a government in accordance with the laws of Islam. If 'Alawis were non-Muslims, as Sunnis held, then they certainly were not the ones to apply Islamic laws; therefore, the Brethren aimed first to eliminate 'Alawi rule. And, indeed, this was the brunt of its message. The Brethren was so effective because it served as the main vehicle for rallying anti-'Alawi sentiment—and not because of its fundamentalist cast. Sunnis joined the Brethren because of its proven record as the most durable and effective organization combatting 'Alawi rule.

Two forms of evidence support this conclusion. First, there is reason to believe that a substantial proportion of the Brethren membership was made up of nonobservant Muslims. A repentant member of the Muslim Brethren, Ahmad al-Jundi, stated in a televised interrogation that he neither prayed nor kept the Ramadan fast, that he knew very little of the Qur'an, and that he drank wine.[137] Second, the Brethren's willingness to work with left-wing and other nonfundamentalist groups in the National Alliance for the Liberation of Syria—including pro-Iraqi Ba'thists and followers of 'Abd an-Nasir—indicated that its first priority was to destroy the Asad regime, not to impose an Islamic order. Foreign fundamentalists sometimes publicly criticized their Syrian colleagues on this score. For example, Zaynab al-Ghazali, leader of the Muslim Sisters in Egypt, regretted that the Syrian Muslim Brethren signed an agreement to join forces with nonfundamentalists.[138]

Muslim Brethren activities began just after the Ba'th Party came to power in March 1963; indeed, the party faced a far more active opposition than had any of the previous military dictators. Nonviolent demonstrations occurred in October 1963; violent incidents followed two months later, provoked by such incidents as the ripping up of a religious book by a Ba'thist teacher. A series of challenges early in 1964, beginning with a clash between 'Alawi and Sunni students in Baniyas and a commercial strike in Homs, were even more threatening. The troubles peaked in Hama, sparked by the arrest of a student for erasing Ba'th slogans from a blackboard. This precipitated riots, a commercial strike, and the shelling of a mosque, killing at least sixty Sunnis.

The 'Alawi consolidation of power in the February 1966 coup made Sunni apprehensions even more acute. This explains their extreme sensitivity to an April 1967 article in the army magazine which condemned God and religion as "mummies which should be transferred to the museums of historical remains."[139] Large demonstrations in all the major cities followed, leading to wide-scale strikes, the arrests of many religious leaders, and considerable violence.[140]

The ascent of Hafiz al-Asad had contrary effects on the Sunni opposition. Initially, Asad won the good will of Sunnis by easing economic and religious pressures. Commercial restrictions (which mostly affected Sunni merchants) were relaxed; private enterprise was permitted more scope. Landlords felt less squeezed, and Damascenes rose to positions of prominence in the government. Foreign policy goals were scaled down, and the army was depoliticized. Further, seeing his main danger coming from the left (especially the Communists and breakaway factions of the Ba'th), Asad initially treated the Muslim Brethren well. He encouraged it to organize and, we are told, even allowed it to open military training camps in the mountains of the 'Alawi region.[141] With government permission, the Brethren made impressive gains in the 1972 local elections.

But Asad's rule also crystallized 'Alawi rule and made it long-lasting. The passage of time exacerbated Sunni discontent, and the stability of Asad's rule foreclosed the possibility of quick change, spurring Sunni antagonism. Life in Syria also became less pleasant in the mid-1970s. The economy suffered from an imbalance between imports and exports, a brain drain, insufficient internal generation of capital, excessive military expenditures, overdependence on oil-related revenues, and too much state interference. Social inequities and cultural repression increased.

These developments plus the alliance between Syrian forces and the Maronites in Lebanon caused the Muslim Brethren to become more active in opposing what it termed "the sectarian, dictatorial rule of the despot Hafiz al-Asad."[142] But the Brethren did not directly challenge the state until September 1976, when it began a major campaign of terror that just three years later seemed on the verge of overthrowing the regime. The Sunni revolt climaxed with two events: in June 1979, the Brethren massacred more than sixty cadets—almost all 'Alawis—at a military school in Aleppo; and in July 1980, they nearly assassinated Asad himself (the attempt was foiled by a guard hurling himself on a live grenade). Not without reason, foreign newspapers at that time featured headlines such as "Time Runs Out for Assad," "Crumbling Regime in Syria," and "Bleak Future for Asad Regime."[143]

Just when it appeared that the regime might fall, Asad responded with a horrible effectiveness. He made mere membership in "the Muslim Brethren gang"[144] a capital crime and hunted down its members without remorse. He took the psychological offensive by having militia groups tear veils off the heads of pious Muslim women. Efforts to destroy the organization peaked in early 1982, when Asad assaulted the city of Hama. Muslim Brethren forces held the city from 2 February for about ten days, killing the governor and several hundred other officials. In response, some twelve thousand troops (almost all of whom were 'Alawi) attacked Brethren strongholds with field artillery, tanks, and air force helicopters. After shelling the city for three consecutive weeks and leveling large portions, soldiers pillaged what remained. In the words of a government official, this city of three hundred thousand "was reduced to the status of a village."[145] In the end, up to thirty thousand Sunni Arabs—a tenth of Hama's population—lost their lives. The anonymous author of a book detailing the events at Hama called it the worst massacre in modern times.[146] Pictures of Hama were shown throughout Syria as an object lesson for Asad's other enemies.

The Hama massacre ended the immediate Muslim Brethren challenge and won the rulers a new lease on life. But it did not make the Sunni danger disappear, as the extraordinary number of bodyguards employed by the regime illustrated. Asad built a palace-fortress for himself high above Damascus and had twelve thousand soldiers in his personal bodyguard. Top generals had sixty soldiers, and prominent apologists for the regime, such as the dean of a dental school and a professor of Arabic literature, had four each.

The Brethren found out what the regime would do to protect itself with "steel, fire, rope, and gallows."[147] Their challenge ended, at least for the next several years. Writing in 1983, Gérard Michaud observed, "today it appears that the repressive machinery has succeeded in dismantling the fundamentalist movement in Syria. But for how long? And at what price!"[148] Indeed, after a quiet four years, the fundamentalists began to attack the government again in early 1986.

Government Strategies

Bedrock Sunni opposition remained the Asad regime's greatest problem. The ʿAlawis, a small and divided minority, knew they could not rule indefinitely against the wishes of more than half the population. As one analyst remarked, "In the long run, it is highly dangerous for the Alawites. If they lose their control, there will be a bloodbath."[149]

One solution, of course, would be to bring Sunnis into the government and share power with them. Asad did take steps in this direction soon after taking power, giving Sunnis greater representation at the expense of minorities other than the ʿAlawis. But beyond that, for the ʿAlawis to have given Sunnis more would have cut into their power, and this they could not do out of fear of a Sunni takeover. Gérard Michaud noted that ʿAlawis "remain persuaded that the slightest concession on their part and they will revert back to their old status of 'damned of the earth.'"[150] To rid the system of sectarian bias would be tantamount to destroying the regime. Thus, Asad sought to win acceptance from the majority population without giving it real power. But what could he offer? Several expedients were tried.

First, he solicited support from the other non-Sunni Arabs (not including ʿAlawis, these constituted 34 percent of the population). Druze, Christians, and Shiʿis enjoyed in diluted form the benefits going to ʿAlawis. For example, representation in the decade before 1976 on the Syrian Regional Command of the Baʿth Party, the most powerful formal body in the country, contained three times as many Druze and five times as many Shiʿis as their shares of the population would justify. Moshe Maʾoz noted: "Hafiz Asad has sought to gain the friendship of the minority communities in order to build an intercommunal alliance for his government. He possibly also recognized that the minorities, in contrast to the Sunnis, would not pose a threat to ʿAlawi dominance in the armed forces."[151] In effect, Asad reverted to the French policy of *politique minoritaire*, that is, ruling Syria through the agency of non-Sunni Arabs.

Second, the regime claimed that all communities enjoyed full representation in the government and constructed a façade of Sunnis in high positions. Indeed, a number of senior officials, such as a vice-president and the defense minister, were Sunni Arabs. Governors and directors of military and civilian intelligence in the provinces were divided among the communities in proportion to their sizes. But this parade of Sunnis fooled no one. Cosmetic efforts notwithstanding, Syrians knew full well who actually ran their country. One source estimated that ʿAlawis held 70 percent of the key posts in the armed forces.[152] A Sunni may have commanded the air force between 1970 and 1978, but ʿAlawis controlled all the major air force bases. That Sunnis were functionaries became most apparent in times of crisis, when ʿAlawi unit commanders carried out tasks properly belonging to Sunni generals.

The same applied to highly placed Sunni civilians, who faithfully served Asad in return for honors and riches. Everyone knew they reported to the regime, not to their own community; unlike ʿAlawis, who had tight family and regional connections to each other, Sunnis in high positions were isolated individuals hailing from all parts of Syria. Cabinet members filled what were ostensibly decision-making positions; in fact, they served as high-level bureaucrats carrying out what ʿAlawis had decided. Should they stray, the ever-vigilant ʿAlawis in their entourage would forestall any mischief. The French political analysts Laurent and Annie Chabry noted that Sunnis in the government were "not so much representatives of alternate policies as hostages . . . ratifying policies made by others."[153]

Only the president's longtime Sunni cronies were exceptions. ʿAbd al-Halim Khaddam had known Asad since childhood and married a woman of Asad's tribe in 1954. Khaddam, a lawyer from Baniyas, Latakia, who filled several high positions after the Asad coup of 1970 (including deputy prime minister, foreign minister, and vice-president), has been called "probably the only Sunni to exercise real influence at the source of power."[154] Reports indicated that Asad befriended Mustafa Tallas, his perpetual defense minister, in 1948.[155]

So sensitive was the Asad regime about the locus of power in Syria, it went so far as to capture and let die in March 1986 Michel Seurat, a French analyst who wrote (under the pen name Gérard Michaud) on decision making in Syria. Seurat characterized such Sunni figures as Mahmud al-Ayyubi, Jabir Bajbuj, ʿAbdallah al-Ahmar, Hikmat Shihabi, and Mustafa Tallas as "Sunni hostages of the dominant minority, held up to ridicule each time they have an impulse to interfere."[156] According to one report at the time of his death, Seurat's worst offense was to point to three hundred ʿAlawi officers as the effective rulers of Syria.[157]

Third, the regime took on a variety of outlooks, including nonsectarianism, Twelver Islam, Pan-Arabism, and Pan-Syrianism, in the effort to win Sunni support.

Nonsectarianism meant a ban on the mention of communal affiliation. The government claimed that Syrians "have never experienced sectarianism" and asserted that Syrians put nationality before ethnic allegiance. When communal violence occurred, it blamed the problem on "enemies both abroad and within the nation."[158] But talk about nonsectarianism and the abolition of communal loyalties failed to bring Sunni Arabs in. Again, no one was fooled; the population knew full well that one small community dominated all the others.

Or the rulers portrayed 'Alawis as Twelver Shi'i Muslims. This effort began in 1922, when the French deemed 'Alawis a kind of Twelver Shi'i in an effort to distinguish them from the Sunnis. The French act was utterly arbitrary, for 'Alawis had no more connections historically to Twelver Shi'ism than to Sunnism. Indeed, Twelvers saw 'Alawism as negatively as did Sunnis; the author of a survey of this topic concluded that "the attitude of the Shi'a toward Ibn Nusayr [founder of 'Alawism] is extremely negative. They ascribe to him extremism, licentiousness, heresy, atheism, and materialism"—and the same attitude extended to Ibn Nusayr's followers.[159] Nonetheless, the French action created a bond that 'Alawis found useful to promote externally; when convenient, they represented themselves as Twelvers. (Among themselves, of course, they rejected any role for Twelver Shi'ism.) At other times, they used the association with Twelver Shi'ism to argue for a distinct 'Alawi form of Shi'ism. Thus, one writer held that "the 'Alawi rite [*madhhab*] is like the other Shi'i rites: its adherents favor 'Ali [the son-in-law of the Prophet Muhammad] and stay within the framework of Islam."[160] Either way, the tie to Twelver Shi'ism helped legitimize the 'Alawi religion in Muslim eyes.

So long as the 'Alawis were a weak and downtrodden sect, the association with Twelver Shi'ism had only moderate importance. But it acquired great utility soon after they took power. Asad's religion became a political issue in January 1973, when the People's Assembly (the nominal parliament) adopted a permanent constitution that made no mention of Islam. Sunnis greeted the new text with riots. To defuse this anger, the government added a clause to the constitution requiring that the head of state be a Muslim. This turn of phrase had the virtue of implicitly affirming Asad's Muslim credentials at the same time that it appeased Sunni sentiments. Unfortunately for Asad, many Syrians rejected this implication; demonstrators carried placards with slogans calling for an end to "'Alawi power"[161] and rioting continued in the cities until troops forcibly intervened.

The riots revealed the hold of venerable Sunni attitudes toward the 'Alawi religion; clearly, it was not enough for Asad and other 'Alawis merely to assert their allegiance to Islam. So they sought to establish their allegiance through practice. Asad began to attend mosque services (something 'Alawis do not normally do) and performed the minor pilgrimage to Mecca in February 1974. The government built mosques at a faster clip than ever before and massively distributed Qur'ans carrying the president's picture (the so-called Asad Qur'ans). Court biographers built up Asad's Islamic credentials, for example, letting it be known that he had memorized one-quarter of the Qur'an by the age of six years.[162] But such claims made very little impression on Sunnis, who instinctively suspected the 'Alawis of *taqiya*. They knew that Asad could practice the rites of Islam and adopt its culture without offending his fellow 'Alawis or being considered an apostate. One Sunni author called 'Alawism "an independent religion with a pagan core and an Islamic appearance";[163] another designated Hafiz al-Asad a "defector from Islam clad in Muslim garb."[164]

To gain more credibility, the regime compelled figures in the Syrian religious establishment to vindicate the Islamic quality of their religion. The mufti of Damascus, for example, personally confirmed Asad's status as a Muslim in good standing. But domestic officials under Asad's control enjoyed little credibility. The government therefore requested the leader of the Twelver Shi'is in Lebanon, Musa as-Sadr, to indicate that the 'Alawis were legitimate Muslims. He did this by calling them "brothers" of his followers in July 1973—in effect, confirming the French decree of 1922.[165] Sadr's ruling has served ever since as the 'Alawis' main defense against those who call them non-Muslims. (In return for this favor, Sadr won authority over the small 'Alawi community in Lebanon and received Syrian government backing—backing which the Amal militia continued to receive long after Sadr's own death in 1978.)

But even Sadr's endorsement did little good, for most Sunnis continued not to recognize 'Alawis as Muslims. Virtually every discussion of this subject in print reached this conclusion. One review of the record determined that "a majority of Sunni and Shi'i scholars concur that the Nusayris are an apostate, irreligious sect."[166] Attitudes reminiscent of Ibn Taymiya's were commonly expressed; indeed, Ibn Taymiya's condemnation of the 'Alawis, repeatedly quoted, turned into a powerful weapon during the Asad presidency.

Tracts accused 'Alawis of heinous religious beliefs (polytheism, resurrection of the dead, the transmigration of souls) and horrible activities (alcoholic consumption, sexual promiscuity, orgies).[167] Muslim Brethren writings recalled the 'Alawis' "ugly crimes through history," claiming they helped Mongols, Crusaders, and French against the Muslim Arabs.[168] Sometimes they were portrayed as the followers of the Crusaders and Zionists. One publication called the 'Alawi religion "a mixture of French, Christian, Buddhist, Hindi, and Mazdaic doctrines" and concluded that "the 'Alawis are complete apostates from Islam."[169] Another saw it as a mixture of Christianity, Freemasonry, and Mazdaism.[170] The mufti of Jerusalem put teeth into these views in June 1983 by declaring in a *fatwa* that "it is the duty of every Muslim to kill Asad, the worst enemy of the Muslims."[171] All this gave the 'Alawis some idea of the fate awaiting them were they to lose power. An 'Alawi official of the Asad regime made it clear that the message was understood: "The Muslim Brethren want to liquidate the 'Alawis. They accuse us of being heretics and schismatics and do not want us to exist as a religious minority."[172]

The Turn to Pan-Syrianism

Nonsectarianism and Islam alike having failed to attract the Sunni majority, the state desperately needed some other way to involve the bulk of its populace. Nationalism offered an obvious vehicle, but as we have seen, allegiance to Syria in its present borders had little appeal to Sunnis. If the Asad regime was to appeal to its people and inspire loyalty on a nationalist basis, it had to look outward. The rulers needed a mechanism of expansion, preferably with a radical tinge. Laurent and Basbous explained this with regard to Lebanon: "From 1920, the Sunni Muslims of Syria felt a constant and almost visceral irredentism toward Lebanon. The ʿAlawis had to match these or, if possible, do better. This is the main reason why they tried so hard to 'recover' Lebanon."[173] The same applied to the other lost lands of Greater Syria.

Two ideologies answered this need: Pan-Arabism and Pan-Syrianism. At first glance, one would expect Pan-Arabism to have been Asad's choice; this would be the logical goal of someone who had been a member of the Baʿth Party since the 1940s. But it was not, in large part because his wing of the Baʿth Party, the Regionalists, had virtually abandoned Pan-Arabism in 1960. Further, ʿAlawis and other minorities perceived Pan-Arabism as equivalent to domination by Sunni Arabs. Discredited for more than a decade among the rulers of Syria, there was no chance that Asad would turn back the clock to this ideology. Pan-Arabist efforts had been given a chance and had failed. With Pan-Arabism unattractive to Regionalists and ʿAlawis, there was only one ideology left to inspire Sunni allegiance: Pan-Syrianism.

After 1974, the drive to establish a Greater Syria became Damascus's outstanding foreign policy goal. Ruling circles in Damascus no longer scorned the notion of special bonds tying the residents of Lesser Syria, Lebanon, Jordan, and Palestine. Indeed, the fate of the regime came to be bound up with the ability to achieve this ambition. Patrick Seale has predicted that "if Asad fails to achieve this role [as arbiter of the region] and his rivals and opponents are victorious in keeping Syria within its present borders, then the regional role of Syria will weaken and the influence of Damascus will shrink. Further, the current regime will not be able to remain in power long."[174]

Although details are unknown, one can speculate about the two critical factors in Asad's path to Pan-Syrianism. First, as was shown in Chapter 2, Pan-Syrianism from 1918 through 1950 was a vital and appealing force. Even though it was hardly visible for twenty-five years, it did not disappear. A force so strong for so long could not be eradicated, only made illicit. Second, Asad had early and extended contact with Pan-Syrianism. When he was growing up, the Baʿth Party and the SSNP shared a similar base of membership and means of recruitment. They competed for adherents primarily among the educated, radically minded non-Sunni minorities. Both recruited heavily in government district high schools, especially in predominantly minority districts such as Latakia. The two blanketed all the high schools of Syria. According to Michael H. van Dusen, "by the early 1950s, there was not a single high school graduate who had not had some exposure to the Baʿth Party or SSNP while in school."[175] The two parties sponsored rival high schools in Latakia during the 1940s; so prevalent was their influence, a high school student asked his religion would likely answer either "Baʿthi" or "Qawmi" (i.e., SSNP).

Even though Asad opted for the Baʿth, he grew up in the period when the SSNP was at its height; and as an ʿAlawi going to school in Latakia during the 1940s, he surely knew Saʿada's thought at close hand. When, a generation later, he sought an alternative to Pan-Arabism, Pan-Syrianism was readily available. The continuity between the vibrant Pan-Syrianism of the 1940s and his revival of it twenty years later is clear.[176]

In conclusion, Damascus's readoption of Pan-Syrianism can be ascribed to a multitude of reasons having to do with the imperatives of domestic Syrian politics:

(1) Rulers of Syria need an ideologically tinged irredentist cause with which to buttress their legitimacy.

(2) Many Syrians turned away from Pan-Arabism after the UAR's failure and favored, instead, an emphasis on Syria's domestic evolution. It was but a step from this to Pan-Syrianism.

(3) The rise of the ʿAlawis brought to power a community that had special reasons to mistrust Pan-Arabism and appreciate Pan-Syrianism. ʿAlawi rulers could more readily dominate Greater Syria than the Arab nation; also, the secularist tradition of Pan-Syrianism appealed to this persecuted minority.

(4) The Asad regime precipitated a revolt by Sunni Arabs, in part because of its sectarian quality, in part because of its policies. It therefore needed an outward-looking ideology to divert attention from internal problems and mobilize support for the government. With Pan-Arabism discredited, Asad turned to Pan-Syrianism.

Conclusion:
A Dangerous Double Game

When Almighty God bestowed riches and resources on the Middle East, he placed Syria in the region so it could assume the devil's role. . . . We ask Almighty God to divide Syria into hundreds of pieces so that the world at large may rest in peace.

Major Sa'd Haddad,
Commander of the South Lebanon forces[1]

Syrian Ba'th leaders have been plagued by a dilemma since the Regionalists emerged as a force in 1960: their ideology and their practice contradict each other. The Regionalists took steps to make Syria a strong and independent state while adhering to a doctrine—Pan-Arabism—that condemned those very steps. This contradiction grew more acute when the Regionalists became rulers of Syria in 1963, for their legitimacy rested partly on a Pan-Arab program. Then the adoption of pragmatic Pan-Syrianism a decade later meant the rulers espoused two opposing ideologies. Surely these inconsistencies must have plagued the Asad regime.

Actually, they seemed not to. Though Pan-Arabism long ago became mere ritual for the Ba'th leaders in Syria, it continued to serve as the party's official credo, and for good reason. Pan-Arabism provided an ideology widely accepted in the Middle East, and any turn by Ba'thists away from Arab unity would have torn the Ba'th Party apart. Renouncing Pan-Arabism in the 1960s would have exposed the Regionalists to attack by 'Abd an-Nasir and other Arab leaders, something the weak Syrian regimes of that period could not afford, and no subsequent leader had reason to stop mouthing the easy pieties of Pan-Arabism. It was easier to pretend that nothing had changed. The 1963 decision to shunt Pan-Arabism aside remained in place but was little known.

One sign of this was the greater rarity of ideologically charged Pan-Arabist statements coming out of Damascus. For example, after a meeting with Libyan diplomats on the eighteenth anniversary of the Ba'th's March 1963 accession to power—two good reasons for trotting out Pan-Arabist rhetoric—the press release only went so far as to note that "the March revolution is still a unionist revolution, struggling to establish one Arab state for the one Arab nation."[2] The word "still" gave the statement a perfunctory, even ritualistic quality. In fact, no Syrian official really subscribed to this ambition anymore, as the bitter comment of the Iraqi ruler, Saddam Husayn, after a visit to Damascus confirmed: "I went to talk about the Arab cause, and I was haggled with like a merchant."[3]

Conversely, Asad had good reason to keep his Pan-Syrian goals quiet. Naomi Joy Weinberger offered two motives: "because its earlier royalist connotations conjured up schemes directed at Syria by ambitious neighbors, and because of reluctance to arouse the anxieties of Syria's contemporary neighbors."[4] The royalist connection seems far-fetched, but the neighbors were a major consideration. Explicit Greater Syrian claims would have unnecessarily complicated relations with Lebanon, Jordan, and the PLO. In the interest of maintaining acceptable relations with its neighbors, the Asad regime did not talk much about Pan-Syrianism; better to retain the tired and by now almost unthreatening language of Pan-Arabism, or else grant that each neighbor has the right to autonomy. "Lip service, at least, had to be paid to Lebanese sovereignty and to the autonomy of the Palestinian Resistance. As long as Syria respected these formal demands of the Arab consensus, its freedom of action remained substantially unconstrained."[5] Were Greater Syrian nationalism formally enshrined, an international uproar would follow, with many consequences for Damascus, all unpleasant.

The deeply held feeling that there is something illicit about Pan-Syrian nationalism suggests another reason to keep quiet about Greater Syria. The bad odor of 'Abdallah's and the SSNP's activities remained pungent; while the high expectations invested in Pan-Arabism lived on. King Hasan of Morocco introduced an anecdote revealing Asad's and Khaddam's Pan-Syrianism (quoted on pp. 131–32) by stressing that he would not have repeated their words except that these had already been made public.[6] Of course, the king would never have hesitated about disclosing parallel Pan-Arab sentiments.

The contradictory nature of government rhetoric also reflected the political ambivalence of Sunni Arabs in Syria. It is hard to ascertain sentiments in the absence of a free press or on-the-ground research, but the following generalization seems likely to be true: Sunni Arabs were simultaneously repelled by the disreputable quality of Pan-Syrianism and drawn to its results. They disdained the theory, but an instinctual imperialism meant their interest was piqued. The regime's devious stance seemed to satisfy this dual sentiment.

Pan-Arabism provided a cover that allowed the regime to deny that Greater Syria represents its ultimate goal. Asad and his aides almost never explicitly referred to Pan-Syrian goals but always presented Pan-Syrianism within the context of Pan-Arabism. *One country, Southern Syria,* and other references compatible with Pan-Arabism turned up in Syrian rhetoric; but a specifically Pan-Syrian and anti–Pan-Arab term such as *Greater Syria* did not. In this way, the Asad regime fit Pan-Syrian practice within Pan-Arab ideology. Further, it showed no intention of wanting formally to annex Lebanon, Jordan, or Palestine. To do so would arouse the animosity of not just the local inhabitants but Arabic speakers everywhere. This would be especially hazardous in Lebanon, where armed groups already showed great ferocity against each other and outsiders. Much safer and smarter than this was to gain hegemonic control, such as Damascus has indeed acquired in large portions of Lebanon.

Pan-Syrian plans were wrapped, as innocuously as possible, in the flag of Arab nationalism. This is the traditional policy of pragmatic Pan-Syrianism: ʿAbdallah adopted it, the SSNP eventually adopted it, and so did Hafiz al-Asad. But being the leader of a Pan-Arabist party, Asad went a step further; he explicitly denied seeking Greater Syrian unity. The result was a striking rhetorical inconsistency. For every overt Syrian claim to take over Lebanon, Jordan, or Palestine, ten or twenty declarations promised to respect the independence of those regions. Thus, in answer to the question "Is your goal to establish Greater Syria, which would include Lebanon?" Asad replied: "The problem is not that of Greater Syria but action leading to Arab unity. . . . We believe in Arab unity and strive in that direction, everywhere and with reference to every Arab country."[7] Jimmy Carter recounted that he asked Hafiz al-Asad in March 1983 why the Syrian government considered Lebanon part of Greater Syria. In reply, Carter reported, Asad "repeatedly disavowed any designs on his western neighbor, insisting that he and his people recognized Lebanon's independence without equivocation."[8]

In a March 1989 question about his ambition to establish Greater Syria through the annexation of Lebanon, Asad began by denying any intentions toward Lebanon, then went on to provide historical background which contradicted his denial. He began by rejecting the term *Greater Syria:*

> In the peace conference in 1919, President Wilson did not say the Syrians sought to establish Greater Syria. He said "Syria should not be divided," and he had differences [over this] with his allies. He did not say "Greater Syria should not be divided," because in his whole life he had never read or heard the term "Greater Syria." In fact, he said only "Syria" because the natural, historic Syria is that Syria which some European officials called Greater Syria after it was divided.

Asad is suggesting that while seventy years may have passed since the Paris Peace Conference, he personally continues to hold on to the 1919 definition of Syria. In his parlance, it appears, Syria means Greater Syria. This equation can perhaps be fully appreciated by drawing a European analogy; it is like the West German chancellor announcing that because Bismarck used the term *Germany* to include what is now East Germany, he will do the same. It is easy to imagine the upheavals that would follow such a statement.

Nor is that all. Asad went on in the same interview to review Syrian history under the mandate:

> Syria in its present shape was divided into four mini-states by French and British colonialism: Damascus, Aleppo, southern Syria, and the coast. But the people struggled and united. Is it possible to say they set up a Greater Damascus [region] or Greater Aleppo [region]? We say they unified whatever parts they could. They are one people that unified themselves. We do not seek to build a Greater Syria nor is it our ambition to do that. Our ambition is to achieve the unity of all Arabs.[9]

By bracketing the unification of Damascus, Aleppo, Jabal Druze, and Latakia with the unification of Syria, Lebanon, Palestine, and Jordan, Asad seems to be equating them. Such unifications, he is saying, are nothing more than preliminary adjustments of boundaries, and so not a major goal in themselves. The major goal remains a single Arab nation. In this subtle but revealing interview, Asad confirmed his intention to unite the regions of Greater Syria while denying it any ideological importance.

To deflect talk about Greater Syria, the government blamed this very notion on the propaganda of enemies. Sometimes the enemy was not specified, as in a June 1985 interview with Vice-President Khaddam, when a Turkish reporter noted that "on official maps of Syria, Alexandretta is still shown as part of Syria" and added, "It sounds as if you are trying to keep the famous Hatay issue alive." Khaddam avoided the question and did a superb job of keeping options open: "I don't think the Turkish people are too concerned about this. I don't think they attach too much importance to it. The only thing the Turkish and Syrian people want is good bilateral relations. This issue is occasionally exploited in certain newspapers under Israeli influence. They want to obstruct a Turkish-Syrian rapprochement and to denigrate Syria." When the reporter pressed, "Well then, can you tell me that Syria never harbors any aggressive intentions?" the vice-president again gave nothing away: "Do you believe Syria is a threat to Turkey? Who would think we are threatening Turkey while we are trying to improve our relations with you and at a time when we want to see you on our side against Israel? We never want tension in our relations."[10]

At other times, Israel was directly accused of spreading calumnies, as Hafiz al-Asad explained in a March 1985 speech:

> Can you and our Arab masses not see with me how premeditated Zionist-imperialist propaganda attacks unity and considers it a form of expansion, annexation, and devouring? Did we not hear them attack Syria and accuse it of having imperialist ambitions? Did we not hear them make statements at high levels in the United States warning that Syria seeks to establish a Greater Syria? It is as if Arab efforts must not be mobilized to prevent the establishment of greater Israel, but to prevent the establishment of Greater Syria. They are trying, of course, to confuse Arab unity with the concept of colonialism.[11]

Sometimes imperialism got the blame. Asked to respond to those Lebanese who suspected Syrian plans to make Lebanon part of Greater Syria, Khaddam accused them of perpetuating "the Western mentality that has divided and disrupted the Arab nation and wants the state of disruption in the Arab homeland to continue."[12]

Asad's amalgam of Pan-Arabism and Pan-Syrianism replicated what the Ba'th and Syrian Social Nationalist Party had both done. The processes of change began in late 1961, when the two parties faced spectacular failures. The UAR breakup in September 1961 discredited the Ba'th Party; three months later, the SSNP failed horribly in an attempt to overthrow the government of Lebanon. These events had the curious effect of compelling each party to adopt elements of the other's ideology. The Ba'th Party of Syria became the Neo-Ba'th and showed new respect for Syria; with time, Pan-Arabism dropped out of its program, giving way to Pan-Syrianism. As for the SSNP, it sought refuge from its failures under the cover of Pan-Arabism. This crossover culminated when a significant number of SSNP members joined the Ba'th Party.[13] By Asad's time, the Neo-Ba'th had become almost indistinguishable from the SSNP. According to David Roberts, "the Ba'th has parted company with the PPS and indeed banned it, but it has quietly absorbed its message."[14] Laurent and Annie Chabry note that the Syrian government "uses the foil of Pan-Arabism to pursue a Pan-Syrian policy of the sort once promoted by the SSNP."[15]

Oddly, the Ba'th and the SSNP turned into the mirror images of each other. The SSNP kept its real doctrines but adopted Pan-Arabism for cover, while the Ba'th Party of Syria adopted a position congenial to the SSNP but pretended to maintain its original ideology. The SSNP talked like the Ba'th; the Ba'th acted like the SSNP. There was, however, a consistency in this behavior; both parties found it advantageous to pursue Pan-Syrian goals under the cover of Pan-Arabist rhetoric.

Asad played a double rhetorical game, equivocating between Pan-Syrianism and Pan-Arabism, espousing and denouncing Greater Syria. This duplicity did not go unnoticed. King Hasan of Morocco pointed out that the Asad regime's policies "come within the framework of a philosophy that it does not declare."[16] Shibli al-Aysami, a leading figure in the Ba'th Party of Iraq, explained Asad's cleverness: "In order to hide his personal ambitions, he has not totally eliminated the Ba'th; he jealously conserves its symbols and institutions, and is content to pervert its ideas and goals."[17]

These complex efforts at dissimulation closely resembled Asad's oft-remarked double game in the domestic arena. The regime kept power in a small circle of minority soldiers but pretended to be a broad-based, representative, civilian government. And so in foreign affairs, where it pursued a Pan-Syrian policy but gave it a Pan-Arabist cast. Just as informal networks counted for more than formal structures domestically, so whispered goals counted more than shouted ones internationally. In all cases, however, ambiguity reigned, allowing the rulers never to be pinned down. Damascus claimed Alexandretta as a part of Greater Syria, and yet it did not; it claimed Lebanon and Jordan yet recognized Lebanon and Jordan as separate polities; it called Palestine "Southern Syria" but acknowledged the PLO as the rightful claimant to Palestine. Projecting two messages simultaneously gave Syrian leaders maximum flexibility in internal and external affairs.

Notes

Introduction

1. *Letter from Lord Palmerston to M. Thiers, Dated Foreign Office, August 31, 1840* (London: T. Brettell, 1840), p. 5. Benjamin Disraeli wrote, in parallel, "Lebanon is the key of Syria." *Tancred, or The New Crusade* (London: Longmans, Green, 1847), pp. 368, 446.

2. Maps of Syria (Damascus: Idarat al-Maslaha al-'Askariya, 1971 and 1977). Although these are official maps of the Syrian armed forces, they are propaganda maps. The Syrian forces would find themselves in enormous trouble if they acted as though Israel did not exist and Alexandretta and the Golan Heights were still under Syrian rule.

3. The party has gone by a variety of names; for simplicity's sake, only Syrian Social Nationalist Party will be used here.

4. Kamal Junbalat, *Adwa' 'ala Haqiqat al-Qadiya al-Qawmiya al-Ijtima'iya as-Suriya* (Beirut, n.d.); Abu Khaldun Sati' al-Husri, *Al-'Uruba bayn Du'atiha wa Mu'aridiha* (Beirut: Dar al-'Ilm li'l-Malayin, 1952); idem, *Difa' 'an al-'Uruba*, 2d ed. (Beirut: Markaz Dirasat al-Wahda al-'Arabiya, 1985).

5. *The Economist*, 10 May 1947, 6 January 1962, 10 August 1985.

6. *The Washington Post*, 23 December 1977.

7. Michael C. Hudson, *The Precarious Republic: Political Modernization in Lebanon* (New York: Random House, 1968), p. 169.

8. Philippe Boulos, Lebanese Minister of Information, Radio Lebanon, January 1962. Text in *Le Liban face è l'Ouragan* (n.p., n.d.), p. 18. The Fertile Crescent plan would join Iraq with Greater Syria in one state.

9. Robert M. Haddad, "Eastern Christianity in Contemporary Arab Society," in Kail C. Ellis, ed., *The Vatican and the Middle East* (Syracuse, N.Y.: Syracuse University Press, 1987), p. 212.

10. George Antonius, *The Arab Awakening: The Story of the Arab National Movement* (Philadelphia: J. B. Lippincott, 1939), pp. 81–91; or A. L. Tibawi, *A Modern History of Syria, including Lebanon and Palestine* (London: Macmillan, 1969), pp. 163–67.

11. Zeine N. Zeine, *The Emergence of Arab Nationalism* (Beirut: Khayats, 1966), pp. 59–67.

12. Memorandum to the Supreme Council at the Paris Peace Conference, 1 January 1919. Text in J. C. Hurewitz, ed., *The Middle East and North Africa in World Politics: A Documentary Record*, 2d ed. (New Haven, Conn.: Yale University Press, 1975–79), Vol. 2, p. 131. By similar token, more than thirty years later, Prince ʿAbdallah held that "we left the Hijaz for the sake of Syria and Palestine." Minutes of a meeting on 28 November 1950, in ʿAbdallah ibn al-Husayn, *At-Takmila*, in *Al-Athar al-Kamila li'l-Malik ʿAbdallah ibn al-Husayn* (Beirut: Ad-Dar al-Muttahida li'n-Nashr, 1976), p. 270.

13. Jon Kimche, *Palestine or Israel* (London: Secker & Warburg, 1973), p. 184.

14. Muhammad Y. Muslih, *The Origins of Palestinian Nationalism* (New York: Columbia University Press, 1988), p. 132.

15. Christopher Sykes, *Crossroads to Israel* (Cleveland: World Publishing Company, 1965), p. 376.

16. Mary C. Wilson, *King Abdullah, Britain and the Making of Jordan* (Cambridge: Cambridge University Press, 1987), p. 101.

17. Philip S. Khoury, *Syria and the French Mandate: The Politics of Arab Nationalism, 1920–1945* (Princeton, N.J.: Princeton University Press, 1987), p. 464. On p. 525, Khoury explains the appeal of the SSNP without any reference to its Pan-Syrian ideology.

18. Stanley F. Reed III, "Dateline Syria: Fin de Régime?" *Foreign Policy* 39 (Summer 1980): 185. Earlier, Eric Rouleau observed that the Baʿth, even in power, "continues to behave more like an occult sect than a political party." See Eric Rouleau, "The Syrian Enigma: What Is the Baath?" *New Left Review*, no. 45 (1967): 54.

19. These are all too often seen as different. For a surprising example, see Moshe Maʿoz, *Asad, The Sphinx of Damascus: A Political Biography* (New York: Weidenfeld & Nicholson, 1988), p. 114.

20. Because of the many meanings of the term "Syria," Syrian nationalism refers to support for either Greater Syria or the Republic of Syria. Pan-Syrian nationalism (or simply Pan-Syrianism) refers only to Greater Syria and will therefore be employed here.

21. David Lloyd George, *Memoirs of the Peace Conference* (New Haven, Conn.: Yale University Press, 1939), pp. 649–50.

22. William Yale, "Strong National Feeling," about 1 July 1919, in the Lybyer Papers. Quoted in Harry N. Howard, *The King-Crane Commission: An American Inquiry in the Middle East* (Beirut: Khayat's, 1963), p. 114. Another skeptic, Robert de Beauplan, wrote that "the nationalists affirm the reality of the Syrian nation, but it is a myth." *Où va la Syrie: Le Mandat sous les Cèdres* (Paris: Éditions Jules Tallandier, 1929), p. 32.

Chapter 1

1. Letter dated 7 February 1928, in Freya Stark, *Letters from Syria* (London: John Murray, 1942), p. 60. Edward Atiyah, *An Arab Tells His Story: A Study in Loyalties* (London: John Murray, 1946), p. 1.

2. Ulrich Kahrstedt, *Syrische Territorien in hellenistischer Zeit* (Berlin: Weidmannsche Buchhandlung, 1926), pp. 1–3.

3. F. M. Heichelheim, "Roman Syria," in Tenney Frank, ed., *An Economic Survey of Ancient Rome* (Baltimore: Johns Hopkins University Press, 1938), Vol. 4, p. 123.

4. Literally, *ash-sham* means "the North;" Arabians used the term in tandem with *al-yaman*, "the South" (in English, "Yemen").

5. For details on the boundaries of Syria as understood by premodern Muslim

geographers, see M. Gaudefroy-Demombynes, *La Syrie à l'époque des Mamelouks* (Paris: Paul Geuthner, 1923), pp. 6–12; also, Guy Le Strange, *Palestine under the Moslems* (Boston: Houghton Mifflin, 1890), pp. 14–43.

6. The letter was published in Arabic a year later in Malta, translated into Arabic by Asʿad ash-Shidyaq, the brother of Faris ash-Shidyaq. Sasson Somekh kindly pointed out this information to me.

7. ʿAbd al-Karim Gharayba, *Suriya fi'l-Qarn at-Tasiʿ ʿAshar, 1840–1876* (Cairo: Maʿhad ad-Dirasat al-ʿArabiya al-ʿUliya, 1961–62), pp. 215–21, 242–45.

8. Manuscript quoted in Kamal S. Salibi, "The 1860 Upheaval in Damascus as Seen by as-Sayyid Muhammad Abu'l-Suʿud al-Hasibi, Notable and Later *Naqib al-Ashraf* of the City," in William R. Polk and Richard L. Chambers, eds., *Beginnings of Modernization in the Middle East: The Nineteenth Century* (Chicago: University of Chicago Press, 1968), p. 189.

9. Ilyas Dib Matar, *Al-ʿUqud ad-Durriya fi Taʾrikh al-Mamlaka as-Suriya* (Beirut: Matbaʿat al-Maʿarif, 1874); Jurji Yanni, *Taʾrikh Suriya* (Beirut: Al-Matbaʿa al-Adabiya, 1881; reprinted by Dar Lahad Khatir, 1986).

10. Volney [pseudonym of Constantin-François Chasseheuf], *Voyage en Égypte et en Syrie* (Paris and the Hague: Mouton, 1959), p. 159.

11. Georg Wilhelm Friedrich Hegel, *The Philosophy of History*, trans. by J. Sibree (New York: Dover, 1956), p. 87. Sarah Barclay Johnson, *Hadji in Syria; or, Three Years in Jerusalem* (Philadelphia: James Challen & Sons, 1858).

12. John Lewis Burckhardt, *Travels in Syria and the Holy Land* (London: John Murray, 1822), p. 368.

13. J. C. Hurewitz, *The Middle East and North Africa in World Politics: A Documentary Record*, 2d ed. (New Haven, Conn.: Yale University Press, 1975–79), Vol. 1, p. 273.

14. H. B. Tristam, *The Land of Israel: Journal of Travels in Palestine*, 4th ed., rev. (London: Society for Promoting Christian Knowledge, 1882), p. 7.

15. "Palestine," *Encyclopaedia Britannica*, 11th ed. (Cambridge: At the University Press, 1911), Vol. 20, p. 600.

16. ʿAbd ar-Rahman al-Jabarti, *ʿAjaʾib al-Athar* (Bulaq, 1290–97/1873–80), Vol. 2, p. 52.

17. *Papers Relating to the Foreign Relations of the United States: The Paris Peace Conference, 1919* (Washington, D.C.: U.S. Government Printing Office, 1942–47), Vol. 12, p. 780.

18. Benoit Aboussouan, *Le Problème politique syrien* (Paris: Librairie de Jurisprudence Ancienne et Moderne, 1925), map at end.

19. Antun Saʿada, *At-Taʿalim as-Suriya al-Qawmiya al-Ijtimaʿiya* (n.p., 1960), pp. 31–32. Saʿada combined the names of Syria and Iraq to come up with the name "as-Suraqiya," which he applied to his later, larger Syria. See Kamal Junbalat, *Adwaʾ ʿala Haqiqat al-Qadiya al-Qawmiya al- Ijtimaʿiya as-Suriya* (Beirut: n.p., n.d.), p. 79.

20. William Libbey and Franklin E. Hoskins, *The Jordan Valley and Petra* (New York: G. P. Putnam's Sons, 1905), Vol. 1, p. 89.

21. A. W. Kinglake, *Eothen* (London: Longmans, Green, 1935), p. 106.

22. Peter Mansfield, "Syria and Jordan: The Desert and the Sown," *Asian Affairs* 16 (1985): 20.

23. Emmanuel de Martonne, "L'Unité géographique de la Syrie," *Congrès Français de la Syrie*, fasc. 2, p. 226. For other geographers on Syria's geographic cohesion, see Nagib Sadaka, *La Question syrienne pendant la guerre de 1914* (Paris: Larose, 1941), chap. 1.

24. Shukri Ghanim of the Central Syrian Commitee, 13 February 1919. Text in *Paris Peace Conference, 1919,* Vol. 3, p. 1025.

25. *Al-Mufid* [Damascus], 1924. Arabic text in Georg Kampffmeyer, "Urkunden und Berichte zur Gegenwartsgeschichte des arabischen Orients," *Mitteilungen des Seminars für Orientalische Sprachen an der Friedrich-Wilhelms-Universität zu Berlin,* 26-27 (1924): 88.

26. K. T. Khaïrallah, "La Syrie," *Revue du Monde Musulman* 19 (1912): 6, 16.

27. ʿAbd al-ʿAziz Muhammad ʿAwwad, *Al-Idara al-ʿUthmaniya fi Wilayat Suriya, 1864–1914* (Cairo: Dar al-Maʿarif, 1969), pp. 66–81.

28. Robert M. Haddad, *Syrian Christians in Muslim Society: An Interpretation* (Princeton, N.J.: Princeton University Press, 1970), p. 6.

29. This term was apparently first used by John Morgan Jones, *La Fin du mandat français en Syrie et au Liban* (Paris: A. Pedone, 1938), p. 142.

30. Omar Djabry, *La Syrie sous le régime du Mandat* (Toulouse: Librairie Générale, 1934), p. 74.

31. Robert de Caix to Raymond Poincaré, Ministère des Affaires Etrangères, Levant, Vol. 47B, no. 265, Beirut, 15 April 1922. Quoted in Meir Zamir, *The Formation of Modern Lebanon* (London: Croom Helm, 1985), p. 142.

32. Isabel Burton, *The Inner Life of Syria, Palestine, and the Holy Land* (London: Henry S. King, 1875), Vol. 1, pp. 105–06.

33. National Register of Archives, London, Shaftesbury (Broadlands), MSS, SHA/PD6, 30 July 1853. Quoted in Geoffrey B. A. M. Finleyson, *The Seventh Earl of Shaftesbury, 1801–1885* (London: Eyre Methuen, 1981), p. 441. *A Handbook for Travellers in Syria and Palestine* (London: John Murray, 1858), Vol. 1, p. xlvi.

34. Gertrude Lowthian Bell, *Syria: The Desert and the Sown,* new ed. (London: William Heinemann, 1919), p. 228.

35. Khaïrallah, "La Syrie," p. 104.

36. T. E. Lawrence, *Secret Dispatches from Arabia* (London: Golden Cockerel Press, n.d.), p. 77.

37. Chief of the Information Service of the French Navy, to Georges Leygues, 12 January 1918, Archives Marines, carton Ea 200, dossier 1918. Quoted in Jan Karl Tanenbaum, *France and the Arab Middle East, 1914–1920* (Philadelphia: American Philosophical Society, 1978), p. 20.

38. Jacques Weulersse, *Paysans de Syrie et du Proche-Orient* (Paris: Gallimard, 1946), pp. 84–85. The dilemma of a government that has no meaning for its citizens is typical of Muslim states, premodern and modern. For an elaboration of this point, see Daniel Pipes, *In the Path of God: Islam and Political Power* (New York: Basic Books, 1983), pp. 57–63.

39. Moshe Maʿoz, "Society and State in Modern Syria," in Menachem Milson, ed., *Society and Political Structure in the Arab World* (New York: Humanities Press, 1973), p. 32.

40. Albert Hourani, *Arabic Thought in the Liberal Age, 1798–1939* (London: Oxford University Press, 1970), pp. 286–87.

41. Stephen Hemsley Longrigg, *Syria and Lebanon under French Mandate* (London: Oxford University Press, 1958), p. 144.

42. Communiqué of 5 October 1918. Text in *Faysal bin al-Husayn fi Khutabihi wa-Aqwalihi* (Baghdad: Matbaʿat al-Hukuma, 1945), p. 181. His father, Husayn, took the title of King of the Arabs in late 1916.

43. *Paris Peace Conference, 1919,* Vol. 5, p. 3.

44. Council of Four Meeting, 20 March 1919. Ibid., p. 4.

45. Quoted in Abu Khaldun Sati' al-Husri, *Yawm Maysalun*, new ed. (Beirut: Dar al-Ittihad, 1965), p. 266. (This speech was originally in French but is translated here from Arabic.) Perversely, the French continued to praise Syrian unity even as they dismembered the region. When General Henri Gouraud sent an ultimatum to Faysal on 14 July 1920 demanding that all powers be handed over to France, he justified this on the grounds that Faysal had "gratefully recognised that it was in the interest of the Syrian population to seek the counsel and help of a great power in order to realise their unity." Quoted in David Lloyd George, *Memoirs of the Peace Conference* (New Haven, Conn.: Yale University Press, 1939), p. 717.

46. Quoted in David Roberts, *The Ba'th and the Creation of Modern Syria* (New York: St. Martin's Press, 1987), p. 13.

47. Resolution of the Comité de l'Asie Française, August 1915, Ministère des Affaires Etrangères, A Guerre 870. Quoted in Christopher M. Andrew, "France, Britain, and the Peace Settlement: A Reconsideration," in Uriel Dann, ed., *The Great Powers in the Middle East, 1919–1939* (New York: Holmes & Meier, 1988), p. 164.

48. According to the King-Crane Commission report, the British government in 1919 subsidized Faysal by $750,000 a month. See *Paris Peace Conference, 1919*, Vol. 12, p. 858.

49. See William I. Shorrock, *French Imperialism in the Middle East: The Failure of Policy in Syria and Lebanon, 1900–1914* (Madison, Wisc.: University of Wisconsin Press, 1976). Not surprisingly, the British saw matters differently. British foreign minister Arthur Balfour explained in a memorandum: "I have never been able to understand on what historic basis the French claim to Syria really rests. Frenchmen's share in the Crusades of the Middle Ages, Mazarin's arrangements with the Turk in the seventeenth century, and the blustering expedition of 1861, lend in my opinion very little support to their far-reaching ambitions." Text in E. L. Woodward and Rohan Butler, eds., *Documents on British Foreign Policy, 1919–39* (London: Her Majesty's Stationery Office, 1952), series 1, Vol. 4, p. 340.

50. Letter to Prime Minister David Lloyd George, 8 March 1919. Text in Lloyd George, *Memoirs of the Peace Conference*, p. 679.

51. 25 April 1919, quoted in Paul Mantoux, *Les Délibérations du Conseil des Quatre (24 mars–28 juin 1919)* (Paris: CNRS, 1955), Vol. 1, p. 379.

52. "Allenby's Condition to Faysal's Provisional Arab Regime at Damascus," 17 October 1918. Text in Hurewitz, *Documentary Record*, Vol. 2, p. 112.

53. Text in Chaim Weizmann, *Trial and Error: Autobiography* (New York: Harper & Row, 1949), pp. 246–47.

54. Dated 13 February 1919. Text in *Paris Peace Conference, 1919*, Vol. 3, p. 1029. Ghanim made an unfortunate impression at the Paris Peace Conference. Given an opportunity to address the Supreme Council, he delivered "a long, ineffective outpouring of pathetic eloquence lasting two and a half hours. Bored by the presentation, Woodrow Wilson before long got up from his chair, wandered over to the other side of the room, and stared out of the windows. Clemenceau spoke over his shoulder to Pichon in a stage whisper . . . asking savagely: 'What did you get this fellow here for, anyway?' Pichon, spreading his hands in impotent protest, said, 'Well, I didn't know he was going to carry on this way.' It was a complete give-away." James T. Shotwell, *At the Paris Peace Conference* (New York: MacMillan, 1937), p. 178.

55. "It is related that when news of the decision reached Faisal's ears he drank champagne for the first time, and drank it as though it were water. Then he went for a drive past the headquarters of the American and British Delegations [those two which had accepted his proposal] and threw cushions at the Crillon, the Majestic and the Quai

d'Orsay, saying that, as he had no bombs, he could only express his feelings in that way." George Antonius, *The Arab Awakening* (Philadelphia: J.B. Lippincott, 1939), p. 288.

56. Speech given on 5 May 1919. Text in *Faysal bin al-Husayn*, p. 196.

57. *Paris Peace Conference, 1919*, Vol. 12, pp. 780, 789.

58. Elie Kedourie, *England and the Middle East: The Destruction of the Ottoman Empire, 1914–1921* (London: Bowes & Bowes, 1956), p. 147. That King and Crane were ill informed was no secret. Indeed, an aide explained that President Woodrow Wilson (in a classic demonstration of American naïveté) "felt these two men were particularly qualified to go to Syria because they knew nothing about it." *Paris Peace Conference, 1919*, Vol. 11, p. 133. This outlook clarifies why European diplomats thought (in Robert de Caix's words) Americans were "too honest to deal with Orientals." Albert Howe Lybyer, "Diary," 12 April 1919, quoted in Harry N. Howard, *The King-Crane Commission: An American Inquiry in the Middle East* (Beirut: Khayat's, 1963), p. 45.

59. Statement of 11 August 1919. Text in Hurewitz, *Documentary Record*, Vol. 2, p. 186.

60. Quoted in ʿAli Rida, *Qissat al-Kifah al-Watani fi Suriya ʿAskariyan wa-Siyasiyan Hatta al-Jalaʾ* (Aleppo: Al-Matbaʿa al-Haditha, 1979), p. 35.

61. Maurice Barrès, "Nos droits seront maintenus en Syrie," *Echo de Paris*, 20 October 1919.

62. Letter to Premier Georges Clemenceau, 18 October 1919. Text in Lloyd George, *Memoirs of the Peace Conference*, p. 707.

63. Text in al-Husri, *Yawm Maysalun*, p. 280.

64. Alaeddin Saleh Hreib, "The Influence of Sub-Regionalism (Rural Areas) on the Structure of Syrian Politics, 1920–73," unpublished Ph.D. dissertation, Georgetown University, 1976, p. 77.

65. Antonius, *Arab Awakening*, p. 304.

66. Alexandre Millerand to General Henri Gouraud, 13 March 1920, Foreign Office (London) 371/5033. Quoted in Ali Mahafzah, "La France et le mouvement nationaliste arabe de 1914 à 1939," *Relations Internationales* 19 (1979): 301.

67. Quoted in al-Husri, *Yawm Maysalun*, p. 99 (this telegram was originally in English but is translated here from Arabic).

68. Arthur Balfour is recorded admitting on 30 July 1920, just six days after French troops entered Damascus: "We had not been honest with either French or Arab, but it was preferable to quarrel with the Arab rather than the French." R. M. Meinerzhagen, *Middle East Diary, 1917–1956* (London: Cresset, 1959), p. 26.

69. The United States had a delegate at San Remo, too, but his instructions failed to arrive. So he "sat in a hotel garden reading the newspapers while the British and French settled the most important matters affecting the Middle East." Edgar Ansel Mowrer, *The Nightmare of American Foreign Policy* (New York: Alfred A. Knopf, 1948), p. 51.

70. The laconic agreement merely stated that "The mandates chosen by the principal Allied Powers are: France for Syria, and Great Britain for Mesopotamia and Palestine." Rohan Butler and J. P. T. Bury, eds., *Documents on British Foreign Policy, 1919–39* (London: Her Majesty's Stationery Office, 1958), series 1, Vol. 8, p. 177.

71. Prime Minister Georges Leygues, quoted in Charles Lord Hardinge of Penhurst (Paris) to George Curzon, 21 December 1920, E16025/2/44 (no. 3786), Foreign Office 406/44. Cited in Aaron S. Klieman, *Foundations of British Policy in the Arab World: The Cairo Conference of 1921* (Baltimore: Johns Hopkins University Press, 1970), p. 51.

72. "Report on the Administration of Palestine, 1920–1925." Text in *Mandate for Palestine* (Washington D.C.: U.S. Government Printing Office, 1927), p. 23.

73. A retronym makes a distinction that previously did not exist. Examples include intact family, genuine leather, whole milk, not-from-concentrate orange juice, natural grass, working fireplace, working farm, analog watch, acoustic guitar, rotary telephone, and manual typewriter.

74. In Arabic, Greater Syria is clearly identified with the aspirations of King 'Abdallah of Transjordan. Other Pan-Syrianists, such as the SSNP members, did not use this term.

75. The term *Small Syria* was used for this purpose in English as early as June 1919. See Howard, *King-Crane Commission*, p. 94. It has also been used in Arabic; thus, the Syrian foreign minister declared in January 1945 that he "preferred to be a low-ranking official in the Greater Arab State to being a Minister or a President of the Republic in a smaller Syria." *Al-Ahram*, 5 January 1945. Quoted in Yehoshua Porath, *In Search of Arab Unity, 1930–1945* (London: Frank Cass, 1986), p. 288. The SSNP usually distinguishes between Lesser and Greater Syria by calling the first *Suriya* and the second *Ash-Sham*, a distinction that cannot be made in English. See *Le Liban face à l'Ouragan* (n.p., n.d), p. 36.

76. Quoted in Elizabeth Monroe, *Britain's Moment in the Middle East, 1914–1956* (Baltimore: Johns Hopkins University Press, 1963), p. 66.

77. *Paris Peace Conference, 1919*, Vol. 12, p. 858.

78. *The Times*, 31 August 1926.

79. *Al-Ayyam*, 26 June 1938. Quoted in Annie Laurent and Antoine Basbous, *Une Proie pour deux fauves?* (Beirut: Ad-Da'irat, 1983), p. 17.

80. Ministère des Affaires Étrangères, Levant, Vol. 200, pp. 71–72. Quoted in Zamir, *Formation of Modern Lebanon*, pp. 114–15.

81. Al-Kataeb Al-Lubnaniat, *Phalanges Libanaises* (Beirut: Parti Democrate Social Libanais, 1956), p. 26. Text in Kemal H. Karpat, ed., *Political and Social Thought in the Contemporary Middle East*, 2d ed. (New York: Praeger, 1982), p. 70.

82. *Nafir Suriya*, 25 October 1860. Quoted in Y. Choueiri, "Two Histories of Syria and the Demise of Syrian Patriotism," *Middle Eastern Studies* 23 (1987): 497.

83. Adil as-Sulh, *Sutur min ar-Risala* (Beirut: Dar al-'Ilm li'l-Malayin, 1966), pp. 98, 100.

84. Fritz Steppat, "Eine Bewegung unter den Notabeln Syriens, 1877–78," *Zeitschrift der Deutschen Morgenländischen Gesellschaft*, suppl. 1, part 2 (1969): 633.

85. Facsimiles in Zeine N. Zeine, *The Emergence of Arab Nationalism* (Beirut: Khayats, 1966), pp. 171–73.

86. George-Samné, *La Syrie* (Paris: Bossard, 1920), p. 523. George-Samné, a member of the Syrian Central Committee, devoted his 733-page book, which went to press at the critical moment of August 1920, to a demonstration of the ways Syria would benefit from French rule.

87. "Memorandum respecting Pan-Arabism," Gilbert MacKereth to Anthony Eden, British Consul in Damascus, 15 May 1936, E 3039/381/65, Foreign Office 371/19980/5925.

88. "Constitution du Parti Ba'th Arabe," of 17 June 1947. Text in André Raymond, ed., *La Syrie d'aujourd'hui* (Paris: Éditions du CNRS, 1980), p. 207.

89. Nuri as-Sa'id, *Arab Independence and Unity: A Note* (Baghdad: Government Press, 1943), p. 12.

90. "Debate Concerning the Political Importance of Pan-Arabism," MacKereth to Anthony Eden, 4 March 1936, in Michael G. Fry and Itamar Rabinovich, eds.,

Despatches from Damascus: Gilbert MacKereth and British Policy in the Levant, 1933–1939 (Tel Aviv: Dayan Center, 1985), p. 136.

91. League of Nations, Permanent Mandates Commission, *Minutes of the 9th Session*, 16th meeting, 17 June 1926, p. 111.

92. Antun Sa'ada, *Mabadi' al-Hizb al-Qawmi al-Ijtima'i wa Ghaybatuhu* (Beirut: n.p., 1972), p. 11.

93. Text in *Qadiyat al-Hizb al-Qawmi* (Beirut: Ministry of Information, 1949), p. 158. Issued by the Lebanese government to justify the execution of Sa'ada, this important source book is to be used only with great caution.

94. One estimate has Muslims making up 20 percent of the SSNP membership in 1959. See W. David Wrigley, "The Orthodox Community in Lebanon on the Eve of the Hostilities, 1974–1975," *Indiana Social Sciences Quarterly* 35 (1982): 49.

95. Yusuf As'ad Daghir, *Masadir ad-Dirasa al-Adabiya* (Beirut: Al-Maktaba ash-Sharqiya, 1972), Vol. 3, part 1, p. 541. Thomas Philipp kindly directed me to this reference.

96. At least four of Sa'ada's father's many books were published in Egypt, including *The Gospel of Barnabas*, *The Secrets of the Russian Revolution* (a novel published in 1906), and an Arabic-English medical dictionary. See Daghir, *Masadir ad-Dirasa al-Adabiya*, Vol. 3, part 1, pp. 543–44.

97. Thomas Philipp, *The Syrians in Egypt, 1725–1975* (Stuttgart: Franz Steiner, 1985), p. 114.

98. Henri Lammens, *La Syrie: Précis historique* (Beirut: Imprimerie Catholique, 1921), Vol. 1, p. 5.

99. Bassam Tibi, *Nationalismus in der Dritten Welt am arabischen Beispiel* (Frankfurt: Europäische Verlagsanstalt, 1971), p. 263.

100. Pierre Rondot, "Quelques aperçus de la doctrine du P.P.S.," *Orient* 40 (1966): 13.

101. Philip K. Hitti, *Suriya wa's-Suriyun min Nafidhat at-Ta'rikh* (New York: Al-Matba'a at-Tijariya as-Suriya al-Amrikiya, 1926), p. 11.

102. Labib Zuwiyya Yamak, *The Syrian Social Nationalist Party: An Ideological Analysis* (Cambridge, Mass.: Center for Middle Eastern Studies, Harvard University, 1969), pp. 53–54.

103. *Faysal bin al-Husayn*, p. 196.

104. In Arabic, these terms are, respectively: *al-umma as-Suriya al-Arabiya, al-bilad al-'Arabiya, al-umma al-'Arabiya, nahiyat Suriya, al-umma as-Suriya, al-qatr as-Suri*. Ibid., pp. 208–12.

105. In Arabic: *kutla Suriya 'Arabiya* and *al-'alam al-'Arabi*. Ibid., pp. 218, 220.

106. *Al-Ahram*, 8 April 1943. Quoted in Porath, *In Search of Arab Unity*, p. 35.

107. Speech on 8 April 1943. Text in Government of Jordan, *Suriya al-Kubra: Al-Kitab al-Urdunni al-Abyad* (Amman: Al-Matba'a al-Wataniya, 1947), p. 77.

108. Undated letter to Sa'dallah al-Jabiri. Text in Government of Jordan, *Suriya al-Kubra*, p. 92.

109. Speech from the Throne, 1 November 1945. Text in ibid., p. 136.

110. Letter to Shukri al-Quwwatli, 28 August 1943. Text in ibid., p. 88.

111. 'Abdallah ibn al-Husayn, *At-Takmila*, in *Al-Athar al-Kamila li'l-Malik 'Abdallah ibn al-Husayn* (Beirut: Ad-Dar al-Muttahida li'n-Nashr, 1976), p. 270.

112. *Al-Hawadith*, 18 July 1975. A rather ignorant interviewer responded to this revelation, "It appears that you were an adherent of the SSNP." In fact, Rifa'i obviously supported 'Abdallah's rival vision, so he answered diplomatically, "I am speaking of natural unity, not of ideology."

113. Facsimiles in Zeine, *Emergence of Arab Nationalism*, pp. 171–73.

114. Negib Azoury, *Le Réveil de la nation arabe dans l'Asie turque* (Paris: Librairies Plon, 1905), p. 245.

115. Anis al-Khuri al-Maqdisi, *Al-Mukhtarat as-Sa'ira* (Beirut: Dar al-'Ilm li'l-Malayin, 1952). Quoted in Nadim K. Makdisi, "The Syrian National Party," unpublished Ph.D. dissertation, American University, 1960, pp. iv–v, 68.

116. Resolutions 3, 5, and 6 of the Arab-Syrian Congress, 21 June 1913. Text in G. P. Gooch and Harold Temperley, eds., *British Documents on the Origins of the War, 1898–1914* (London: His Majesty's Stationery Office, 1926–38), Vol. 10, part 2, p. 826. Shukri Ghanim, the adamant Pan-Syrian nationalist, was vice-president of this congress.

117. Makdisi, "Syrian National Party," p. 67.

118. Kemal Joumblatt, *Pour le Liban* (Paris: Stock, 1978), p. 177.

119. Edmond Rabbath, *Unité syrienne et devenir arabe* (Paris: Marcel Rivière, 1937), p. 33.

120. Kassim Sallam, *Le Ba'th et la patrie arabe* (Paris: Éditions du Monde Arabe, 1982), p. 97.

121. *Qadiyat al-Hizb al-Qawmi*, p. 158.

122. Muhammad Jamil Bayhum, *Lubnan Bayn Musharriq wa-Mugharrib* (Beirut: author, 1969), p. 22.

123. Fiches du Monde Arabe, II 110. Quoted in Laurent and Basbous, *Une Proie pour deux fauves?*, p. 17.

124. Ahmad 'Arif az-Zayn, "Mu'tamar as-Sahil wa'l-Aqdiya al-Arba'a," March 1936. Quoted in Hisan 'Ali Hallaq, *Mu'tamar as-Sahil wa'l-Aqdiya al-Arba'a, 1936* (Beirut: Dar al-Jami'iya, 1403/1983), p. 45.

125. Fawzi Barudawil [spelling unsure], "Mu'tamar as-Sahil wa'l-Aqdiya al-Arba'a," March 1936. Quoted in ibid., p. 48.

126. David Ben-Gurion, *My Talks with Arab Leaders*, trans. by Aryeh Rubinstein and Misha Louvish (New York: Third Press, 1973), pp. 49–55.

127. Rabbath, *Unité syrienne et devenir arabe*. Rabbath defines Syria as Greater Syria on p. 71.

128. Aboussouan, *Le Problème politique syrien*, p. 238.

129. Terence Shone to Anthony Eden, 22 March 1945, no. 47 (60/311/45), in the Foreign Office archives.

130. "Weekly Political Summary No. 156, Syria and the Lebanon," 27 March 1945, E 2381/5/89, Foreign Office 371/45553/7504. Faysal II was king of Iraq, 1939–58.

131. Patrick Seale, "Madha Yurid Hafiz al-Asad?" *Al-Majalla* [London], 23 July 1983, p. 23.

132. *At-Tadamun*, 7 September 1985.

133. Antun Sa'ada, *Al-Islam fi Risalatayh al-Masihiya wa'l-Muhammadiya*, 3d ed. (Beirut: n.p., 1958), p. 216.

134. Sa'ada, *Mabadi'*, p. 32.

135. Sa'ada, *Al-Islam fi Risalatayh*, p. 216.

136. Quoted in Hisham Sharabi, *Al-Jamr wa'r-Ramad: Dhikrayat Muthaqqaf 'Arabi* (Beirut: Dar at-Tali'a li't-Tiba'a wa'n-Nashr, 1978), p. 74.

137. Quoted in Junbalat, *Adwa' 'ala Haqiqat al-Qadiya*, p. 90.

138. Ministry of the Interior permit, dated 2 May 1944. Text in *Qadiyat al-Hizb al-Qawmi*, p. 148.

139. *Al-Hayat*, 8 October 1963. Text in *Arab Political Documents 1963*, p. 418.

140. Quoted in Rondot, "Quelques aperçus," 16.

141. Sadiq ʿAta [pseud.], "Al-Ahzab fi Lubnan wa'l-Jaysh." *Al-ʿAmal* [Cairo] 14 (1979): 174–80, provides abundant detail on cooperation with the PLO. On SSNP efforts in Palestine in the 1935–48 period, including failed efforts to work with Amin al-Husayni, see Bayan N. al-Hut, *Al-Qiyadat wa'l-Muʾassasat as-Siyasiya fi Filastin, 1917–1948* (Beirut: Muʾassasat ad-Dirasat al-Filastiniya, 1981), pp. 496–502.

142. For example, *Foreign Report*, 19 March 1987, which refers to it as "a Marxist group."

143. Text in *Le Liban face à l'Ouragan*, p. 3.

144. Muhammad al-Baʿalbakki, quoted in Rondot, "Quelques aperçus," p. 20.

145. ʿIsam al-Mahayiri, *Fi'l ʿUrubat as-Suriya al-Qawmiya al-Ijtimaʿiya* (Beirut: n.p., 1958), p. 9. The title of this collection of short pieces translates, revealingly, as "The Arabism of Syrian Social Nationalism."

146. *At-Tadamun*, 24 August 1985.

147. Tawfiq Muhanna, SSNP Secretary for Radio and Information, Voice of the Mountain, 25 January 1987.

Chapter 2

1. Quoted in Annie Laurent, "Syrie-Liban: Les faux frères-jumeaux," *Politique Étrangère* 48 (1983): 594.

2. The Palestinian movement is the topic here, not the Yishuv or Israel, because the focus is on inter-Arab politics.

3. Abu Khaldun Satiʿ al-Husri, *Yawm Maysalun*, new ed. (Beirut: Dar al-Ittihad, 1965), p. 330.

4. Damad Ahmad Nami Bey, quoted in *The Times*, 30 April 1926.

5. Muhammad ʿIzzat Darwaza, *Hawl al-Haraka al-ʿArabiya al-Haditha* (Sidon: Al-Matbaʿa al-ʿAsriya, 1950–?), Vol. 1, pp. 89–91. Also Muhammad ʿIsmat Shaykhu, *Suriya wa-Qadiyat Filastin, 1920–1949* (Damascus: Dar Qutayba, 1402/1982) pp. 71–72.

6. Yehoshua Porath traces the term *Southern Syria* to French. Until World War I, French diplomatic usage did not distinguish between *Syria* and *Palestine*. Then *Southern Syria* emerged and passed from French into Arabic. See Yehoshua Porath, *The Emergence of the Palestinian-Arab National Movement, 1918–1929* (London: Frank Cass, 1974), pp. 73–74.

7. Appeal by the Syro-Palestinian Congress to the League of Nations, 21 September 1921. Text in Bayan al-Hut, ed., *Watha'iq al-Haraka al-Wataniya al-Filastiniya, 1918–1939: Min Awraq Akram Zuʿaytar* (Beirut: Muʾassasat ad-Dirasat al-Filastiniya, 1979), p. 164.

8. *Alif Ba*, 14 May 1925 and 12 June 1925. Summarized in *Oriente Moderno* 5 (1925): 357.

9. Petition dated 15 January 1925. Text in Muhi ad-Din as-Safarjalani, *Ta'rikh ath-Thawra as-Suriya* (Damascus: Dar al-Yaqza al-ʿArabiya, 1381/1961), pp. 118–19.

10. Proclamation by Sultan al-Atrash, President of the Provisional National Government, 23 August 1925. Text in Amin Saʿid, *Ath-Thawra al-ʿArabiya al-Kubra* (Cairo: Matbaʿat ʿIsa al-Babi al-Halabi, 1934), Vol. 3, p. 312. Similar demands were made over an extended period. For earlier ones, see *The Times*, 2 January 1925. For the claims of 27 January 1926, see League of Nations, Permanent Mandates Commission, *Minutes of the 9th Session*, 16th meeting, 17 June 1926, p. 114.

11. Quoted in Jean Lapierre, *Le Mandat français en Syrie* (Paris: Recueil Sirey, 1936), pp. 133–34.

12. "Mulakhkhas Mahadir Mushawarat al-Wahda al-'Arabiya," unpublished documents at the League of Arab States, pp. 23–29. Summarized in Ahmed M. Gomaa, *The Foundation of the League of Arab States* (London and New York: Longman Group, 1977), p. 181.

13. Text in Government of Jordan, *Suriya al-Kubra: Al-Kitab al-Urdunni al-Abyad* (Amman: Al-Matba'a al-Wataniya, 1947), pp. 105–6.

14. Agence France Presse, 17 February 1946, carried in *L'Orient-le Jour*. Quoted in Annie Laurent and Antoine Basbous, *Une Proie pour deux fauves?* (Beirut: Ad-Da'irat, 1983), p. 19.

15. For an exposition of these views, see Nader Kuzbari, *La Question du cessation du mandat français sur la Syrie* (Paris: Éditions A. Pedone, 1937), pp. 89–97.

16. Text in Safarjalani, *Ta'rikh ath-Thawra as-Suriya*, p. 296.

17. For example, ibid., p. 312.

18. C. Ernest Dawn, "The Project of Greater Syria," unpublished Ph.D. dissertation, Princeton University, 1948, p. 14. Dawn says this passage is quoted in *Oriente Moderno* 16 (1936): 347, but it is not.

19. Text in Sami Hakim, *Mithaq al-Jami'a wa'l-Wahda al-'Arabiya* (Cairo: Maktabat al-Anglo al-Masriya, 1966), p. 208.

20. Damascus recently chose to reinterpret its recognition of Lebanon in 1943 to justify the interventions since June 1976, saying that Lebanon agreed then not to "become a place or staging area for aggression menacing the security of the Arab world or of Syria" (Radio Damascus, 9 May 1983). Asad told an interviewer in February 1977 that Syria withdrew from the four Muslim provinces that became Lebanon to prevent "sectarian statelets" from emerging (*Ar-Ra'y al-'Amm*, 10 February 1977). Neither of these statements has a basis in fact.

21. *Al-Kawbab*, 10 February 1920. Text in al-Hut, *Watha'iq*, p. 36.

22. Letter dated 15 May 1920. Facsimile in Khayriya Qasimiya, *Al-Hukuma al-'Arabiya fi Dimashq bayn 1918–1920* (Cairo: Dar al-Ma'arif, 1971), p. 329.

23. Letter to Foreign Secretary Arthur James Balfour, 25 August 1919. Quoted in Simha Flappan, *Zionism and the Palestinians* (London: Croom Helm, 1979), p. 48.

24. Statement of 13 February 1919. Text in *Papers Relating to the Foreign Relations of the United States: The Paris Peace Conference, 1919* (Washington: U.S. Government Printing Office, 1942–47), Vol. 3, p. 1037.

25. Musa Kazim al-Husayni to the Executive Committee of the Palestinian Arab Congress, no. 6, 19 December 1922. Israel State Archives, Arab Executive Committee, 1541. Quoted in Porath, *Emergence*, p. 118.

26. These and other examples of Syrian interest and Palestinian reluctance can be found in ibid., pp. 116–22.

27. Petition of 15 June 1936, Ministère des Affaires Étrangères, doc. 3547. Text in Abu Musa al-Hariri, *Al-'Alawiyun—an-Nusayriyun* (Beirut: n.p., 1400/1980), p. 230. (See chapter 4, page 167 for information on this letter and further references to it.)

28. Text of statements in al-Hut, *Watha'iq*, pp. 448–52.

29. Yehoshua Porath, *The Palestinian Arab National Movement, From Riots to Rebellion, 1929–1939* (London: Frank Cass, 1977), pp. 246, 275. See also al-Hut, *Watha'iq*, p. 708.

30. Faris al-Khuri, quoted in *Bourse Égyptienne*, 18 January 1946. Cited in *Cahiers de l'Institut d'Études de l'Orient Contemporain* 5 (1946): 16.

31. Quoted in N. Bar-Yaacov, *The Israel-Syrian Armistice: Problems of Implementation, 1949–66* (Jerusalem: Magnes Press, 1967), p. 47.

32. Adib Nassur, *Qabl Fawat al-Awan* (Beirut: Dar al-'Ilm li'l-Malayin, 1955), p. 32. The original newspaper column was published on 28 March 1949.

33. Quoted in Majid Khadduri, "The Scheme of Fertile Crescent Unity: A Study in Inter-Arab Relations," in Richard N. Frye, ed. *The Near East and the Great Powers* (Cambridge, Mass.: Harvard University Press, 1951), p. 143.

34. Quoted in Hakim, *Mithaq al-Jami'a*, p. 46.

35. High Commissioner for Transjordan to the Colonial Office (copy), secret telegram no. 49, 12 September 1944, 48(2), 44/117, Foreign Office 921/221. Sir E. Spears to the Foreign Office, no. 587, 22 September 1944, E 5813/41/65, Foreign Office 371/39990. Paraphrased in Yehoshua Porath, *In Search of Arab Unity, 1930–1945* (London: Frank Cass, 1986), pp. 37–38, 280.

36. Statement of 15 September 1947. Quoted in Khadduri, "Scheme of Fertile Crescent Unity," p. 150.

37. *Journal d'Egypte*, 27 April 1949. Quoted in Patrick Seale, *The Struggle for Syria: A Study of Post-War Arab Politics, 1945–1958* (London: Oxford University Press, 1965), p. 57. Shortly after, Za'im announced: "I am and shall remain categorically opposed to the establishment of a Greater Syria." *Gazette de Lausanne*, 1 July 1949, quoted in Seale, p. 61.

38. *Al-Jam'iya al-'Arabiya*, as reported by the British Consul in Damascus, Gilbert MacKereth, in Michael G. Fry and Itamar Rabinovich, eds., *Despatches from Damascus: Gilbert MacKereth and British Policy In the Levant, 1933–1939* (Tel Aviv: Dayan Center, 1985), p. 112.

39. Quoted in G[eorge] E. K[irk], "Cross-Currents within the Arab League: The Greater Syria Plan," *The World Today*, January 1948, p. 24.

40. Dhuqan Qarqut, *Tatawwar al-Haraka al-Wataniya fi Suriya, 1920–1939* (Beirut: Dar at-Tali'a li't-Tiba'a wa'n-Nashr, 1975), pp. 110–11.

41. Sir Francis Humphrys to Sir John Simon, no. 683, 26 October 1933, E 6747/5250/93, Foreign Office 371/16924. Quoted in Porath, *In Search of Arab Unity*, p. 21.

42. Yusif Ilyan, 30 October 1944, as recorded in a Beirut dispatch of 19 December 1944, Foreign Office 371/45556/7592.

43. Not to be confused with a party by the same name founded in 1925.

44. *Gazette de Lausanne*, 1 July 1949. Quoted in Seale, *Struggle for Syria*, p. 61.

45. Muhammad Kurd 'Ali, *Khitat ash-Sham*, 2d ed., (Beirut: n.p., 1389-90/ 1969–70), Vol. 1, p. 9.

46. *At-Taqaddum* [Aleppo], 10 August 1945. Quoted in Avedis K. Sanjian, "The Sanjak of Alexandretta (Hatay): Its Impact on Turkish Syrian Relations (1939–1956)," *Middle East Journal* 10 (1956): 382.

47. Bashir Da'uq, ed., *Nidal al-Ba'th* (Beirut: Dar at-Tali'a, 1963–74), Vol. 1, p. 221.

48. "Mudhakkirat Abna' as-Sahil ila'l-Mandub as-Sami Weygand," 1923, quoted in Hisan 'Ali Hallaq, *Mu'tamar as-Sahil wa'l-Aqdiya al-Arba'a, 1936* (Beirut: Dar al-Jami'iya, 1403/1983), p. 18. For a facsimile of the last page of this petition, see Muhammad Jamil Bayhum, *Lubnan Bayn Musharriq wa-Mugharrib* (Beirut: author, 1969), p. 25. Hallaq's book contains forty-one appendices replete with petitions, speeches, and other documents demanding Lebanese unity with Syria.

49. Program of the Central Committee of the Union of Syrian-American Associations. Text in Eugene Jung, *La Révolte arabe* (Paris: Librairie Colbert Ch. Bohrer, 1924–25), Vol. 2, p. 135.

50. Meir Zamir, *The Formation of Modern Lebanon* (London: Croom Helm, 1985), p. 182. Zamir provides an extraordinarily lucid and complete account of the intricacies surrounding the history of Lebanon between 1912 and 1926; this section on Lebanon draws heavily from his study.

51. Text in Safarjalani, *Ta'rikh ath-Thawra as-Suriya*, p. 343.

52. Text in ibid., p. 346.

53. Fonds Henri de Jouvenal, Rapport Journalier, 4 March 1926. Quoted in Zamir, *Formation of Modern Lebanon*, p. 212.

54. March 1926 conference, quoted in *Oriente Moderno* 6 (1926): 202.

55. "Mu'tamar Abna' as-Sahil," June 1926, quoted in Sa'id, *Ath-Thawra al-'Arabiya al-Kubra*, Vol. 3, pp. 545–47.

56. "Mu'tamar Abna' as-Sahil," June 1928, quoted in Hallaq, *Mu'tamar as-Sahil wa'l-Aqdiya al-Arba'a, 1936*, p. 21.

57. "Mu'tamar as-Sahil," November 1933, and telegram from Hashim al-Atasi, quoted in ibid., pp. 24–25.

58. League of Nations, Permanent Mandates Commission, *Minutes of the 26th Session*, 18th meeting, 9 November 1934, p. 186.

59. Salah Labki [spelling unsure], March 1936, "Mu'tamar as-Sahil wa'l-Aqdiya al-Arba'a," quoted in Hallaq, *Mu'tamar as-Sahil wa'l-Aqdiya al-Arba'a, 1936*, pp. 46–47.

60. Yusuf Yazbak, March 1936, "Mu'tamar as-Sahil wa'l-Aqdiya al-Arba'a," quoted in ibid., p. 49.

61. *Bulletin du Comité de l'Asie Française*, November 1936, p. 308.

62. Damien de Martel to the French Foreign Ministry, 20 November 1936, Ministère des Affaires Étrangères, Syrie-Liban, 1918–1930, E-492. Quoted in Annie Laurent and Antoine Basbous, *Guerres secrètes au Liban* (Paris: Gallimard, 1987), p. 82.

63. Quoted in ibid., p. 83.

64. J. N. Camp's letter to the Foreign Office, 371/4153/41476/f275. Quoted in Taysir Jbara, *Palestinian Leader Hajj Amin al-Husayni, Mufti of Jerusalem* (Princeton, N.J.: Kingston Press, 1985), p. 29.

65. Akram Zu'aytir papers, File A/Manuscript 16, 5 February 1919, Institute for Palestine Studies. Quoted in Muhammad Y. Muslih, *The Origins of Palestinian Nationalism* (New York: Columbia University Press, 1988), p. 177.

66. Akram Zu'aytir papers, File A/Manuscript 16, Institute for Palestine Studies; and Record Group L4, File 768, Central Zionist Archives. See ibid., p. 180.

67. Akram Zu'aytir papers, File A/Manuscript 16, Institute for Palestine Studies. Quoted in ibid., pp. 181–82.

68. Text in Neil Caplan, *Futile Diplomacy*, Vol. 1, *Early Arab-Zionist Negotiation Attempts, 1913–1931* (London: Frank Cass, 1982), p. 157.

69. Ahmad ash-Shuqayri, *Hiwar wa-Asrar ma'a'l-Muluk wa'r-Ru'asa* (Beirut: Dar al-'Awda, [1970?]), pp. 15, 24.

70. Letter dated 8 December 1919, Israel State Archives, pol. 2095. Quoted in Aaron S. Klieman, *Foundations of British Policy in the Arab World: The Cairo Conference of 1921* (Baltimore: Johns Hopkins University Press, 1970), p. 62.

71. Muslih, *Origins of Palestinian Nationalism*, p. 199.

72. Text in al-Hut, *Watha'iq*, pp. 9–11.

73. *Al-Mufid*, February 1920. Text in ibid., pp. 35–36. In a letter to the author (dated 30 June 1986), Yehoshua Porath suggests that this meeting was not a real congress but "a meeting of some representatives who were members of the General Syrian Congress." Muslih (*Origins of Palestinian Nationalism*, p. 199) believes it was a group of what he calls Younger Politicians who convened their own meeting.

74. Horace B. Samuel, *Unholy Memories of the Holy Land* (London: Hogarth Press, 1930), p. 57. The British police report corroborates this account.

75. Jbara, *Hajj Amin al-Husayni*, p. 33.

76. Paul-Marie Durieux to Georges Picot, 4 December 1918, Ministère des Affaires Étrangères, Levant, 1918–1929, Palestine, Vol. 11, fols. 250–51. Quoted in Jan Karl Tannenbaum, *France and the Arab Middle East, 1914–1920* (Philadelphia: American Philosophical Society, 1978), p. 26.

77. J. N. Camp report, Foreign Office 371/4153/41476, 2 February 1919. Quoted in Flappan, *Zionism and the Palestinians*, p. 59.

78. Jerusalem Muslim-Christian Association to the Governor of Jerusalem, 11 February 1919; "Copy of the Power of Attorney Given to Prince Faysal," 10 February 1919. Both in Israel State Archives, Chief Secretary, 156, and quoted in Porath, *Emergence*, pp. 85-86.

79. Quoted in Benoit Aboussouan, *Le Problème politique syrien* (Paris: Librairie de Jurisprudence Ancienne et Moderne, 1925), p. 247.

80. Interview with Darwaza by Muhammad Y. Muslih on 17 May 1979. Recounted in Muslih, *Origins of Palestinian Nationalism*, p. 176.

81. Archives Diplomatiques, Paris, E, Turkey, Vol. 274, 26 August 1921. Quoted in Marie-Renée Mouton, "Le Congrès syrio-palestinien de Genève (1921)," *Relations Internationales* 19 (1979): 322.

82. Porath, *Emergence*, chap. 2.

83. *Paris Peace Conference, 1919*, Vol. 5, p. 3.

84. Porath, *Emergence*, pp. 114, 103.

85. Zionist Archives, Z/4, 2800 II, Report no. 138, 5 August 1920. Quoted in ibid., p. 107.

86. Interview with Dajjani by Muhammad Y. Muslih on 11 March 1979. Quoted in Muslih, *Origins of Palestinian Nationalism*, p. 203.

87. *Al-Jami'a al-'Arabiya*, 4 August 1932. Quoted in Porath, *From Riots to Rebellion*, p. 125.

88. Susan Lee Hattis, *The Bi-National Idea in Palestine during Mandatory Times* (Haifa: Shikmona Publishing, 1970), p. 123.

89. Quoted in David Ben-Gurion, *My Talks with Arab Leaders*, trans. by Aryeh Rubinstein and Misha Louvish (New York: Third Press, 1973), p. 27.

90. Quoted in ibid., p. 50.

91. Text in al-Hut, *Watha'iq*, p. 76.

92. Ibrahim 'Abd al-Hadi, "Proposals," Israel State Archives, Arab Executive Committee, 1771, 22 August 1922; quoted in Porath, *Emergence*, p. 111.

93. Palestine Arab Delegation, "Statement Submitted to the President of the League of Nations," 10 September 1921. Text in al-Hut, *Watha'iq*, p. 147.

94. Executive Committee of the Palestine Arab Congress, "Report on the State of Palestine," 6 October 1924. Text in ibid., p. 314.

95. Executive Committee of the Third Arab Palestine Congress, "Report on the State of Palestine," 28 March 1921; Arab Palestine Legation in London, "A Brief Statement of the Demands of the Arab People of Palestine." Texts in ibid., pp. 72, 120.

96. Party of Arab Independence in Palestine, "Bayan ila Ahali Suriya Hawl al-Matami' as-Sahyuniya fi Biladihim," 22 June 1933. Text in ibid., p. 376.

97. Palestine National League, New York, "Palestine's Cry for Justice." Text in ibid., p. 199.

98. Translation of threat dated 23 October 1937, enclosed with report from Gilbert MacKereth to Anthony Eden, Foreign Office 371/20819/5930.

99. Text of the conversation in Walter Laqueur and Barry Rubin, eds., *The Israel-Arab Reader: A Documentary History of the Middle East Conflict*, 4th ed. (New York: Penguin Books, 1984), p. 80.

100. Text in *Qadiyat al-Hizb al-Qawmi* (Beirut: Ministry of Information, 1949), p. 202.

101. Interview with Husayni by Muhammad Y. Muslih on 23 February 1979. Quoted in Muslih, *Origins of Palestinian Nationalism*, p. 209.

102. For example, King ʿAbdallah, "Nidaʾ ilaʾsh-Sha῾b as-Suri waʾl-῾Alim al-῾Arabi," 8 March 1943. Text in Government of Jordan, *Suriya al-Kubra*, p. 76.

103. ῾Awni ῾Abd al-Hadi, *Mudhakkirat*. Quoted in Sulayman Musa, *Taʾsis al-Imara al-Urdunniya, 1921–1925*, 2d ed. (Amman: n.p., 1972), p. 85.

104. Laurence Oliphant, *The Land of Gilead* (New York: D. Appleton, 1881), p. 179. On the very next page, however, Oliphant wrote: "Salt now contains a population which is estimated at six thousand souls, and is the only center of population to the east of the Jordan."

105. Suleiman Mousa, "The Rise of Arab Nationalism and the Emergence of Transjordan," in William W. Haddad and William Ochsenwald, eds., *Nationalism in a Non-National State: The Dissolution of the Ottoman Empire* (Columbus: Ohio State University Press, 1977), p. 248.

106. Selah Merrill, *East of the Jordan* (New York: Charles Scribner's Sons, 1881), p. 112.

107. William Libbey and Franklin E. Hoskins, *The Jordan Valley and Petra* (New York: G. P. Putnam's Sons, 1905), Vol. 1, p. 152. Also John Lewis Burckhardt, *Travels in Syria and the Holy Land* (London: John Murray, 1822), p. 360.

108. J. S. Buckingham, *Travels in Palestine* (London: Longman, Hurst, Rees, Orme, and Brown, 1822), Vol. 2, p. 92.

109. Jonathan Franklin Swift, *Going to Jericho* (New York: A. Roman and Company, 1868), p. 273.

110. *Cook's Tourists' Handbook* (London: Thomas Cook & Son, 1876), p. 27.

111. For more on Transjordan's features, see Daniel Pipes and Adam Garfinkle, "Is Jordan Palestine?" *Commentary*, October 1988, pp. 38–39.

112. Albert Abramson to Wyndham Deedes, 29 August 1921, Foreign Office 371/6462.

113. Avi Shlaim, *Collusion Across the Jordan: King Abdullah, the Zionist Movement, and the Partition of Palestine* (New York: Columbia University Press, 1988), p. 33.

114. To British High Commissioner to Palestine, Sir Herbert Samuel, 4 June 1921, Colonial Office 733/6. Quoted in Walid Kazziha, "The Political Evolution of Transjordan," *Middle Eastern Studies* 15 (1979): 247.

115. British High Commissioner to Palestine, Sir Herbert Samuel. Quoted in *Mandate for Palestine* (Washington D.C.: U.S. Government Printing Office, 1927), p. 23.

116. "Report on Middle East Conference Held in Cairo and Jerusalem (Secret), March 12 to 30, 1921," p. 8, Foreign Office 371/6343. Quoted in Porath, *In Search of Arab Unity*, p. 23.

117. ῾Abdallah ibn al-Husayn, *At-Takmila*, in *Al-Athar al-Kamila liʾl-Malik ῾Abdallah ibn al-Husayn* (Beirut: Ad-Dar al-Muttahida liʾn-Nashr, 1976), p. 269. See also Government of Jordan, *Suriya al-Kubra*, p. 66. In an earlier account, ῾Abdallah related that Churchill asked him "to remain in Trans-Jordan where I should endeavor by a policy of peace and loyalty to attract the attention and gratitude of France . . . in order to ensure its assent to the uniting of the four Syrian cities and Trans-Jordan."

'Abdallah to the High Commissioner, 22 February 1936, Foreign Office 371/20065/7573.

118. This foreshadowed 'Abdallah's practice three decades later of bringing Palestinians from the West Bank into the Jordanian cabinet.

119. "Organic Law of Transjordan," 16 April 1928, and "Constitution of the State of Syria," 14 May 1930. Texts in Helen Miller Davis, ed., *Constitutions, Electoral Laws, Treaties of States in the Near and Middle East* (Durham, N.C.: Duke University Press, 1947), pp. 303, 263.

120. For details and the Syrian reaction, see C. H. F. Cox to Arthur G. Wauchope, 26 March 1936, Foreign Office 371/20065/7573.

121. *Daily Telegraph*, 30 March 1936, quoted in *Oriente Moderno* 16 (1936): 180-81. Transjordanian comments from *Al-Jihad*, 15 April 1936, can be found in ibid., pp. 278–79.

122. *Al-Ahram*, 21 June 1937. Summarized in *Oriente Moderno* 17 (1937): 337.

123. See the passage from Alec Seath Kirkbride quoted on page 83.

124. Gabriel Puaux, telegram of 10 June 1939, in Ministère des Affaires Étrangères, Papiers Puaux, Syrie-Liban, carton 255, dossier. Quoted in Ali Mahafzah, "La France et le mouvement nationaliste arabe de 1914 à 1939," *Relations Internationales* 19 (1979): 309.

125. On this most unlikely alliance, see "The Present State of Syria and the Lebanon," Suppl. II, 23 March 1945, Foreign Office 371/45562/7505.

126. Letter from Faris Bey al-Khuri to Amir 'Abdallah, undated. Text in Government of Jordan, *Suriya al-Kubra*, pp. 51–52.

127. Terence Shone, 3 April 1945, Foreign Office 371/45611/7539.

128. Mary C. Wilson, *King Abdullah, Britain and the Making of Jordan* (Cambridge: Cambridge University Press, 1987), p. 138.

129. Decision 337 of the Transjordanian Council of Ministers, 1 July 1941. Text in Government of Jordan, *Suriya al-Kubra*, pp. 34–35.

130. *Al-Ahram*, 3 and 18 March 1943. Quoted in Porath, *In Search of Arab Unity*, p. 35.

131. 'Abdallah ibn al-Husayn, *Mudhakkirat* (Jerusalem: Bayt al-Muqaddas, 1945), pp. 226–27.

132. "Weekly Political Summary no. 196, Syria and the Lebanon," 27 November 1945, E 9925/5/89, Foreign Office 371/45554/7587.

133. Charter of the League of Arab States, text and discussion in Government of Jordan, *Suriya al-Kubra*, p. 107. For the charter's full text, see Hakim, *Mithaq al-Jami'a*, p. 233.

134. Prince 'Abdallah, 11 November 1946. Text in Government of Jordan, *Suriya al-Kubra*, p. 240.

135. Prince 'Abdallah, *Middle East Opinion* [Cairo], 2 December 1946, p. 12.

136. Foreign Minister Philip Taqla, 13 and 22 November 1946. Texts in Government of Jordan, *Suriya al-Kubra*, pp. 250, 255.

137. King 'Abdallah, quoted in *Kull Shai*, March 1947. Cited in *Cahiers de l'Orient Contemporain* 9–10 (1947): 51.

138. *Bayan Maliki: Suriya al-Kubra wa'l-Ittihad al-'Arabi*, 4 August 1947. Quoted in Dawn, "Project of Greater Syria," p. 86.

139. Nizar Kayali, "Syria: A Political Study (1920–1950)," unpublished Ph.D. dissertation, Columbia University, 1951, p. 227.

140. Bishara al-Khuri and Shukri al-Quwwatli, communiqué of 27 August 1947, quoted in *Cahiers de l'Orient Contemporain* 11–12 (1947): 206.

141. Government of Jordan, *Suriya al-Kubra: Al-Kitab al-Urdunni al-Abyad* (Amman: Al-Matba'a al-Wataniya, 1947).

142. Text of 6 September 1947 in *Kalimat as-Suriya wa'l-'Arab fi Mashru'at Suriya al-Kubra*, edited by "A Group of Educated Arab Youth" (Damascus: n.p., 1947), p. 87.

143. September 1947 statement, quoted in Johannes Reissner, *Ideologie und Politik der Muslimbrüder Syriens* (Freiburg: Klaus Schwarz, 1980), pp. 216, 412.

144. According to Terence Shone in a report to Anthony Eden, 26 March 1945, E 2336/8/89, Foreign Office 371/45562/7505.

145. Memorandum from Dean Acheson to President Truman, 18 February 1947. Text in Ibrahim ar-Rashid, ed., *Documents on the History of Saudi Arabia* (Salisbury, N.C.: Documentary Publications, 1980), Vol. 5, pp. 72–74.

146. Statement of 22 December 1947, quoted in *Cahiers de l'Orient Contemporain* 11–12 (1947): 206.

147. *Daily Telegraph*, 30 March 1936. Quoted in *Oriente Moderno* 16 (1936): 180–81.

148. *The New York Times*, 27 June 1936.

149. Quoted in Wilson, *King Abdullah*, p. 127.

150. *Az-Zaman* [Beirut], 13 March 1948. Quoted in *Cahiers de l'Orient Contemporain* 13 (1948): 21.

151. *The Washington Post*, 9 April 1988.

152. Central Zionist Archives, S25/9038, 27 October 1947. Quoted in Shlaim, *Collusion Across the Jordan*, p. 110.

153. Quoted in Benjamin Shwadran, *Jordan: A State of Tension* (New York: Council for Middle Eastern Affairs Press, 1959), p. 280.

154. Avi Plascov, *The Palestinian Refugees in Jordan 1948–57* (London: Frank Cass, 1981), p. 13.

155. Resolutions of 1 December 1948. Text in 'Abdallah at-Tall, *Karithat Filastin: Mudhakkirat 'Abdallah at-Tall* (Cairo: Dar al-Qalam, 1959), p. 378.

156. Quoted in Plascov, *Palestinian Refugees in Jordan*, p. 13.

157. According to Yigal Allon, 'Abdallah at this time considered renaming his kingdom Palestine. See Susan Hattis Rolef, "Jordan and Palestine," *Middle East Focus*, Spring 1987, pp. 6, 8, 9. Had 'Abdallah taken this step, the kingdom might have had a different role in the future of Pan-Arab, Pan-Syrian, and Palestinian politics.

158. Alec Kirkbride, *From the Wings: Amman Memoirs, 1947–1951* (London: Frank Cass, 1976), p. 96.

159. 'Abdallah, *Mudhakkirat*, quoted in Aqil Hyder Hasan Abidi, *Jordan: A Political Study, 1948–1957* (New York: Asia Publishing House, 1965), p. 79.

160. *Al-Hayat*, 18 February 1958. Quoted in ibid., pp. 79–80.

161. *Al-Hawadith*, 18 July 1975.

162. P. M. Crosthwaite, minutes on Sir Harold MacMichael's telegram, 24–25 June 1941, E 3225/62/89, Foreign Office 371/27296. Quoted in Porath, *In Search of Arab Unity*, pp. 208–09.

163. Wilson, *King Abdullah*, p. 140.

164. 'Abdallah to the High Commissioner, 22 February 1936, Foreign Office 371/20065/7573.

165. Wilson, *King Abdullah*, p. 147.

166. R. W. Rendel, "The Palestine Report, Preliminary Department Comments," 23 June 1937, Foreign Office 371/20807/ Quoted in ibid., p. 136.

167. Breasted explains in *Ancient Times: A History of the Early World*, 2d ed. (New York: Ginn and Company, 1935), p. 135, note 1, that he found no name to describe the

great semicircle between the mountains and the desert. "Hence in the first edition of this work (1916) the author was obliged to coin a term. It was called, therefore, the Fertile Crescent. The term has since become current and is now widely used." Indeed, so widely used did it become that Nagib Sadaka, in *La Question syrienne pendant la guerre de 1914* (Paris: Larose, 1941), pp. 26, 28, wrote that the term "Fertile Crescent" was used by medieval Arab geographers. I find no confirmation of this claim, however.

168. Alec Seath Kirkbride, *A Crackle of Thorns* (London: John Murray, 1956), pp. 18–19. These goals have been challenged by Mary C. Wilson, who argues that Husayn's ambitions were limited to the Arabian peninsula; in effect, he had himself acclaimed not "king of the Arabs" but "king of the Arabians." Also, she locates 'Abdallah's early ambitions in Yemen, not Iraq. See Wilson, *King Abdullah*, pp. 31, 33.

169. But see other views on p. 100.

170. Majid Khadduri, *Political Trends in the Arab World* (Baltimore: Johns Hopkins University Press, 1970), p. 189.

171. Rashid al-Barrawi, *Mashruʿ Suriya al-Kubra* (Cairo: Maktabat an-Nahda al-Misriya, 1947), p. 36.

172. Francis Humphreys, British High Commissioner for Iraq, E 347, Foreign Office 371/16854. Quoted in Khaldun S. Husry, "King Faysal I and Arab Unity," *Journal of Contemporary History* 10 (1975): 324.

173. Colonel Nieger, "Choix de documents sur le Territoire des Alaouites," *Revue du Monde Musulman* 49 (March 1922): 3.

174. Nuri as-Saʿid, *Arab Independence and Unity* (Baghdad: At the Government Press, 1943), p. 11.

175. Political Summary, Syria and the Lebanon, 16 February 1944, E 1486/23/89, Foreign Office 371/40300/7543.

176. For references, see note 133 on p. 209.

177. *The New York Times*, 12 February 1946.

178. Reeva S. Simon, "The Hashemite 'Conspiracy': Hashemite Unity Attempts, 1921–1958," *International Journal of Middle East Studies* 5 (1974): 323.

179. George Adam Smith, *Syria and the Holy Land* (London: Hodder and Stoughton, 1918), pp. 53, 48.

180. Naval Intelligence Division, *A Handbook of Syria* (London: His Majesty's Stationery Office, 1920), p. 9. By the time of the next edition in 1943, Syria came to be defined as the states of Syria and Lebanon. Naval Intelligence Division, *Syria* (London: His Majesty's Stationery Office, 1943), p. 1.

181. Arnold J. Toynbee, *A Journey to China: Or Things Which Are Seen* (London: Constable & Co., 1931), p. 111.

182. *The Near East and India*, 5 November 1925, p. 547.

183. Sir Edward Spears, British Minister to Syria and Lebanon, quoted in Porath, *In Search of Arab Unity*, p. 292. As the many references in the following pages make clear, materials in this section derive in large part from Yehoshua Porath's research in the British archives.

184. Christopher Sykes, *Crossroads to Israel* (Cleveland: World Publishing, 1965), p. 192.

185. Lord Lloyd to Sir Harold MacMichael, 24 September 1940, Colonial Office 733/444l/75872/115. Quoted in Porath, *In Search of Arab Unity*, p. 116.

186. Sir John Martin, memorandum of 21 November 1940, PREM 4/5/51. Quoted in ibid., p. 117.

187. Anthony Eden, *The Times*, 30 May 1941.

188. Dawn, "Project of Greater Syria," p. 99.

189. Hamilton A. R. Gibb, memorandum of 9 June 1941. Quoted in Porath, *In Search of Arab Unity*, p. 117.

190. Humphrey Bowman, notes of 5 and 7 July 1941, E 3824/53/65, Foreign Office 371/27044. Quoted in ibid., pp. 117–18.

191. Sir Harold MacMichael's note (copy), September 1941, E 6210/53/65, Foreign Office 371/27045. Quoted in ibid., p. 252.

192. Leo Amery to Winston Churchill, 29 April 1943, PREM 4/52/1. Quoted in ibid., p. 128.

193. Sir Harold MacMichael's memorandum, Middle East War Council (43) 2, 21 April 1943, E 3577/2551/65, Foreign Office 371/34975. Quoted in ibid., p. 290.

194. Middle East War Council (43) May 1943, E 3577/2551/65, Foreign Office 371/34975. Quoted in ibid., p. 291.

195. Freya Stark, *East Is West* (London: John Murray, 1945), p. 125.

196. Quoted in the report of a lecture by W. W. Astor, "The Middle East and the War," *Journal of the Royal Central Asian Society* 30 (1943): 139.

197. Lord Moyne to Richard K. Law, 29 November 1943, E 7575/506/65, Foreign Office 371/31338. Quoted in Porath, *In Search of Arab Unity*, p. 306. Porath (pp. 306–08) provides information on other officials' backing for Nuri's plan and shows how this created the impression that the British government sought Arab unity.

198. Richard Casey to Anthony Eden, 6 November 1943, E 6866/2551/65, Foreign Office 371/34976. Quoted in ibid., p. 138.

199. Sir Winston Churchill's minute, 16 January 1944, P(M)(44)4, 21 January 1944, E 665/95/31, Foreign Office 371/40133. Quoted in ibid., p. 139.

200. Sir Douglas Harris in a meeting of 15 October 1943, E 6027/87/31, Foreign Office 371/35039. Quoted in ibid., p. 135.

201. Cabinet 95/14, P(M)(43)16], 1 November 1943. Discussed in Gomaa, *Foundation of the League of Arab States*, pp. 141–42. Gomaa explains the problems of this scheme and the reasons why it was eventually dropped on pp. 143–50.

202. Sir Winston Churchill's minute, 16 January 1944, P(M)(44)4, 21 January 1944, E 665/95/31, Foreign Office 371/40133. Quoted in Porath, *In Search of Arab Unity*, p. 139.

203. Richard Casey to Sir Winston Churchill, 17 January 1944. Quoted in ibid.

204. Sir Harold MacMichael's memorandum, 4 February 1944, E 1425/95/31, Foreign Office, 371/40144. Quoted in ibid., p. 143.

205. Enclosure from Lord Moyne to Anthony Eden, 9 May 1944, E 2987/95/31, Foreign Office 371/40135. Quoted in ibid., p. 145.

206. Dated September 1944, E 5658/95/31, Foreign Office 371/40137. Quoted in ibid., p. 146.

207. E 9493/E9734, Foreign Office 371/61960. Quoted in Richard L. Jasse, "Great Britain and Abdallah's Plan to Partition Palestine: A Natural Sorting Out," *Middle Eastern Studies* 22 (1986): 506.

208. Arthur Wauchope to 'Abdallah, 30 March 1936, Foreign Office 371/20065/7573.

209. R. M. A. Hankey, 7 February 1945, Foreign Office 371/45236/7801.

210. Hector McNeil, Minister of State, on 14 July 1947, in *Parliamentary Debates: House of Commons* (London: His Majesty's Stationery Office, 1947), 5th series, Vol. 440, col. 9.

211. P. M. Crosthwaite, minutes on Sir Harold MacMichael's telegram, 24–25 June 1941, E 3225/62/89, Foreign Office 371/27296. Quoted in Porath, *In Search of Arab Unity*, pp. 208–09.

212. Oliver Lyttleton, telegram no. 6 to the Foreign Office, 6 February 1942, E 901/541/31, Foreign Office 371/31381. Quoted in ibid., p. 212.

213. Harold A. Caccia, minutes on Lyttleton telegram. Quoted in ibid., p. 212.

214. Sir Maurice Peterson, minutes on 15–16 April 1942, E 2310/541/31, Foreign Office 371/31381. Quoted in ibid., p. 213.

215. Letter to D. G. Pearman, *The Letters of T. E. Lawrence*, ed. David Garnett (New York: Doubleday, Doran & Co., 1939), p. 577.

216. Quoted in Dominique Chevallier, "Lyon et la Syrie en 1919: Les Bases d'une intervention," *Revue Historique* 224 (1960): 306. Ghanim and George-Samné sought financial help from the Lyons Chamber of Commerce but were turned down (p. 314). See also Wajih Kawtharani, *Bilad ash-Sham* (Beirut: Ma'had al-Inma' al-'Arabi, 1980), pp. 187–96.

217. Quoted in Michel Seurat, "Le Rôle de Lyon dans l'installation du Mandat français en Syrie: Intérêts économiques et culturels, luttes d'opinion (1915–1925)," *Bulletin d'Études Orientales* 31 (1979): 139.

218. Quoted in *Paris Peace Conference, 1919*, Vol. 5, p. 13.

219. James Morris, *The Hashemite Kings* (New York: Pantheon, 1959), p. 99.

220. League of Nations, Permanent Mandate Commission, *Minutes of the Eighth Session (Extraordinary)*, 16 February–6 March 1926, pp. 74, 207.

221. Bayan N. al-Hut, *Al-Qiyadat wa'l-Mu'assasat as-Siyasiya fi Filastin, 1917–1948* (Beirut: Mu'assasat ad-Dirasat al-Filastiniya, 1981), p. 435.

222. *Al-Ahram*, 21 June 1937. Summarized in *Oriente Moderno* 17 (1937): 337.

223. Quoted in Seale, *The Struggle for Syria*, p. 92.

224. Quoted in ibid, p. 97.

225. Statement of 14 August 1951, quoted in Jon Kimche, *Seven Fallen Pillars: The Middle East, 1945–1952*, rev. ed. (New York: Praeger, 1953), p. 321.

226. *Al-Jarida ar-Rasmiya* 33 (1956): 4762. Quoted in *Al-Kitab as-Sanawi li'l-Qadiya al-Filastiniya l-'Amm 1971* (Beirut: Mu'assasat ad-Dirasat al-Filastiniya, 1975), p. 133.

227. United Nations General Assembly, *Official Records*, S/PV.724, 31 May 1956, p. 10. That this remark was spoken by Ahmad ash-Shuqayri, later to serve as the PLO's first chairman, makes it especially noteworthy.

228. George Tomeh, United Nations Security Council, *Official Records*, S/PV.1352, 9 June 1967, p. 15.

229. Sanjian, "The Sanjak of Alexandretta," p. 389.

230. *Al-Ahram*, 17 July 1960.

231. Middle East News Agency, 11 February 1961. Quoted in *Middle East Record* 2 (1961): 513.

232. *Al-Ba'th*, 29 November 1965. Text in *Arab Political Documents 1965*, pp. 426–27.

233. Y. Harkabi, *The Palestinian Covenant and Its Meaning* (London: Valentine, Mitchell, 1979), p. 34. The full implications of this article are discussed on pp. 33–39.

234. Quoted in Asher Susser, *Bayn Yardayn l'Filastin: Biografiya Politit shel Wasfi al-Tall* (Tel Aviv: Kibbutz Ha-Me'uchad, 1983), pp. 168–69.

235. *Shu'un Filastiniya*, June 1972.

236. Voice of Palestine, Cairo, 15 May 1965. Quoted in Susser, *Bayn Yardayn l'Filastin*, pp. 78–79. Susser notes that some of Shuqayri's speeches from Cairo were written for him and in some cases were broadcast under his name without his knowledge.

237. *Ruz al-Yusuf*, 4 July 1966, and Radio Cairo, 25 October 1966. Quoted in ibid., p. 95.

238. Shafiq al-Hut, quoted in M. Nisan, "The Palestinian Features of Jordan," in Daniel J. Elazar, ed., *Judea, Samaria, and Gaza: Views on the Present and Future* (Washington: American Enterprise Institute, 1982), p. 206.

239. *Ad-Difaʿ* [East Jerusalem], 24 August 1959; Radio Amman, 23 August 1959. Quoted in Moshe Shemesh, *The Palestinian Entity, 1959–74: Arab Politics and the PLO* (London: Frank Cass, 1988), p. 24.

240. *The Jerusalem Times* [East Jerusalem], 17 March 1960.

241. *Jordan: The Palestine Problem and Inter-Arab Relations* (Amman: Government of Jordan, 1962). Quoted in Nisan, "The Palestinian Features of Jordan," p. 202.

242. *Standard Postage Stamp Catalogue, 1984* (New York: Scott Publishing, 1983), Vol. 1, p. 424, col. 4.

243. Radio Amman, 13 May 1965.

244. *Filastin* [East Jerusalem], 5 October 1965. Quoted in Clinton Bailey, *Jordan's Palestinian Challenge, 1948–1983: A Political History* (Boulder and London: Westview Press, 1984), p. 24.

245. David Roberts, *The Baʿth and the Creation of Modern Syria* (New York: St. Martin's Press, 1987), pp. 140, 161.

246. See Moshe Maʿoz, *Asad, The Sphinx of Damascus: A Political Biography* (New York: Weidenfeld & Nicholson, 1988), pp. 47, 112–13, 178.

247. Majid Khadduri, *Political Trends in the Arab World* (Baltimore: Johns Hopkins University Press, 1970), p. 190.

248. Antun Saʿada, *Mabadiʾ al-Hizb al-Qawmi al-Ijtimaʿi wa Ghaybatuhu* (Beirut: n.p., 1972).

249. Authors writing in German are especially prone to this error. See Harald Vocke, *Was geschah im Libanon?* (Frankfurt: author, 1977), p. 45; *Frankfurter Allgemeine Zeitung*, 20 September 1986. For examples in English, see Kamel S. Abu Jaber, *The Arab Baʿth Socialist Party* (Syracuse, N.Y.: Syracuse University Press, 1966), p. 31; *Foreign Report*, 25 September 1986.

250. For example, see the decree signed by Salim Khuri, 27 October 1947. Text in *Qadiyat al-Hizb al-Qawmi*, p. 162. Also Hisham Sharabi, *Al-Jamr waʾr-Ramad: Dhikrayat Muthaqqaf ʿArabi* (Beirut: Dar at-Taliʿa liʾt-Tibaʿa waʾn-Nashr, 1978), pp. 73–74.

251. Sami al-Jundi, *Al-Baʿth* (Beirut: Dar an-Nahar liʾn-Nashr, 1969), p. 49.

252. Hashim ʿUthman, "Adonis waʾl-Bidayat al-Ula . . . Shiʿriya waʾn-Nathiriya," *Al-Mawqif al-Adabi* 1 (1982): 156–58.

253. When Hawrani broke with the SSNP is in doubt. Michael Hillegas Van Dusen, "Intra- and Inter-Generational Conflict in the Syrian Army," unpublished Ph.D. dissertation, Johns Hopkins University, 1971, p. 312 wrote that he left the SSNP "about 1941." *Qadiyat al-Hizb al-Qawmi*, pp. 219–20 contains the text of a decree expelling Akram al-Hawrani from the SSNP, signed by Antun Saʿada and dated 30 February 1949.

254. *Lebanon News*, 30 June 1986. This account is replete with factual mistakes; further, Yossi Melman, *The Master Terrorist: The True Story Behind Abu Nidal* (New York: Adama Books, 1986), p. 61, says that Banna attended the University of Cairo.

255. Mustafa Juha, *Lubnan fi Zilal al-Baʿth: Fusul fiʾl-Harb as-Suriya al-Lubnaniya* (n.p., n.d.), p. 26. Juha writes that ʿAflaq and al-Bitar also suggested to Saʿada that the SSNP be renamed the "Arab Social Nationalist Party."

256. Abu Khaldun Sati῾ al-Husri, *Al-῾Uruba bayn Du῾atiha wa Mu῾aridiha*, 4th ed. (Beirut: Dar al-῾Ilm li'l-Malayin, 1961), p. 70.

257. Muhammad Harb Farzat, *Al-Hayah al-Hizbiya fi Suriya bayn 1908–1955* (Damascus: Dar ar-Rawwad, 1955), p. 141.

258. Undated text in *Qadiyat al-Hizb al-Qawmi*, p. 265.

259. Quoted in *Le Liban face à l'Ouragan*, p. 37.

260. "Taqrir Muwajjah li-῾Umdat ad-Dakhiliya," 28 November 1947. Text in *Qadiyat al-Hizb al-Qawmi*, pp. 203–4.

261. Agence France Press, 14 March 1947. Text in ibid., p. 167.

262. "Taqrir ῾Amid ῾Abdallah Muhsin al-Muwajjah ila az-Zu῾ama," 30 September 1947. Text in ibid., p. 204.

263. "Jalsa Munaffidhiya Hums al-῾Amma," 2 September 1947. Text in ibid., p. 264.

Conclusion

1. This paragraph summarizes an analysis of the significance of the rivalry between three Arab states and the Palestinian movement in my article "Arab vs. Arab over Palestine," *Commentary*, July 1987, pp. 17–25; reprinted in Daniel Pipes, *The Long Shadow: Culture and Politics in the Middle East.* (New Brunswick, N.J.: Transaction, 1989), pp. 119–43.

2. David Roberts, *The Ba῾th and the Creation of Modern Syria* (New York: St. Martin's Press, 1987), p. 15.

3. Bassam Tibi, *Nationalismus in der Dritten Welt am arabischen Beispiel* (Frankfurt: Europäische Verlaganstalt, 1971), p. 187.

Chapter 3

1. Quoted in *MERIP Reports* 61 (1977): 17.

2. *Watha'iq al-Filastiniya al-῾Arabiya li-῾Amm 1974* (Beirut: Mu'assasat ad-Dirasat al-Filastiniya, 1976), p. 211.

3. Letter to the Jordanian Student Congress in Baghdad, *The Washington Post*, 12 November 1974.

4. ῾Isam Sakhnini, "Muhawila Ula fi Utruha: Sharq al-Urdunn al-Filastiniya," *Shu'un Filastiniya*, September 1975, pp. 25–27. The title of this piece, "A First Attempt at a Thesis: Palestinian Transjordan," suggests tentativeness.

5. *Newsweek*, 14 March 1977.

6. *Trouw* [Amsterdam], 31 March 1977.

7. Voice of Palestine, 18 November 1978.

8. Radio Damascus, 18 May 1979. Note also ῾Arafat's statement, Radio Damascus, 15 April 1981.

9. The very terms *Northern Palestine* and *Northern Jordan* betray this. When Jordanian and Palestinian politicians truly hoped to expand to Lesser Syria, they referred to it as "Northern" or "Interior" Syria. See Government of Jordan, *Suriya al-Kubra: Al-Kitab al-Urdunni al-Abyad* (Amman: Al-Matba῾a al-Wataniya, 1947), p. 104. Bayan al-Hut, ed., *Watha'iq al-Haraka al-Wataniya al-Filastiniya, 1918-1939: Min Awraq Akram Zu῾aytar* (Beirut: Mu'assasat ad-Dirasat al-Filastiniya, 1979), pp.

36, 376. Conversely, Lesser Syrians used these terms when they aspired to move south; Muhammad 'Ismat Shaykhu, *Suriya wa-Qadiyat Filastin, 1920–1949* (Damascus: Dar Qutayba, 1402/1982), pp. 6, 79, 81, 87.

10. *Al-Hawadith*, 18 July 1975.

11. Radio Amman, 25 December 1981.

12. "Al-Mu'tamar ad-Duwali li-Ta'rikh Bilad ash-Sham (Filastin)." Several publications came out of this conference. See, for example, Vol. 3 on Gaza, by 'Abd al-Karim Rafiq, *Ghazza: Dirasa 'Umraniya wa-Ijtima'iya wa-Iqtisadiya* (n.p., 1981).

13. For example, Ibrahim Husayn 'Abd al-Hawdi al-Fayyumi, *Al-Waqi'iya fi'r-Riwaya al-'Arabiya al-Haditha fi Bilad ash-Sham (Suriya, Lubnan, Filastin, al-Urdunn) min 1929–1967* (Amman: Dar al-Fikr, 1983).

14. Dhuqan al-Hindawi and 'Abd al-Bari Durra, *Al-Qadiya al-Filastiniya*, 11th ed. (Amman: Wizarat at-Tarbiya wa't-Ta'lim, 1407/1987), p. 12. This book was first used in 1977.

15. Radio Amman, 18 July 1983. On *Northern Jordan*, see note 9 above.

16. Radio Amman, 27 February 1986.

17. *Shu'un al-Ard al-Muhtalla* (Amman: Mudiriyat ad-Dirasat, Wizarat Shu'un al-Ard al-Muhtalla, May 1986).

18. I have catalogued some of these in Daniel Pipes, "The Unackowledged Partnership," *National Interest* (Winter 1987–88): 95–98.

19. *Ash-Sharq al-Awsat*, 30 June 1986.

20. *Al-Anba'* [Kuwait], 26 October 1986.

21. Minister of Defense General Mustafa Tallas, *Ar-Ra'y al-'Amm*, 1 October 1983; idem, Radio Damascus, 9 September 1980; Hafiz al-Asad, *Ar-Ra'y al-'Amm*, 6 December 1980.

22. *Al-Anwar*, 10 August 1972.

23. *Jaysh ash-Sha'b*, 28 August 1973. Quoted in Moshe Ma'oz, *Asad, The Sphinx of Damascus: A Political Biography* (New York: Weidenfeld & Nicholson, 1988), p. 89.

24. Ahmad Iskandar, January 1975. Quoted in Anne Sinai and Allen Pollack, eds., *The Syrian Arab Republic: A Handbook* (New York: American Academic Association for Peace in the Middle East, 1976), p. 148.

25. Radio Damascus, 20 July 1976.

26. *Le Monde*, 27 July 1976.

27. 'Abd ar-Ra'uf al-Kasm, Radio Damascus, 14 April 1982.

28. *Al-Mustaqbal*, 8 May 1982.

29. *The Christian Science Monitor*, 18 August 1983.

30. *The New York Times*, 24 December 1983.

31. *Le Monde*, 24 May 1985.

32. Quoted in David Roberts, *The Ba'th and the Creation of Modern Syria* (New York: St. Martin's Press, 1987), p. 14.

33. *Der Spiegel*, 22 September 1986, p. 163.

34. *Ar-Ra'y al-'Amm*, 7 January 1976.

35. Naomi Joy Weinberger, *Syrian Intervention in Lebanon: The 1975–76 Civil War* (New York: Oxford University Press, 1986), p. 212.

36. Quoted in Gérard Michaud, "Terrorisme d'état, terrorisme contre l'état: Le Cas syrien," *Esprit*, October–November 1984, p. 199.

37. Quoted in Antun Khuwayri, *Al-Harb fi Lubnan 1976* (Junya: Al-Bulusiya, 1977), p. 154.

38. *As-Safir*, 10 February 1978.

39. Quoted in Erish Gysling, "An Assad führt kein Weg vorbei," *Schweizer Monatshefte* 64 (1984): 232.

40. Radio Damascus, 17 July 1986.

41. Asad has, by contrast, made a number of informal visits to areas of Lebanon under Syrian control. He and his spokesmen have even received the foreign press there; see *Le Nouvel Observateur*, 7 November 1986.

42. Agence France Presse, 7 January 1975. Quoted in Laurent, "Syrie-Liban: Les faux frères-jumeaux," *Politique Étrangère* 48 (1983): 592.

43. Associated Press, 23 June 1977.

44. Radio Damascus, 27 March 1989.

45. Ahmad Iskandar, *Ash-Shira'*, 7 March 1983.

46. Radio Damascus, 27 August 1979. For the significance of the absence of diplomatic relations, see Annie Laurent and Antoine Basbous, *Une Proie pour deux fauves?* (Beirut: Ad-Da'irat, 1983), pp. 41–43, 84–85; also idem, *Guerres secrètes au Liban* (Paris: Gallimard, 1987), pp. 90–92.

47. Quoted in Laurent, "Syrie-Liban," p. 599.

48. This list was compiled by comparing the diplomatic representation in Beirut in 1974 and 1985.

49. Reuven Avi-Ran, "The Syrian Military-Strategic Interest in Lebanon," *The Jerusalem Quarterly* 46 (Spring 1988): 141.

50. The Economist Intelligence Unit, *Quarterly Economic Review of Syria, Lebanon, Cyprus* (3d quarter 1976): 11.

51. Quoted in Karim Pakradouni, *La Paix, manquée: Le Mandat d'Elias Sarkis (1976–1982)* (Beirut: Éditions Fiches du Monde Arabe, 1983), p. 170.

52. *The New York Times*, 30 December 1983.

53. *The Christian Science Monitor*, 18 March 1983.

54. *The Washington Post*, 23 July 1984.

55. Voice of Hope, 9 September 1985.

56. Middle East News Agency, 28 May 1988.

57. *Al-Watan al-'Arabi*, 3 June 1988.

58. *As-Sayyad* [Beirut], 9 September 1976.

59. Voice of the Mountain, 2 December 1988.

60. This wing came into existence shortly after the Syrian *coup d'état* of February 1966. Asad used his influence to get the leader of the Lebanese Ba'th Party put in jail for criticizing a foreign state, then proceeded to set up a new Ba'th organization.

61. Quoted in Antun Khuwayri, *Hawadith Lubnan 1975* (Juniya: Al-Bulusiya, 1976), p. 304.

62. Agence France Presse, 14 November 1975.

63. Associated Press, 23 June 1977.

64. Voice of Lebanon, 2 August 1986.

65. Radio Beirut, 6 August 1985.

66. Radio Damascus, 7 August 1985.

67. Voice of the Mountain, 31 August 1985.

68. Radio Damascus, 29 December 1985.

69. Damascus Television, 9 September 1985; Voice of Lebanon, 10 September 1985. Samir Ja'ja' called Hubayqa a "parrot" who "repeats what the Syrians say." Radio Free Lebanon, 30 January 1988.

70. Radio Monte Carlo, 19 February 1986.

71. Voice of the Mountain, 22 October 1986.

72. Voice of the Mountain, 5 November 1985.

73. Radio Jerusalem, 24 July 1985.

74. *Ma'ariv*, 11 April 1985.

75. *At-Tadamun*, 24 August 1985.

76. Harald Vocke, *Was geschah im Libanon?* (Frankfurt: author, 1977), p. 45.

77. *Ath-Thawra*, 17 August 1976.

78. *Ath-Thawra*, 18 January 1977. See also notes 110 and 179 to Chapter 3.

79. Radio Beirut, 2 August 1985.

80. Ehud Ya'ari, "Behind the Terror," *The Atlantic*, June 1987, p. 19.

81. *Ma'ariv*, 16 July 1985.

82. The statement by the previously unknown group that took responsibility for the explosion combined two usually incompatible ideals, fundamentalist Islam and Pan-Syrian nationalism. It read as follows: "The movement declares its full support for the Greater Syria policy, which calls for the return of Palestine to the Palestinians and the liberation of Lebanon from imperialism and isolationism and strengthening the Islamic revolution throughout the Arab world." Agence France Presse, 23 October 1983. This statement hinted at cooperation between the SSNP and Hizbullah.

83. Floyd I. Clarke, "Affidavit," dated 10 May 1988 and attached to the "Memorandum in Aid of Sentencing," in the case of *United States of America* v. *Walid Kabbani et al.*, considered by the U.S. District Court for the District of Vermont.

84. Damascus Radio, 4 May 1985.

85. Ya'ari, "Behind the Terror."

86. Damascus Televsion, 10 July 1985.

87. Damascus Television, 10 April 1985. SSNP gunmen subsequently took to wearing the portrait of this girl around their necks.

88. *The New York Times*, 3 August 1985.

89. On this unusual case, see *The New York Times*, 28 January and 18 May 1988; *The Wall Street Journal*, 11 February 1988; *The Los Angeles Times*, 18 May 1988.

90. 'Isam al-Mahayiri and In'am Ra'd, Radio Damascus, 11 June 1986.

91. Roberts, *Ba'th*, p. 15.

92. Ya'ari, "Behind the Terror."

93. Hafiz al-Asad, Radio Damascus, 20 July 1976.

94. Radio Damascus, 18 June 1985. Also Defense Minister Mustafa Tallas: "Who is Arafat? He is nothing more than a puppet in the hands of the United States." Vienna Television, 22 September 1987.

95. Damascus Television, 13 June 1985.

96. *Tishrin*, 25 October 1987. In private conversations, Syrian officials have been known to add, "we may someday want to negotiate on the Palestinians' behalf ourselves."

97. Radio Damascus, 5 December 1980; Hafiz al-Asad, *Ar-Ra'y al-'Amm*, 6 December 1980.

98. Radio Damascus, 25 June 1983.

99. Radio Damascus, 28 November 1980.

100. Radio Monte Carlo, 20 May 1983.

101. *Ar-Ra'y al-'Amm*, 6 December 1980.

102. *The Christian Science Monitor*, 8 January 1986.

103. Radio Damascus, 8 March 1974.

104. Sami al-'Attari, on behalf of President Asad, Radio Damascus, 24 May 1978.

105. 'Abd ar-Ra'uf al-Kasm, *Al-Mustaqbal*, 29 March 1980.

106. Radio Damascus, 23 April 1980.

107. Radio Damascus, 3 June 1980.
108. Assistant Secretary of the Ba'th Party Regional Command Muhammad Mash-ariqa, Radio Damascus, 17 April 1983.
109. Henry Kissinger, *Years of Upheaval* (Boston: Little, Brown, 1982). p. 954.
110. Radio Damascus, 20 September 1976.
111. *As-Sayyad*, January 1981.
112. Radio Amman, 21 February 1981.
113. Radio Damascus, 1 April 1981.
114. 'Abdallah al-Ahmar, *Ath-Thawra*, 18 August 1982.
115. Radio Damascus, 9 May 1983.
116. Radio Damascus, 27 February 1986.
117. *L'Humanité*, 17 June 1976; Kamal Joumblatt, *Pour le Liban* (Paris: Stock, 1978), p. 177.
118. Radio Rabat, 7 August 1986.
119. 'Abd al-Karim Rafiq, *Al-'Arab wa'l-'Uthmaniyun, 1516–1916* (Damascus, 1974), p. 602. I used a reprint, Acco: Maktabat wa-Matba'at as-Suruji, 1978.
120. Shaykhu, *Suriya wa-Qadiyat Filastin, 1920–1949*, pp. 5, 45, 47, 48, 63, 81. For similar sentiments, see Hissan 'Ali Hallaq, *Mu'tamar as-Sahil wa'l-Aqdiya al-Arba'a, 1936* (Beirut: Dar al-Jami'iya, 1403/1983), pp. 11–12, 15.
121. Palestine as Southern Syria: Shaykhu, *Suriya wa-Qadiyat Filastin, 1920–1949*, pp. 5, 6, 43, 62, 87. The Republic of Syria as Northern Syria: pp. 6, 79, 81, 87. The present borders are discussed on p. 43.
122. *An-Nahar*, 20 and 25 January 1976. Quoted in Weinberger, *Syrian Intervention in Lebanon*, p. 187.
123. Radio Damascus, 20 July 1976.
124. Defense Intelligence Agency, *International Terrorism: A Compendium, Volume II—Middle East*, Secret (Washington D.C.: D.I.A., July 1979), pp. 37–38. This is one of the classified documents captured from the U.S. Embassy in Tehran, then reprinted by the Muslim Students Following the Line of the Imam as *Documents From the U.S. Espionage Den (43): U.S. Interventions in the Islamic Countries: Palestine (2)*. Writing from a completely different viewpoint, Yasser Ali also dubbed Sa'iqa "Asad's Trojan horse." See "Le 'petit' Croissant fertile de la Syrie," *Khamsin* 4 (1977): 33.
125. *International Terrorism*, p. 37.
126. Radio Damascus, 8 March 1975.
127. 'Arafat to Anwar as-Sadat, Middle East News Agency, 12 April 1976. Quoted in P. Edward Haley and Lewis W. Snider, eds., *Lebanon in Crisis: Participants and Issues*, edited by P. Edward Haley and Lewis W. Snider (Syracuse, N.Y.: Syracuse University Press, 1979), p. 144.
128. *An-Nahar*, 11 April 1976. Quoted in Weinberger, *Syrian Intervention in Lebanon*, p. 200.
129. Legislative Decrees nos. 7, 9, and 12, as reported by Damascus Television, 13 May 1985.
130. *Al-Ba'th*, 27 October 1974.
131. *Trouw*, 31 March 1977.
132. Damascus Voice of Palestine, 27 June 1983 (as monitored by the BBC).
133. *Le Monde*, 1 January 1986, and Yossi Melman, *The Master Terrorist: The True Story of Abu-Nidal* (New York: Adama Books, 1986), p. 80. See also the interview Banna granted to *France-Pays Arabes*, February 1985.
134. According to one account (Melman, *The Master Terrorist*, p. 56), Sabri al-Banna had a Palestinian father and a Syrian mother.

135. *Der Spiegel*, 14 October 1985, pp. 194, 197.

136. *Monday Morning*, 17 July 1977.

137. Radio Damascus, 16 July 1980.

138. *Ash-Sharq al-Awsat*, 7 August 1985.

139. Radio Damascus, 5 January 1985.

140. *Tishrin*, 9 July 1983.

141. Radio Baghdad, 6 September 1985.

142. Hungarian Television, 20 March 1986.

143. Na'if Hawatma and Yasir 'Abd Rabbu, quoted in Matti Steinberg, "The Worldview of Hawatmeh's 'Democratic Front,'" *Jerusalem Quarterly* 50 (Spring 1989): 35.

144. *The Christian Science Monitor*, 5 August 1981.

145. Baghdad Voice of the PLO, 23 July 1983.

146. Baghdad Voice of the PLO, 13 March 1989.

147. *Tishrin*, quoted in *The New York Times*, 13 July 1983; *The Washington Post*, 6 August 1983; Mustafa Tallas, Damascus Television, 6 October 1986.

148. Radio Damascus, 18 June 1985.

149. Radio Damascus, 24 March 1984.

150. Voice of Lebanon, 20 April 1986.

151. Simon Malley, "Hafez El-Assad: Guerre a l'O.L.P.! . . ." *Afrique-Asie*, 25 October 1982, p. 13.

152. *Davar*, 18 August 1985.

153. Baghdad Voice of the PLO, 6 October 1988.

154. *The Washington Post*, 1 January 1985.

155. San'a Voice of Palestine, 25 September 1985.

156. Salah Khalaf, *Al-Majalla*, 26 November 1983.

157. *Tishrin*, 3 August 1985.

158. Radio Damascus, 23 March 1980.

159. Radio Damascus, 30 November 1980; also *Tishrin*, 4 December 1980.

160. *Tishrin*, 26 March 1981.

161. *Al-Khalij*, 15 March 1981. See also *Ath-Thawra*, 14 July 1981.

162. *Ar-Ra'y al-'Amm*, 6 December 1980.

163. Radio Damascus, 9 January 1981.

164. *Ath-Thawra*, 14 January 1981.

165. Ibid., 18 February 1981.

166. *Tishrin*, 21 February 1981.

167. Radio Damascus, 15 April 1981.

168. Radio Damascus, 26 April 1981.

169. *Tishrin*, 5 December 1980.

170. *Ar-Ra'y al-'Amm*, 6 December 1980.

171. Radio Damascus, 10 June 1975; also Radio Amman, same date.

172. Radio Amman, 25 July 1985.

173. Radio Amman, 6 February 1981.

174. *Le Monde*, 27 July 1976.

175. Élisabeth Picard, "Retour au Sandjak," *Maghreb-Machrek*, January–March 1983, p. 58.

176. Anatolia, 18 March 1987.

177. 'Abd al-Halim Khaddam, *Tishrin*, 17 May 1980. Alexandretta province (now officially known as Hatay) covers 1,814 square miles; Mandatory Palestine covered 10,800 square miles.

178. Muhammad Mashariqa, *Ta Nea* [Nicosia], 15 February 1981.

179. Shawqi Khayrallah, *Ath-Thawra*, 29 August 1976.

180. Kamal Shatila, Secretary General of the National Front, writing in *Tishrin*, 22 November 1976.

181. *The Los Angeles Times*, 7 May 1981.

182. Paris Domestic Service, 18 November 1984.

183. *Ath-Thawra*, 14 July 1981.

184. Ma'oz, *Asad*, p. 113.

185. Legislative Decrees nos. 7, 9, and 12, as reported by Damascus Television, 13 May 1985.

186. Quoted in Malley, "Hafez El-Assad," p. 13.

187. Voice of Hope, 25 March 1983.

188. Voice of Hope, 30 July 1983. For a more alarmist analysis, see the statement quoted in Nicolas Nasr, *Faillité syrienne au Liban, 1975–81* (Beirut: Dar el-Amal, 1982), Vol. 1, pp. 169–70.

189. *La Vanguardia* [Barcelona], 25 May 1986.

190. *Le Journal de Dimanche*, 24 April 1988.

191. Reuters, 19 March 1985. See also Voice of Lebanon, 15 June 1987; Radio Free Lebanon, 29 August 1987; Voice of Lebanon, 15 September 1987.

192. Radio Free Lebanon, 30 September 1987.

193. Joumblatt, *Pour le Liban*, pp. 177, 197; also pp. 124, 180. *Asad* means "lion" in Arabic.

194. Ibid., pp. 168, 34.

195. Ibid., p. 167; also pp. 31, 37, 48, 49, 181–91.

196. Abdullah Sa'idi, *MERIP Reports* 61 (1977): 17.

197. Quoted by Lally Weymouth, *The Los Angeles Times*, 7 August 1983.

198. *Al-Quds*, 21 June 1976.

199. Quoted in Pakradouni, *La Paix, manquée*, p. 229.

200. Voice of the PLO, Baghdad, 12 December 1986.

201. Sadat usually expressed this mock title in French (*le Lion de la Grande Syrie*). See Joseph Kraft, "Letter from Egypt," *The New Yorker*, 28 May 1979, pp. 97–98; United Press International, 4 June 1981.

202. *Le Figaro*, 15 October 1986.

203. *Al-Ahram*, 9 June 1976.

204. *Al-Ahram*, 14 November 1988.

205. *Ma'ariv*, 22 July 1983.

206. Reuters, 5 April 1981.

207. *The New York Times*, 10 November 1983.

208. *The Washington Post*, 1 September 1978.

209. IDF Radio, 17 December 1985.

210. Reuters, 20 November 1983; see also *The New York Times*, 17 November 1983.

211. Maurice Couve de Murville, "La Crise libanaise et l'évolution du Proche-Orient," *Politique Étrangère* 41 (1976): 100.

212. Reuters, 7 February 1983.

213. Roberts, *Ba'th*, pp. 15, 124, 141, 152, 161.

214. *The Economist*, 6 February 1988. Survey on "The Arab East," p. 23.

215. Kissinger, *Years of Upheaval*, p. 935. In a discussion with the author (on 29 September 1986), Kissinger noted that the Syrians view Lebanon and Jordan similarly.

216. *The New York Times*, 20 October 1983. The same point was made in public

and private remarks later that month; see ibid., 29 October 1983, and Associated Press, 29 October 1983.

217. United Press International, 25 October 1983.

218. *The New York Times*, 15 March 1984. Some politicians went further; Gary Hart, for example, disregarded facts, writing that before World War II, "Lebanon was part of Greater Syria." *The Los Angeles Times*, 6 October 1988.

219. Fouad Ajami, "The Arab Fascination with the Forbidden," *U.S. News & World Report*, 31 October 1988.

220. Najib E. Saliba, "Syrian-Lebanese Relations," in Halim Barakat, ed., *Toward a Viable Lebanon* (London: Croom Helm, 1988), pp. 147–48.

221. Adeed Dawisha, "The Motives of Syria's Involvement in Lebanon," *Middle East Journal* 38 (1984): 229. See also his book *Syria and the Lebanese Crisis* (New York: St. Martin's Press, 1980), p. 72.

222. Itamar Rabinovich, "The Changing Prism: Syrian Policy in Lebanon as a Mirror, an Issue and an Instrument," in Moshe Ma'oz and Avner Yaniv, eds., *Syria under Assad: Domestic Constraints and Regional Risks* (New York: St. Martin's Press, 1986), p. 180. Rabinovich's thinking on this matter has evolved. Earlier, in *The War for Lebanon, 1970–1983* (Ithaca, N.Y.: Cornell University Press, 1984), pp. 53–54, he argued that "Asad's decision to intervene in Lebanon was not made in order to implement that notion [i.e., Greater Syria]. But when the conflict with the Palestinians and the Lebanese left developed, this vision became useful to justify their subjugation."

223. Ma'oz, *Asad*, p. 113. Ma'oz argued that although Asad's efforts to build Greater Syria reached their apogee in 1977 (p. 132) and had "virtually failed" by 1979 (p. 178), he "has not relinquished" this ambition (p. 181).

224. *The Observer*, 6 March 1977.

225. Patrick Seale, "Madha Yurid Hafiz al-Asad?" *Al-Majalla*, 23 July 1983, pp. 22–23.

226. Laurent and Basbous, *Une Proie pour deux fauves?* p. 84.

227. Laurent, "Syrie-Liban," p. 599.

228. Charles Saint-Prot, *Les Mystères syriens: La Politique au Proche-Orient de 1970 à 1984* (Paris: Albin Michel, 1984), pp. 124, 147.

229. Dominique Chevallier, preface to Ghassan Tuéni, *Une Guerre pour les autres* (Paris: Éditions Jean-Claude Lattès, 1985), pp. 18–19. For a similar view, see Charles Villeneuve and Jean-Pierre Péret, *Histoire secrète du terrorisme: Les Juges de l'impossible* (Paris: Plon, 1987), p. 150.

230. Gudrun Krämer, "Syriens Weg zu regionaler Hegemonie," *Europa-Archiv* (1987): 670.

231. John F. Devlin, "Syrian Policy in the Aftermath of the Israeli Invasion of Lebanon," in Robert O. Freedman, ed., *The Middle East after the Israeli Invasion of Lebanon* (Syracuse, N.Y.: Syracuse University Press, 1986), p. 302.

232. "Why Syria Invaded Lebanon," *MERIP Reports* 51 (1976): 10.

233. Weinberger, *Syrian Intervention in Lebanon*, p. 267.

234. William Harris, "Syria in Lebanon," in Altaf Gauhar, ed., *Third World Affairs 1988* (London: Third World Foundation for Social and Economic Studies, 1988), p. 90.

235. Radio Tripoli, 1 September 1985..

236. *Al-Ba'th*, 19 May 1976.

237. *Al-Iqra'*, 21 March 1985.

238. Joumblatt, *Pour le Liban*, p. 180.

239. *Al-Qabas*, 10 August 1985.

240. Congressional testimony of Assistant Secretary of State for Near Eastern and

South Asian Affairs Richard Murphy, *The Philadelphia Inquirer*, 19 November 1983. This statement raises obvious questions. When has Lebanon ever threatened Syria? How could it do so in the future?

241. *The New York Times*, 10 April 1984.

242. Richard F. Nyrop, ed., *Syria: A Country Study* (Washington, D.C.: U.S. Government Printing Office, 1979), p. 181.

243. Moshe Ma'oz and Avner Yaniv, "The Syrian Paradox," in Ma'oz and Yaniv, *Syria under Assad*, pp. 251–52.

244. *Newsweek*, 19 December 1983.

245. Reuters, 4 October 1983.

246. Krämer, "Syriens Weg zu regionaler Hegemonie," p. 670.

247. Harris, "Syria in Lebanon," p. 90. Harris explained what this policy means for the Lebanese army, internal security services, and the country's foreign policy on p. 91.

248. Quoted in Kati Marton, "Peril or Possibility: America and Syria at the Crossroads," *Middle East Insight* 4 (1986): 17.

Chapter 4

1. David Roberts, *The Ba'th and the Creation of Modern Syria* (New York: St. Martin's Press, 1987), p. 152.

2. Daniel Dishon, "The Lebanese War—An All Arab Crisis," *Midstream*, January 1977, p. 27. For an extended version of this argument, see Moshe Ma'oz, *Asad, The Sphinx of Damascus: A Political Biography* (New York: Weidenfeld & Nicholson, 1988), pp. 45–48, 110–13.

3. Notably Nikolaos van Dam, *The Struggle for Power in Syria: Sectarianism, Regionalism and Tribalism in Politics, 1961–1978* (New York: St. Martin's Press, 1979); John F. Devlin, *The Ba'th Party: A History from Its Origins to 1966* (Stanford, Calif.: Hoover Institution Press, 1976); Itamar Rabinovich, *Syria under the Ba'th 1963–1966: The Army Party Symbiosis* (Jerusalem: Israel Universities Press, 1972); Patrick Seale, *The Struggle for Syria* (London: Oxford University Press, 1965).

4. As a polity, Syria closely resembles the states of sub-Saharan Africa. In both, artificial boundaries bear mute testimony to the interests of fallen empires. In both, hostile ethnic groups compete outside the national framework. Politically, the religious communities of Syria equal the tribes of Africa.

5. Quoted in Daniel Lerner, *The Passing of Traditional Society* (New York: Free Press, 1964), p. 272.

6. *Al-Barada*, 25 October 1953. Quoted in Seale, *Struggle for Syria*, p. 130.

7. Roberts, *Ba'th*, p. 14.

8. Henry Kissinger, *Years of Upheaval* (Boston: Little, Brown, 1982), p. 779.

9. Abu Khaldun Sati' al-Husri, *Al-Iqlimiya: Judhurha wa Budhurha* (Beirut: Dar al-'Ilm li'l-Malayin, 1963), p. 178.

10. *The Times*, 24 February 1926; League of Nations, Permanent Mandates Commission, *Minutes of the 9th Session*, 16th meeting, 17 June 1926, p. 119. See also Safiuddin Joarder, *Syria under the French Mandate: The Early Phase 1920–27* (Dacca: Asiatic Society of Bangladesh, 1977), pp. 170–71.

11. The Ba'th Party also had important branches in Iraq and other Arab countries, but the concern here is only with Syria; therefore, *the Ba'th Party* will be shorthand for *the Ba'th Party of Syria*.

12. Bashir Da'uq, ed., *Nidal al-Ba'th* (Beirut: Dar at-Tali'a, 1963–74), Vol. 4, pp. 140–41. Ba'th Party internal development during this period is known in detail because

of the publication of Ba'th documents in Da'uq's multivolume book and the capture of documents on the Golan Heights by Israeli troops in 1967.

13. The party dissolution was only in Syria, it should be noted; branches of the Ba'th Party existed in many other Arab countries, most importantly Iraq. Again, remarks here refer only to the Ba'th Party in Syria.

14. Michel 'Aflaq, quoted in *At-Taqrir al-Watha'iqi li-Azmat al-Hizb*, p. 16. Reference in Rabinovich, *Syria under the Ba'th*, p. 145. See also *Al-Hayat*, 26 February 1966.

15. Husri, *Al-Iqlimiya*, p. 167.

16. Da'uq, *Nidal al-Ba'th*, Vol. 4, pp. 195–96.

17. Ibid., p. 196.

18. Al-Hizb al-Ba'th al-'Arabi al-Ishtiraki, Al-Qiyada al-Qawmiya, *Ba'd al-Muntalaqat an-Nazariya*. Text in ibid., Vol. 6, pp. 254–55.

19. Devlin, *Ba'th Party*, p. 227.

20. Munif ar-Razzaz, *At-Tajriba al-Murra* (Beirut: Dar Ghandur, 1967), p. 95.

21. Martin Seymour, "The Dynamics of Power in Syria since the Break with Egypt," *Middle Eastern Studies* 6 (1970): 44.

22. Quoted in Charles Saint-Prot, *Les Mystères syriens: La Politique au Proche-Orient de 1970 à 1984* (Paris: Albin Michel, 1984), p. 77.

23. Quoted in Eric Rouleau, "The Syrian Enigma: What Is the Ba'th?" *New Left Review* 45 (1967): 63.

24. This story resumes on p. 180.

25. Apologists have constructed an elaborate argument to prove that 'Alawi was the sect's original name. See 'Ali 'Aziz Ibrahim, *Al-'Alawiyun: Fida'iy ash-Shi'a al-Majhulun* (n.p., 1392/1972), pp. 9–14.

26. For accounts of 'Alawi theology and doctrines, see many of the books cited in the following notes, especially those by Sulayman Efendi al-Adhani, Halm, Lammens, Lyde, Moosa, de Sacy, and Sharaf ad-Din.

27. Ibn Kathir, *Al-Bidaya wa'n-Nihaya* (Cairo: Matba'a as-Sa'ada, 1351–58/1932–39), Vol. 14, p. 83.

28. See Wolff, "Auszüge aus dem Katechismus der Nossairier," *Zeitschrift der Deutschen Morgenländischen Gesellschaft* 3 (1849): 308.

29. And just as Muslims traditionally accused Christians of making Jesus divine, so they accused 'Alawis of doing the same to 'Ali; the parallel is striking.

30. T. E. Lawrence, *Seven Pillars of Wisdom: A Triumph* (Garden City, N.Y.: Doubleday, Doran & Company, 1935), p. 329.

31. Henri Lammens, "Les Nosairis: Notes sur leur histoire et leur religion," *Études*, 1899, p. 492.

32. Sami al-Jundi, *Al-Ba'th* (Beirut: Dar an-Nahar li'n-Nashr, 1969), p. 145.

33. Pierre May, *L'Alaouite: Ses croyances, ses moeurs, les cheikhs, les lois de la tribu et les chefs* (Beirut: Imprimerie Catholique, 1931?), pp. 42–43.

34. F. Walpole, *The Ansayrii (or Assassins) with Travels to the Further East, in 1850–51* (London: Richard Bentley, 1851), Vol. 3, p. 64.

35. Heinz Halm, *Die islamische Gnosis: Die extreme Schia und die 'Alawiten* (Zurich: Artemis, 1982), p. 316.

36. Hamza ibn 'Ali, *Ar-Risala ad-Damigha li'l-Fasiq ar-Radd 'ala an-Nusayri*. Text in Silvestre de Sacy, *Exposé de la religion des Druzes* (Paris: À l'Imprimerie Royale, 1838), Vol. 2, pp. 571–73.

37. For a wild novelistic account of 'Alawi religious orgies, see Jehan Cendrieux, *Al-Ghadir ou le Sexe-Dieu* (Paris: Bibliothèque-Charpentier, 1926), pp. 10–11.

38. "An Oriental Student," *The Modern Syrians: or, Native Society in Damascus,*

Aleppo, and the Mountains of the Druses (London: Longman, Brown, Green, and Longmans, 1844), p. 281.

39. Sulayman Efendi al-Adhani, *Kitab al-Bakura as-Sulaymaniya fi Kashf Asrar ad-Diyana an-Nusayriya*. Summary and Arabic extracts in Edward E. Salisbury, "The Book of Sulaiman's First Ripe Fruit: Disclosing the Mysteries of the Nusairian Religion," *Journal of the American Oriental Society* 8 (1866): 285, 306. According to Sulayman Efendi, this practice originated in an esoteric interpretation of the Qur'an, sura 33, verse 49.

40. Ibn Battuta, *Ar-Rihla* (Beirut: Dar as-Sadr and Dar Bayrut, 1384/1964), pp. 79–80.

41. Matti Moosa, *Extremist Shiites: The Ghulat Sects* (Syracuse, N.Y.: Syracuse University Press, 1988), p. 271.

42. Ignaz Goldziher, *Vorlesungen über den Islam* (Heidelberg: C. Winter, 1910); trans. by Andras and Ruth Hamori as *Introduction to Islamic Theology and Law*, (Princeton, N.J.: Princeton University Press, 1981), p. 228.

43. Sulayman Efendi al-Adhani, *Kitab al-Bakura*. Extracts in al-Husayni 'Abdallah, ed., *Al-Judhur at-Ta'rikhiya li'n-Nusayriya al-'Alawiya* (Cairo: Dar al-I'tisam, 1400/1980), p. 55.

44. Sulayman Efendi al-Adhani, *Kitab al-Bakura*, in Salisbury, "Book of Sulaiman's First Ripe Fruit," p. 298. The third sentence in this quote comes from Henri Lammens, *L'Islam, croyances et institutions*, 2d ed. (Beirut: Imprimerie Catholique, 1941), p. 228.

45. Paulo Boneschi, "Une fatwà du Grand Mufti de Jérusalem Muhammad 'Amin al-Husayni sur les 'Alawites," *Revue de l'Histoire des Religions* 122, 2–3 (September–December 1940): 152.

46. Henry Maundrell, *A Journey from Aleppo to Jerusalem in 1697* (London: J. White & Co., 1810), pp. 16–17.

47. Benjamin Disraeli, *Tancred, or The New Crusade* (London: Longmans, Green, 1847), pp. 374–75.

48. Sulayman Efendi al-Adhani, *Kitab al-Bakura*, in Salisbury, "Book of Sulaiman's First Ripe Fruit," p. 298.

49. Muhammad Rida Shams ad-Din, *Ma'a al-'Alawiyin fi Suriya* (Beirut: Matba'at al-Insaf, 1376), pp. 5–6.

50. Annie Laurent and Antoine Basbous, *Guerres secrètes au Liban* (Paris: Gallimard, 1987), pp. 71–72.

51. Hamza ibn 'Ali, *Ar-Risala ad-Damigha*, Vol. 2, p. 570. This accusation resembles those used by medieval Christians to explain the popularity of Islam.

52. Quoted in 'Izz ad-Din al-Farisi and Ahmad Sadiq, "Ath-Thawra al-Islamiya fi Suriya," *Al-Mukhtar al-Islami* [Cairo], October 1980, p. 39.

53. Ahmad ibn Taymiya, "Fatwa fi'n-Nusayriya." Arabic text in M. St. Guyard, "Le Fetwa d'Ibn Taimiyyah sur les Nosairis," *Journal Asiatique*, 6th series, 16 (1871): 167, 168, 169, 177. For other premodern Sunni assessments of the 'Alawis—including al-Ash'ari, 'Abd al-Qadir al-Baghdadi, Ibn Hazm, ash-Shahrastani, and Fakhr ad-Din ar-Razi—see As-Sayyid 'Abd al-Husayn Mahdi al-'Askari, *Al-'Alawiyun aw an-Nusayriya* (n.p., 1400/1980), pp. 49–53.

54. Text in Robert Mantran and Jean Sauvaget, eds., *Règlements fiscaux ottomans: Les provinces syriens* (Paris: Librairie d'Amerique et d'Orient, 1951), p. 76. See also pp. 77, 88, 93.

55. Jacques Weulersse, "Antioche, un type de cité d'Islam," *Comptes Rendus du Congrès International de Géographie, Varsovie 1934* (Warsaw: Kasa Im. Mianowskiego, 1937), Vol. 3, p. 258.

56. Martin Kramer, "Syria's Alawis and Shi'ism," in Martin Kramer, ed., *Shi'ism, Resistance, and Revolution* (Boulder, Colo.: Westview Press, 1987), p. 238.

57. Samuel Lyde, *The Asian Mystery: Illustrated in the History, Religion, and Present State of the Ansaireeh or Nusairis of Syria* (London: Longman, Green, Longman, and Roberts, 1860), p. 196; Walpole, *Ansayrii*, Vol. 3, p. 115.

58. Ibn Battuta, *Ar-Rihla*, p. 80; Muhammad Amin Ghalib at-Tawil, *Ta'rikh al-'Alawiyin*, 2d ed. (Beirut: Dar al-Andalus, 1386/1966), p. 342. Tawil, a leading 'Alawi shaykh, published the first edition of his history in 1924.

59. Jacques Weulersse, *Le pays des Alaouites* (Tours: Arrault, 1940), Vol. 1, p. 54.

60. E. Janot, *Des Croisades au mandat: Notes sur le peuple Alouïte* (Lyons: Imprimerie L. Bascon, 1934), p. 37.

61. Paul Jacquot, *L'État des Alaouites: Guide* (Beirut: Imprimerie Catholique, 1929), p. 10.

62. R. Strothmann, "Die Nusairi im heutigen Syrien," *Nachrichten der Akademie der Wissenschaften in Göttingen*, phil.-hist. Kl. Nr. 4 (1950): 35.

63. George-Samné, *La Syrie* (Paris: Bossard, 1920), p. 340.

64. John Lewis Burckhardt, *Travels in Syria and the Holy Land* (London: John Murray, 1822), p. 141.

65. Lyde, *Asian Mystery*, pp. 219–20.

66. *Handbook for Travellers in Syria and Palestine* (London: John Murray, 1858), p. xli.

67. Weulersse, *Pays des Alaouites*, Vol. 1, pp. 73, 317; idem, *Paysans de Syrie et du Proche Orient* (Paris: Gallimard, 1946), p. 272. Étienne de Vaumas shows the similarities of the Lebanese and 'Alawi regions, then explains the profound differences of their populations, in "Le Djebel Ansarieh: Études de géographie humaine," *Revue de Géographie Alpine* 48 (1960): 267–311.

68. According to Nawfal Iliyas, a lawyer who worked for the 'Alawi tribes during those decades; reported by Laurent and Basbous, *Guerres secrètes au Liban*, p. 70. On Iliyas, see Jurj Gharib, *Nawfal Iliyas: Siyasa, Adab, Dhikriyat* (Beirut: Dar ath-Thaqafa, 1975).

69. Tawil, *Ta'rikh al-'Alawiyin*, p. 470.

70. Lyde, *Asian Mystery*, p. 222.

71. Weulersse, "Antioche," p. 258.

72. Weulersse, *Paysans de Syrie*, p. 85.

73. Van Dam, *Struggle for Power in Syria*, p. 22.

74. Yusuf al-Hakim, *Dhikriyat al-Hakim*, Vol. 3, *Suriya wa'l-'Ahd al-Faysali* (Beirut: Al-Matba'a al-Kathulikiya, 1966), p. 94.

75. Lammens, *L'Islam*, p. 228.

76. Gouraud to premier and foreign minister, 29 December 1919, Ministère des Affaires Étrangères, Series E, Levant, Syrie-Liban, Vol. 20, pp. 226–33. Quoted in Wajih Kawtharani, *Bilad ash-Sham* (Beirut: Ma'had al-Inma' al-'Arabi, 1980), p. 211.

77. Taqi Sharaf ad-Din, *An-Nusayriya: Dirasa Tahliliya* (Beirut: n.p., 1983), pp. 73–75.

78. Arrêté no. 623, 15 September 1922. Quoted in E. Rabbath, *L'Évolution politique de la Syrie sous mandat* (Paris: Marcel Rivière, 1928), p. 185.

79. Sharaf ad-Din, *An-Nusayriya: Dirasa Tahliliya*, p. 80.

80. 77 percent voted in the 'Alawi state, 20 to 25 percent in Aleppo, and so few in Hama that elections were canceled. League of Nations, Permanent Mandates Commission, *Minutes of the 9th Session*, 16th meeting, 17 June 1926, p. 116.

81. 'Alawis made up the 1st, 2d, and much of the 5th battalions; Armenians appear to have made up the 4th; and Christians made up the 8th. The composition of the 3d, 6th, and 7th battalions is unknown. 'Alawis had no cavalry role. The 2d battalion, for example, had 773 soldiers, of whom 623 were 'Alawi, 73 Sunni, 64 Christian, and 13 Isma'ilis. See R. Bayly Winder, "The Modern Military Tradition in Syria," unpublished draft dated 5 March 1959, pp. 14–15; and Jacquot, *L'État des Alaouites*, p. 11.

82. President of the 'Alawis State Representative Council, League of Nations, Permanent Mandates Commission, *Minutes of the 9th Session*, 16th meeting, 17 June 1926, p. 112.

83. Petition dated 4 March 1936, *Bulletin du Comité de l'Asie Française*, April 1936, p. 131.

84. 11 June 1936, Ministère des Affaires Étrangères, Levant 1918–1930, Syrie-Liban, Doc. E-492, fol. 195. Quoted in Laurent and Basbous, *Guerres secrètes au Liban*, p. 74.

85. Document 3547, dated 15 June 1936, Ministère des Affaires Étrangères. Text in Abu Musa al-Hariri, *Al-'Alawiyun—an-Nusayriyun* (Beirut: n.p., 1400/1980), pp. 228–31. See also *International Impact*, 28 March 1980; al-Farisi and Sadiq, "Ath-Thawra al-Islamiya fi Suriya," p. 39; Anon., *Al-Muslimun fi Suriya wa'l-Irhab an-Nusayri, 1964–1979* (Cairo: n.p., n.d.), p. 6; Annie Laurent, "Syrie-Liban: Les faux frères-jumeaux," *Politique Étrangère* 48 (1983): 598; Annie Laurent and Antoine Basbous, *Une Proie pour deux fauves?* (Beirut: Ad-Da'irat, 1983), p. 96. Moosa, *Extremist Shiites*, pp. 287–88, provides a full English translation of the letter.

Laurent and Basbous report (*Guerres secrètes au Liban*, p. 76) that the letter is missing from the Quai d'Orsay and speculate that its absence has to do with the embarrassment it causes the Asad regime.

Four other memoranda from the 'Alawis to the French high commissioner are quoted extensively in Sharaf ad-Din, *An-Nusayriya: Dirasa Tahliliya*, pp. 87–92.

86. Note dated 3 July 1936, quoted in Sharaf ad-Din, *An-Nusayriya: Dirasa Tahliliya*, p. 57, n. 67.

87. Petition dated 26 September 1936, *Bulletin du Comité de l'Asie Française*, December 1936, p. 340.

88. Arrêté of 5 December 1936, *Échos de Syrie*, 13 December 1936. FO 371/20067/7579

89. Stephen Helmsley Longrigg, *Syria and Lebanon under French Mandate* (London: Oxford University Press, 1958), p. 210. British officials called him a "notorious brigand." See "Weekly Political Summary, Syria and the Lebanon," 2 February 1944, E 1049/23/89, Foreign Office 371/40299/7543. For photographs of this strange figure, see Weulersse, *Pays des Alaouites*, Vol. 2, pp. XCI–XCII.

90. "Weekly Political Summary, Syria and the Lebanon," 22 March 1944, E 2211/23/89, Foreign Office 371/40300/7543.

91. "The Present State of Syria and the Lebanon," suppl. II, 23 March 1945, Foreign Office 371/45562/7505.

92. Seale, *Struggle for Syria*, p. 37.

93. Fadlallah Abu Mansur, *A'asir Dimashq* (Beirut: n.p., 1959), p. 51. The total number of army officers at this time, it should be noted, was less than two hundred.

94. The 'Adnan al-Maliki affair of 1955, which eliminated the SSNP from political power in Syria, was an exception, for the SSNP included many 'Alawis (including Sergeant Yusuf 'Abd al-Karim, the man who assassinated Maliki). For some years after this event, 'Alawis in the army lay low.

95. On the Ba'th-SSNP rivalry, see Daniel Pipes, "Radical Politics and the Syrian Social Nationalist Party," *International Journal of Middle East Studies* 20 (1988): 313–16.

96. The most prominent exception to communal alignment was the cooperation between Amin al-Hafiz, a Sunni, and Salah Jadid and Hafiz al-Asad, both 'Alawis. In subsequent years, as non-'Alawis increasingly served 'Alawi purposes, cross-communal ties became unbalanced.

97. Rabinovich, *Syria under the Ba'th*, p. 181.

98. Syrian Regional Command of the Ba'th Party, *Azmat al-Hizb wa Harakat 23 Shubat* (Damascus, 1966), pp. 20–21. This document was classified as a "secret internal publication exlusively for members."

99. *Ad-Difa'* [Jerusalem], 14 September 1966; *An-Nahar*, 15 September 1966; *Al-Hayat*, 29 September 1966. Quoted in van Dam, *Struggle for Power*, pp. 75–76. For many more examples of suspicion about 'Alawis, see ibid., pp. 110–24. Much of my information on the rise of the 'Alawis derives from van Dam's meticulous study.

100. The family name was originally Wahsh, meaning "wild beast" or "monster," then was changed to Asad, meaning "lion." Michael Hillegas van Dusen, "Intra- and Inter-Generational Conflict in the Syrian Army," unpublished Ph.D. dissertation, Johns Hopkins University, 1971, p. 315. The meaning of the two names is akin, but the tone is entirely different. There is some disagreement over the year of the change in name. Patrick Seale, *Asad of Syria: The Struggle for the Middle East* (Berkeley: University of California Press, 1989), p. 6, gives 1927 as the year of the change. Ma'oz, *Asad*, p. 24, has it around 1944. Seale's date fits with other evidence (such as his grandfather signing his name as Sulayman Asad in 1936).

101. According to Ahmad Sulayman al-Ahmad, *Al-Watan al-'Arabi*, 5 August 1988.

102. Laurent, "Syrie-Liban," p. 598.

103. Moosa, *Extremist Shiites*, p. 297.

104. *Al-Irhab an-Nusayri*, p. 46.

105. For the fullest account of these meetings, see Hariri, *Al-'Alawiyun—an-Nusayriyun*, pp. 234–37.

106. Devlin, *Ba'th Party*, pp. 319–20.

107. Alasdair Drysdale, "The Syrian Political Elite, 1966–1976: A Spatial and Social Analysis," *Middle Eastern Studies* 17 (1981): 27.

108. Yahya M. Sadowski, "Ba'thist Ethics and the Spirit of State Capitalism: Patronage and Party in Contemporary Syria," in Peter J. Chelkowski and Robert Pranger, eds., *Ideology and Power in the Middle East: Studies in Honor of George Lenczowski* (Durham: Duke University Press, 1988), p. 168.

109. Michael van Dusen, "Syria: Downfall of a Traditional Elite," in Frank Tachau, ed., *Political Elites and Political Development in the Middle East* (Cambridge, Mass.: Schenkman Publishing, 1975), p. 136.

110. Kramer, "Syria's Alawis and Shi'ism," p. 245.

111. Van Dusen, "Syria: Downfall of a Traditional Elite," p. 115. Also idem, "Political Integration and Regionalism in Syria," *Middle East Journal* 26 (1972): 125.

112. Ma'oz, *Asad*, pp. 62, 65.

113. Jabir Rizq, *Al-Ikhwan al-Muslimun w'al-Mu'amara 'ala Suriya* (Cairo: Dar al-I'tisam, 1980), p. 108, has 270; *Ad-Da'wa*, August 1979, p. 10, has 286. See also *Le Monde Diplomatique*, October 1979.

114. *Filastin ath-Thawra* [Baghdad], December 1986.

115. For a chilling account by an American of a year visiting Tishrin University, see

Samuel Pickering, Jr., "Pedagogica Deserta: Memoir of a Fulbright Year in Syria," *American Scholar* 50 (1981): 163–77.

116. Kamal Joumblatt, *Pour le Liban* (Paris: Stock, 1978), p. 193.

117. Muta' Safadi, *Hizb al-Ba'th* (Beirut: Dar al-Adab, 1964), pp. 338–39.

118. Quoted in Chris Kutschera, "Syrie: L'Opposition démocratique et la difficile intégration du mouvement islamique," *Le Monde Diplomatique*, March 1983, p. 12.

119. *Filastin ath-Thawra*, December 1986.

120. Rizq, *Al-Ikhwan al-Muslimun*, p. 81.

121. *Al-Hayat*, 5 May 1966. Quoted in Eliezer Be'eri, *Army Officers in Arab Politics and Society* (Jerusalem: Israel Universities Press, 1969), p. 337.

122. Muta' Safadi, *Hizb al-Ba'th* (Beirut: Dar al-Adab, 1964), p. 334.

123. Rizq, *Al-Ikhwan al-Muslimun*, p. 97. *Al-Irhab an-Nusayri*, p. 50, accuses 'Alawis of taking all Syria and a minor part of Lebanon, leaving the bulk of Lebanon for the Maronites. These accusations would seem to be contradicted by the evidence of 'Alawi dispersal from Latakia to other parts of Syria (noted above). They also appear incompatible with the accusation that the 'Alawis are preparing to break Latakia off from Syria (see below).

124. Quoted in Elizabeth Picard, "Y a-t-il un problème communautaire en Syrie?" *Maghreb-Machrek* 87 (January–March 1980): 15.

125. Radio Damascus, 12 April 1976.

126. Document 3547, dated 15 June 1936, Ministère des Affaires Étrangères. Text in Abu Musa al-Hariri, *Al-'Alawiyun—an-Nusayriyun*, p. 230. (See note 85 above for background on this letter and more references.) Such views were at the time not unique to 'Alawis; for a similar outlook among the Druze, see Yehoshua Porath, *The Palestinian Arab National Movement: From Riots to Rebellion* (London: Frank Cass, 1977), p. 271.

127. Laurent and Basbous, *Guerres secrètes au Liban*, p. 66.

128. See Khalil Mustafa, *Suqut al-Jawlan!?* (Amman: Dar al-Yaqin, 1969), pp. 97–315. This calumny has even found its way into responsible, scholarly analyses; for example, see Moosa, *Extremist Shiites*, p. 307–8.

129. Saint-Prot, *Les Mystères syriens*, pp. 22–23.

130. "Mithaq al-Jabha al-Islamiya fi Suriya," quoted in Umar F. Abd-Allah, *The Islamic Struggle in Syria* (Berkeley, Calif.: Mizan Press, 1983), p. 257.

131. *Ad-Dustur*, 24 January 1983.

132. *Al-Irhab an-Nusayri*, p. 72.

133. Anon., *As-Siyasa al-Kharijiya li-Nizam Hafiz al-Asad* (Beirut: Dar Bardi, n.d.), p. 46.

134. For elaboration of this argument, see Daniel Pipes, "Syria's Imperial Dream," *The New Republic*, 9 June 1986, pp. 13–16.

135. Joumblatt, *Pour le Liban*, p. 193; Middle East News Agency, 24 July 1985. A foreshadowing of these thoughts is found in Benjamin Disraeli's 1847 novel, *Tancred*: "if the Shehaabs [the Maronite rulers] and the Ansarey [the 'Alawis] are of one mind, Syria is no longer earth, but indeed paradise" (p. 418).

136. Laurent, "Syrie-Liban," p. 593; Laurent and Basbous, *Guerres secrètes au Liban*, p. 80. See also *Le Nouvel Observateur*, 30 April 1982.

137. Transcript in *Ath-Thawra*, 28 September 1980.

138. Kutschera, "Syrie," p. 12.

139. Ibrahim Khalas, *Jaysh ash-Sha'b*, 25 April 1967. Quoted in Rizq, *Al-Ikhwan al-Muslimun*, p. 111. Rizq quotes other provocative material on the same page.

140. The regime attempted to mollify public sentiment by sentencing the article's author and two of *Jaysh ash-Sha'b*'s editors to life imprisonment on 11 May 1967. Interestingly, Mustafa Tallas, then a lieutenant colonel, presided over the military court which meted out these punishments; subsequently, he became Asad's minister of defense.

141. Saint-Prot, *Les Mystères syriens*, p. 84.

142. *Al-Irhab an-Nusayri*, p. 38.

143. *The Economist*, 22 March 1980; *Foreign Report*, 26 March 1980; *Impact International*, 11 April 1980.

144. This expression was first used by Interior Minister 'Adnan Dabbagh, Radio Damascus, 22 June 1979.

145. *The Wall Street Journal*, 6 May 1982.

146. *Hama: Ma'sat al-'Asr Allati Faqit Majazir Sabra wa-Shatila* (Cairo: Dar al-I'tisam, 1984), p. 7. The before-and-after pictures in the book (for example, on p. 42) and the grim details of the twenty-seven-day siege make the events of Hama uniquely vivid.

147. *Al-Irhab an-Nusayri*, p. 92.

148. Olivier Carré and Gérard Michaud [Michel Seurat], *Les Frères musulmans: Égypte et Syrie (1928–1982)* (Paris: Collection Archive, 1983), p. 160. Michaud wrote the section on Syria.

149. *The Washington Post*, 22 January 1982.

150. Gérard Michaud [Michel Seurat], "Terrorisme d'état, terrorisme contre l'état: Le cas syrien," *Esprit*, October–November 1984, p. 193.

151. Moshe Ma'oz, "'Alawi Military Officers in Syrian Politics, 1966–1974," in Harold Z. Schiffren, ed., *Military and State in Modern Asia* (Jerusalem: Jerusalem Academic Press, 1976), p. 286.

152. Saint-Prot, *Les Mystères syriens*, p. 59.

153. Laurent Chabry and Annie Chabry, *Politique et minorités au Proche-Orient* (Paris: Maisonneuve & Larose, 1984), p. 185. Asad's use of a façade resembled the Soviet practice of putting members of the ethnic minorities in nominal charge of the republics in the USSR, then surrounding them with Russians.

154. Saint-Prot, *Les Mystères syriens*, p. 64.

155. Lucien Bitterlin, *Hafez el-Assad: Le Parcours d'un combattant* (Paris: Les Éditions du Jaguar, 1986), p. 33. Tallas may have had an 'Alawi mother.

156. Gérard Michaud [Michel Seurat], "L'Etat de barbarie: Syrie 1979–1982," *Esprit*, November 1983, p. 26.

157. *At-Tali'a al-'Arabiya* [Paris], 10 March 1986. This may be a faulty reference to a passage in Seurat's article, "L'Etat de barbarie," p. 26, in which he referred to the thirty 'Alawis, mostly officers, who composed the Central Committee of the Ba'th Party in Syria.

158. *Tishrin*, 19 September 1979.

159. Al-'Askari, *Al-'Alawiyun aw an-Nusayriya*, p. 48. For excerpts of Twelver Shi'i writings on the 'Alawis, see pp. 31–47.

160. Munir ash-Sharif, *Al-Muslimun al-'Alawiyun: Man Humma? Wa-Ayna Humma?* 3d ed. (Damascus: Al-Matba'a al-Umumiya, 1381/1961), p. 106. This title translates to *The 'Alawi Muslims: Who Are They? Where Are They?*

161. *The Economist*, 10 March 1973.

162. Bitterlin, *Hafez el-Assad*, p. 18.

163. Al-'Askari, *Al-'Alawiyun aw an-Nusayriya*, p. 61.

164. Quoted in Emmanuel Sivan, *Radical Islam: Medieval Theology and Modern Politics* (New Haven, Conn.: Yale University Press, 1985), p. 106.

165. *Al-Hayat*, 7 July 1973, quoted in Kramer, "Syria's Alawis and Shi'ism," p. 247. This account derives largely from Kramer's excellent review of 'Alawi-Twelver relations.

166. Al-Farisi and Sadiq, "Ath-Thawra al-Islamiya fi Suriya," p. 39.

167. *Al-Irhab an-Nusayri*, pp. 35, 9; *Ad-Da'wa* editorial staff, *An-Nusayriya fi'l-Mizan* (Cairo: Dar al-Ansar, 1980).

168. Al-Farisi and Sadiq, "Ath-Thawra al-Islamiya fi Suriya," p. 39.

169. *Al-Irhab an-Nusayri*, p. 7.

170. Rizq, *Al-Ikhwan al-Muslimun*, p. 85.

171. *Fatwa* of 25 June 1983 issued by Mufti Sa'd ad-Din al-'Alami. Quoted in Laurent, "Syrie-Liban," p. 598, and Saint-Prot, *Les Mystères syriens*, p. 215. See also *Der Spiegel*, 4 July 1983, and Radio Jerusalem, 26 June 1983.

172. Saint-Prot, *Les Mystères syriens*, p. 88.

173. Laurent and Basbous, *Guerres secrètes au Liban*, p. 81.

174. Patrick Seale, "Madha Yurid Hafiz al-Asad?" *Al-Majalla*, 23 July 1983, p. 23.

175. Van Dusen, "Downfall of a Traditional Elite," p. 141.

176. Itamar Rabinovich, stressing the long period of quietude that preceded the present efforts, disagreed with this assessment. He wrote that "the present regime's allusions to the existence of a Greater Syrian entity and its contingent claim to a special and direct relationship between Syria and Palestine do not represent a continuous policy line, but rather, novel elements in a new policy." Rabinovich supported this argument with the observation that "no Syrian government tried to promote the idea of a Greater Syria" in the preceding fifty years. Itamar Rabinovich, "Syria, Israel and the Palestine Question, 1945–77," *Wiener Library Bulletin* 31 (1978): 135.

Conclusion

1. Sawt Amal, 30 July 1980.

2. Radio Damascus, 8 March 1981.

3. Quoted in Charles Saint-Prot, *Les Mystères syriens: La Politique au Proche-Orient de 1970 à 1984* (Paris: Albin Michel, 1984), p. 74.

4. Naomi Joy Weinberger, *Syrian Intervention in Lebanon: The 1975–76 Civil War* (New York: Oxford University Press, 1986), p. 266.

5. Ibid., p. 268.

6. Radio Rabat, 7 August 1986.

7. 3 March 1976, quoted in Pierre Rondot, "Le Couple Syrie-Liban dans le mouvement arabe," *Défense Nationale*, May 1976, p. 74.

8. Jimmy Carter, *The Blood of Abraham: Insights into the Middle East* (Boston: Houghton Mifflin, 1985), p. 80. Carter observed, with justice: "I suspect that Syria prefers a strong hand in Lebanon's affairs rather than annexation, something like the Soviets' relationship with the more submissive Eastern European countries."

9. Radio Damascus, 27 March 1989.

10. *Milliyet*, 6 June 1985.

11. Radio Damascus, 12 March 1985.

12. *Al-Majalla*, 25 June 1986.

13. Elizabeth Picard, "L'Évolution recente du Parti populaire syrien à la lumière des

éditoriaux de Shawqi Khairallah dans 'Al-Thawra,'" *Maghreb-Machrek*, October–December 1977, p. 76.

14. David Roberts, *The Baʿth and the Creation of Modern Syria* (New York: St. Martin's Press, 1987), p. 15.

15. Laurent Chabry and Annie Chabry, *Politique et minorités au Proche-Orient* (Paris: Maisonneuve & Larose, 1984), pp. 166–67.

16. Radio Rabat, 7 August 1986.

17. Quoted in Saint-Prot, *Les Mystères syriens*, p. 56.

Index

Boldface type indicates a principal entry.